ORAL CULTURE AND CATHOLICISM IN
EARLY MODERN ENGLAND

ORAL CULTURE AND CATHOLICISM IN EARLY MODERN ENGLAND

ALISON SHELL

CAMBRIDGE UNIVERSITY PRESS
Cambridge, New York, Melbourne, Madrid, Cape Town, Singapore, São Paulo, Delhi

Cambridge University Press
The Edinburgh Building, Cambridge CB2 8RU, UK

Published in the United States of America by Cambridge University Press, New York

www.cambridge.org
Information on this title: www.cambridge.org/9780521883955

© Alison Shell 2007

This publication is in copyright. Subject to statutory exception
and to the provisions of relevant collective licensing agreements,
no reproduction of any part may take place without
the written permission of Cambridge University Press.

First published 2007

Printed in the United Kingdom at the University Press, Cambridge

A catalogue record for this publication is available from the British Library

ISBN 978-0-521-88395-5 hardback

Cambridge University Press has no responsibility for the persistence or accuracy of URLs for external or third-party internet websites referred to in this publication, and does not guarantee that any content on such websites is, or will remain, accurate or appropriate.

Contents

List of illustrations	*page* vi
Preface	vii
Note on conventions	xii
List of abbreviations	xiii
— Introduction	1
1 Abbey ruins, sacrilege narratives and the Gothic imagination	23
2 Anti-popery and the supernatural	55
3 Answering back: orality and controversy	82
4 Martyrs and confessors in oral culture	114
Conclusion: orality, tradition and truth	149
Notes	170
Index	237

Illustrations

1 Ephraim Udall, *Noli Me Tangere* (1642), engraved title page.   *page* 29
2 Netley Abbey: from Francis Grose, *Antiquities of England*,
   1783–7 edn, vol. II, plate opposite p. 211.   38
3 Garnet's straw: a contemporary engraving, reproduced in
   Henry Foley, *Records of the English Province of the Society of Jesus*
   (1878), vol. 4 (ninth, tenth and eleventh series), plate opposite
   p. 133.   136

All illustrations are reproduced by permission of the Syndics of Cambridge University Library.

Preface

My first book, *Catholicism, Controversy and the English Literary Imagination, 1558–1660* (1999), presented the English and Latin writing of post-Reformation Catholic Englishmen and women as a topic suitable for serious literary-critical consideration in the academic mainstream. While writing it I had moments of feeling like a lone crusader, since I was less aware than I should have been that I was part of a movement: what Ken Jackson and Arthur Marotti have identified as the 'turn to religion', which has been such a defining feature of early modern literary studies for the last decade or so.[1] In part, this has surely been due to the long-term effects of new historicism; while often characterised by reductive attitudes to religion in its heyday, the movement spread a tolerance of non-canonical writing and an attentiveness to the historical moment which remain essential stimuli to any research that attempts to span literature and history. Researchers who operate from within English departments, as I do, have also been able to draw upon huge recent historical advances in our understanding of the English Reformation, for which we must thank such scholars as John Bossy, Patrick Collinson, Eamon Duffy, Christopher Haigh, Peter Lake, Nicholas Tyacke and Alexandra Walsham. While our preoccupations have often been different from those of historians, this has led to creative cross-fertilisation, and historians have sometimes repaid the compliment by engaging with material more usually the province of literary critics.[2] It would be shockingly ungrateful to occlude or play down the importance of earlier scholars, particularly easy to do in a field such as post-Reformation Catholic history, where much of the best research has come from outside conventional academic circles, or been inspired by denominational motives. Nevertheless, within the academy, this has been a remarkable decade for the topic. There can be few fields where so much has happened, or where interest has permeated so far down, in so short a time: as this preface goes to press, a reader of early modern Catholic texts intended for undergraduate use is just about to appear from a major academic publisher.[3] Always an exciting field of study, this is now a fashionable one too; there is, as it were, a Catholic revival going on.

Perhaps this has been most visible in the case of recognisable names. The fact that post-Reformation English Catholicism has become a more popular area of study than I could have dreamed when writing my first book is in large part due to the hypotheses, strongly advanced by some Shakespeare scholars and as strongly denied by others, that Shakespeare's father was an adherent to the old faith, and that Shakespeare himself spent some time in a recusant household in Lancashire in his early years.[4] While neither contention is especially new, and the vociferous debate to which they have recently given rise is inconclusive, the combat has at least had the effect of drawing attention to the writings of those who, unlike Shakespeare, are proven Catholics.[5] One major monograph on Robert Southwell, the martyr-poet arguably more responsible than anyone else for disseminating Counter-Reformation literary ideals in England, has recently been published, and another is about to appear as this book goes to press, authored by a scholar who has also co-edited a new paperback edition of his English and Latin verse, designed for the undergraduate market.[6] Not all Catholic writers were as exemplary representatives of their faith as Southwell, and Donna Hamilton's stimulating work on Anthony Munday sketches a picture of a complex, contradictory individual who wrote as a Catholic even while persecuting Catholics; she impels her successors to look out for similar pragmatic accommodations that Catholics may have made with the times.[7] The Catholic convert and pioneer woman writer Elizabeth Cary, best known for *The Tragedy of Mariam*, has been another point of entry into the field, representing two minority groups for the price of one.[8]

Those interested in the recovery of submerged testimonies have, almost by definition, to range beyond obvious canonical sources. The academic rediscovery of early modern women's writing has inspired enquiry into literary genres not traditionally the territory of the literary critic, such as letters and household memoranda; the current interest in Catholic writing is having a similar effect, though the types of source are often very different. Peter Davidson's forthcoming work on the international baroque, with its stress on the importance of Latin as an international language and the baroque as a mode especially responsive to cultural assimilation, looks set to expand a number of disciplinary paradigms.[9] His valorisation of a truly British, thoroughly international literary heritage is one which future scholars of Catholic literature should take to heart; it would be a shame if its rediscovery were to be impaired by too narrow a concentration on English-language 'recusant' writing. Edmund Campion's Latin verse history of the early church, recovered and transcribed by Gerard Kilroy in his in-depth study of manuscripts produced by the English Catholic community, is just one example of what non-English-language sources can yield. Given what a byword for eloquence Campion was among his contemporaries, relatively little of his work survives; here as elsewhere in his writing, Kilroy is keenly aware of the special relationship between manuscript sources and the writing of a community who often found it difficult to exploit print.[10] His interest in manuscripts is shared by Arthur Marotti, in a substantial volume which is, as yet, the nearest we have to a survey of post-Reformation English Catholic and anti-Catholic literature.[11]

The present study too has a concern to expand canonical boundaries, looking at ballads, onomastics and anecdotes alongside more conventionally literary genres, and it makes heavy use of manuscript sources, though less for their own sake than as a means of recovering the overlap between the oral and the literary. Chapter 1 looks at sacrilege narratives: stories which circulated among Catholics and others concerning the terrible fates overtaking individuals who desecrated ruined abbeys, and families who benefited from monastic impropriations. Chapter 2 assesses the afterlife of Catholic liturgical fragments in spells and unofficial religious practice, and comments on how the conceptual gulf that existed between literate commentators and the uneducated could affect definitions of popish idolatry. Drawing largely on ballads and other popular verse, chapters 3 and 4 discuss how the Catholic oral challenge worked in relation to polemical material and the depiction of martyrs and confessors; while the conclusion asks how the English situation prompted reflection on the relationship between oral tradition and religious authority.

Acknowledgements are always a pleasure to write. Arnold Hunt has been the acutest, most knowledgeable critic that any academic could wish for, and the most facilitating of husbands. John Morrill has been a kind mentor of the project, especially in encouraging me to think of my initial unwieldy manuscript as two books rather than one. As my editors at Cambridge University Press, Josie Dixon, then Ray Ryan, were unfailingly efficient, sympathetic and positive, and I must also express my gratitude to Maartje Scheltens, Jo Breeze and Hywel Evans. The two anonymous readers for the Press made several helpful suggestions, and the book, I know, is better as a result; a stringent word-count has prevented me from responding as fully as I would like to their useful suggestions, but in many cases they have given me ideas for future projects. For access to unpublished work, helpful advice, the checking of references, and in many cases reading chapters too, I am enormously grateful to Paul Arblaster, James Austen, Kate Bennett, Richard Bimson, Patricia Brückmann, Fr Michael Brydon, Daniela Busse, Peter Davidson, Anne Dillon, Eamon Duffy, Alex Fotheringham, Adam Fox, Tom Freeman, Anne Barbeau Gardiner, Jan Graffius, Helen Hackett, John Harley, Eileen Harris, Stanley Hauerwas, John Hinks, Sarah Hutton, Phebe Jensen, Gerard Kilroy, Jenny McAuley, Thomas McCoog, SJ, Peter Marshall, the late Jeremy Maule, John Milsom, John Newton, Anne Parkinson, Jane Pirie, Diane Purkiss, Michael Questier, Fr Terence Richardson, Andrew Rudd, David Salter, Jason Scott-Warren, Bill Sheils, Judith Smeaton, Diane Spaul, Jane Stevenson, Alexandra Walsham, Nicola Watson, Heather Wolfe and Henry Woudhuysen. Though I have been unable to locate Margaret Sena, I would like to express my deep gratitude to her for sharing with me her excellent transcriptions from William Blundell's 'Great Hodge Podge', which saved me a lot of work. Among archivists, I would especially like to thank Anna Watson at the Lancashire Record Office and Mauro Brunello at the Archivum Romanum Societatis Jesu, Rome; the staff of the British Library and Durham University Library deserve collective commendation, but among the latter, Judith Walton should be singled out.

Many colleagues and ex-colleagues from Durham University, inside and outside the English Department, have had a hand in the book: for reading portions of it, and for providing me with useful leads, I am grateful to Chris Brooks, Robert Carver, Pamela Clemit, Douglas Davies, Alison Forrestal, Mandy Green, Margaret Harvey, John McKinnell, Barbara Ravelhofer, Fiona Robertson and Sarah Wootton. During their respective terms as Heads of Department, Michael O'Neill, David Fuller and Patricia Waugh were tremendously kind and supportive; I must also acknowledge my gratitude to the departmental research committee for several grants towards research trips, and to the university for periods of research leave during which I was able to work on the book. Thanks are due as well to the Lewis Walpole Library, Yale University, and its librarian Maggie Powell, for awarding me a fellowship in September 2001, during which most of the work for chapter 1 was undertaken. Various portions of this book were delivered at conferences run by the MLA, BSECS and the Catholic Record Society, at colloquia at Stirling University, Aberdeen University and the University of East Anglia, and at seminars at Durham University, York University and the University of Central England; thanks are due to all my audiences for enabling me to try out ideas, and commenting so usefully. For permission to quote from manuscripts, I am grateful to the Blundell family and the

County Archivist at Lancashire Record Office; Staffordshire Record Office; Somerset Record Office; the Beinecke Library, Yale University; the Bodleian Library; the British Library; the Folger Shakespeare Library; Hull University Library; Lambeth Palace Library; the National Art Library, London; and the National Library of Wales.

I dedicate this book to Arnold Hunt.

Note on conventions

In quotations from contemporary texts, i/j and u/v have been normalised, though all other contemporary spelling has been retained; no attempt has been made to represent italics in most cases; and unusual scribal features have been commented on where appropriate.

Punctuation has been omitted before an ellipsis except where its retention is helpful to interpreting the quotation.

Unless otherwise indicated all Bible references have been taken from the King James Bible and all Shakespeare references from *William Shakespeare: The Complete Works*, general editors Stanley Wells and Gary Taylor (Oxford: Clarendon, 1988).

Abbreviations

ARCR   A. F. Allison and D. M. Rogers, *The Contemporary Printed Literature of the English Counter-Reformation between 1558 and 1640. Volume I: Works in Languages Other Than English. Volume II: Works in English* (Aldershot: Scolar, 1989–94)
BL   British Library, London
Bod   Bodleian Library, Oxford
Clancy   Thomas H. Clancy, *English Catholic Books, 1641–1700: A Bibliography* (Aldershot: Scolar, 1996)
CSPD   *Calendar of State Papers, Domestic*
EHR   *English Historical Review*
ELH   *English Literary History*
ELR   *English Literary Renaissance*
ESTC   *English Short-Title Catalogue*, online version
Foley   Henry Foley (ed.), *Records of the English Province of the Society of Jesus*, 7 vols. in 8 (London: Burns & Oates, 1875–83)
Frank   Frederick S. Frank, *The First Gothics* (New York: Garland, 1987)
Guiney   Louise Imogen Guiney, *Recusant Poets*, vol. I (no vol. II) (London: Sheed & Ward, 1938)
HJ   *Historical Journal*
JEH   *Journal of Ecclesiastical History*
Milward   Peter Milward, *Religious Controversies of the Elizabethan Age* (London: Scolar, 1977)
ODNB   *Oxford Dictionary of National Biography*
OED   *Oxford English Dictionary*, 3rd edn (online)
P & P   *Past and Present*
PMLA   *Proceedings of the Modern Language Association*
PRO   Public Record Office, London
RES   *Review of English Studies*

STC W. A. Jackson, F. S. Ferguson and Katharine F. Pantzer, *A Short-Title Catalogue of Books Printed in England, Scotland and Ireland and of English Books Printed Abroad, 1475–1640*, 2nd edn, 3 vols. (London: Bibliographical Society, 1976–91)

Wing Donald Wing, Revd Timothy J. Crist and John J. Morrison, *Short-Title Catalogue of Books Printed in England, Scotland, Ireland, Wales, and British America and of English Books Printed in Other Countries, 1641–1700*, 2nd edn, 3 vols. (Baltimore: Modern Language Association of America, 1972–88)

Introduction

> ... as for oral Traditions, what certainty can there be in them? What foundation of truth can be laid upon the breath of man? How do we see the reports vary, of those things which our eyes have seen done? How do they multiply in their passage, and either grow, or die upon hazards?[1]

What impact did post-Reformation Catholicism have on England's oral culture? The Protestant theologian Joseph Hall provides one point of entry in an influential passage from his tract *The Old Religion*, usually held to be the first occasion in English when oral tradition is named as such.[2] Attacking Catholics for investing tradition with an authority comparable to the written word of God, he makes pejorative use of the familiar idea that traditions could be passed down verbally as well as contained in writing, and links oral tradition, oral transmission and unreliability in a way that implies a strong pre-existing association between Catholics and orality.[3] As against the fixedness of print, oral communication was seen as having infinite potential to distort, and it became a powerful metaphor to express the fears about the fertility of ignorance that are so common in anti-Catholic polemic.

But this is only one reason why the association between orality and Catholicism was a natural one in post-Reformation England. An antiquarian would have pointed to the rich anecdotal tradition surrounding ruined abbeys, which kept England's Catholic past and the depredations of the Reformation alive in the popular memory, a puritan minister in a rural parish might well have deplored the use of popish spells among his flock, while a seminary priest would have recognised the missionary usefulness of ballad-singing to drive home the anti-Protestant message and commemorate martyrs. The four essays which make up the main body of this study address all these topics, while the conclusion asks how a specific body of mid-seventeenth-century radical Catholic scholars confronted the challenge of demonstrating a relationship between oral transmission and religious truth.

When I was researching my first book,[4] the Catholic presence in the oral culture of early modern England forced itself on my attention like an insistent background noise. This study is the result: written in a time when the study of orality has come of age, and benefiting from recent work which has charted the changes and continuities within England's oral culture during the couple of centuries following the advent of print.[5] Keith Thomas has drawn attention to the complexity of 'the interaction between contrasting forms of culture, literate and illiterate, oral and written', which gives this period of English history its 'peculiar fascination';[6] and certainly, attempts to determine what is covered by the term 'oral culture' at this time and place have been much improved by recent attempts to plot it against the continuance of written culture and the beginnings of print culture.[7] Loosely, one can say of early modern English society or any other that oral communication affects every branch of human activity, but one gets a better purchase on any culture that is not pre-literate by asking which functions of oral communication have been supplemented, altered or taken over by writing and print, and which remain the same.

Recent studies, notably those by Adam Fox, D. R. Woolf and Bruce R. Smith, have also done much to minimise the frustration brought about by the fact that, for this period, one's sources are necessarily at one remove or more from spoken discourse.[8] The essays that comprise this study draw, as these earlier works have also tended to do, from an eclectic range of sources: among them, Gothic novels, antiquarian and folklore studies, ballads in print and in manuscript, letters and polemical theology. This eclecticism is necessary because oral culture operates on many different levels of formality, ranging from extemporised conversational interchange to anecdotes refined in the retelling, and the scripted voicings of drama, liturgy and song; but in introducing a book which is bound to betray its author's training in university English departments, one needs to stress from the outset that consciously 'literary' texts at this period could have as close a relationship to orality as less formal communications. Edward Doughtie has written of the sixteenth century what continues to be true for some time after: 'Most of the really vital literary texts ... were written with the possibility of oral performance in mind: sermons, plays, and song lyrics, of course – even romances and long poems were probably read aloud to small groups.'[9] Conversely, this book attempts to point up the literariness of texts recovered from, designed for or dependent upon oral transmission, whose particular formalities, sophistications and allusive complexities remain under-discussed by scholars: ballads, anecdotes, spells, even the powerful metaphors and hagiographical allusions inherent in an assumed name.[10] A great deal of this material remains, and much of it is powerfully evocative.

THE ORAL WORLD OF POST-REFORMATION ENGLAND: SURVIVAL, LOSS AND CHANGE

Whether one looks at this kind of material or at oral communication in general, an emphasis on the oral experience of early modern England is hardly denominationally specific in itself. Nevertheless, choosing a denominational filter is useful for a number of reasons: most of all because looking at oral culture can tell us a good deal about what happens to a once unchallenged religious body, after it has been driven underground. Because of the difficulty of controlling or censoring oral discourse, records of it are a natural place to find opinions running counter to the prevailing orthodoxy – perceived offensiveness is often the only reason why remarks get recorded at all. Besides, there is a strong link between religious conservatism and illiteracy at this date, and oral discourse was the only means which illiterates had of making their opinions felt.[11]

Records of conversations and of popular opinion testify to the potent afterlife of the old religion in the historical memories of both Catholics and non-Catholics, at all levels of society.[12] These memories could be merely factual, or – especially among the unlearned – numinous in a way that could invite accusations of superstition. William Fulke, for instance, cites a memory of medieval church-art called forth by sunbeams raying from behind a cloud, 'The common people cal it the desce[n]ding of the holy ghost, or our Ladies Assumption, because these things are painted after suche a sort', which from someone of Fulke's puritan sympathies is hardly a neutral observation.[13] The use of a present tense is striking in a pamphlet of the 1560s: perhaps an acknowledgement that several church windows and wall-paintings survived the early Tudor reformers, but also suggesting how what remained would have been a constant reminder of what was gone.[14] Medieval Catholicism also had a protracted afterlife in local legends with a supernatural element: especially those surrounding the ruins of abbeys and other religious houses, or commemorating a local saint.[15]

These memories could go beyond the specific to a generalised nostalgia. Surfacing obliquely in elite literary culture, most famously in the evocation of 'bare ruined choirs' in Shakespeare's Sonnet 73, this spirit finds a more direct expression in a widespread, stubborn, wistfully enhanced popular memory of more pleasant and charitable times.[16] As always with nostalgia, one does not need to have a first-hand memory of old times to regard them as intrinsically happier; so, as Protestant polemicists like John Favour suspected, this was an attitude which could be and was orally conveyed between the generations.

> Are not these words . . . in the mouthes of all the old superstitious people of this land? And do not the yong learne of the old? *When we prayed to our Lady, and offred tapers on Candlemasse day, and heard Masse as we have done . . . then we had plentie of all things, and were well, we felt no evill. But since we have left the religion of our fathers . . . we have scarsnesse of all things.* The old superstitious people of Christ-Church in Hampshire, would say, that there came fewer Salmons up their River, since the masse went downe: for they were wont to come up when they heard the sacring Bell ring . . . the pretence is still, that the former way was the Old way, and that Old way was the best way.[17]

A ballad of the 1590s, 'A pleasant Dialogue between plaine Truth, and blind Ignorance', sets the scene by a ruined abbey. Truth asks Ignorance why he 'keepe[s] such gazing / on this decaied place: / The which for superstition / good Princes downe did race', to which Ignorance – a papist talking broad Mummerset – replies:

> Ah, ah, che zmell thée now man,
> che well know what thou art:
> A vellow of new learning,
> che wis not worth a vart:
> Vor when we had the old Law
> a mery world was then:[18]
> and every thing was plenty,
> among all sorts of men . . .
>
> Chill tell thée what good vellow,
> bevore the Vriers went hence,
> A bushell of the best wheat
> was zold for vortéene pence:
> And vorty Eggs a penny,
> that were both good and new:
> All this che say my selfe haue séene
> and yet ich am no Jew.[19]

But one should not assume, as this ballad does, that Catholic nostalgia and Catholic practice necessarily went together. As Eamon Duffy comments, 'nostalgic idealization of the Catholic past [became] as much the voice of the church papist, and of some backward-looking parish Anglicans, as of conscientiously recusant Catholics'.[20] In addition, some educated hearers of this type of oral memory, like John Aubrey, would have recorded it primarily for the evidence it yielded of a vanished past. But this in turn illustrates the intimate relationship between England's medieval past and the antiquarian spirit, which drew so many outright Catholics, crypto-Catholics and religious conservatives towards this kind of scholarship during penal times, and so spectacularly informed England's Catholic revival in the nineteenth century.[21] Ironically, pejorative records like Favour's are almost as efficacious in preserving evidence of the old religion, and have been plundered by later commentators for reasons which would have distressed the original collectors.[22] The numerous scholars to cite the puritan John Shaw's 1644 examination of an old man who saw a late performance of a Corpus Christi play in his youth, 'there was a man on a tree and blood ran down', are less interested in Shaw's complaint about religious ignorance in Lancashire than in the incidental evidence he gives about the continuance of medieval drama after the Reformation.[23]

Certainly, any survey of Catholicism's afterlife in post-Reformation oral culture must consider those literary genres which had a religious content, depended on oral delivery to get their message across, and were disliked by the Reformers. Drama, as Shaw's quotation suggests, is one such. Despite governmental hostility towards traditional popular religious drama from the time of the Henrician Reformation, it took a surprisingly long time to die out altogether – the Corpus Christi play which figures in the old man's reminiscence was last performed in 1603 – and had a profound effect on later secular drama.[24] But drama was vulnerable because of its high-profile collective nature, because of the expenditure it entailed and because public performances had to be regulated.[25] Carols fared better, despite falling foul of Protestantism because of their use of non-biblical legends and their association with religious festivals at a time when emphasis was shifting away from the liturgical year. It is obviously easier to sing a carol than put on a play; besides, sacred songs were more religiously versatile than theatrical performances which would have invited accusations of blasphemy and idolatry from protestantised authorities. Some pre-Reformation carols were capable of causing offence to Protestants, but survived nevertheless; most could have been sung by anyone who did not have a puritan objection to the genre.[26] In the climate of the 1630s, given the backing of traditional festive custom by Archbishop Laud and the Crown, carols could even have been seen as conspicuously orthodox; and later, Royalist members of the Church of England during the Interregnum developed considerable interest in the genre as part of an attempt to keep beleaguered Christmas traditions alive. New carols went on being composed after the Reformation, by both

Catholics and Protestants; and other devotional verse related to the church's year, both Catholic- and Protestant-authored, could be co-opted into this tradition.[27] Thus, carols would often have fitted into mainstream culture as easily as many other texts from a Catholic source; though, given the large number of manuscript and print miscellanies with a Catholic provenance or including identifiably Catholic material which preserve carols, they might well have played a particularly prominent part in Catholic liturgical festivity and general merrymaking.[28]

Whenever a nineteenth-century antiquarian collected an oral rendition of a medieval carol containing Catholic matter, his text was not necessarily a reliable guide to the carol's original wording, but it did at least testify to the fact of its journey.[29] Carol-singing – sometimes with help from printed or written sources, sometimes perhaps independently of them – was a means of bearing medieval devotion through one of the most religiously alert and combative phases in England's history.[30] Whereas physical survivals from pre-Reformation England primarily depend on something being left alone, oral survivals imply a conscious decision to transmit. The reasons for this would have been various, ranging from an informed, polemicised desire to keep the old ways alive, to situations where the religious content was rendered unnoticeable by familiarity. Religious behaviour, even among the well-informed, is not always perfectly integrated, and ostensibly Protestant individuals might have transmitted doubtful carols for tradition's sake. Thus, carolling presents a picture of continuity and widely acceptable survival, perhaps one of the points where the oral cultures of Catholics, conformists and even dissenters would have overlapped or blurred – which must surely have been helped by the fact that, though associated with religious festivals, it was an optional extra as far as liturgy went, and had strong secular roots.[31]

To set against this, though, is the liturgical change that took place when Latin was replaced by the vernacular in church services and other set forms of prayer. Any assessment of how oral experience shifted when England became a Protestant nation must give full weight to the very differing responses that this change would have elicited.[32] It could have represented an impoverishment of spiritual experience at all social levels, not only among those who understood Latin – even if one should not expect either Catholic or Protestant commentators at this date to endorse what Rudolf Otto has called 'the spell exercised by the only half intelligible or wholly unintelligible language of devotion, and . . . the unquestionably real enhancement of the awe of the worshipper which this produces'.[33] As the history of Bible translation proves, it would be mistaken to equate

Catholicism with a blanket hostility towards the vernacular, either in England or on the Continent; nevertheless, Catholics and religious conservatives during the English Reformation repeatedly asserted that the vernacular was irreverent and that translating sacred texts would invite heretical readings from unqualified interpreters.[34] In this context, it may seem paradoxical that the Latin Mass should ever have been a means of widening access. But by keeping Latin alive as a spoken language outside school and university contexts, post-Reformation Catholic liturgy would have given those who had no other access to classical education an impressionistic familiarity with Latin; and its usefulness would have gone beyond the merely educative, since the shared experience of difference would have been a means of reinforcing communal solidarity. Most of all, perhaps, it would have been a comforting reminder of the wider church.[35] A seventeenth-century Catholic dialogue marshals a number of these arguments, contending that even women and children understand 'not only the substance of the whole Mass, but the very words, as little children learne any language by often hearing it', and that the use of the vernacular isolates the English church from mainland Christendom. Latin, it reminds us, is the 'vulgar language of the Church', and by using it, Christians can be brought together in the way that they were before the Tower of Babel, whereas the 'learned'st clerk of any other nation cannot serve the poorest Parish in England upon a Sunday for want of a book of common prayer in his owne language'.[36]

Though the writer here is obviously giving an educated person's view of the changes, one should not necessarily assume that all uneducated worshippers would have preferred a vernacular liturgy, especially when the reforms first came in. The writer of a mid-sixteenth-century Catholic lament, commenting on the liturgical changes, explicitly identifies himself with the common voice in his lament that services in English only make people hypocritical, and may be picking up on a real grass-roots feeling:

> For our reverend father hath set forth an order,
> Our service to be said in our seignours tongue;
> As Solomon the sage set forth the scripture;
> Our suffrages, and services, with many a sweet song,
> With homilies, and godly books us among,
> That no stiff, stubborn stomacks we should freyke [i.e. 'humour']:
> But wretches nere worse to do poor men wrong;
> But that I little John Nobody dare not speake.
>
> For bribery was never so great, since born was our Lord,
> And whoredom was never les hated, sith Christ harrowed hel,
> And poor men are so sore punished commonly through the world,

> That it would grieve any one, that good is, to hear tel.
> For al the homilies and good books, yet their hearts be so quel,
> That if a man do amisse, with mischiefe they wil him wreake
>   [i.e. 'pursue revengefully'];
> The fashion of these new fellows it is so vile and fell:
> But that I little John Nobody dare not speake.[37]

As the poem ends, the speaker chooses a solitary existence, with his whereabouts known only to the other complainant. Using speech to lament enforced silence, the piece is consciously paradoxical in its very existence, and this is driven home by the multiple negations of the ending:

> Thus in NO place, this NOBODY, in NO time I met,
> Where NO man, ne NOUGHT was, nor NOTHING did appear;
> Through the sound of a synagogue[38] for sorrow I swett,
> That Aeolus through the eccho did cause me to hear.
> Then I drew me down into a dale, whereas the dumb deer
> Did shiver for a shower; but I shunted from a freyke:
> For I would no wight in the world wist who I were,
> But little John Nobody, that dare not once speake.

If it does nothing else, the current book should give the lie to Little John Nobody – though his complaint, and even his name, remind us that the association between Catholic literature and anonymity or pseudonymity is a pronounced one, which has had its effect on mainstream recognition of the material.[39] Besides, saying that one is unable to speak becomes less paradoxical if one reads the complaint as identifying impediments in communication, rather than the utter impossibility of communicating. Interpreted in this way, the libel is prophetic in foretelling many such impediments for the Catholic community during England's Protestant ascendancy, and not only among the uneducated.

Post-Reformation English Catholic priests, obliged to be citizens of Europe during their education, did not always find this a straightforwardly enabling experience, and perhaps it is not surprising that the most literary among them were often the most conscious of deficiency in their mother tongue. The prodigiously eloquent Edmund Campion, journeying back to England after several years on the Continent, believed his English might have become rusty and gave his companions a practice address. As it turned out, he need not have worried – an eyewitness reported that 'so rapid was the torrent of his words, that with impetuous violence [his speech] seemed to overflow its barriers'.[40] But Robert Southwell, who left England very young, had to re-learn English almost from scratch in preparation for the English mission, and wrote to the Rector of the English College in Rome just after his arrival in England stressing the enormous importance of training seminarians to preach in English.[41] Even so, over a century later, some missionaries were still not well enough equipped in their mother tongue. Philip, Cardinal Howard, told Bishop Burnet, on the latter's visit to Rome in 1685, that 'They came over young and retained all the English that they brought over with them, which was only the language of boys: But their education being among strangers they had formed themselves so upon that model that really they preached as Frenchmen or Italians in English words' – a factor which could only have exacerbated the usual polemical association of Catholicism with foreignness.[42]

Most of all, perhaps, the writer of 'Little John Nobody' pinpoints the sense of oral inhibition which pervades post-Reformation English Catholic discourse, both conversational and written, and which comes through in occasional anecdotes. One such survives of Richard Cosen, a Colchester keeper who was accused of having engaged in wild talk when cutting hay in 1562 with William Blackman. Praising the Duke of Guise, Cosen repeated a rumour that the Queen had had a child and died of it, and drew from Blackman an admission that he could hardly understand the changes over the past fifteen years. Thinking over the conversation later, Blackman's conscience became troubled and he unburdened himself to an alderman. Cosen was arrested and tried, and his statement makes it clear that he was trying to elicit an admission of religious allegiance from Blackman. The background to this altercation is hinted at by another of the witnesses, Cosen's maid Margaret Sander, in her testimony that Cosen and his wife 'talke moche agenst the use of the Curche that nowe is apointed And that they sytte singing together the old messe in myrthe by the fyresyde in the house . . .'.[43]

Set against the original exchange between Cosen and Blackman, this testimony vividly demonstrates the different conversational registers which Catholics would have needed: tentative advances and retreats when trying to draw out someone whose sympathies were unclear, unbuttoned talk when relaxing in the company of one's co-religionists. In the report of the Cosens 'singing together the old messe in myrthe', a defiantly polemicised use of Catholic matter not polemical in itself, one can see one way that the Catholic oral response to the English Reformation took shape. But literary material bearing the marks of engagement with the reformers, and designed for easy oral transmission, is perhaps a clearer sign than informal conversations of the Catholic oral challenge: and the next section will consider how, while denied official access to print and the pulpit, English Catholics deliberately attempted in other ways to match and counteract the effect that Protestant evangelism had had on the oral world of early modern England.

PROTESTANT CHALLENGES, CATHOLIC RESPONSES: THE REFORMATION INFLUENCE ON ORAL CULTURE

Almost from the beginning, the message of the English Reformation was addressed to a range of audiences: from the university-educated theologian to the labourer who could neither write nor read.[44] Inevitably, this affected how religious controversy and doctrinal affirmation came to be delivered. The oral medium of the sermon continued to be employed as a direct means of transmitting doctrine to the laity; the ideal of preaching was often used to signify the whole of the reformers' mission, and preachers themselves were sophisticated and entertaining communicators whose sermons stood up to comparison with plays.[45] As Andrew Pettegree has recently stressed, music was another important pedagogic tool for the Reformers in both ecclesiastical and popular contexts.[46] Most relevantly of all to the current study, popular literary genres were also used to spread the new message: ballads, liturgical parodies, or the rhymed taunt of an epigram. These had a strong presence within popular print culture, and invited oral dissemination – sometimes, as in the case of ballads, by a conjunction of illustrations, words and music.[47] Maximising evangelical effectiveness in a world shaped by the advent of print, the ubiquity of oral methods of communication, and remaining widespread illiteracy, they would have been used to provoke or enhance the millions of spoken arguments by which the Reformation was established, or resisted, within the population in general: arguments which, inside and outside the schools, must themselves have had their trajectories determined to some degree by patterns of disputation already embedded in European oral culture.[48]

Few ideological battles have foregrounded linguistic concerns so much as the Reformation, or been fought in such a rhetorically self-conscious manner; as Brian Cummings has recently pointed out, the points at issue between Catholic and Protestant demanded constant awareness to grammatical minutiae and linguistic nuance. The amount of attention paid at this period to the terms of debate had literary knock-on effects, engendering raptly attentive animadversion and utterly serious wordplay.[49] Lengthy, ritualistic and imaginatively charged dissociation was undertaken not only from the rhetoric of opponents, but from individual elements of their vocabulary. This is as noticeable in verse as in prose; in particular, verse is better fitted than prose to exploit iteration, and display a number of possible verbal associations in a succinct manner. One Catholic poem uses its refrain to criticise the doctrine of justification by faith alone, with almost palpable quotation marks around its first three words, 'Alone and onely in a wrong scole, / have brought to error many a foole.' The verses link the idea of the undivided Trinity with the foolhardiness of supposing that faith and works can be separated. As used in this poem, the terms 'only' and 'alone' become personified, both in the service of the writer's opponents and as interlocutors in their own right:

> Manye under god, & yett god alone
> workethe godds pleasure, as godds wyll ys
> so onlie or a lone can make no reson
> Wy man as a minister may doo that or this
>
> Onlie and a lone have beyne so abused
> to dissevere faythe & charitie a sonder
> as charitie in Justification clerelye refused
> hathe made religion talke & worldlye wonder
>
> Yett some saye onlie and not alone
> mans fayth dothe worke his Justification
> w[ith] charitie p[re]sent & myche they mone
> men can not co[n]ceyve there fonde conclusion⁵⁰.

The notion that language speaks its user would have come as no surprise to a Reformation polemicist. A sense that religious language has a quasi-autonomous power runs through poems like these, and posed the question of how far it was legitimate to handle enemy propaganda. Even using the terms of the reformers could be interpreted as a concession to their doctrine; a notebook of this date contains the injunction:

Let us keepe our forefathers words and we shal easily keep our old and true faith that we had of the firste Christians. Let them say, Amendement, abstinence, the Lordes Supper, the Com[m]union table, Elders, ministers, Superintendant, Congregatio[n], so be it, praise ye the Lord, morning praier, Evening prayer, and the reste as they will: Let us avoide these novelties of words . . . and keepe the old termes Penance, Fasting, Priest, Church, Bishop, Masse, Mattines, Evensong, the B. Sacrament, Alter, Oblation, Host, Sacrifice, Alleluia, Amen, Lent, Palme Sunday, Christmas, and the very wordes wil . . . condemne the new apostatates (sic) new f[a]ith and phrases.⁵¹

Differences between Catholic and Protestant doctrine were often epitomised by word-choice, usually on the part of translators: Tyndale's choice of 'elder' rather than 'priest' to translate 'πρεσβύτερος' is a well-known example.⁵² Thus, denominational differences in vocabulary had the effect not only of endorsing a supposedly preferable meaning, but of distancing oneself from the other side. As the above quotation shows, this alertness would have carried over from specialised theological discourse into everyday life. While some of the listed words and phrases are more charged than others, all are potentially signals of allegiance. Its author is unusually extreme in advocating a complete refusal to employ the other side's terminology, a view which would render polemic nearly impossible if taken literally. Yet this throws into relief the usual concessions which any polemicist, Catholic or Protestant, was obliged to make. To condemn something one needs to evoke it, and where Reformation writers evince squeamishness about voicing one's opponent, this reflects a wider anxiety about the potential entrapments of spontaneous everyday speech.

Nevertheless, oral debates took place between Catholics and Protestants at every level from ecclesiastical conference to brawl, with some occasions being preserved in contemporary partisan accounts such as Daniel Featley's *The Romish Fisher Caught and Held in his Owne Net* (1624).[53] While participants on both sides would have aimed to attract converts, disputations must sometimes have had the opposite effect of bringing about disaffection; certainly, the Catholic and Protestant disputants of this period often seem caught up in a linguistic round-game as interminable as that figured by Samuel Fisher, where the words SO and NO, typeset in two concentric circles, chase each other endlessly.[54] Michael Questier has remarked upon this stalemate, stressing the importance of outside factors in converts' decisions to go over.[55] But the deadlock could be broken in certain situations, such as trials or executions, which would have stimulated sympathy for the underdog at their most inequitable. Future confessors and martyrs had unparalleled opportunities to win souls by an impressive performance in the dock or on the scaffold; even when – tortured, imprisoned and deprived of books – they were not as effective as their opponents, they would have scored a moral victory in the eyes of sympathetic observers.[56] Yet though trials of Catholics could bring about *parrhesia*, the act of speaking out frankly, they were also occasions when questions of casuistry and equivocation were to the fore.[57] Equivocation, the practice of using words in more than one sense, was a protective rhetorical device for those under trial, where ambiguity could be seen as shading into falsehood; and all early modern Englishmen, Catholics or not, would have identified a particularly close relationship between the ordeals of Catholic priests and the occasions on which it might, or might not, be acceptable to be economical with the truth.[58] The practice was particularly associated with Jesuits, though the Catholic secular priest William Rushworth claims in his *Dialogues* that equivocation is incident to all writing. Though this might be read now as reinforcing his argument that Scripture has limits – as well as anticipating post-structuralist thought – it would also have had distinct defensive overtones at the time.[59]

The work of Rushworth and his followers, discussed in the conclusion to this study, illustrates how questions of truth-telling, and reliability in general, constantly spiralled back to questions of how message could be affected by medium.[60] But the sharp distinctions they make between oral and written means of communication are only helpful up to a point. Practice constantly complicated theory in an era characterised by energetic use of oral, written and printed media, and distinctions between speech, script and print were easy to collapse. Writing to the Pope in 1581, Robert Persons includes both literary and non-literary forms of verbal attack in a complaint about English Protestants: 'Against us they publish the most threatening proclamations, books, sermons, ballads, libels, lies and plays.'[61] Metaphors drawn from speech were easy to apply to books, and a valediction appended to Alexander Cooke's *Worke, More Worke, and a Little More Worke for a Masse-Priest* epitomises this tight relationship between orality, print and the propagation of Protestant doctrine.

> Goe little booke, make speed, apply the season,
> Propound thy Quaeres with undanted cheere:
> Bid learned Priests and Cardinalls speake reason.
> The vulgar dare not reade, but make them heare.[62]

But if polemicists like this writer routinely distinguished between learned literates and the illiterate vulgar, present-day scholars would be wrong to take these oppositions too literally. The notions of oral culture and written do not imply a binary divide; nor do those of literacy and illiteracy, since the population of early modern England contained within itself an incalculable number of possible gradations between these states.[63] Everyone was affected to some degree by writing and print, since uneducated England was not pre-literate in the same sense as a tribe that has never been exposed to either. Yet the abilities to write and read were far from universal, and rural England, in particular, could still show many characteristics of pre-literate cultures.[64] These inspired what can often seem an *a priori* lack of sympathy with the ignorant among educated commentators, whereby mental habits associated with a pre-literate culture were automatically read as foolish or superstitious.[65] Walter Ong has asked 'What was the hermeneutic situation in cultures that mingled an intensive textuality with a high residual orality?', and answered himself, in part, by quoting another scholar: 'The most injurious consequence . . . [was] the notion that literacy is identical with rationality.'[66] The equation of literacy with progress is familiar to us: European reformers would have put it differently, arguing first and foremost that literacy gave one greater access to truth through the ability to read the Scriptures. The supposed tendency of papists to discourage literacy meant that, though the prejudice against illiterates was by no means restricted to Protestants, it became deeply embedded in anti-Catholic polemic.[67]

The verse quoted above has a more sympathetic view of illiterates than one often finds, implying that they can recognise rational argument when they hear it, but also that their illiteracy is not intrinsic to their condition. Arguing that common people were irrational could arise from a conviction that they were irredeemably stupid, but also a feeling that they had been short-changed by those in power. The author's exhortation in the last line of his verse suggests the latter; it contains a double sneer at his religious opponents, implying that the 'vulgar' have been cowed into illiteracy by popish clerics who are not even interested in giving them oral instruction. Overall, the quatrain has a suggestively ambiguous take on oral transmission, suggesting both the importance which the reformers ascribed to it, but also how it could be thought of as second-best to reading. Despite the immense importance given by the reformers to the oral delivery and hearing of sermons, and despite the fact that 'entry into the Kingdom of Heaven was not conditional on being able to read', this is not the only occasion on which one catches a Protestant happiest when endorsing print.[68] The need for oral transmission could imply illiteracy in an audience, which was thought in turn to engender credulity and ignorance: defects which, in England as elsewhere in Protestant Europe, were believed to be typical of papists. Certainly both illiteracy and Catholicism did tend to remain strong in outlying areas of England, areas which Christopher Hill famously dubbed – not altogether in quotation marks – the 'dark corners of the land';[69] and given the tenacious afterlife of liturgical fragments in spells, it may not have been entirely unfair to perceive a link between Catholicism and superstitious beliefs.[70]

The verse identifies two potential audiences among Catholics, not merely the 'vulgar' but 'learned Priests and Cardinalls'. Prejudices against popish oral tradition had a similarly wide social remit, criticising esoteric high politics as well as the garbled distortions and fantasies of the uneducated.[71] Among English Protestants from very early times, polemical connections between popery and oral tradition routinely linked tales of Robin Goodfellow with papal *arcana imperii*: a sign of how attitudes towards the uneducated could affect notions of authority further up the line. This should, perhaps, alert one to the fact that, on the question of orality, English Catholic theory and practice could have an equally broad notion of audience. Some English Catholic theologians gave a demotic emphasis to theories of oral tradition, drawing out the full implications of the idea that salvation had to be available to illiterates and literates alike.[72] The emphasis that Protestantism placed on individual reading of the Bible seems, in at least one documented case, to have resulted in a conversion to Catholicism: the Jesuit annual letters for 1624 recount the tale of how an illiterate woman became a Catholic after she understood a Protestant preacher to say that people like her could not be saved.[73] It could also lead Catholics to stress how orthodoxy, common sense and sound debating skills could all be found among illiterates: more than just a counter-gambit, this displays considerable sensitivity to the fact that early modern England was a place of limited educational opportunities. Peter Talbot's *A Treatise of the Nature of Catholick Faith, and Heresie* (1657) makes a special point of backing the commonsensical, quick-witted Catholic illiterate against the Protestant with only scholarship to recommend him:

If Protestancy be . . . contrary to reason, and common sense . . . what wonder is it, that any illiterate Catholick should convince the most learned Ministers, and pillars of Protestant Churches; unlesse it be supposed that we are deprived, or at least, know not how to make use of our reason, and common sense? . . . I do seriously averre, that every Countreyman, who hath wit, and judgement enough to except, at the Assises, against an illegall, and false witnesse, hath learning enough to convince in controversies of Religion, the most learned Protestant Minister. And every carrier, or husbandman, who hath so much wit, and judgement, as not to believe an extravagant, and incredible history, or ballads, of some strange feigned Monster, hath wit, and judgement enough to convince any Protestant whosoever. (pp. 75–6)

To prove the point, Talbot includes a dialogue between a 'Catholick Clowne' and a learned Protestant. The unlearned participant walks away with all the honours, from his cheeky opening inquiry stressing the novelty of the reformed faith, 'What newes good Master Doctor of your English Protestant Church?' (p. 76), to the end, where the Protestant fails to make a convincing case that his sense of Scripture is the sense that God intended.[74] The exchange is lively, but not facetious, and Talbot intends it to be taken seriously; it acts as a refreshing counterpoint to the suspicion of illiterates' reasoning powers so often shown by clerics on both sides of the religious divide, and finds an echo in the scholarship of our own day that critiques the invariable equation of literacy with progress.[75]

But those Catholic writers and publicists who exploited orally transmissible media would often have done so not simply as a means of targeting illiterates, but of reaching as wide an audience as possible. The scope, ingenuity and success of their efforts, described in chapters 3 and 4, entitles one to speak of a Catholic oral challenge, counterparting and complementing the challenges thrown down by Catholics to Protestants in printed media.[76] The latter claim perhaps still needs justifying. Scholars have rightly emphasised the dynamism of the reformers' attitude to printed and oral communication, but until recently have paid less attention to the other side of the debate; indeed, they have sometimes believed the reformers and assumed there was little to say on the topic of Catholics and print.[77] Mary I's reign in particular, despite the propagandist efforts of writers like Miles Huggarde, has been seen as a time when Protestants gained a decisive lead here.[78] But if Mary's reign appears mildly disappointing from the propagandist point of view, that may, paradoxically, stem from English Catholicism's enormous residual strength at the time rather than its weakness. Reversions to a popular *status quo ante bellum* may be inherently unlikely to inspire propagandists; besides, as Christopher Haigh has pointed out, English Catholics could hardly have guessed that Mary I would only reign five years, and had some reason to assume that heresy had gone for good.[79] Certainly, once Protestantism appeared to have become permanent in Elizabeth's reign, Catholics were more than capable of mounting a counter-attack in all kinds of media, including print, and of using print to sustain the spiritual lives of those loyal to the old religion.[80] Manuscript circulation, vital to so many aspects of early modern English literary culture, had especial importance within a community whose access to the press was so constrained.[81]

Minority groups often give the historian particular cause to read gaps as well as looking at the surviving evidence; and this is certainly true in relation to Catholics and popular print, the area where crossovers with oral culture are most marked.[82] Ballads are occasionally to be found among the products of secret presses or material printed on the Continent for distribution in England – most importantly, the rhymed version of Allen's 'Articles', discussed below in chapter 3 – while ballads from a Catholic source occasionally find their way into texts published in the mainstream.[83] But as far as format goes, very little survives from post-Reformation English Catholic print culture that is comparable to the broadside ballad: a gap which has, for instance, led to Catholic material figuring hardly at all in Tessa Watt's study of broadside ballads between 1550 and 1640.[84] Given the low survival rate for this kind of ephemeral publication, it is possible that Catholic broadside ballads existed at the time: the production and distribution of Catholic ballads is a subject which begs more questions than this study can answer, but the pedlars who hawked illicit Catholic books, pictures and artefacts around the country could certainly have carried broadsides as part of their stock.[85] But printing for Catholics was illegal on the English mainland and logistically complicated at all times, the occasion for a ballad often ephemeral and the genre relatively low-ranking. Manuscript distribution was bound to be a more obvious complement than print to oral dissemination, and certainly, the Catholic ballads addressed in this study most commonly survive in one of two ways: in manuscript copies of a single item and within manuscript miscellanies, or printed side-by-side with Protestant refutations.[86]

This is not the only reason for postulating a close relationship between oral and manuscript means of transmission. At all times, early modern England was an environment where orality cross-fertilised with both script and print. Adam Fox, one of the recent generation of scholars whose work has addressed the relationship between these three media, has said of England in the sixteenth and seventeenth centuries that '[it] was a society in which the three media of speech, script, and print infused and interacted with each other in myriad ways. Then, as now, a song or a story, an expression or a piece of news, could migrate promiscuously between these three vehicles of transmission as it circulated around the country, throughout society and over time.'[87] But different interest-groups would have made different use of these three media, and oral communication and manuscript circulation would have had extra importance to a religious body whose access to the press was circumscribed.[88] Sieving manuscript and printed material, as all those interested in early modern orality are obliged to do, opens a researcher's eyes to how interdependent oral and written sources are – as well as demonstrating how randomly the evidence of extemporised oral exchange is preserved, and how strongly its preservation depends on records made by the literate.

CATHOLICS AND POPULAR CULTURE: THE BONDS OF DISEMPOWERMENT

The term 'orality' has come to describe two things: the interface between oral and literate which is inseparable from all communication in a literate society, and the experience of societies or societal groups among whom literacy is partial or non-existent. In the field of early modern cultural studies, the second has been made more visible by the term 'popular culture', and certain bodies of evidence have been scrutinised for what they can yield about the habits of the semi-literate. Thus, though oral culture and popular culture are not identical concepts at all, interest in oral culture has been stimulated by attempts to recover a notional popular voice.[89] This has had especially fruitful results in the field of popular culture and politics. Several recent studies have analysed the workings of rumour, which Ethan Shagan has called 'a medium through which communities monitored their own vital signs, canvassing beliefs and reactions and testing the boundaries of the sayable'. While disparaged by members of the political elite, rumour was vital to other groups who sought to be influential, and Tim Harris and others have alerted us to the link between orality and political intervention among those excluded from the main channels of power.[90] This suggests how the history of communication and news-gathering is part of a broader concern with the operations of influence, which the recent fashion for Jürgen Habermas's work has encouraged. This development is a useful one for scholars interested in groups who, like Catholics, had an access to the public sphere which was problematic at best, and it illustrates how the quest to recover the oral dimension of political interchange can open up broader issues of marginalisation.[91]

Oral history, which Ronald Hutton has defined as 'personal experience, usually of the person making the statement, described directly to a researcher in conversation', is to be distinguished from the study of oral transmission and oral tradition, with which a book on early modern England must necessarily be most concerned.[92] Yet the areas overlap, not least because oral history has traditionally functioned as a way of giving platform-time to groups marginalised – at least until recently – by conventional historical narrative.[93] Catholics certainly fall into this category, though certain provisos must be issued. Marginalisation of this kind often occurs when a group is illiterate or has little access to education; and so, in arguing that the study of orality has something to tell the scholar interested in early modern English Catholics, one should point out that several models devised by oral historians are not fully applicable to this particular case. Catholics were of all degrees, and were therefore to be found at all levels of educational attainment; what unified them was not social homogeneity but a denominational bond, and the quasi-feudal arrangements by which the old faith was so commonly maintained would, if anything, have reinforced traditional societal divisions.[94] Thus, linking orality and marginalisation is most helpful not as a comment on Catholics' educational opportunities or lack of them, but on their general disempowerment, drawing attention to how things could be said or sung that could not easily be printed.

Broadly speaking, though, looking at orality within post-Reformation Catholic culture is bound to give more space than usual to the experience of the uneducated, and the religious world of the Catholic illiterate concerned to defend his faith. Some of the material treated in this book derives from the unlettered – though, as ever, it is dangerous to assume one is gaining unproblematic access to the popular voice – and much more of it is devised to be accessible to them.[95] At all times, one needs to gauge the relationship between producer and audience, asking firstly whether there is a social divide between the two, and secondly how any difference in station affects the writer's or speaker's mode of address.[96] This is, perhaps, particularly relevant to popular missionary material. Where evidence for the authorship of this survives at all, it can be seen to emanate from the clerical hierarchy and educated laymen – just as one would expect – and sometimes it is difficult to get an idea of how widespread such material really became, or who actually read it.[97] All the same, it is powerful evidence that opinion-forming Catholics were anxious to target the lower orders, or at the very least to appropriate a popular voice. Some of these texts ventriloquise the common man, like 'Little John Nobody' above, while the authors of others tried to cross the barrier erected by educational deficiency.

This could have varying literary effects. Publishing his religious verses at the end of the seventeenth century, the Catholic writer John Parlor wrote:

> I . . . make an Apology for these plain Verses, which I dedicate unto the Poor, who indeed stand most in need of Instructions, which must be given to them in an humble and low stile, befitting their capacities. Wherefore, I hope, no pious person will carp at them, which are beneath a Poets censure: since I pretend not to Poetry in them: but only have put such Instructions, as I think needful to the Poor People, in Meeter, fitted for tunes . . .[98]

Other authors, though, wrote in genres associated with popular dissemination but in a manner which displays considerable allusive complexity, even elegance. One should not assume that their work would have gone over the heads of the illiterate – or, indeed, that illiterates were incapable of inventing or appreciating rich metaphor and narrative surprise. Scholars working on the early modern period and beyond are used to examining how the categories of orality and literacy diverge and interweave, but are perhaps less conscious of the interface between orality and literariness than those who work on material of an earlier date, or on non-European cultures.[99] Hence, this study aims to demonstrate how material that tends to fall outside the literary scholar's purview can be read for reasons other than factual content, curiosity value and political correctness; often enough, it is well able to stand up to close reading, and yields a surprising level of complexity on successive encounters. The unambitious metre of ballads can initially prevent one's noticing their sophistication in other respects; anecdotes frequently yield formal satisfactions; fictional tropes can derive from oral culture and be grafted back into it; and looking at popular culture can at all times yield unexpected insights into canonical writing.

As Christopher Haigh has pointed out, historians working on early modern Catholicism have always tended to concentrate on gentry and priests: 'we badly need more work on Catholicism among the lower orders'.[100] More literary-critical work is needed too on material from the world of popular culture, which more often than not falls outside the literary canon. One way to do both jobs at once is perhaps to look, as this study does, at the world of ballad, anecdote, reminiscence, inscription, rhymed prayer and onomastic which had the potential to influence the self-definition of so many Catholics, and must have been particularly important for those of low degree. This material, though very various indeed, can all be classified under the heading of popular mnemonic. Less resolvable into theory than the scholar's art of memory or pedagogical methods of increasing efficiency, popular mnemonic nevertheless had a practical effectiveness, and each chapter in this book describes one of its social operations. But oral culture is an almost limitless topic, and this is not a survey. Some of the areas which this book does not attempt to cover, or mentions only in passing, have been given detailed treatment elsewhere: proverbs, drama, music, disputations between Catholics and Protestants, and how Catholic priests exploited the theatre of the prison, courtroom and scaffold.[101] The relationship of orality to prayer and devotional practice, and the Catholic sermon in post-Reformation England, are two obvious gaps, less well covered in secondary literature;[102] post-Reformation Catholics' missionary sensitivity to minority languages across Britain and Ireland is another.[103] While the essays which comprise this book are primarily about English Catholicism, they include some examples from Scotland, Wales and Ireland: partly for comparative purposes, partly for simple embellishment, but also to point up how each region ought to receive separate study in the future.

One surprising methodological feature may need explanation. In so far as one can be specific when dealing with material which is often difficult to date, and where dating matters less than with some subjects, the chronological span of this study mostly runs from Elizabethan to late Stuart England. But these chronological limits have sometimes been stretched, for reasons specific to individual subjects. For instance, as discussed in Chapter 1, sacrilege narratives hinted that the impropriators of monastic goods would see their families die out, thereby ensuring that gossip and genealogical scrutiny would continue for several generations after the original offence. To discuss these narratives effectively, one needs to stride centuries – one example among many of how memories of pre-Reformation Catholicism survived and resonated. Oral culture is stubbornly preservative, and when reflecting on the workings of historical memory, one cannot be too fastidious about terminal dates.[104] Post-Reformation English Catholics were anxious that the old faith should not be forgotten, and the most spectacularly diachronic moments of this study are the greatest testimony to their success – after all, though many of England's post-Reformation Catholic martyrs were only canonised in the twentieth century, this was the culmination of a cult which began at their executions and had never been allowed to lapse.[105]

Since this study was first conceived, an interest in the interface of collective or cultural memory with historical trauma has become commonplace in literature and history departments.[106] As Elizabeth Jelin has put it, 'memory and forgetting, commemoration and recollections become crucial when linked to traumatic political events or to situations of repression and annihilation, or when profound social catastrophes and collective suffering are involved'.[107] The impossibility of forgetting the medieval past, and the horrors of remembering it, permeate post-Reformation English culture both inside and outside Catholic circles, sometimes welling up in literary contexts which, on the face of it, might seem far removed: it is no coincidence that, as editors of *Hamlet* regularly point out, the madness of the traumatised Ophelia embodies itself in snatches of Catholic material, evoking lost worlds of pilgrimage and purgatory: 'How should I your true love know / From another one? / By his cockle hat and staff / And his sandal shoon', 'God a' mercy on his soul. And of all Christians' souls, God buy you.'[108] Trying to give early modern English Catholic culture popular relevance by labouring a comparison with Holocaust studies would be a particularly tasteless academic pastime, but neither should one neglect any insights forged by studying the traumatic events of the twentieth century, or be afraid to read them back onto previous eras. One such is the move away from seeing an aggregate of personal, emotionally charged memories as somehow less authoritative than official history – especially pertinent to a topic such as this, where protestantised historical narrative has dominated the field for so long, and where so much Catholic counter-evidence comes down to us in a relentlessly emotional form. Oral history is an obvious, frequently employed way to recover cultural memory, and even if this latter term post-dates early modern English commentators, the concept itself is certainly being evoked by the rhetorical tactics of Catholic writers like Edward Francis Eyston:

> Number I pray the dayes of the yeer, over run the Parishes of your native soil, England, and you will believe what I say to be true. What is Michaelmas, Christmas, Candlemass, Ashwednesday, Palm-Sunday, Corpus Christ day, All Souls day, &c. But words expressing the dread Sacrifices and divine Ceremonies of the Cath[olic] Roman Faith? what Town or City can you enter but instantly you discover the track of this Religion? when the old wals of Churches and Monasteries, the defaced ruins of Altars, images, and crosses do cry with a loud voice, that the Romain Catholique faith of Christ Jesus did tread this way? behold the words and deeds of the Christian world: behold the Characters of our Cath[olic] belief printed on the frontispiece of all times and places.[109]

Though this prosopopoeia beautifully illustrates how *lieux de mémoire* inspire oral remembrance, stones do not really cry out; Eyston's audience would have known that this was a literary injunction to actual communal effort, a call to use their day-to-day experience of language and landscape as a means of remembering the terrible past, of keeping faith and even of evangelising.[110] One is not surprised to find this passage followed by a prayer for sectarians to be converted, or to find this followed in turn by a rhyme: 'Brave English soul that (by thy Will / and Satans wiles) art drown'd / In sordid pleasures turn, embrace / that Faith that is most sound' (p. 180). As the rest of this study aims to demonstrate, England's post-Reformation Catholics knew all about the potency of cheap verse and the rallying powers of nostalgia.

I

Abbey ruins, sacrilege narratives and the Gothic imagination

The Catholic antiquary Charles Eyston, writing in *The History and Antiquities of Glastonbury*, has a story to tell about the market house in the town:

> It is a neat Pile of Building, built of late Years with some Materials the Town had from the old Abbey. But I was told by a Man of Credit, living in the Neighbourhood of Glastonbury, that the Town hath lost, in a great measure, their Market since it's (*sic*) Building, which he imputed to it's (*sic*) being built with Materials that belonged to the Church; and whoever reads Sir Henry Spelman's History of Sacrilege, will not wonder, that such a Fate should attend it.[1]

This is one example of a sacrilege narrative, a story which demonstrates God's providence by showing the dire consequences of violating or demeaning a person, object or place publicly dedicated to the worship of God. The notion that sacrilege provokes divine wrath has a long history; as John Weever put it, 'the depredation of Churches, Church robbing, or Sacriledge, was in all ages held most damnable . . . he that steals any thing from the Church, may be compared to *Judas* the traitour'.[2] But Englishmen after the Reformation had particular cause to be nervous, since Henry VIII's dissolution of religious houses was held by many to be the worst example of sacrilege that England had ever seen. Eyston was a kinsman of the Edward Francis Eyston quoted at the end of the introduction to this book, and like him, he would have been aware that 'the old wals of Churches and Monasteries, the defaced ruines of Altars, images, and crosses do cry with a loud voice, that the Romain Catholique faith of Christ Jesus did tread this way'.[3] In preserving this snippet of local gossip, he is giving a warning that sacred stones cry out against sacrilege, calling down divine vengeance on the perpetrator.

Though the secular landowners who acquired monastic property during the Henrician Reformation had a legal title to their newly acquired land, their families' moral claim on it, during the Reformation and for centuries afterwards, was felt by many to be considerably more dubious. Not all such families, one needs to remember, adhered to the reformed religion; though many later became Protestant, others were more mixed in their allegiance and some stayed Catholic, sometimes even receiving papal absolution for any wrong done.[4] But where they or their family had not personally benefited from monastic impropriations, Catholics like Charles Eyston tended to be happy to cite sacrilege narratives as instances of divine justice.[5] In addition, over the period covered by this study, many Protestants, especially High Churchmen and those of antiquarian interests, would have tended to agree with Catholics on two points: that widespread sacrilege had taken place during the English Reformation, especially at the time of the dissolution of religious houses; and that divine vengeance for sacrilege could be extremely long-term. The concern encompassed both land and architecture, and especially at issue was the very common practice of using the fabric of ecclesiastical properties for secular uses: as a basis for houses, or as a quarry for building stone and lead.[6]

Many writers on the topic believed that the sacrilegious sins of the fathers could be visited on the children to the third and fourth generation, or even beyond;[7] and here, already, is one reason to try and span decades and centuries when assessing the imaginative consequences of Reformation thought. The long time span covered by this chapter, from the Reformation to the growth of the Gothic novel in the late eighteenth century, is responding to the material in other ways too. As this chapter will argue, sacrilege narratives have a certain similarity to ghost stories, and like oral tradition itself, the ghost story is spectacularly diachronic; ghosts mean nothing if not the defiance of time, and the impossibility of closure where a wrong remains unrighted. The relentless periodisation of undergraduate courses can sometimes obscure the relationships between English Reformation literature and later works;[8] all the same, critics have long recognised that the Gothic novel of late eighteenth-century England takes many of its imaginative bearings from orally transmitted anecdote concerning the supernatural, especially from those stories attached to ruined abbeys, martyrs' relics, and other highly visible signs of Reformation violence.[9] But they have been so much more interested in Gothic novels than in orally transmitted anecdote that they have tended only to discuss one half of the equation. This chapter is an attempt to invert the picture: firstly by looking at sacrilege narratives within conventionally literary texts such as Horace Walpole's *The Castle of Otranto*, the most trend-setting Gothic novel of them all; and secondly, by discussing imaginative and antiquarian retellings of the sacrilege narrative associated with Netley Abbey in Hampshire.[10]

SIR HENRY SPELMAN AND THE SACRILEGE NARRATIVE

In the quotation with which this chapter began, it may at first seem surprising to see a Catholic author citing a conformist, Sir Henry Spelman; but there are two reasons why this gambit would have made sense. In an attempt to disarm his non-Catholic readers, Eyston – like many other Catholic scholars – used Protestant authorities wherever possible.[11] But, more than that, Spelman's *The History and Fate of Sacrilege* (1698) was a book which any believer in the ill consequences of monastic impropriations would automatically have turned to. Spelman was an early seventeenth-century antiquarian who became interested in the topic of sacrilege for family reasons, after both he and an uncle had encountered difficulties relating to their ownership of church lands; and it bulks so largely in Spelman's writings that it becomes an organisational principle of his thought: '*Sacrilege* was the first sin, the Master-Sin, and the common Sin at the beginning of the World, committed in Earth by Man in Corruption, committed in Paradise by Man in Perfection, committed in Heaven it self by the Angels in Glory ... The Sacrilege [of Adam and Eve] was a Capital Sin, that contained in it many other specifical Sins, Pride, Ambition, Rebellion, Hypocrisie, Malice, Robbery, and many other hellish Impieties.'[12]

The *History of Sacrilege*, compiled during the 1620s and 1630s, was by no means the only work of Spelman's to address the topic, but it had perhaps the widest impact outside the circle of those interested in antiquarianism and canon law. It combines his most extended and outspoken theoretical exposition of sacrilege with a number of anecdotal case histories, demonstrating the different ways in which Spelman believed Church lands had proved unlucky to their owners. For a long time, it was not the easiest of works to lay one's hands on. Spelman himself kept the *History* in manuscript form – in itself a common practice among antiquarians of the era, but his harsh words about many of England's noble families would probably have rendered the book too offensive to be printed during his lifetime. However, it seems to have circulated in manuscript while Spelman was alive or just after his death in 1641, to judge by the comments below from near-contemporary sources.[13] Spelman's literary executor Jeremy Stephens made an abortive attempt to print it in 1663; but in a sequence of events that defy providentialist exposition, the copy was thought to have been lost in the Fire of London, and then re-emerged in incomplete form among Thomas Barlow's manuscripts in the Bodleian.[14] Edmund Gibson omitted it from his 1698 edition of Spelman's collected works, where Spelman's writing on sacrilege is represented principally by the less personal, somewhat more moderate *De Non Temerandis Ecclesiis*;[15] but the first edition, bearing a deliberately, tauntingly anonymous editorial preface, was published later in the same year.[16]

The work had an extended afterlife, but Spelman's legacy was never other than controversial. Spelman himself certainly had enthusiastic advocates, and his own restoration to the Church of England of an impropriation on his estate was an action copied by several others:[17] the High Churchman Martin Lluelyn, in his elegy on Spelman's death, declared, 'No such confusion now, now no rash Arme / Dares seize the *Chappel* to enlarge the *Farme*. / Lest his offence his Issues Plague beget, / As th'*poyson'd Spring* infects the *Rivulet*.'[18] But not everyone agreed. In his *Church-History*, Thomas Fuller briskly summarised Spelman's argument and concluded, with a tongue sharpened by the events of the Civil Wars, 'this old and trite subject has now grown out of fashion, men in our Age having got a new object to fix their eyes, and observation thereon, taking notice how such Church-lands doe thrive, which since hath been derived into the hands of new possessors'.[19] The school of thought Spelman represented was condemned by the testy Low Churchman Edmund Hickeringill as 'a most Theological and Ecclesiastical Scare-Crow, to 'fright the Rooks and other Vermine from feeding on Church-lands . . .';[20] yet the story of Walter Taylor, associated with Netley Abbey and discussed below, illustrates how even some nonconformists could have qualms about sacrilege.[21]

It became, though, most characteristic of High Churchmen to condemn popery while abhorring the general principle of stealing from the Church, and pointing to dreadful fates suffered by those individuals and families who benefited from the Dissolution.[22] It was not the only topic that preoccupied non-Catholic writers on sacrilege; they covered several issues, some of which – such as the right to tithes, and the manner in which clergymen should be brought to trial – are a long way from supernatural concerns.[23] There is a considerable difference, too, between believing in principle that sacrilege was likely to incur divine wrath, and identifying specific instances of this happening. Nevertheless, if one can use the term 'superstition' neutrally, then a belief in the malefic consequences of sacrilege was a familiar superstition in England for a very long time after the Reformation: commonly between the Dissolution itself and the age of the Gothic novel, and long past that in some cases.

An interest in sacrilege had partisan overtones, tending as it did to coexist with High Church clericalism, and one could be accused of popery or impiety by one's religious opponents, depending on one's interpretation of such stories. But rather as with ghost stories, nothing more than a free vote was ever officially demanded on the interpretation of sacrilege narratives.[24] Spelman's rhetoric was at its most widely compelling when it bypassed party concerns, and recited plain lists of tragic events. This was partly fortuitous; the *History of Sacrilege* has an undigested, provisional presentation only to be expected in a book which the author himself never refined for print. But an anti-analytical stance, letting the facts speak for themselves, was also crucial to the effect Spelman wished to create. As he himself said, 'God's Judgments are his Secrets; I only tell Concurrences', and his was perhaps the greatest influence on the studiedly neutral reportage that, even now, the topic tends to invite.[25]

Particularly illustrative of this, and particularly relevant to the subject matter of the rest of this chapter, is the expression of Spelman's views on how sacrilegious impropriators harm not only themselves, but their posterity. An unusually laconic case history from the *History of Sacrilege* gives a fair impression of the doom which Spelman believed the sacrilegious might expect: 'The Abbey of *Radegundis* at *Bradefalk* in *Kent* by *Dover* is now Sir *Tho. Edolph's* Knight, who did lately build a fair House upon the Site of the Monastery, and it hath fallen down three times; his two Brothers lunatique.'[26] Recognising that by the nature of the subject fact may have been contaminated by fiction, Spelman is anxious to present himself as a responsible chronicler. 'I urge nothing, as not medling with the secret Judgments of Almighty God, but relate *rem gestam* only as I have privately gotten notice of it, and observed living in these parts almost all my life, and endeavouring faithfully to understand the truth, yet no doubt many things have been mistaken by those who related them unto me; and therefore I desire that wheresoever it so falleth out, my Credit may not be engaged for it' (p. 245). Thus, for every version of familial misfortune that Spelman sets down, one can postulate rejected and irrecoverable anecdotal versions that would have been a good deal less scrupulous: short on fact, heavy on myth.

For the believer in sacrilege, if someone inherits monastic land, their home is likely to fall down and their family to decay: thus, two potential meanings of the word 'house' are being invoked. The implication is that they have usurped: that, whatever the sins and idolatries of the monkish occupants, they had a right to the land and the buildings which the present owners do not. The author of *Sacrilege a National Sin* (1718), a tract heavily influenced by Spelman, gives a comprehensive list of misfortunes which the families of impropriators are liable to incur.

If those Persons and Families which have been, as we term them, Unfortunate, since their Acquisition of Church-Spoils, would well consider [God's forgiveness]; methinks they should be desirous to rid their Hands of them as soon as possible, . . . And therefore if his Hand lies heavy upon them in temporal Afflictions, in Pains and Diseases of Body, or in Distractions, Troubles, Ill-bodings and Uneasiness of Mind; if their Enterprizes are blasted; if their reasonable Expectations are disappointed by calamitous Accidents; if their Name and Estates decay; if their Children and Heirs are cut off in the Flower of their Age; or if they survive only to increase their Grief . . . They would do well to consider whether they have not made themselves justly liable to GOD's Anger, by any sacrilegious Usurpation? (p. 71)

Over a century earlier, according to Isaak Walton, Archbishop Whitgift had declared to Elizabeth I: 'Church land added to an ancient and just inheritance, hath proved like a moth fretting a garment, and secretly consumed both; or like the Eagle that stole a coal from the altar, and thereby set her nest on fire, which consumed both her young eagles and herself that stole it.'[27] The emblem of the eagle unwittingly killing its young was commonplace in the context of sacrilege, and received its most vivid theoretical exposition in Ephraim Udall's *Noli Me Tangere* (1642). Udall's remarkable engraved title page and frontispiece show an eagle bearing back sacrificial flesh from an altar to his nest, destroying his chicks as a result of the live coal still attached to the meat, with the motto *Ardet carbone nidus quo perit soboles impiae genetricis*.[28] In the text, he expounds the emblem, and even recommends it for use in the interior decoration of stately homes:

I could therefore wish, That all our Gentry that would preserve their Inheritances, without ruine to their posterity; would beware they bring not any spoiles of the Church into their Houses, lest they be spoyled by them: . . . And to preserve them from this sin, That they would have a Tablet hung up alwaies in the Dining Roome, where they ordinarily take their repast; in which should be drawne an Altar with Flesh and Fire on it, for Sacrifice, with an Eagle ready to take wing, having in her Talons a piece of Flesh, with a burning coale at it . . . and . . . a tall Tree, with an Eagles Nest in it,, [sic] and the Heads of her young ones discovered above the Nest, and the Nest flaming with a light fire about them, with this Inscription over the Altar, *Noli me Tangere, ne te & tuos perdam*:[29] For things belonging to the Altar, will certainly prove a snare to the devourers of them . . . (pp. 32–3)

1. Ephraim Udall, *Noli Me Tangere* (1642), engraved title page.

RELIGIOUS HOUSES AND SECULAR OCCUPANCY:
SEVENTEENTH-CENTURY ATTITUDES

The sacrilege narrative, like the more conventional ghost story, demands that its listeners engage with questions of fictionality and belief. The fact that neither kind of story was universally believed made them particularly tempting subjects for fictional treatment via individual authorship or collective anecdotal embroidery, though the term 'fictional' seems inadequate as a description of all possible audience reactions; paradoxically, the audience must have gained a frisson both from the suspension of disbelief, and a half-entertained fear that the stories might be true after all. The link between the two genres does not end there, since hauntings were consistently identified by believers as being among the consequences of sacrilege.[30] One of the richest and most sustained traditions of English ghost story, long predating the Gothic novel, is that where a new house is built on the site of a religious house, or with building materials from it, and strange things happen as a result. In *Pandaemonium, or the Devil's Cloyster* (1684) Richard Bovet gives an anecdotal account of such a haunting: 'About the year 1667. (*sic*) being . . . at the House of a Nobleman in the West Country, which had formerly been a *Nunnery*: I must confess I had often heard the Servants . . . speak much of the noises, stirs, and Apparitions that frequently disturbed the House . . .' (p. 202). Bovet witnesses, among other strange sights, five spectral women who – though he does not make the connection – are veiled like nuns. But while stories like this instil a powerful sense of the original owner's continued presence, not all sacrilege narratives relate ghostly manifestations in human form. Some, as with the story of Walter Taylor below, relegate the spectre to a prophetic dream; others leave them out altogether, telling tales of supernatural immanence as displayed in other kinds of occult or providential activity.

But both the new inhabitants of the properties and their apologists felt the necessity to assert the legitimacy of the new line against the remembered presence of the buildings' former occupants. Their responses to the mute historical reproach represented by the building are often set up to show them having the last word. By means of mottoes and other textual additions to a building, a dialogue could be set up between the current and former occupants of a house. Describing the house built on the site of Clerkenwell Priory by Sir Thomas Challoner, John Weever – himself a good example of the nostalgic conformist – quotes the verses from its frontispiece: 'Does chaste faith survive, even though the veiled sisters are missing, banished from this house? Now revered Hymen guards nuptial vows here, and studies in his mind how to keep warm the vestal hearth.'[31] The motto can be seen as defusing the conflict of interest between the displaced owners and the current ones, simply by admitting it. But more polemically, an imaginative case could be made for the religious inhabitants having been the wrongful owners all along. In 'Upon Appleton House', Andrew Marvell gives a decadent allure to the notion of a house being built on the site of a nunnery. Previously a Cistercian priory, Nun Appleton House had been given to the Fairfax family at the Dissolution, and one of Marvell's aims in the poem is to stress the legitimacy of the descendants' – and thus his employers' – claim to the property.

Retelling the story of how the early sixteenth-century heiress Isabel Thwaites had been confined within its walls by her guardian, the Prioress, and seized by her betrothed, an ancestor of the Fairfaxes, Marvell sketches the disreputable nature of the nuns' existence.[32] But the building can still, Marvell assures the reader, be redeemed through the virtue of its new occupants: 'Though many a nun there made her vow, / 'Twas no religious house till now' (279–80). This is only one of the tactful stratagems by which Marvell deflects attention from the unpleasant circumstances of the Dissolution. He begins his relation of the house's history with a metaphor which brilliantly combines a sense of genealogical inevitability and an anti-Catholic sneer at nuns' bastards – 'A nunnery first gave it birth / (For virgin buildings oft brought forth)' (85–6). A similar sense of inevitability, narrative rather than historical, informs Marvell's description of Fairfax's triumphant retreat with his beloved. Folk tale conventions dictate that the enchanted castle fall into ruins when the spell is broken, and the convent is in any case 'dispossessed' (272) now Isabel Thwaites has left it. The 'demolishing' (273) can, with deliberate ambiguity, be interpreted either as referring to the above events or, more obliquely, to the Dissolution itself;[33] and again, genealogical laws are invoked to commend the appropriateness of the outcome.

> Thenceforth (as when th' enchantment ends,
> The castle vanishes or rends)
> The wasting cloister with the rest
> Was in one instant dispossessed.
> At the demolishing, this seat
> To Fairfax fell as by escheat [i.e. reversion].
> (269–74)

Marvell gives to the anxious Fairfax, waiting outside the convent walls, a speech addressing the offending nuns, which asserts that even the building's architecture has become infected by wrongful religious practice. This deliberately inverts many of the sacrilege narrative's commonplaces, since to picture stones crying out in condemnation of the usurper was a standard imaginative response to sacrilege directed against buildings.

> Were there but, when this house was made,
> One stone that a just hand had laid,
> It must have fall'n upon her head
> Who first thee from thy faith misled.[34]
> And yet, how well soever meant,
> With them 'twould soon grow fraudulent:
> For like themselves they alter all,
> And vice infects the very wall.
> But sure those buildings last not long,
> Founded by folly, kept by wrong . . .
>   (209–18)

Writing out of a sensibility affected by childhood Catholicism, Patrick Cary uses the trope more straightforwardly, setting out the image of a house built with gravestones to condemn the impiety of those who oppress the defenceless. While money may be saved by reusing building materials, Cary argues, such buildings will always be haunted by the ghosts of the oppressed. Crucial to the poem's effect is its invocation of the general correspondence between sacrilegious despoilation and poverty. One did not have to be Catholic to pick up the wider implication that to use any building material salvaged from sacred sites was sacrilegious, or to understand that, while the use of gravestones might not directly impoverish anyone, stones from other sacred sites had only become available as a direct result of evicting the previous occupants. Cary's poem illustrates how the visual elements of a landscape can bespeak changing ownership, and sometimes silently complain at it:

> Who, without Horrour, can that HOVSE behold
> (Though n'ere soe fayre) which is with TOMBE-STONES made;
> Whose Walls, fraught with INSCRIPTIONS writt of old,
> Say still, *Here underneath SOME-BODY'S layde.*
> Though such translated CHVRCH-YARDS shine with GOLD,
> Yett They the BVILDER'S SACRILEDGE up-brayde;
> And the wrong'd GHOSTS, there haunting uncontrol'd,
> Follow Each-one his Monumentall Shade.
> But They, that by the POORE-MAN'S DOWNE-FALL rise,
> Have sadder EPITAPHES carv'd on their CHESTS:

As Here, the WIDDOW; Here, the ORPHAN lyes.
Who sees their WEALTH, their AVARICE detests;
Whilst th'Injured, for REVENGE urge HEAV'N with CRYES;
And, through Itt's GVILT, th'Oppressour's Mind n'ere rests.³⁵

HORACE WALPOLE, HENRY SPELMAN AND THE SACRILEGE NARRATIVE

To assert that Horace Walpole drew on fears about sacrilege when writing *The Castle of Otranto*, more than a century after most of the writers quoted above, may at first seem unexpected. Strawberry Hill, after all, incorporates Gothic carving in its fabric;³⁶ and looking at the biography of the author who has been claimed as the first Gothic novelist, it is not hard to identify a pronounced vein of anti-popery. Walpole's fascination with Catholic ritual, and deep imaginative involvement with Catholicism itself, coexisted with an explicit, often hostile disengagement from it; he described himself as the 'Protestant Goth', and promoted anti-Catholicism both as author and as patron.³⁷ *The Castle of Otranto*, so often described as the founding text of English Gothic fiction, is anti-Catholic in a way which, despite the novel's foreign setting, Walpole takes pains to locate in an English context. As part of his authentication strategy, the very first sentence in the preface to the first edition says that the story comes from a black-letter book found in the library of an 'ancient catholic family in the north of England'.³⁸

But Walpole's real ambivalence towards Catholicism is nowhere better demonstrated than in his use of ideas familiar from commentators on sacrilege. As Kenneth W. Graham has observed, *The Castle of Otranto* 'is really about the ownership of property and problems in title', and the story is a prolonged meditation on two ownership issues central to sacrilege narratives: usurpation and the longevity of curses.³⁹ The novel begins with Manfred, a prince of Otranto born to a usurping line, trying to marry off his sickly son Conrad too early, as a ploy to fend off a prophecy 'that the castle and lordship of Otranto should pass from the present family, whenever the real owner should be grown too large to inhabit it' (p. 17). The threat of growing too large, the reader soon learns, is to be taken quite literally – the most famous scene in the novel is the first, in which the enormous helmet of Alfonso the Good, the unjustly despoiled ancestor of the rightful owner, supernaturally appears and presages disaster to come.⁴⁰ Walpole's emphasis is on a growing retribution, one which does not lapse with the death of the initial usurper, but swells in proportion to the length of time that the grievance has gone unavenged. This is a trajectory directly in line with how sacrilege narratives take the temporal unpredictability of divine justice for granted, and emphasise how the sins of the fathers will be visited upon the children. It might be the first impropriator who suffers, or it might be his descendants – but sooner or later, the family will be held to account. In keeping with this, Manfred sees his son Conrad and daughter Matilda die, before he abdicates the principality and retires into a religious house for the rest of his life.

The sin of sacrilege could, however, be defrayed to some extent by gifts to the church. Still pretending that the tale has been authored by a sixteenth-century Italian, Walpole scolds himself in his own preface: 'I could wish he had grounded his plan on a more useful moral than this; that *the sins of the fathers are visited on their children to the third and fourth generation* . . . And yet this moral is weakened by that less direct insinuation, that even such anathema may be diverted by devotion to saint Nicholas' (p. 7).[41] Here, Walpole is referring to the way in which the original usurper, Manfred's grandfather Ricardo, delays the action of the curse by founding a church to St Nicholas – whereupon the saint appears to him in a dream and promises that he will reign in Otranto 'until the rightful owner should be grown too large to inhabit the castle, and as long as issue-male from Ricardo's loins should remain to enjoy it' (pp. 113–14). In *The Castle of Otranto*, Walpole is pursuing two aims which are rationally incompatible but able to be synthesised imaginatively: expressing disbelief in the type of curse which the sacrilegious are supposed to incur, but giving powerful imaginative realisation to the working out of just such a curse.[42]

Writing as editor, Walpole admits the power of his superstitious construction in the preface, and equates it with religious polemic. Pretending to guess at the date when the story was first told, he hazards that it was in the humanist era when 'letters were . . . in their most flourishing state in Italy, and contributed to dispel the empire of superstition, at that time so forcibly attacked by the reformers. It is not unlikely that an artful priest might endeavour to turn their own arms on the innovators; and might avail himself of his abilities as an author to confirm the populace in their ancient errors and superstitions . . . Such a work as the following would enslave a hundred minds beyond half the books of controversy that have been written from the days of Luther to the present hour' (pp. 5–6).[43] A dialogue is going on here between Walpole as imaginative conceiver of supernatural events – famously, *The Castle of Otranto* was inspired by a nightmare – and the equally imaginary but elaborately rationalistic activities of Walpole as self-styled editor and translator, distancing himself from his own invention.

Walpole, together with all his family, would have had particular cause to be familiar with the *History of Sacrilege*. Spelman's case histories of families who impropriated monastic lands, and subsequently failed to prosper, are divided into two parts.[44] The first gives the history of some of England's great families at the time of the Reformation; the second concentrates on the environs of Spelman's own home in Norfolk. Spelman tells the reader about a statistical experiment he conducted around the period 1615–16, when he took a compass and drew a circle twenty-four miles in diameter round his own home on a map of Norfolk.

> I inclosed the Mansion-houses of about 24 Families of Gentlemen, and the sight of as many Monasteries all standing together at the time of Dissolution; and I then noted that the Gentleman's Seats continued at that day in their own Families and Names. But the Monasteries had flung out their Owners with their Names and Families (all of them save 2) thrice at least, and some of them 4 or 5 or 6 times, not only by fail of Issue, or ordinary Sale, but very often, by grievous Accidents and Misfortunes. (pp. 243–4)[45]

Because of the slur cast on the ancestors of the impropriating families mentioned, and because Spelman implies that the present-day occupants of the land should make retrospective reparation, this was plainly one of the parts of the book most likely to cause offence. By the same token the landowners in question are sure to have known about it, by repute or in detail: perhaps from the time Spelman conducted his experiment, and certainly after the book began to be circulated in manuscript, with a revival of interest after it was printed in 1698.

It has never previously been noticed that the Walpole family are among those whose genealogies Spelman scrutinises, and that Spelman lists the Walpole family home at Houghton in his study of estates. Happily, the Walpoles were designated by Spelman as one of the 'good' families who did not receive impropriations and therefore prospered. But for a Gothicist coming of a family within a small area where, uniquely for all England, systematic genealogical enquiries had been conducted to estimate the human cost of sacrilege conducted at the Reformation, the imaginative effects would have been profound and various. When in residence at Houghton, Walpole and members of his family would have had daily intercourse with families who had been named and shamed; would have heard gossip about bloodlines that had died out entirely; and would have walked in a landscape where certain buildings and parcels of land were thought to carry God's curse.

Walpole was familiar with Spelman's work, and outside an imaginative context would probably have been dismissive of Spelman's attitude towards sacrilege, given the tone of his other recorded remarks on the topic.[46] Writing to Sir David Dalrymple, he calls sacrilege 'the lightest species [of robbery] which injures nobody'; in another letter, discussing church plate, he jokingly claims that Dr Johnson believed sacrilege to be 'the sin against the Holy Ghost, who, I suppose, he thinks has a particular fondness for silver basins and ewers'. Elsewhere, discussing the execution in Italy of a criminal who stole a cup from a church, his tone is sadder: 'I could not sleep for thinking about the poor creature, who was to suffer for so trivial a fault . . . To me, 'tis shocking, that what they have branded with this formidable title *sacrilege*, should be a capital crime.'[47] A disproportionate emphasis on sacrilege is invested with all the irrationality of which Walpole, and most of his audience, would have convicted the Roman church in general – and High Churchmen like Johnson are considered foolish to believe in it.

In the end Walpole's novel may repudiate the claims made by believers in sacrilege, but it does so only after a prolonged, detailed and imaginatively compelling exploration of them. The sacrilege narrative is, prior to Gothic fiction, the only genre to link two topics which were to become pervasive in that fiction: family curses, and medieval architecture. Walpole's story utilises both, and in addition explicitly engages with questions of sacrilege. How much of an influence this had on his copyists and successors is a far more open question. As Gothic fiction gathered pace, it became rapidly clear that both themes were capable of much wider application; the family curse, especially, developed a multivalency and wide suggestiveness which could tend away from Walpole's original emphases. Moreover, much Gothic writing, in the late eighteenth century and after, has no bearing on sacrilege at all, other than a standard invocation of awe at ruins. But as has been commented, 'Gothicists seized materials wherever they found them',[48] and in the genealogy of Gothic, the sacrilege narrative must surely rank as one of its ancestors.

The early twentieth-century writer John Meade Falkner, in *The Nebuly Coat* (1903), is one of the rare exponents of Gothic who returns to source. In this novel, the noble house of Blandamer has impropriated lands among its possessions, and the plot relates the downfall of Lord Blandamer. The narration is heavy with themes of providence, and at one point, Falkner explicitly refers to the *History of Sacrilege*.[49] Perhaps the most significant imaginative writer to refine Walpole's use of the sacrilege narrative was not one of Walpole's immediate successors, but a near-contemporary of Falkner's, M. R. James.[50] While his famous ghost stories hardly reflect at all on the sacrilege of the English Reformation, they show James relocating features of the sacrilege narrative to other periods and locations. Like Walpole, he imaginatively reinvents the idea that one incurs supernatural penalties by encroaching upon territory, or appropriating possessions, which are rightfully another's; though where Walpole explores the idea of a gradually accruing penalty for knowingly undertaken sacrilegious action, James's protagonists incur instant and automatic shocks, whether or not they are aware they have trespassed. Treasure hunters may awaken malign sleeping entities, as in 'The Treasure of Abbot Thomas', but so too, in 'The Rose Garden', can people innocently engaged upon horticultural improvements. James is issuing a warning to the curious, but also a warning against disturbance of any kind. His ghosts are hard to read as anything but evil; but they are not actively so, since they are only called up by meddlesome or thieving actions. One is not allowed to sympathise with the precipitators of supernatural revenge, since the ghosts have an atavistic right to do what they do. James's stories unsettle sceptics in a way that Spelman himself would have endorsed.[51]

STONES CRYING OUT: NETLEY ABBEY AND THE FATE OF WALTER TAYLOR

Walpole, like Spelman, was employing theories about sacrilege which had a symbiotic relationship with gossip, anecdote and folklore; he gives them a sustained imaginative treatment which mounts a critique of Spelman's theological interpretation, even while drawing upon it. This section supplements the previous one by tracing reactions to a real sacrilege narrative: a story attached to Netley Abbey, one of the monastic ruins most admired by early Gothicists. The tale is first reported by antiquarians in the early eighteenth century, significantly before the age of the Gothic novel, and it continued to attract interest into the nineteenth century, when imaginative reactions to Gothic ruin had become more standardised. Some treatments of it are fictional, others are not, though most of the non-fictional accounts address the question of whether sacrilege narratives are to be believed. The story offers an example of how the authors of written texts entered into scholarly and imaginative dialogue with orally transmitted material – though, as ever, one should remember that one has no access to anything other than a retelling, and that antiquarians were not immune from the temptation to embellish a story.

Folklore itself is, *inter alia*, an explanatory mechanism. Stories attach themselves to prominent and distinctive features in a landscape, and so when a landscape changes, they evolve too. Ruins have always demanded exposition, both for the educated and the uneducated observer:[52] John

2. Netley Abbey: from Francis Grose, *Antiquities of England*, 1783–7 edn, vol. II, plate opposite p. 211.

Wootton's 'Riders pausing by the ruins of Rievaulx Abbey', painted around the mid-eighteenth century, is one of this era's first pictorial recognitions of how ruined abbeys may be objects of interest.[53] Educated landowners could do this by landscaping their grounds around them – the ruins of Fountains Abbey, for instance, form part of the moral perambulation demanded of those who walk in the gardens of Studley Royal – and frequently, too, they became local occasions for literary reflection.[54] Myth-making of a more chthonic variety, feeding off the stereotypical association of Catholicism with elaborate secrecy, was perpetuated by tour-guides – like so many doubtful stories since. Discussing a picture of the Abbot's Kitchen at Netley Abbey, drawn around 1772, Francis Grose says: 'The hole seen on the right hand was, in all likelihood, a vault: according to the vulgar opinion, it is deemed a subterraneous passage, formerly leading to the neighbouring castle, and is always pointed out as such by the person who shows the ruins.'[55]

Netley Abbey inspired a number of more literary narratives, and one could write a micro-history of imaginative reactions to Gothic ruin simply by drawing upon the writings of those who were inspired by it.[56] As with many other medieval ruins, it was believed by some locals to be haunted. Describing his visit there in November 1764, Thomas Gray told his correspondent Norton Nicholls how 'the Ferryman, who row'd me, a lusty young Fellow, told me, that he would not for all the world pass a night at the Abbey, (there were such things seen near it,) tho' there was a power of money hid there'. The incident, which Gray also mentions in another letter, gives an authentic picture of the mixture of fear, fascination and greed which must have coloured local conversation about the Abbey.[57] As in *The Castle of Otranto*, published that same year, superstitious members of the servant classes are brought into play to voice the fears inseparable from Gothic: fears which gentlemen can allow themselves to enjoy, but not to endorse.

Gray, as self-aware a letter-writer as he was a poet, is also using the ferryman's words to throw into relief his own, more artful evocations of Catholic ghosts. Invoking the medieval inhabitants of the Abbey, he muses: '[The Abbot] is walking slowly (good Man!) & bidding his beads for the souls of his Benefactors, interr'd in that venerable pile, that lies beneath him . . . did not you observe how, as that white sail shot by & was lost, he turn'd and cross'd himself, to drive the Tempter from him, that had thrown that distraction in his way.' As George Keate reflected in an elegy discussed below, 'Scenes such as these, with salutary change, / O'er flatt'ring Life their melancholy cast; / Teach the free thoughts on wings of air to range, / O'erlook the present, and recall the past!' (l.85–8). Certainly Netley Abbey was regarded as especially fine by eighteenth-century gothicists, and inseparable from aesthetic pleasure in ruins was the imaginative ability to summon up the ghosts of former occupants.[58] Horace Walpole, suggesting ways that his correspondent Lady Ossory can amuse herself in Hampshire, explicitly recommends this technique: 'When by the aid of some historic vision and local circumstance I can romance myself into pleasure, I know nothing transports me so much. Pray, . . . try this secret at . . . Nettley Abbey.'[59]

One of the local circumstances of Netley Abbey would have engendered more painful meditation: a story illustrating the ill-advisedness of sacrilege, orally transmitted in the first instance, and widely disseminated by antiquarians.[60] This story, which is a very characteristic example of a sacrilege narrative, dates from the first years of the eighteenth century and first saw print in the antiquarian Browne Willis's *A History of the Mitred Parliamentary Abbies, and Conventual Cathedral Churches* (1718–19). Willis's preamble to it runs as follows:

. . . about 15 Years ago, . . . Sir B[erkeley] L[ewis],[61] who had the Propriety of the Abbey, sold the whole Fabrick of the Chapel to one Taylor a Carpenter of Southampton, who took off the Roof (which was entire till then) and pull'd down great part of the Walls. The entire Ruin of this noble Fabrick, which the principal Undertaker did not live to finish, having been since compleated, and the Chapel and Abbey being both now quite destroy'd, it may may (*sic*) not be improper to give some account of it; and add hereunto the History of the Fate of the Undertaker Taylor, in regard that 'tis a thing so particular, and so generally known in the Neighbourhood, and may be attested by divers Evidences, and very credible Witnesses. (p. 205)

Willis's concern with trying to authenticate the story is manifest. Nor is it merely a matter of common knowledge in the neighbourhood, but 'credible Witnesses' are willing to testify to it; and the suggestive initials denoting Sir Berkeley Lewis's name hint at how the matter is still a living scandal. The authentication strategies so characteristic of later, avowedly fictional ghost stories are all in place, as Willis proceeds to retell the supernatural element of the story; but well aware that his readership would be eager both for thrills and moral exposition, Willis had this story indexed under 'Sacrilege, the consequences of it'.

During the time that this Taylor (who was a Dissenter) was in treaty with Sir B– for the Chapel, he was much disturbed in his Sleep by frightful Dreams, (and, as some say, Apparititions (*sic*), in particular of a Person in the Habit of a Monk) representing to him the Mischief that would befall him in destroying the Chapel; and one Night he dreamt, that a large Stone out of one of the Windows of the Chapel fell down upon him and kill'd him. He was so affected with this Dream in particular, that he told what had happen'd to him in his Sleep to a Person of the same Perswasion with himself, *viz.* one Mr. W – a serious Man, who had a good Esteem with him, who examining particularly into the Disturbance that had been thus given him, advised him not to proceed in his Contract, there being reason to fear, that some Mischief would befall him if he did; and that the Notice which had been given him was to be looked upon as the kind Admonition of Heaven to prevent his Hurt. The Undertaker, tho' he was somewhat stagger'd with those Intimations that had been given him, yet (forasmuch as his other Friends Advice, to whom he had universally imparted it, was different) moved by the Gain he propos'd to himself, finish'd his Agreement with Sir B, – and soon after set to work on pulling down the Chapel; but he was not far advanced in it, when endeavouring with a Pickax to get out some Stones at the bottom of the West Wall of the Church or Chapel, in which there was a large Window, the whole Body of the Window fell down suddenly upon him, and crushed him in pieces. (pp. 205–6)

Antiquarians other than Willis would have ranked fears of sacrilege high among the several good reasons not to destroy ecclesiastical ruins; all the same, Willis's interpretation was not the only possible one.[62] Some antiquarians, telling the story of Walter Taylor, used Willis's account but took pains to demonstrate their own scepticism, using a surprising variety of rhetorical stratagems. Writing in 1798, William Gilpin went so far as to give the whole story a facetious treatment. Referring, not without irony, to 'that renowned antiquarian Brown (*sic*) Willis', he adds his own improvements to the fictional structure:

From [Willis] we have an anecdote, which, *he assures us*, is founded on fact, of a carpenter, who once trafficked with the owner of Netley for this elegant roof, which he meant to pull down and convert into gain. As he retired to rest, his slumbers were disturbed with dreadful dreams. These having no effect, the next night visions appeared; venerable old men in Monkish habits, with frowning faces and threatening hands. Still he pursued his wicked purpose. But the next night he had scarce fallen asleep, when a monstrous coping-stone fell plumb upon his head. He started with horror, and was hardly at length persuaded it was a dream. All this having only a momentary effect, in the morning he went to work on the execution of his design. No farther warning was given him. He had scarce mounted a ladder, when a coping-stone fell in earnest from the roof, and put him to instant death. Others, however, it seems, have been found, notwithstanding this example, who have pursued the design, for a mere fragment of the roof only now remains.[63]

Gilpin's beautifully orchestrated crescendo of threats has only the smallest basis in Willis, but by elaborating upon the story in this manner, Gilpin is giving an ironist's response to it. E. W. Brayley took an opposite approach. While admitting that the ruins 'have often furnished a theme for poetical description, and moral precept', his account of the story is more explicitly rationalistic. He scoffs that the accident 'has been regarded by the vulgar as a judgment inflicted by Heaven, for [Taylor's] presumed guilt, in undertaking to destroy a sacred edifice; but more enlightened understandings can only regard it as the effect of a fortuitous combination of circumstances, in perfect accordance with the established laws of Nature'. All the same, several generations after the event, it is still enough of an issue for Brayley's source to engage in a point-by-point amendment of Browne Willis, and to make an enquiry about the facts of the case from Taylor's family. These investigations result in a considerably emended version of the story which now includes the warning of Taylor's friends, the identity of 'Mr W' – Isaac Watts, father of the hymn writer of the same name – and the sequel of Taylor dying while being operated upon.[64] As Brayley further comments, sacrilege narratives are entirely beneficial in so far as they prevent the destruction of ruins: 'Whether this accident occasioned a direct stop to be put to the demolition of the Abbey is uncertain, but the superstitious gloom which it generated, has had an evident tendency to the preservation of the ruins in more modern times.'

Brayley is self-consciously writing as an heir to the Enlightenment, but some of his Victorian successors were to exhume the half-buried fears about sacrilege. In his guide to Southampton, Philip Brannon agonised about the sacrilegious actions of the destroyers in terms less guarded than his antiquarian forebears, which the Catholic revival in England was beginning to make more acceptable.[65] An intriguing question, which lies beyond the scope of this chapter, is the extent to which the sacrilege narrative helped prepare the ground in nineteenth-century England for the wide interest outside Catholic circles in the polemicised connection of Gothic and Englishness associated with the priest and architectural historian John Milner, and the Catholic architect A. W. N. Pugin.[66] A consciousness of the depredations suffered by England's medieval buildings, and a desire to put things to rights by refurbishing them in an archaeologically correct manner, was certainly fundamental to England's Gothic Revival, and it may not be too large an imaginative leap to see it as motivated in part by instincts of reparation. As in previous centuries, High Churchmen were likeliest of all to take sacrilege narratives seriously, and Spelman's *The History and Fate of Sacrilege* was edited, and ringingly endorsed, by the prominent Anglo-Catholic J. M. Neale in 1846 – with the last reprint in 1895.[67] But perhaps the sacrilege narrative's increasing lack of credibility, as England moved into the twentieth century and Catholicism became a more unremarkable confessional choice, is best demonstrated by Cardinal Gasquet, a writer not slow elsewhere to comment reproachfully on the English Reformation. Mentioning the story of Walter Taylor in an account of Netley Abbey, he refrains from commenting on it, beyond calling it an accident.[68]

Via antiquarian accounts, the earlier sacrilege narratives surrounding Netley Abbey became an inspiration to imaginative writers. For instance, in *Netley Abbey*, an imitation of Gray's *Elegy* showing a nostalgic sympathy for Catholics, the poet George Keate makes use of the story. The manner in which he does is suggestive. In his preface he takes care to demonstrate a concern with reliable evidence, and says of Browne Willis that he was 'possessed of a happy Credulity . . . [crowding] a Page or two in his *History of Mitred Abbies*, with every Circumstance of every old Woman's Story he could meet with' (p. 13). This, however, does not stop him repeating the Walter Taylor story in generalised form – Sir Berkeley Lewis's various purchasers are said 'by the Neighbours, to have been visited by Judgements, proportioned to the different Degrees of their imagined Sacrilege' – and repeating a less well-known sacrilege narrative, inspired by one of the heaps of stone on the Abbey floor.

A PURITAN, in the Reign of JAMES I . . . is said to have defaced many of [the Abbey's] Ornaments, and to have intended the Demolition of the whole; but, while he was giving Orders to his Workmen, was crushed to Death by the Fall of Part of the Building. The Heap of Stones under which he is supposed to lie buried, is still pretended to be shown. Superstition made its proper Use of this Fable, and was very probably the Means of protecting the Fabric . . . (pp. 13–14)

Nothing could demonstrate the licence given to imaginative genres more vividly than the difference between Keate's preface, pragmatic and cynical as it is, and the treatment he gives the story in the actual poem. He begins with a suggestion that readers suspend their disbelief, and attend to what oral tradition has to relate:

> Here too (Belief could old Tradition claim)
> Where swells the rocky Mound in shapeless Heaps,
> (His Name forgot, his Guilt divulg'd by Fame)
> Some rude Dismantler of this Abbey sleeps.
>
> Long, long in Thought the patient Earth he curs'd,
> That bore the Fabric's then unbroken Spires;
> Long wish'd the Pow'r to bid Volcano's burst,
> Or call from Heav'n thought-executing Fires.
>
> 'Wide wave (he cry'd) all bright with golden Grain
> The neighb'ring vales, while this proud cumb'rous Mass
> For many a barren Furlong chills the Plain,
> And draws with idle Zeal the Crowds that pass:
>
> No more the Vot'ries of each time-shook Pile,
> As Ruin's Heirs, shall call these Shades their own,
> For blazon'd Arms explore the pageant Isle,
> Or search dark Registers of faithless Stone.'
>
> He spoke – resolv'd. – The menac'd Arches frown'd,
> The conscious Walls in sudden Conflict join'd,
> Crush'd the pale Wretch in one promiscuous Wound,
> And left this Monument of Wrath behind.
>
> (pp. 23–4)[69]

Another anonymous elegy on Netley Abbey is very different in approach.[70] The author is careful to distinguish between what are, in his view, valid and invalid oral traditions – for instance, details on the number of people in the

Abbey during its period as a private residence are vouched for as coming from two old men of undoubted veracity, who remember their fathers describing it. But relating Walter Taylor's story, and a supplementary one telling how the purchaser of the leads from the abbey roof was killed by falling into the vessel in which they were melting, the author comments: 'The common people idly imagine it was a judgment upon them, and tell a long story of a dream Taylor had the night before, warning him of it; but such nonsense as that is from the present purpose, and at no time indeed at all worth relating.' Even if the author is slightly disingenuous in relating it anyhow, he makes, unlike Keate, no imaginative use of what he disdains to endorse in a factual preface. The elegy, which is very close in date to Keate's, may even be intended as a riposte to it.[71]

A more oblique commentary on the Abbey's history is William Pearce's *Netley Abbey: An Operatic Farce* (1794). Poking fun at the fashion for sham ruins, and boasting in its last act a spectacular backdrop of the Abbey drawn by John Inigo Richards, this highly successful production manifested a topical engagement with the Gothic throughout.[72] Expressing the concern with the theme of dispossession characteristic of all writers on sacrilege, the plot turns on the frustration of plans by Oakland, a landlord, to knock down the cottage of his poverty-stricken god-daughter Ellen in order to improve the vista through from his land to the Abbey. Oakland contemptuously dismisses his daughter Lucy's objections as fanciful nonsense inspired by Gothic romance, 'while I go on improving, she, as if in direct opposition, goes on reading' (p. 2). Nevertheless, the denouement vindicates readers and condemns improvers. The threat to the cottage is removed, and Ellen is restored to her rightful inheritance when – in an update of oral traditions surrounding ecclesiastical ruins – her lost fortune of India bonds and exchequer bills is discovered buried in the Abbey. Less slight than it seems, the play is making a serious point in its portrayal of the immoral Gothicist: one who enjoys the sight of picturesque ruins, but risks repeating the sin of the original impropriators. Paul Ranger may even be correct in suggesting that Pearce intends some members of the audience to pick up a specific allusion to the Walter Taylor story, among the more general references to dispossession.[73]

The clergyman Richard Warner's *Netley Abbey: A Gothic Story* appeared the year after Pearce's farce; the novel, though emphatically not borrowing from the play, was perhaps suggested by it. As a prolific antiquarian, living locally, Warner was well aware of the legends surrounding the Abbey, and he discusses them in *Collections for the History of Hampshire*, also of 1795. But as an imaginative writer, he seems to have chosen not to give further currency to any pre-existent orally transmitted legends which he considered dangerously fanciful. Commenting on the so-called Abbot's Kitchen, for instance, he remarks on the 'dark aperture, which the rustic antiquarian of the spot points out as extending a considerable distance under ground. These subterraneous passages are annexed, by vulgar credulity, to almost every old convent in the kingdom, and supposed to contain the masses of riches which the Monks by their avarice were enabled to heap together; an idea which probably arose from the reports of the visitors in Henry VIII.'s time, who invented and diligently propagated various stories to lower the cloistered ecclesiastics in the opinion of the people in general' (p. 36).[74] Quoting the story of Walter Taylor from Browne Willis's account, Warner calls it 'superstitious' (p. 32), and though he uses supernatural machinery in his novel, it is striking how strongly he reverts to standard-issue Gothic tropes which have no particular connection with Netley. One scene exhibits particularly well the ambivalence with which Catholic spectres were regarded. The hero is wandering by the Abbey at midnight: 'A religious awe now took possession of his soul, for the scene around was calculated to excite serious emotions. He trod on consecrated ground.' A benign phantom directs him to seek for happiness within the walls of the Abbey, whereupon he hears a woman's shriek; hurrying towards it, he discovers the heroine walled up in the building by the monks at her wicked cousin's request.[75]

A very similar contradictoriness is visible in the first of two poems written by Mary Russell Mitford about Netley Abbey. Mitford characterises herself as alive to reverberations of the sacred, while deploring popery itself:

> 'Tis sweet, – though memory loves to tell
> The cloister'd forms that sleep beneath;
> Pale ghosts in every shadow dwell;
> And spirits sigh in every breath;
> Still with that sweetly solemn fear,
> A softer, better feeling blends; –
> 'Twas Superstition govern'd here,
> And here her sullen empire ends.[76]

Published in 1811 and 1827 respectively, Mitford's two poems on the same subject show an interesting modulation in the author's sympathies at a time when questions of Catholic toleration had assumed an enormous political prominence. Sixteen years later, Mitford was to use no such proviso when she described Netley's numinous qualities – though, in its seemingly unconscious equation of enchantment with divine intercession, the last line is particularly suggestive of the associations which Catholic devotion conjured up in the mind of the Romantic.

> There in each moss-grown stone we trace
> The pious tenants of the place;
> There in each lingering footstep tread
> Upon the unmonumented dead.
> Yes, image of Rome's fallen power,
> This, this is Netley's hallowed bower!
> And it is holy still. Each wall
> And silent aisle and roofless hall . . .
> Each mark of ruined grandeur there
> All to the charmed heart whisper prayer.[77]

While both Warner and Mitford could equally well have used any other Gothic ruin as a starting-point for spectral reflection, William Sotheby's 'Netley Abbey. Midnight' makes use of the Walter Taylor story to initiate his own Catholic seance, citing Francis Grose in the margin as his authority.

> Upon the mossy stone I lie reclin'd,
> And to a visionary world resign'd,
> Call the pale spectres forth from the forgotten tombs.
> Spirits! the desolated wreck that haunt,
> Who frequent by the village maiden seen,
> When sudden shouts at eve the wanderer daunt,
> And shapeless shadows sweep along the green;
> And ye, in midnight horrors heard to yell
> Round the destroyer of the holy cell,
> With interdictions dread of boding sound;
> Who, when he prowl'd the rifled walls among,
> Prone on his brow the massy fragment flung; –
> Come from your viewless caves, and tread this hallow'd ground!
> (l.18–30)[78]

Sotheby continues with reminiscences about his own boyhood, when he 'saw gleaming far the visionary croud / Down the deep vaulted aisle in long procession float' (l.39–40); but, in the end, he sighs:

> Farewell, delightful dreams, that charm'd my youth! . . .
> Now while this shrine inspires sublimer truth . . .
> In the deep stillness of the midnight hour,
> Wisdom shall curb wild fancy's magic pow'r . . .
> (l.51, 53, 55–6)

Catholicism is equated with all imagination, and the avengers of Walter Taylor's sacrilege, outgrown spectres from Sotheby's fanciful childhood, are dismissed with regretful finality alongside the rest of the visionary crowd.

GHOST STORIES OF THE ANTIQUARIES

It was not only poets who dreamt up spirits in a place like Netley Abbey. Ruins of this kind, fascinating both to antiquarians and locals, became a particular stimulus to the visions, hallucinations and supernaturally charged dreams which Jan Vansina has identified as frequent in oral societies, and which were familiar enough too in the more mixed conditions of early modern England.[79] Frequently from the seventeenth to the nineteenth centuries, and occasionally thereafter, antiquarian descriptions of ecclesiastical ruins are punctuated by ghost stories. Typical is an account of Kirkstall Abbey, West Yorkshire, in the *Gentleman's Magazine* for 1805. Describing the former public path through the abbey, the writer confides: 'In this path, while a thoroughfare, were seen *monstrous prodigies*. The most curious relation was that of a peasant, who scampered from a long retinue of mourners, shrouded in white, and marching in slow funeral procession, at the dead hour of midnight.'[80]

This brief anecdote takes us in several directions. Its date of 1805 is a reminder that the Gothic novel was a dominant imaginative genre in the 1790s, and that subsequent accounts of ruined abbeys were liable to attract supernatural literary association. However, there was a well-established tradition of reporting local ghost stories in antiquarian works long before the official advent of the Gothic novel; as commented above, the beginnings of this are usually ascribed to Horace Walpole and *The Castle of Otranto* (1764), though the genre only came into high fashion in the closing decade of the century.[81] One must notice, too, that the story is said to come from a peasant, but is only conveyed to us via the report of someone literate enough to be a correspondent of the *Gentleman's Magazine*. Ghost stories reported by antiquarians are most typically ascribed, as here, to uneducated observers. This reporter, like many others, does not positively endorse the story, but leaves the possibility of wider belief and corroboration titillatingly open. A range of other rhetorical opportunities could be taken by the antiquarian interested in ghost stories; sceptics used them to illustrate the credulity of the ignorant, while believers in the demonic quality of apparitions could marshal them in support of a solemn theological warning.

There was a constant interplay, among both antiquarians and their informants, between popular moralisation and popular superstition. Ghost stories themselves are not morally neutral: cross-culturally, revenants are believed to wander because of un-righted wrongs, while ghost stories tend to attach themselves to sites of violent death.[82] The dissolution of abbeys, monasteries and convents would have reverberated for several generations in the memories of those living near the sites.[83] Many ecclesiastical ruins came to have ghost stories attached to them, and all of them were seen as exuding a sense of the uncanny, which imaginative writers in the Gothic tradition encouraged but did not invent. While there is an obvious anti-Catholic element to some of this mythologisation, in other cases the ghost stories attached to abbey ruins reflect a perception of the ruins' original inhabitants as wronged rather than evil. Theo Brown has argued that such stories are a form of social correction, the externalisation of a collective bad conscience about the Reformation;[84] certainly, they can often be interpreted as expressing nostalgia for medieval Catholicism, or at least an indignation at the manner of its downfall.[85] Reformers under Henry VIII might have hoped they were doing away with superstition by suppressing England's religious houses; all the same, England's inheritance of ghost stories would be impoverished without the ecclesiastical ruins they left in their wake, and sacrilege narratives should be read as part of this wider tradition.[86]

CONCLUSION: CATHOLICS, THE GOTHIC AND THE RETURN OF THE REPRESSED

The orally transmitted sacrilege narrative, like Gothic writing itself, fictionalises a wide variety of topics – from ruined abbeys to secular great houses, from celibate religious communities to the continuance of noble bloodlines, from human relics to architectural fragments – but all have some bearing on how the English experienced, fictionalised and framed in anecdote the conscientious cruxes of the English Reformation.[87] It is nothing new, in itself, to remark how much the Gothic writers owed to stories, plots and themes influenced by the Reformation; critics have, for instance, been conscious of the earliest Gothic novelists' debt to revenge tragedy, not least because Gothic drama came to vie for popularity with the Gothic novel.[88] That late eighteenth-century Britain's growing interest in orally transmitted ballads and regional literature also contributed to the lineaments of the Gothic is similarly indisputable.[89] But critics have been less interested in what those same novelists borrowed from non-literary fiction or non-fictional literature: and this chapter has suggested that those interested in the antecedents of Gothic fiction should look more closely at the works of early modern church historians and antiquarians in which sacrilege narratives are preserved, with an especial eye to the creative ambivalence with which England's Catholic heritage was regarded.

Appropriately enough for sources which have so much to say about architecture, this is in keeping with the current rethinking of English Gothic, which architectural historians are undertaking. As Chris Brooks puts it, 'Around the start of the seventeenth century, and in England most importantly, the Gothic revival began.'[90] Side-by-side with a continuing, unreflective tradition of Gothic building and ornamentation, and a care among antiquarians to preserve and record the threatened remains of the medieval past, there arose further evolutions such as Tudor Gothic, and in the early seventeenth century, the style's self-conscious deployment by Bishop Cosin and others for ideological ends. Though interest in the Gothic took a decisive new turn in mid-eighteenth-century England, the Gothic revival was not inaugurated with the designs for Strawberry Hill, and English Gothic fiction did not begin with Horace Walpole's bad night. Moreover, just as there is no one-to-one correspondence between religious denomination and style of building, Gothic fiction is capable of taking on many different denominational or secular casts.

When the Gothic literary mode began in England it certainly had explicit religio-polemical overtones deriving from the manner in which England had handled the Reformation, but these did not all work one way. Despite the trend set by Walpole, and the powerful use of anti-Catholic tropes by writers as central to the Gothic canon as Ann Radcliffe and Matthew Lewis, Gothic fiction is not necessarily anti-Catholic.[91] There is more work to be done on Catholic, and pro-Catholic, remodellings of fictional Gothic. *A Simple Story*, by the Catholic writer Elizabeth Inchbald, is set among English Catholic gentry, drawing on certain Gothic tropes like the tyrannical father and the persecuted heroine, while rather ostentatiously avoiding others that could be perceived as directly reflecting on the Catholic faith: no coincidence, perhaps, that critics are divided as to whether to call it a Gothic novel or not.[92] Other novelists make use of subject matter directly related to the Reformation in a manner which foregrounds the romance of Catholicism, rather than its evil: Sophia Lee's early Gothic novel *The Recess* (1785) tells the story of Mary Stuart's secret daughters, brought up as Catholics under the ruined abbey of St Vincent, where there exists a system of tunnels designed by a nobleman after the Dissolution to house dispossessed monks discreetly.[93]

Rosetta Ballin's less well-known *The Statue Room* (1790), more consciously sympathetic to Catholicism than Lee's novel, also comments on the Reformation by means of a counterfactual genealogy. The novel, which is based on the idea that Catherine of Aragon was pregnant at the time of her banishment from Henry VIII, ends despondently with its heroine, the rightful queen, going mad and firing a pistol at Elizabeth I before committing suicide.[94] The novel vividly illustrates Robert Miles's contention that Gothic texts engage with issues of genealogy and descent, while picking up on Catholic controversialists' awareness of how Protestant success in England had been helped by the accidents of the Tudor line.[95] Ballin and Lee both use counterfactual history to bring out the themes of dispossession omnipresent in Gothic writing: to quote another analysis, 'there is broad agreement that the Gothic represents the subject in a state of deracination, of the self finding itself dispossessed in its own house, in a condition of rupture, disjunction, fragmentation'.[96] Like the ghost stories and sacrilege narratives discussed above, their novels testify to England's imaginative preoccupation with the human cost of the Reformation; and *The Recess* in particular, with its stress on architectural ruin, evokes a chronological period closer to Lee's own time than that of Mary Stuart's.[97] English Protestants thought they knew that popery was oppressive and tyrannical; but the abbey ruins scattered across the English countryside also inspired sympathetic speculation and pity towards their former inhabitants, and Gothic fiction often became a way of expressing this double reaction.[98]

Should one, therefore, argue that because no exact counterpart to England's ruined abbeys was to be found elsewhere in early modern Europe, there was nowhere else that Gothic writing could have arisen? Literary historians have tended to identify the genre as smelted in England and further refined in Germany, two countries which had overpowering reason to express the conflict between Catholic and Protestant in their national literature.[99] But it would be wrong not to recognise the appeal that Gothic fiction had for other nationalities; it was, for instance, also seen as peculiarly topical at the time of the French Revolution, as commentators from the Marquis de Sade onwards have recognised.[100] Anticlericalism, blending with the hatreds of the revolutionaries, tended in French Gothic to obscure the characteristically English emphasis on unjust dispossession and providential intervention – but this is because the presence of Catholic themes in Gothic writing has always acted as a lightning-conductor for strongly divergent imaginative emphases.[101] The revolutionaries' anticlericalism and violent prejudice against the aristocracy would have made myths of aristocratic decadence, ecclesiastical corruption and tumbling edifices highly congenial to them, however and wherever those myths arose.

Linking the French Revolution with the knock-on effects of the English Reformation is nothing new. One of the founding texts of Gothic criticism,

Maurice Lévy's *Le Roman 'Gotique' Anglais* (1968), asserts that England's revolution of 1688, by which England's Protestant ascendancy was finally established, was a more determining factor on Gothic fiction than the French Revolution.[102] But the rise of Gothic fiction has been related as well to other causes of historical anxiety. In an influential study, David Punter has argued that the Gothic is a literature of self-analysis emerging at the stage when the English bourgeoisie began to explore the conditions and history of their own ascent, and that the preoccupation in this literature with issues of ancestry, inheritance and the transmission of property betrays anxieties about the nature of their ascendancy.[103] An uneasiness of the kind Punter suggests is certainly prevalent in the period – if more overtly among the detractors of social climbers than elsewhere – and could certainly have found metaphorical reflection in the dubieties of English Protestantism. But issues of religious etiology are, arguably, more directly related to Gothic fiction's overt preoccupations than are issues of class; and given the monopoly still wielded by Christianity over ideas of heaven and hell, religious anxiety would have been just as natural a cause of terror at that date as social.

Historical moods and events may fortuitously become a mirror for psychological dramas, and this is never more true than in the preoccupation with inheritance manifested in the Gothic novel. As a number of critics have recognised, it is very easy to dehistoricise family dramas, and that has its own dangers.[104] But there should be no problem in combining historical and psychoanalytical criticism, since a particular, fortuitous combination of political and religious circumstances may spring the lock on a pre-existent chamber of family secrets.[105] Parental metaphors are basic to Christian doctrine and discipline; the Reformation rendered it necessary to endorse certain aspects of one's inheritance while repudiating others; and thus, from the imaginative if not the social point of view, Protestantism can be said to have imposed a desperate ambivalence about the family on all its followers. As George E. Haggerty has put it, 'The devices typical of Gothic fiction have not been chosen by accident. They offer the most complex vocabulary for Gothic expression because they have the power to objectify subjective states of feeling.'[106]

Another series of psychological insights, those gleaned from Freud's essay on the uncanny, has already been fruitful as a means of combining historical criticism with the psychological.[107] It is now commonplace to think of the Enlightenment period as one plagued by instabilities and phantasmagorias, offsetting its glorification of rationality and progress; and discussing Gothic fiction, Terry Castle has made an attractive case for reading the Enlightenment period in the light of Freud's essay.[108] Freud sees the return of the repressed as reopening world-views belonging to an earlier stage of development; and if one firmly historicises this, it has some relevance to the subject matter of this chapter.[109] While it was never fair to equate Catholicism with the dark, the irrational and the unspeakable, such an equation would have been routine for most pre-modern Protestant Englishmen at most times, including the time at which the first Gothic novels were being written.[110] Moreover, what distinguishes the late eighteenth century from previous periods in England is, precisely, the return of the repressed in the form of increasing conspicuousness and legal toleration for Catholics.

Throughout the late eighteenth and early nineteenth centuries, Catholics were becoming more assertive, and successfully gained an ever-increasing degree of toleration from the government.[111] The first Catholic Relief Act, whereby Catholics could legally purchase and inherit land if they subscribed to a new oath of loyalty, was granted in 1778; and the early 1790s, the period when the Gothic novel first enjoyed widespread success, began with the second Catholic Relief Act (1791) which widened provision for Catholic worship and admitted Catholics to the professions. In addition, John Bossy has argued that from about 1770 the English Catholic community began a fast expansion because of a number of factors: increased toleration, Irish immigration and demographic trends in general. Thus, at the period when the Gothic novel was most popular, Protestant Englishmen would have experienced an intensification of the anti-Catholic fears that were so central to their sense of nationhood – fears to which the Gordon Riots of 1780 bore earlier witness, and which must have operated at the psychological level as well as the political.[112] The central paradox in Freud's essay is how the genuinely unknown is not frightening at all, because uncanniness depends on a previous, outgrown familiarity. To many English Protestants of the late eighteenth century, nothing could have seemed more familiar, more superseded or more threatening than medieval Catholicism; and its growing legal toleration would perhaps, at both conscious and subconscious levels, have been almost as terrifying as seeing monks move back into the ruined abbeys.[113]

Thus, one can only partly agree with Robert Kiely when he writes, on the topic of irrationality within *Otranto* and other English Gothic novels, that Catholic 'energy seemed largely a thing of the past. Heightened emotion was the objective for which the Roman Church was a convenient excuse.'[114] For the first Gothic novelists, Catholic topics certainly acted as a way into many different facets of unreason, as they undertook imaginative explorations which might seem to leave denominational questions far behind. But one should be wary of forgetting the initial inspiration, whether responding to novels of the 1790s or to those later critics who have found it irresistible to polarise daemonic Catholic irrationality with Protestant scepticism, reason and science. Using just such an opposition, Joel Porte commented some years ago that 'Gothic fiction [is] the expression of a fundamentally Protestant theological or religious disquietude'; and while this attitude has largely been supplanted by a widespread critical empathy with 'irrational' elements in the genre, one should still beware ancestral memories of anti-popery in any criticism which equates the Gothic too fluently with horror and unreason.[115]

But is the 'heightened emotion' of irrationality 'an objective for which the Roman church was a convenient excuse'? In an age of vigorous antipopery, Catholicism was likely enough to be the object of strong emotion in itself; yet to invert Kiely's first remark, 'things of the past' are exactly what does generate Gothic energy. Generally speaking, Gothic has less intrinsic connection with subject matter than with a manner of approach; any element of superseded belief can be gothicised, but this has a particularly powerful effect in cases where the belief is still held by some, and looks set for revival. This chapter has aimed both to identify anti-Catholic elements in the Gothic novel, and to assess how the genre both drew on and repudiated the more tolerant sensibility displayed in the sacrilege narrative. For an age when anti-popery and Catholic toleration were both matters of the highest political interest, this goes some way to explain why the Gothic novel grew popular when it did, and why it borrowed what it did from oral tradition. The sacrilege narrative, after all, is above all an expression of rights.

More generally, religious themes in the Gothic novel should not invariably be read as a metaphor for something assumed to be more relevant to today's undergraduates: family romances, class struggles, the oppression of women or the disjunctions of incipient modernity. If one does this, one is likely to pass over the intuitions of injustice which find expression in the sacrilege narrative, and over-simplify the mixture of sympathy and repulsion which characterises the treatment of Catholic medievalism and Continental popery in so many Gothic novels.[116] This is not simply an argument against present-day teleological readings, though teleology is certainly a problem at a time when topics relating to Christianity are so frequently elided, or misread, because of our contemporary sensitivities, blindnesses and terrors. Secularism has had the effect of diminishing the kind of general knowledge which the authors discussed in this chapter could all take for granted, and has in some ways coarsened our response to a genre for which a knowledge of England's religious history is so necessary – but, as so often, ignorance may act as an imaginative stimulus. The less recognisable the specificities of Christianity become, the more they can be taken as standing for something other than themselves; and secularism in its more polemical modes, associating Christianity and all organised religion with oppressiveness, has also given this generation a new way of reading the Gothic novel, and new opportunities to frighten itself. Since nothing now is uncannier than Christianity within the confines of literary-critical orthodoxy, it has become a Gothic enterprise in itself to disinter and anatomise religious elements within the Gothic novel.[117]

2

Anti-popery and the supernatural[1]

Thirty-five years before this chapter was completed, Keith Thomas's *Religion and the Decline of Magic* (1971) redefined early modern folklore studies. Since he wrote, a greater respect for the texts of non-elite culture has become standard; and more recently, Ronald Hutton has asked for historians to pay more attention to the deposits of folkloric evidence patiently collected by specialist and local societies.[2] Though a number of mantraps lie hidden in the fairy woods of folkloric scholarship, this challenge ought to be taken up by literary critics too.[3] This chapter considers anonymous, collectively written texts which had a prophylactic or magical meaning, and stories or descriptions concerning local landmarks and natural phenomena, both of which have traditionally been seen as the province of the folklorist; but since they are also formal generic constructions, they repay literary attention. They are, too, often Catholic texts – or were once. But this chapter is concerned less with individual scraps of folklore than with early modern Englishmen's attitudes towards folklore as a whole, and with setting out how Protestants defined it as popish.

This emphasis on English Protestants reflects the fact that more material on this topic survives from their pens than from those of post-Reformation English Catholics. It should certainly not be thought that the latter would not have noticed the interplay between religion and folklore, or that they would necessarily have approved of it; across Europe at this date, both Reformers and Counter-Reformers presented themselves as disliking superstition and aiming to purify popular culture. Catholics, it is true, were in some ways more willing to accommodate themselves to the mindset of the uneducated – surely often for pragmatic reasons, though Catholic theology lent itself well to the exploitation of sacred objects in a way that, to the hostile Protestant observer, would have borne comparison with the superstitious practices being eliminated.[4] Given that England presented different problems from most of continental Europe for Catholic missionaries, one might expect them to have maximised on whatever remnants of Catholic devotion remained within popular culture, and indeed this is sometimes the case – particularly, as argued below, in relation to holy wells.[5] But where folkloric material is commented on at all, it seems to have engendered distrust from Catholics as well as Protestants, even in instances which would have reinforced popular Catholic piety. Concluding his account of the pious legends surrounding St Patrick's Purgatory, a site in County Donegal, Edmund Campion reflects: 'Touching the credit of those matters, I see no cause but a Christian man assuring himself that there is both hel and heaven, may . . . be persuaded that it might please God . . . to reveale by miracles the vision of joyes & paines eternal, but that altogether in such sort, & so ordinarily, & to such persons, & by such means as the common fame & some records therof doe utter, I neither believe, nor wish [them] to be regarded.'[6] This is remarkably similar in tone to the Protestant William Camden's account of the same site: 'some persons devoutly credulous, affirme, that Patrick the Irishmens Apostle, or else some Abbat of the same name, obtained . . . that the punishments & torments which the Godlesse are to suffer after this life, might here bee presented to the eye'.[7] One writer believes in purgatory, one does not, but both distrust devout credulity.

Whether they were Protestant or Catholic, educated individuals consciously held themselves at a distance from the rest of the population on the topic of folklore. England – certainly at the beginning of the period of this study, perhaps at the end – would have had fully oral communities, fully literate ones and everything in between; but literates were educated into various kinds of dissociation from illiterates, which fostered the artificially sharp distinctions of polemic, and were fostered by them in turn. Consequently, there could occur a polemical isolation of the educated from the rest; literates' suspicion of illiterates is one of the great underexamined prejudices of the early modern period.[8] Differences between literate and illiterate ways of thinking were often used to define superstition, even down to matters of style and genre rather than content: for instance, George Sinclair's account of the witch Agnes Sympson attacks her for using mnemonic devices, 'Nonsensical Rhyms, for the instructing of ignorant people', and for 'teaching them to pray . . . in Meeter, in set Forms to be used Morning and Evening, and at other times, when occasion offered'.[9] These slights went largely unanswered, since the challenge would have made little sense to those primarily being accused. Certainly the victims of superstition tend not to be the intended addressees of diatribes against superstition; more usually, one literate Protestant is writing to others, sorrowing over the plight of the illiterate papist.[10]

CATHOLICISM, ANTI-POPERY AND THE SPELL

Polemicists' assertions could have been supported by a number of factors at work in the late medieval English church. The fact that snatches of Catholic prayer and Catholic liturgy were a well-established element of popular religion, medicine and magic at that date made it possible to condemn the Latin Mass as nothing but occult gibberish.[11] As Eamon Duffy has pointed out, charms and invocations were widespread: not only among the unlettered, but in devotional collections 'whose overall sophistication and orthodoxy cannot be doubted'.[12] The emphasis of Catholicism on the miraculous could lead – as the church was well aware – to an equation of priest and magus wherever a firm definition of Christian orthodoxy was not operative.[13] Inspired in some instances by clerical initiatives to christianise pagan sites, folk beliefs across Europe before the Reformation could synthesise Christian devotion with non-Christian practice – as Christianity has so often done.[14] If these factors were not especially endorsed by the medieval church, they were at least containable within it, or tolerated and exploited as a stage on the way to greater orthodoxy.

The Reformation, and the Catholic church's own internal reforms, caused the Catholic clerisy to become warier of superstition, more concerned with defining it and more anxious to dissuade the laity from it.[15] But Protestants went further, often seeing no distinction between Catholic sacramental theology and pagan superstition: to take one example among thousands, in *Polimanteia* (1595) William Covell argues that the consecrations of salt, water and oil are charms that derive from the Chaldaeans and ultimately from Satan (ff. I4b–K1a). Thus, it was hardly surprising that, in England, the outlawing of Catholic practices should have led to such an intimate, long-lasting polemical association of popery with supernatural folklore. An entire body of belief, one already vulnerable to ecclesiastical attack, was annexed for anti-Catholic purposes within and outside imaginative literature. Because popery was linked with non-Christian mythology and ritual by the reformers, and the two were persecuted side by side, their post-Reformation association went beyond the polemical. Real life imitated controversial commonplaces as, forcibly yoked together, popery and paganism were driven out into the wilderness of polemical exclusion. One can imagine a syncretism of the disallowed, which would have been achieved all the more easily because of the complex, often uneasy relationship that already prevailed between Catholicism and superstition.[16]

This post-Reformation linkage of Catholic and non-Christian mythology and ritual has often been observed, and explained in varying ways. It contributes to the model of survivalism, the idea that aspects of an essentially pre-Reformation religious culture lingered long after England became Protestant; and to notions of resistance, which point to the fact that, under successive Protestant governments, many aspects of Catholic ritual were practised covertly in opposition to the current ecclesiastical regime.[17] There is something apologetic about the admission which usually accompanies this argument: how, lacking a regular clerisy and the other normative checks of official religion, it was only natural for lay initiatives to interbreed with superstition. But traditional rituals for which the reformed religion offered no substitute, and which came to be practised independently of parish control, can also be defined as a sign of conscious nonconformity, whether or not they adhered to pre-Reformation standards of orthodoxy. In an important article, Ronald Hutton has argued that there took place a 'privatisation' of services no longer supplied by the official church, such as Candlemas, or prayers for the dead on All Souls' Day.[18]

One did not, of course, need to be a Catholic to mutter a spell.[19] Among the meaner sort, both Catholics and Protestants, spells might not have been seen as incompatible with Christianity, while spells with recognisably Catholic matter might have been employed across the board, out of a feeling that the old religion was more supernaturally efficacious than the new. Certainly, if polemic can be taken as evidence, even orthodox Catholic prayers might have been used quite straightforwardly by the purveyors of spells. In an early seventeenth-century manuscript tract inveighing against white witches and wise women, by the Sussex physician Edward Poeton, a dialogue takes place between the educated Dr Dreadnought and Gregory Groshead, a papist who – like others in this study – is made to talk in broad Mummerset. Groshead explains that he sees no harm in white witches: 'theyle tawke o god as well as tha best ome all: An I ha hurd um ze good prayers meny a time and oft.' Dreadnought asks what these prayers are, and Groshead replies: 'Tiz Our Vather. &c. an I beleeve in god. &c. Hayle Mary vull a grace &c. An zum wother zuch leek good prayers . . .' The threefold connection between spells, rote prayer and popery could not be clearer, extending even to implicit condemnation of two texts which Catholics and Protestants would have had in common, the Lord's Prayer and the Creed; to Groshead's revelations, Dreadnought responds: 'Alas poore man I much pitty your absurd ignorance . . .'[20] In contrast, the testimony of John

Rudgely, preserved at the English College in Rome, suggests that the sign of the Cross could be recognised as a sign of orthodox Catholic intention in both a devotional and a demonifugal context: having learnt it from his godfather, he used to make it both when he went to bed, and if he met women on the road who looked like witches or enchantresses.[21] So far from being the fruits of priestcraft, such shifts might have filled a devotional vacuum caused by the frequent lack of priests.

The Chinese whispers of orality could, though, have changed or distorted orthodox Catholic texts in a way which laid them open to reformist mockery, particularly where the original had been in Latin.[22] What purports to be a phonetic rendition of the way that Catholic lay people pronounce the Credo is preserved within John White's controversial pamphlet *The Way to the True Church* (1st edn 1608):

Creezum Zuum patrum onitentem creatorum eius anicum Dominum nostrum qui cum sops, virigini Mariae: crixus fixus, Ponchi Pilati audubitiers, morti by sonday . . . Creezum sprituum santum, ecli Cathóli, remissurum, peccaturum, communiorum obliuiorum, bitam and turnam again. (f. **7b)

In this almost Joycean gibberish, each linguistic distortion, however minute, speaks of what popery and orality were believed to have done to the Gospel; and it is no accident that the text chosen should be the Credo. Though White's intention is obviously humorous, he is also forging a serious polemical connection between misunderstanding and dangerous linguistic mutability. Yet however ridiculous the oral distortion of Catholic texts might have seemed to the reformers, orthodox intentions may have clung around them for a long time; it was, after all, possible to be an exemplary medieval Christian without understanding one word of the Latin Mass.

Deliberate travesties of Catholic religious and liturgical language are another kind of inaccurate oral rendition. As a feature of anti-Catholic mockery from the first years of the English Reformation, they could imply Protestant orthodoxy; but they also had occult potential. Where Catholic language was borrowed for non-Christian or anti-Christian ritual, the reasons why would have altered when Protestantism became the official version of Christianity in England. An occult liturgical travesty, such as the Black Mass was imagined to be, would always have represented a perversion of language originally intended as sacred. But before the Reformation, the force of any perversion would have depended on the sanctity of the original and even reinforced it; thereafter, anti-popery would have encouraged a belief that Catholic religious language was spiritually void, and therefore wide open to occult influence.[23] How often this kind of self-conscious perversion actually took place, though, is very hard to tell. Witch-trials demonstrate just how easy it was to confuse prayers and spells, and though witch-hunters would have attributed this to satanic cunning, it arises from a genuine generic overlap between the two.[24]

It has been commented that 'the distinction between a charm and a prayer was subtle', and certainly, many spells invoke the efficacy of the Christian God.[25] What makes them less orthodox to the educated observer – if, perhaps, no less pious – is the range of invocations they commonly employ. In the parody of the Credo quoted above, corruption of language is held to mean that the suppliants – whether they are conscious of this or not – are praying to something indefinite. But even where God or the saints feature among those summoned, a spell positively suggests a range of auditors wider, at the very least, than in a traditional Christian invocation. Sometimes evil spirits are told to get themselves gone in God's name; sometimes the second-person singular is less directive, as in the following charm 'to helpe drinke that was forspoken or bewitched', quoted at the trial of the Lancashire witches in 1613, and actually called a 'prayer' by the examinee, Anne Whittle.

> Three Biters hast thou bitten,
> The Hart, ill Eye, ill Tonge:
> Three bitter shall be thy Boote,
> Father, Sonne, and Holy Ghost
> a Gods name.
> Five Pater-Nosters, five Avies [i.e. Ave Marias],
> and a Creede,
> In worship of five wounds
> of our Lord.[26]

In effect, the drink-spell quoted above is a lay exorcism. In so far as it resembles the processes of sanctification that the medieval church had developed, it would have been subject to reformist disapproval, while Catholic clerics would have disapproved of it because of how the notion and language had been garbled by laymen.[27] As so often with exorcisms, some confusion is forgivable: is it the drink that is being addressed, or God, or His heavenly agents, or some demonic power? The effect of multiple addressees would have been complicated, and to some extent legitimised, by recollections of past heavenly hierarchies: Catholic prayers, after all, were attended to not merely by the Trinity, but by saints and angels. One cannot, perhaps, recover the mindset of the unsophisticated user: a spoken spell might not have been directed *at* any supernatural ear in particular, but simply have been seen as efficacious in itself, with the catalogue of names performing a function analogous to the combination of ingredients in a recipe.[28] But those unsophisticated enough to use spells, yet sufficiently analytical to recognise the problem of the addressee when it was pointed out, would have relied on definitions of orthodoxy framed by their superiors, and especially vulnerable where those orthodoxies conflicted. John Aubrey sums up the dilemma in his neatly framed anecdote of a woman who made use of a spell to cure an ague, by the advice of the mathematician John Napier. 'A Minister came to her, and severely reprimanded her . . . and commanded her to burn it. She did so, and her Distemper returned severely; insomuch, that she was importunate with the Doctor to use the same again: She used it, and had ease. But the Parson . . . thundred Hell and Damnation, and frighted her so, that she burnt it again. Whereupon she fell extremely Ill, and would have had it a Third time; but the Doctor refused, saying, That she had contemned and slighted the power and goodness of the Blessed Spirits (or Angels) and so she died.'[29]

One can guess that – here as elsewhere – it was the puritans who helped to articulate the question of exactly where devotions were going. Just as puritans disapproved of the practice of bowing to the altar on the grounds that an altar was not a worthy object of worship, they would have been alert to signs that texts mimicking prayer were not being directed solely to God.[30] Non-puritans were often critical of this literal-mindedness, and anti-puritanism may even have helped the cause of the spell, in saving it from unanimous disapproval among the educated. Spells certainly veer from the path of puritan-defined rectitude; yet many other English Protestants took the pragmatic view that some folkloric texts were more pernicious than others, and most were harmless. This difference of opinion resonates with another contemporary controversy: that surrounding the Book of Sports, the document instituted by James I which endorsed traditional religious pastimes in English parishes.[31] Both debates pit elite tolerance of popular culture against elite repudiation of it, and take place between writers who differ radically on the question of what is and is not tolerable. Thus, what we know of reactions to the Book of Sports may give some clue as to how folkloric texts like the spell would have been regarded – though admittedly in less extreme form.

Wherever the Book of Sports was endorsed, one may assume a *de facto* acceptance of many Catholic – or non-Christian – elements within popular religious behaviour: an acceptance that did not necessarily imply outright approval, but a feeling that such elements were not especially significant or threatening. Despite the Book of Sports' royal sponsorship, and what Leah Marcus has called the 'wave of antiquarian nostalgia' surrounding its republication by Charles I in 1633, this was an equilibrium that depended on not being publicly articulated.³² But much of the coterie verse written by the High Church poets of the 1620s and 1630s is what the Book of Sports could never have been: an exposition of the paradox, which translates into a mischievous anti-puritanism combined with a self-consciously daring tolerance of non-Christian elements in popular worship. Robert Herrick mocks pagan and papistical activity, but he also writes spells; a correct reading of his poems depends on an initiate audience who will appreciate the brinkmanship, but not be humourless enough to question the author's own conformity.³³

THE ANTIQUARIAN AND THE SPELL: RECORDING POPISH FOLKLORE

Spells, of course, were not the only way that Catholic matter could be transmitted in metrical form amongst the uneducated. The famous Lyke-Wake Dirge, which Aubrey records as being sung at Yorkshire funerals in the 1620s, sets forth an unreconstructed Catholic doctrine of the afterlife. The song would never have been part of the official order of service at a funeral, and so cannot be said to be a liturgical survival; but it conserves the Catholic doctrine of purgatory for which, notoriously, the reformed church had no emotional substitute.

> This ean night this ean night;
> every night and awle:
> Fire and Fleet and Candle-light
> And Christ receive thy Sawle . . .
>
> From Brig of Dread that thou mayst pass,
> every night etc:
> To Purgatory fire thou com'st at last
> and Christ etc:
>
> If ever thou gave either Milke or drinke,
> every night etc:
>
> The fire shall never make thee shrink
> and Christ etc.
> But if milk nor drink thou never gave nean,
> every night and awle:
> The Fire shall burn thee to the bare bane
> and Christ receive thy Sawle.³⁴

The way in which Aubrey preserves this material, contextualising what he finds by quotations from *The Iliad*, Plautus and Ovid's *Tristia*, is as suggestive as what he preserves. More generally, discussions of English custom owe a good deal to notions of classical paganism gleaned from Virgil and Theocritus: both imaginative writers, cited in a manner which hardly acknowledges how poetic convention might problematise the historical evidence they appear to preserve – and leading one, in turn, to suspect that the educated observer of folk ritual might have classicised what he saw by unconscious selection.[35] Aubrey's accounts are unusually non-judgmental, as so often with him – which may be due, in part, to the fact that so many of his collections survive in note form only.[36] But as a general rule, this conflation of English custom and classical literary motif could only have aided the common controversial identification of similarities between Catholicism, paganism and fictionality. Juxtapositions like Aubrey's, which occurred naturally to the classically educated mind, could become condemnatory evidence in themselves. To the polemicist, popery and paganism were natural partners, united against the reformed gospel like fictions against fact; since truth was unitary, and error many-headed, Catholicism and its personnel could easily be received into the pagan pantheon.

In the preface to *Antiquitates Vulgares* (1st edn 1725),[37] Henry Bourne asserts that popular customs ought to be judged by the sole criterion of whether or not they are sinful in practice, while adopting an almost all-inclusive definition of whether a custom is sinful.[38] Some, originally good, have lost their 'true Meaning and Design' through the accretions of 'Folly and Superstition'; others are a 'Scandal to Religion', though superficially harmless. In conclusion, he comments bluntly that 'the ignorant Part of the World' are almost all superstitious: 'the Opinions they hold . . . being generally either the Produce of Heathenism; or the Inventions of indolent Monks, who having nothing else to do, were the Forgers of many silly and wicked Opinions, to keep the World in Awe and Ignorance' (pp. x–xi).

Bourne's collection in itself can be seen as a form of opposition to the folkloric text: a stratagem which was not new. Aubrey's *Remains of Gentilisme and Judaisme*, compiled in the latter half of the seventeenth century, is often called the first collection of English folkloric material: in fact, it is only the first designated collection of folkloric material.[39] Aubrey's approach was innovative because it was unprecedentedly detailed and systematic: in the earlier part of the period covered by this book, a more usual antiquarian attitude to charms and popish rhymes can be illustrated by the 1610 edition of Camden's *Britain*, which records the fact that the Irish use charms but does not quote the charms themselves (pp. 143–7). But simply as a recorder, Aubrey was pre-empted by the controversialists. A number of small collections of folkloric texts were created during the sixteenth and early seventeenth centuries as part of various controversial initiatives, often in pamphlet form. Some are explicitly anti-Catholic, others – like condemnations of witchcraft – exercises in anti-satanic rhetoric which often co-opted anti-popery;[40] the notes to this chapter give some examples. Though Aubrey's collection is far larger than any of these, the main distinction between an accumulation and a collection is not size, but manner of assemblage: the former is an accidental aggregate of individual items, while the latter is deliberately brought together to make an evidential point. Aubrey's motive was, overridingly, an anxiety to preserve vulnerable traces of the past; but many other texts survive because they were presented for condemnation.

Most of these small collections are preserved in polemical writing. But others survive – and many more must have been thrown away – among the papers of government officials whose task it was to gauge levels of Catholic survivalism and anti-Protestant reaction. Some folkloric texts are undoubtedly more threatening than others on a political level. It is hardly surprising that a government should be anxious to quell prophecies of its downfall, or spells to bring that downfall about – nor that, in sixteenth- and seventeenth-century England, those prophecies and spells should so often have emanated from Catholics.[41] G. R. Elton has described how Thomas Cromwell's administration sought out and punished prophecies and spells levelled against the government: 'With a nation so volatile, at a time when even the truth of events was demolishing concord and threatening all good order, no government could afford to ignore the less rational attacks on the general state of mind. It was necessary not only to put down disaffection, but also to prevent the dissemination of false hopes and fears.'[42]

If bricolage is a manipulation of the impersonal elements of myth as demanded by specific occasion, then prophecies are almost pure bricolage. Enacted by a cast of quasi-historical characters and allegorical designations, they show an amalgam of learned, popular and heraldic references, and borrow from both English and foreign mythologies. Now that awareness is increasing of how written, printed and oral methods of transmission cross-fertilised, and of how this affects evidence that has previously been regarded as exclusively oral in nature, prophecies fit more centrally than ever into both learned and folkloric traditions. But for several reasons, they are a genre dependent on orality. When spoken rather than written, their message was inseparable from the manner of personal delivery and could be altered by topical improvisation. Even where they were written down, their enigmas would have placed the interpretive onus on the hearer, and suggested different, even conflicting possibilities. Often, too, prophecies were voiced by the uneducated. But as far as reception went, they behaved like many other texts geared towards oral dissemination, and found an audience at all levels of the social hierarchy.

The riddling incognito of the prophecy makes it a kind of folk allegory, and exploits allegory's ability to convey defiance in disguise. But precisely because allegories lend themselves to multiple interpretation, and because the whole authority of the historical prophetic text depends on elements authored earlier, the idea of a *specifically* Catholic prophecy is hard to sustain – as it would be for any disaffected group that utilised historical prophecy to justify itself. For the most part, one must speak of Catholic interpretations and emphases rather than Catholic inventions.[43] The cluster of traditionalists executed in the 1530s for calling Henry VIII the moldwarp 'that turned all up' were employing a metaphor wonderfully apt for religio-political upheaval, but one already to be found within the Merlinic prophetic tradition.[44] Subversion, as Howard Dobin suggests in his recent study of early modern English prophecy, was central to the conception of the prophet, and drew on Old Testament exemplars as well as Merlinic: 'these would-be prophets are nothing less than have-been priests . . . Although inspired and sanctioned by the same claim of divine legitimacy, the priestly Catholic voice, simply by being evicted from the centre of power, becomes the marginalised and criminalised voice of the prophet.'[45] Long after the Henrician Reformation, when Catholics had become well used to political marginality, they continued to use prophecy as a rallying device;[46] and accordingly, prophecies continued to be impounded as evidence of treasonous sympathies. Pursuivants searching for incriminating material after the discovery of the Babington Plot found prophecies beginning 'When the cock in the north has buylded his neste . . .' and 'A serpent shall arrise owt of the North ungraciouslye to conquer England', among the papers of Anthony Babington.[47]

More surprising, perhaps, is that spells and prophylactic rhymes could be collected side-by-side with prophetic threats to the state. The report on Babington's treacherous library survives within the portion of the British Library's Lansdowne papers originally amassed by Lord Burghley, which also contains folkloric texts of a popish nature. Endorsed 'A Popish Charm or Spil' and unattributed to person, locality or occasion – at least as the records survive – they stand as a general sign of civic disobedience and spiritual darkness. Among them are a rhyme to say on seeing the new moon, a rhymed prayer at night-time and the following 'Friday spell'. The latter potentially reinforces a connection between popery and superstition because of its reference to a Catholic pattern of fasting, and its emphasis on repetition of formulaic prayer as a means of obtaining divine forgiveness.[48]

> This daye is fridaye faste while we maye
> While wee heare knyll / our lordes owne bell
> our lorde in his Chappell stoode w[i]th his xij appostells soe good
> There came a Saynte throughe ryghte robe
> What is yt that shynes soe bryght / our lorde god almyghte
> he was naled sore / farre and in goore
> Throughe lyver throughe longe / throughe harte throughe tonge
> Throughe the holye brayne panne / well is that man /
>   that frydaye spell can
> he for to saye and his fellowes for to learne /
> So manye tymes as youe saye this one frydaye before noone
> So manye tymes shall your synnes be forgeven youe att domesdaye Amen[49]

Other collections of folkloric texts can survive because the dangers of popular superstition were preached about, or inveighed against in an explicitly moral and religious context. In *The Way to the True Church*, John White records a prophylactic rhyme.

> I blesse me with God and the rood,
> With his sweet flesh and precious blood:
> With his Crosse and his Creed,
> With his length and his breed,
> From my toe to my crowne,
> And all my body up and downe,
> From my backe to my brest,
> My five wits be my rest:
> God let never ill come at ill,
> But through Jesus owne will,
> Sweet Jesus Lord, Amen.
>   (f. **8a)

It is hard not to think that the rhymes are being criticised as much as the content, because of their indecorous jingling sound and the mindless repetition they encourage – which, in turn, betrays a hostility to the mnemonic devices of popular verse.[50]

The generic commonplaces of prophylactic verse were common to most pieces of this type – rhymes, enumeration of body parts and diseases, embedded Christian references and liturgical formulas – and were simultaneously mimicked and condemned in the reformers' parodies from the beginning, as in this snatch of dialogue from John Bale's *Three Laws of Nature*:

INFIDELITAS: Is not thy name Ydolatrye?
SODOMISMUS: Yes, an wholsom woman verelye . . .
>   She can by sayenge her Ave Marye,
>   And by other charmes of sorcerye,
>   Ease men of toth ake by and bye,
>   Yea, and fatche the devyll from hell.
>   She can mylke the cowe and hunte the foxe,
>   And helpe men of the ague and poxe,
>   So they brynge moneye to the boxe,
>   Whan they to her make mone.
>   She can fatch agayne all that is lost,
>   And drawe drynke out of a rotten post,
>   Without the helpe of the holye Ghost:
>   In workynge she is alone.[51]

But popish words, like idols, could be thought to have an autonomous malign power, which was why even the hostile reporting of popish rhymes could be criticised. In the 1650s Thomas Larkham, the puritan vicar of Tavistock, was accused of bringing in 'many ridiculous rimes, and impertinent stories in his Sermons, very unbefitting the seriousness which becomes one that hath to deal in the name of God'.[52] These include charms for toothache and scalds ('Out fire, in frost: / In the name of the Father, Son, and Holy Ghost'),[53] and a rhyme that might even have had an anti-Catholic provenance, or have been altered to summarise aspects of the Catholic devotional life which Protestants found objectionable:

> I give my dole when I am dead,
> I eat my maker in my bread,
> I knock my brest at every post,
> I pray to God, and heavenly host:
> And doing this still day by day,
> My venial sins shall wash away.

But if so, the anonymous writers of the complaint are unaware of it. They admit that Larkham was not using the rhymes seriously, but their terms reveal an uneasiness about the act of saying them at all: 'True it is . . . he reproved them when he reported them, but whither charming might not be reproved without all this Gibble-gabble, let wise men judge.'[54]

Philip Stubbes described the idolatrous maypole with an obsessive detail that has proved invaluable to later historians, and similarly, polemical writers like White and Larkham's critics have unwittingly preserved evidence for future antiquarians.[55] But the contemporary link between folklore, antiquarianism and polemic was stronger still. It was no coincidence that, although their relative emphases on past and present were different, antiquarians and polemical writers were both interested in popular legends and customs, and often reacted to them with a similar hostility. No antiquarian in early modern England could have avoided engaging with England's Catholic past, and for many non-Catholic antiquarians, the shift into anti-Catholic polemic was easy to make wherever an appropriate fact was surrounded by commentary.

Writing in the 1570s, the antiquarian William Lambarde yields an example of this. *A Perambulation of Kent* (1576) records a popularly transmitted pious legend about Chetham, which Lambarde justifies preserving because 'it is . . . profitable to the keping under of fained & superstitious religio[n], to renewe to minde, the Priestly practises of olde time (which are declining to oblivio[n])' (p. 286).[56] In the story, the church's statue of the Virgin comes alive and goes to the house of the parish clerk to complain about a drowned corpse who has recently been buried in the churchyard, on the grounds that he is a 'sinfull person, whiche . . . offended her eye with his gastly grinning'. The clerk accompanies her to the churchyard to dig up the body, 'but the goode Ladie (not wonted to walk) waxed wearie of the labour, and therfore was inforced for very want of breath to sit downe in a bushe by the way, and there to rest her: And this place (forsooth) as also the whole track of their journey, (remaining ever after a greene pathe) the Towne-dwellers were wont to shew' (p. 287). As Lambarde goes on to comment, the anecdote is tinctured – or tainted – by the hermeneutics of faery lore. 'For no doubte, if that age had ben as prudent in examining spirits, as it was prone to beleve illusions it should have found, that our Ladies pathe was some such greene trace of grasse, as we daily behold in [th]e fields, proceeding in deed of a naturall cause, thoughe by olde wives, and superstitious people, reckoned to be the dau[n]cing places of night Spirites, which they call Fayries' (p. 288).[57] This illustrates, in microcosm, how unusual local features could be explained as demonstrating either Christian or non-Christian supernatural immanence – which clearly helped the reformers' case.

'TOPICKE GODS': IDOLATRY AND THE NATURAL WORLD

What the story also shows is something which recent historians, informed by anthropology, have increasingly come to recognise. Daniel Woolf comments how, in early modern rural England, 'the sense of the past was focused less on time than on space, less on dates than on locations. Almost every rural community contained or abutted on a field, hill, river or ruin which it associated with a saint or local hero or with a memorable event.'[58] It would have been natural for this type of community to read onto their immediate surroundings the theological topoi of Christian narrative and the moral landscapes of man's life.[59] One can detect traces of this in the Lyke-Wake Dirge, where the theologically defined space of purgatory and the wholly allegorical Brig-O'Dread are both arrived at by crossing Whinny-Muir, a moor covered with whins or furze-bushes. This may well have been a specific place name, but it carries a double metaphorical charge: banishment from the centres of habitation, and a passage across thorns which, to inhabitants of moorland country, would have been an acutely felt metaphor for penitence. The two tropes of thorn and bridge are conflated in the satirical pamphlet *Tarltons Newes out of Purgatorie* (1590), where the speaker describes the 'hie way to Purgatory': 'after you have wandered a while, you come to a bridge, framed all of Needle points and over that must you passe bare footed, as the first penance for your formost offences' (p. 4). As the comments about St Patrick's Purgatory in the introduction to this chapter demonstrate, the idea of a transitional space between mortality and immortality, or the known and the unknown worlds, could also lend itself more variously to topographical mythologising.

Among features in a landscape, holy wells demonstrate particularly clearly how educational differences could cut across denominational considerations, since they were a type of site which invited reverence from traditionally minded common people of assorted religious allegiances, pragmatic exploitation from the educated Catholic and contempt from the educated Protestant.[60] Describing the holy well of Wanswell in the early seventeenth century, and utilising a mistaken but forgivable etymology, John Smyth of Nibley commented that it was 'Anciently called Woden well or Wodenswell, from the Goddesse Woden the Idoll of our old Ancestors the paynim Saxons . . . ffrom which goddesse and this her well, have byn by our forefathers as tradition tells related so many miracles and strange cures there wrought, that from the concurrence and confluence of all ages and sexes, meetinge at this un-holy well, The proverbe arose, which yet continueth; That all the maids in Wanswell, may dance in an egshel . . .'[61] The well is a site of misbehaviour, destroying social distinctions, undermining sexual segregation and promoting promiscuity. The proverb, too, is replete with double entendre: because their community is hydrolatrous, chastity among the young women of Wanswell is as fragile as an egg, and so there are no maids in Wanswell.

Only literates were in the position of being able to analyse where oral and literate mentalities clashed with each other, and by literates, the difference was sometimes called idolatry. This passage is dominated by the assumption that the uneducated are naturally idolatrous – here and usually elsewhere, an assumption rather than a fully worked-out position. While the problems with oral transmission were minutely analysed by Protestants as a reason for distrusting the Catholics' high doctrine of tradition, the feeling that habits of mind characteristic of oral cultures were superstitious seldom received the same expository treatment.[62] This is not to say that analysis did not exist: in *Origines Sacrae* (1662), Edward Stillingfleet uses heathen cultures' supposed dependence on oral tradition as a stick to beat them with, an argument shaped – as Gerard Reedy remarks – by Catholic–Protestant polemic.[63] But on both social and denominational fronts, the debate suffered badly from one-sidedness. Illiterates, after all, would probably not even have known they were being criticised; and while the average post-Reformation Catholic priest working in England would have tended to be pragmatic about exploiting whatever instances of Catholic piety were near at hand, Catholic writers on religion had other preoccupations than defending the mental habits of the unlearned.[64] Thus, the discussion about religion, the landscape and the common people was largely one confined to Protestants, and tended to employ protestantised terms of abuse.

A sophisticated and reflexive discussion of the topic, which problematises the usual association between idolatry and the vulgar, can be found in *A Treatise Containing the Originall of Unbeliefe* (1625) by the High Churchman Thomas Jackson. Here, the author laments man's inherent propensity towards idolatry: 'The multiplicitie of Topicke gods amongst the heathen could hardly have been hatcht without a conjunction of the ... imbecillity of mans understanding, or confused apprehensions of time, and place, as cogenitors of effects begotten in them, and of such affections or dispositions as the holy Ghost deciphers in Balaam' (p. 160).[65] This refers to the episode in the Book of Numbers where Balaak and Balaam curse the Israelites. When this proves to be in vain, Balaak superstitiously fears that the place itself has had an ill effect on the outcome: 'Come, I pray thee, I will bring thee unto another place; peradventure it will please God that thou mayest curse me them from thence.'[66]

Here the enemies of the Israelites are to be read as unregenerate souls, but not necessarily popish, heathen or uneducated.[67] Though Jackson renders unusually explicit the doubts which surface in other writers about the wisdom of allowing the uneducated to interpret nature, he is aware of very similar dangers lying in wait for those who cultivate an uncritical appreciation of verse written by pagans: an awareness that sometimes cuts across his Christian humanism and at other times draws on its inherent contradictions, echoing Plato's own wariness of poetry. Especially striking for the literary scholar is a further statement of his: 'That the seminaries of Poetrie should be the chiefe nurses of Idolatry, argues how apt the one is to bring forth the other; or rather how both lay like twinnes in the wombe of the same unpurified affection, usually begotten by one spirit. Woods and fountaines, as every Schoole-boy knoweth, were held chiefe mansions of the Muses . . . to attentive and composed thoughts, they inspire a secret seede or fertilitie of invention, especially sacred' (pp. 190–1). Poetry is the blood relation of idolatry; *loci amoeni* inspire both the educated and the vulgar, and may corrupt anyone whose imagination has never been corrected.[68] Jackson's description of how evil spirits operate in places of natural beauty demonises the tutelary deities of classical mythology:

And because superstition can hardly sprout, but from the degenerate and corrupt seeds of devotion, wicked spirits did haunt these places most, which they perceived fittest for devout affections. As sight of such groves and fountaines . . . would nourish affection: so the affection naturally desirous to enlarge it selfe, would, with the helpe of these Spirits sleights and instigations, incite the superstitious to make their groves more retired, and sightly . . . the eye would easily seduce the heart to fasten his affections to the place, wherein they appeared, as more sacred than any other . . . groves were as the banquetting houses of false gods . . . (p. 192)

Though Jackson is a firm believer in the instructive powers of nature, he is anxious to warn his audience that nature may teach wrongly as well as rightly – in part, precisely because it elicits such powerful feelings. Quoting Seneca's Epistle 41 on how religious emotion may be elicited by groves and overhanging rocks, Jackson comments on how this passage suggests a 'maine head or source of heathenish Idolatrie, which well cleansed might adde fertilitie to Christian devotion' (p. 191). On several counts, this admission is striking. Conventional scientific scholarship of the date when Jackson was writing described nature as God's book, and so does Jackson; yet, as he acknowledges, it is a book which idolatrous interpreters have the power to misread. Jackson's call for purgation evokes the contemporary debate between puritans and conformists about whether objects tainted with superstition can ever recover devotional usefulness, and his assertion that they can be cleansed places him squarely in the conformist camp.

More affirmatively, Jackson comments that 'the frequency of Sermons seemes most necessary in Citties and great Townes, that their Inhabitants, who . . . see for the most part but the workes of men, may daily heare God speaking unto them: whereas such as are conversant in the fields and woods, continually contemplate the workes of God' (p. 196). But here again, the onus is on the interpreter not to make God's revelation an occasion of idolatry: a slant which characterises Jackson's discussions both of natural sites like woods and groves, and of individual species. When considering plants, he asserts that their more striking quiddities are another possible source of idolatry, because they command an unusual degree of attention. 'Some whether halfe-Christians or meere Pagans, ranked by the auncient in the bed-rolle of heretickes, have held the Marigold, and like flowers, not uncapable of divine honour, by reason of their live-sympathie with the Sunne . . . So easily are mindes, apt to admire things strange and uncouth, drawne through curiositie of observation, unto superstitious and idololatricall performances' (pp. 198–9).[69]

This is an unusual take on a commonplace doctrine which, as noted above, Jackson himself would have accepted. Most considerations of natural history in the 1620s, and for some time subsequently, stressed how nature revealed God by means of similitude.[70] Levinus Lemnius's *An Herbal for the Bible*, translated into English by Thomas Newton in 1587, gives a typical account:

> [The prophets] use so manie Similitudes, & make so many Comparisons of things fetched out of the verie secrets and bowels of Nature; as namely from beasts, fouls, wormes, creeping and swimming creatures, Herbes, Trees, the Elements . . . and likewise from the humours in a mans bodie . . . wherewith they learnedly beautifie their matter, and (as it were) bravely garnish and deck out their termes, words, and sentences with tropes and figurative Phrases, Metaphors, Translations, Parables, Comparisons, Collations, Examples, Schemes, and other ornaments of speech, giving therby unto their matter a certaine kind of livelie gesture . . . stirring up thereby mens drowsie minds . . . to the consideration and acknowledgement of the truth . . . (pp. 6–7)[71]

Given the widespread acceptance of this idea, and how often the didactic meanings of images in Renaissance discourse depend on a knowledge of natural lore, Jackson's strictures can seem startling in their acute consciousness of the spiritual dangers which such comparisons might pose. Crucifixes and marigolds could both be seen as dangerous because the imaginatively undisciplined observer might commit idolatry by confusing signifier with signified, and carrying admiration too far – but though crucifixes could be confiscated from churches, nothing could be done about the English meadow.

This Protestantised caution could extend to the names of plants. Jack Goody has argued that a suspicion of flowers, especially of those that have no other purpose than ornamentation, is characteristic of Protestantised cultures;[72] but one does not need to assent to all the details of his argument to recognise that, in Europe, flowers have often been the inspiration for Catholic-inspired imaginative nomenclature. To this day

English flower names, although anonymously authored and communally transmitted, are remarkably imaginative, foregrounding startling religious metaphor of which a baroque poet could have been proud. Writing in the 1950s, Geoffrey Grigson collected over seventy names for the bird's foot trefoil, including such christianised ones as Devil's Claws, God Almighty's Thumb and Finger, Lady's Cushion, Lady's Fingers and Lady's Slipper.[73] Sometimes, as here, these names derive their religious conceits from the physical shape of a flower, or they can embody a dedication.[74] Nicholas Culpeper sarcastically commented of St John's wort, 'It may be if you meet with a Papist . . . he wil tel you St. John made it over to him by a Letter of atturney.'[75] Seasonal by nature, flowers with religiously inspired names became fantastic accessories to the Catholic liturgical year, and by virtue of their names acted – depending on one's viewpoint – as reflections of sacrality or instances of idolatry.

Keith Thomas has maintained that, by objecting to some plant names and the symbolic use of plants in general, reformers tried to cut the associational links between popular botany and religion.[76] It is a statement that can bear qualification, partly because consciousnesses took some time to be raised: throughout this period herbals are characterised more by the neutral accumulation of plant lore than a Protestant-inspired winnowing of it, and the impeccably Protestant Milton was happy, in the imaginative context of *Comus*, to exploit the demonifugal associations of haemony, or St John's wort.[77] Nevertheless, it is against this background that one must see the objections to plant lore made by some botanists: notably, as above, Nicholas Culpeper. Discussing the properties of angelica, he makes it clear how the names of many plants were felt to be offensive.

In times of Heathenism, when men had found out any excellent Herb . . . they dedicated it to their gods, As the Bay tree to Apollo . . . These the Papists following as their Patriarchs, they dedicate them to their Saints, as our Ladies-Thistle to the Blessed Virgin, St Johns Wort to St. John . . . Our Physitians must imitate like Apes . . . for they Blasphemously cal Pansies, or Hearts ease, an Herb of the Trinity, because it is of three colors: . . . The Heathens and Papists were bad, and ours worse; the Papists giving Idolatrous Names to Herbs for their Vertues sake, not for their fair looks, and therefore some called this, an Herb of the Holy Ghost, others more moderate called it Angelica, because of its Angelical Vertues, and that Name it retains stil, and al Nations follow it so neer as their Dialect wil permit.[78]

If anything, it is the professional herbalists whom Culpeper suspects of this idolatry: in his description of the archangel he rages, 'To put a gloss upon their practice, the Physitians cal an Herb (which Country people vulgarly know by the name of dead Nettles) Arch angel, wherein whether they savor of more Superstition or Folly, I leave to the Judicious Reader' (pp. 15–16). But, conspicuously, it is one more area where folklore would have attracted criticism for popery.

The assumption that God was directly revealed in the natural world structured scientific thinking throughout the period covered by this study, which made it very easy for scientific discourse to slide into religious apologetics. Commenting on the foundation of the Royal Society, Thomas Sprat famously remarked how both it and the Church of England had passed by corrupt copies and referred themselves to perfect originals, 'the one to the Scripture, the other to the large Volume of the Creatures'.[79] With the difference that he is asserting the similarity of conformist Protestantism to the new scientific methodology, he compares the word of God and the work of God as piously as his predecessors; God is still directly revealed within the natural world, if no longer by signatures. Within both theology and science, literacy had helped to fix written records against which interpretations could be compared. Elizabeth Eisenstein uses Sprat's quotation to underpin her influential comparison of the new science and the new biblical scholarship, as developments which were both facilitated by the rise of the printing press.[80] But though it is not a comparison made in her book, reformist suspicion of the illiterate can be very similar to the medieval Catholic wariness of uneducated laypeople.[81] Literacy brought about greater possibilities of verification, and this had the effect of creating a new conception of fact; in both medieval and early modern England the educated were, above all, opposing themselves to the rest. Nevertheless, Protestantism benefited from the link between print and verifiability, and this in turn encouraged reformers and other Protestant writers to reframe a suspicion of the independent imagination, particularly where the imaginative agents were illiterate. An educated disapproval of religious metaphors developed within oral cultures, and a feeling that discredited techniques within natural science must originally have been disseminated by those interested in promoting theological error, both contributed to a widespread intuition of popish rural idolatry.

Efforts to reform botany would have been spurred by the known use of flowers in pagan ritual, and classically educated clergy would have been especially alert to popish uses of flowers which could be paralleled within Latin and Greek texts.[82] Thomas Jackson comments that 'the use of Vervine, of our Ladies gloves, and S. Johns grasse at this day [is] in no lesse request amongst some rude and ignorant Christians, than sometimes they were amongst the ancient Grecians or Romanes, to whose manners Theocritus and Virgil in their poems doe allude' (p. 176), and White complains at greater length:

Many also use to weare Vervein against blasts: and when they gather it for this purpose, first they crosse the herbe with their hand, and then they blesse it, thus:

> Hallowed be thou Vervein, as thou growest on the ground,
> For in the mount of Calvary there thou was first found:
> Thou healedst our Saviour Jesus Christ, and stanchedst his bleeding wound:
> In the name of the Father, the Son, and the holy Ghost, I take thee fro[m] the ground.

And so they pluck it up, and weare it. Their prayers and traditions of this sort are infinite, and the ceremonies they use in all their actions are nothing inferiour to the Gentiles in number and strangenesse.[83]

POPERY AND FAERY

White's condemnation, like the title of Aubrey's manuscript compilation, 'Remaines of Gentilisme and Judaisme', suggests how easy it was to classify together all popular non-Protestant religious practice. Hitherto defined by the traditional opposition of Judaism and the gentile or heathen religions, the subject could incorporate Catholic survivals without difficulty, because the mixed character of popular Catholic devotion had always been part of the reformers' condemnation. In this context, the tendency was to equate papists with heathens rather than Jews, and frequently with believers in classical paganism, though not exclusively; the description of Wodenswell quoted above shows, for instance, how sacred Catholic sites might be interpreted in terms of Nordic myth. Fairies were even more prominent mythological representatives of the old religion, and in an English context, Jackson's observation that groves are 'as the banquetting houses of false gods', discussed above, may owe something to faery lore:[84] a link that is made more explicit in another quotation from Sprat's *History of the Royal Society*.

The Poets began of old to impose the deceit. They to make all things look more venerable than they were, devis'd a thousand false Chimæras; on every Field, River, Grove, and Cave, they bestow'd a Fantasm of their own making: . . . And in the modern Ages these Fantastical Forms were reviv'd, and possess'd Christendom, in the very height of the Scholemens time: An infinit number of Fairies haunted every house; all Churches were fill'd with Apparitions; men began to be frighted from their Cradles . . . All which abuses if those acute Philosophers did not promote, yet they were never able to overcome; nay, even not so much as King Oberon and his invisible Army. (p. 340)

Sprat is utilising a standard polemical linkage which shows not only how previously existing folkloric material came to be interpreted in a Catholicised – and usually anti-Catholic – light, but how strongly popery was linked with belief in fairies. This involved controversialists' appropriation of a coherent, detailed native British mythology, much used within imaginative literary texts at both elite and popular levels.[85] Pleading for godly preachers in Wales, for instance, John Penry complained of the danger posed in many areas by 'obstinate idolaters that would fain be again in execrable Rome':

Hence flow our swarmes of south-saiers, and enchanters, such as will not stick openly, to professe that they walke, on Tuesdaies, and Thursdaies at nights, with the fairies, of whom they brag themselves to have their knowlege. These sonnes of Belial, who shuld die the death . . . have stroken such an astonishing reverence of the fairies, into the hearts of our silly people, that they dare not name the[m], without honor . . . Hence proceed open defending of Purgatory & the Real presence, praying unto images &c. with other infinit monsters.[86]

As this illustrates, faery lore was not the only element of folklore or popular culture that could be used to condemn popery, and it is sometimes striking how little the differentiations of genre seem to matter. John Harvey wrote in 1588 how 'idle Cloistermen, mad merry Friers, and lusty Abbey Lubbers'[87] used to keep alive 'tales of Hobgoblin, Robin Goodfellow, Hogmagog, Queene Grogorton, King Arthur, Bevis of Southhampton, Lancelot du Lake, Sir Tristram, Thomas of Lancaster, John a Gaunt, Guy of Warwike, Orlando furioso, Amadis du Gaul, Robin Hood and little John, Frier Tuck and maid Marian, with a thousand such legendaries . . . to busie the minds of the vulgar sort . . . and to avert their conceits from consideration of serious graver matters'.[88] In this indictment, real and quasi-history jostles with native faery lore and – in the case of *Orlando Furioso* – imaginative writing from an elite source, perhaps filtered down through chapbooks. In so far as the characters in question are legendary or fictional, they all have the power to pervert the attention of the uneducated from the true God. Superstition could, indeed, come to stand for all fictionality. Reginald Scot makes a suggestive link in one of the chapter headings to his *Discovery of Witchcraft*: 'What miraculous actions are imputed to witches by witchmongers, papists, and poets.'[89]

This, though, is not the whole story. Faery lore was used by Protestants for a number of imaginative purposes, negative, positive, neutral or all three:[90] for instance, in William Warner's *Albion's England*, a mock-pastoral about a shepherd's dream of popish fairies, Puck ironically praises the bad old days of Catholicism but also condemns contemporary ecclesiastical abuses.[91] Spenser's faery allegory in *The Faerie Queene* may be employed for polemical purposes within the narrative, but is certainly not anti-Catholic in itself; on the other hand, in the glosses to Spenser's *Shepheardes Calendar*, E. K. turns a description of a fairy-haunted dell into an opportunity to explain how friars 'soughte to nousell [nurture] the comon people in ignorounce'.[92] Because of its hold among the English unlearned, faery lore was more suitable than classical myth for illustrating one of the reformers' favourite topics, the stupidity of superstition. Because it was a non-Christian belief-system, it could also be easily appropriated for anti-Catholic imaginative polemic – an association which would have been reinforced by the real and supposed syncretisms of the vulgar. Here one must revert to Thomas Larkham. The shortest rhyme his critics quote, 'Mary fary, fary Mary', shows neatly how the imaginary inhabitants of the common people's countryside were held to include figures associated with Catholicism. It may contain another phonetic transcription of dialect,[93] but the reference to fairies, literal or punning, was one that the reader was intended to recognise and condemn, and hints that the Queen of Heaven and Queen Mab could be conflated.[94]

Still, there is something almost affectionate in the way that High Church poets in the early seventeenth century routinely equated Catholics with fairies. A poem like Richard Corbett's 'The Fairies' Farewell' is certainly not endorsing Catholicism, but if anyone is being demonised, it is the Puritan:

> Farewell, Rewards & Faeries,
> Good Houswives now may say;
> For now foule Slutts in Daries
> Doe fare as well as they;
> And though they sweepe theyr Hearths no less
> Then Maydes were wont to doe,
> Yet who of late for Cleaneliness
> Finds sixe-pence in her Shoe?[95]

Here, Corbett uses a familiar topos, the association of dairies and fairies. It derives from the fact that butter- and cheese-making is unpredictable, making it particularly tempting to placate whatever tutelary spirit might be in charge of the process, it often crops up in imaginative writing – partly, no doubt, because of the serendipitous rhyme. Hobbes uses it in the famous ending of *Leviathan*, though with suggestively different emphases from Corbett's. In his first verse Corbett comments, with some tolerance, that the erroneous belief systems of popery used to have a beneficial effect in encouraging dairymaids to perform their duties well. Though the point would have been taken by Hobbes, *Leviathan*'s critique is of the system itself: the interest, as it were, that fairies have in encouraging dairy products. 'The Ecclesiastiques take the Cream of the Land, by Donations of ignorant men, that stand in aw of them, and by Tythes: So also it is in the Fable of Fairies, that they enter into the Dairies, and Feast upon the Cream, which they skim from the Milk.'[96] Even this, though, was a point that could sometimes backfire. In his anti-witchcraft polemic *A Candle in the Dark* (1656), Thomas Ady quotes a dairymaid's charm: 'Come Butter come, come Butter come, Peter stands at the Gate, waiting for a buttered Cake, come Butter come' (p. 59). He uses the rhyme to reinforce the standard equation of popery and superstition, and it could also have lent itself to a more specific reading along the same lines: the numinous power of St Peter's successors at the pearly gates can be channelled for butter-making because priests live off the fat of the land. Still, in context, it does not entirely bear out the anti-clerical point which Ady wants to make. He quotes his informant, an old woman, as saying that it was 'taught my Mother by a learned Church-man in Queen Maries days, when as Church-men had more cunning, and could teach people many a trick, that our Ministers now a days know not' (p. 59). As this suggests, it is in a dairymaid's interests as well as a priest's that butter should be made, and the anecdote preserves Catholic nostalgia too.

In his *Reliques* (1765) Thomas Percy comments of English folklore: 'The reader will observe that our simple ancestors had reduced all these whimsies to a kind of system, as regular as, and perhaps more consistent than, many parts of classical mythology.'[97] Hobbes would have concurred, as his emphasis is firmly on the structural analogies between the two hierarchical systems of popery and faery. 'The Fairies in what Nation soever they converse, have but one Universall King, which some Poets of ours call King Oberon; but the Scripture calls Beelzebub, Prince of Daemons. The Ecclesiastiques likewise, in whose Dominions soever they be found, acknowledge but one Universall King, the Pope . . . The Fairies are not to be seized on; and brought to answer for the hurt they do. So also the Ecclesiastiques vanish away from the Tribunals of Civill Justice.' Elsewhere, Hobbes allegorises: church-Latin is literally 'the Ghost of the Old Romane Language' and 'Ecclesiastiques walke in Obscurity of Doctrine' just as 'Fairies and Ghosts inhabit Darknesse, Solitudes, and Graves'.

Hobbes ends: 'To this, and such like resemblances between the Papacy, and the Kingdome of Fairies, may be added this, that as the Fairies have no existence, but in the Fancies of ignorant people, rising from the Traditions of old Wives, or old Poets: so the Spirituall Power of the Pope . . . consisteth onely in the Fear that Seduced people stand in, of their Excommunication;

upon hearing of false Miracles, false Traditions, and false Interpretations of the Scripture.' It was an accusation of which many educated Catholics would have seen the force. Just as they were not necessarily more tolerant than Protestants towards the intrusion of pagan elements into Christian festivity – when imprisoned at Wisbech Castle in 1597, the priest Christopher Bagshaw objected when a Christmas hobby horse was brought into the jail – they must constantly have been embarrassed by having belief in popular superstitions imputed to them.[98] Aubrey reports of France in the 1660s that 'much of the fulsome Superstition and Ceremonies were left-off, with the last 30 yeares. The Jesuites (clearer sighted than the other Orders) doe omitt them, as being ridiculous and giving scandall.'[99] The Catholic church's continued endorsement of miracle made it all the more important for its apologists to maximise the distance between real and spurious supernaturalism: in a work devoted to celebrating Marian miracles, Philips Numan remarks on the 'perticular and zealous hatred' that Catholics bear to superstition, and the fact that they are forbidden to read or own books of magic, chiromancy or astrology.[100] Nor is it impossible to find Catholics writing dismissively about phenomena already mentioned in this chapter: Thomas Lodge referred contemptuously to charms, while both Edmund Campion's and Richard Stanihurst's accounts of Ireland are sceptical about the visions which pilgrims claimed to have seen at St Patrick's Purgatory.[101]

Imaginative writing could also be a way to redirect accusations of superstition: in *The Hind and the Panther*, written after Dryden's conversion to Catholicism, the monk Chanticleer is undeservedly depicted adoring 'stocks of sainted trees', and sectarians are compared to fairies.[102] But perhaps the most authoritative Catholic riposte to Protestant accusations of promiscuous superstition comes from the early eighteenth century, in an imaginative work which generates enormous energy from the tension between fantasy and rationalism. In *The Rape of the Lock*, Alexander Pope mocks fairies, but also encompasses more orthodox supernatural machinery in his sceptical vision. Addressing Belinda, the sylph Ariel equates fairies and angels:

> If e'er one Vision touch'd thy infant Thought,
> Of all the Nurse and all the Priest have taught,[103]
> Of airy Elves by Moonlight Shadows seen,
> The silver Token, and the circled Green,
> Or Virgins visited by Angel-Pow'rs,
> With Golden Crowns and Wreaths of heav'nly Flow'rs,
> Hear and believe! thy own Importance know,
> Nor bound thy narrow Views to Things below.
> (29–36)[104]

Pope's real injunction is, of course, just the opposite: hear and disbelieve, unless you are of the credulous sex or of a credulous age. But anti-priestcraft though Pope is, his succeeding lines deflect accusations of superstition temporarily away from Catholics and onto weak wits or the unlearned. Catholicism, like any other peculiarity, made a satirist vulnerable; and to those aware of Pope's religious persuasions, this reattributing of superstition would have mitigated the accusations which he himself directed at his co-religionists, and enhanced his own poetic authority.

> Some secret Truths from Learned Pride conceal'd,
> To Maids alone and Children are reveal'd:
> What tho' no Credit doubting Wits may give?
> The Fair and Innocent shall still believe.
> (37–40)

Writing in confidence to a fellow Catholic, Pope was more prepared to be explicit about where their denomination was vulnerable to attack. The first version of *The Rape of the Lock* was written in 1711 and published in 1712, while the second, which includes the epic machinery, was written in 1713 and published in 1714. Later in 1714, on the topic of the siege of Barcelona and poetic supernaturalism in general, Pope was to write to Edward Blount: 'That siege deserves as fine a poem as the Iliad, and the machining part of poetry would be the juster in it, as they say the inhabitants expect Angels from heaven to their assistance. May I venture to say, who am a Papist, and say to you who are a Papist, that nothing is more astonishing to me, than that people so greatly warm'd with a sense of Liberty, should be capable of harbouring such weak Superstition, and that so much bravery and so much folly, can inhabit the same breasts?'[105] Letter and poem, considered together, add up to a rueful double acknowledgement: that all Catholics are indiscriminately accused of superstition by Protestants, but that this lack of discrimination is unfair, because it is impossible for a reasonable Catholic to justify the superstitions of many co-religionists. Though the occult hierarchies of the Comte de Gabalis are Pope's ostensible source for the supernatural element in *The Rape of the Lock*, the poem also demonstrates the particular association of Catholicism with the personnel of folk superstition. It found its first audience within a Catholic coterie, but in a non-supernatural version; in making it less of a coterie poem Pope may have made it more of a Catholic one, simultaneously defending his own kind and criticising them for the polemical opportunities they gave to their adversaries.[106]

The fear of superstition haunted generations even later than Pope's. Nathan Drake defined 'the awful ministrations of the Spectre, or the innocent gambols of the Fairy' as 'vulgar Gothic' – potentially a useful term to resurrect – and comments that it is a 'mode of superstition so assimilated with the universal apprehension of superior agency, that few minds have been altogether able to shake it off'.[107] This echoes Thomas Jackson's much earlier intuition, and helps to explain why the material covered in this chapter was often found so personally disturbing by those who preserved it. Many of the above-mentioned writers demonstrate – consciously or otherwise – an anxiety about the imagination which, though stimulated by Catholics or the unlearned, is not confined to them. Through a suspicion that popish superstition has pagan and gentile antecedents, they expressed a common early-modern ambivalence about the classical heritage, seeing it as potentially productive of idolatry. All the same, if learning was not enough to save one, ignorance was a far more dangerous companion to imagination. Unlike the producers of anti-puritan polemic, these authors identified a lack of learning as the problem with their subjects, rather than an attitudinous new literacy;[108] but whether error arose through attending to orally transmitted nonsense or misinterpreting the Scriptures through private reading, conventionally educated controversialists tended to be scared by the combination of worship with wayward language and undisciplined imaginings. When these factors accompanied illiteracy, low social status and a version of Catholicism unendorsable by orthodox Catholics, educated individuals on both sides of the divide would have had reason to fear the gods that might be invoked.

3

Answering back: orality and controversy

A Catholic balladeer of the late sixteenth century complained of his controversial opponents: 'Thei play upon advantages / which makes the[m] be so stowte, / They knowe what is against them sayde / shall not be published out.'[1] On one level, his chagrin is understandable; but given his own poem, and the many other Catholic controversial ripostes which survive from this period, it can also seem thoroughly disingenuous. Officially at least, most Catholics were debarred access to the press at most times when censorship was operating in Tudor and Stuart England. But just as this could be circumvented by printing confessional material on the Continent or on illicit presses in England, print itself was supplemented by means of manuscript transmission. Besides, it is the contention of this chapter and the next that one can speak of a Catholic oral challenge to the religious status quo in Protestant England, manifesting itself through a number of media, accessible to those at many social levels, and acting as a supple and evasive means of popularising dissident ideas.

On this front as on so many others, the connection that Protestants made between orality and popery was true, despite being polemically motivated. But it is differently true for the material treated in the preceding chapter, and for that discussed below. One basic division can be gauged by how the Protestant polemicist locates himself in relation to the enemy, and the type of response he expects. When he talks of superstition, his reproach concerns the common folk; yet he is addressing not the offenders, but those who are responsible for their education or the cure of their souls.[2] But complaints about popish ballads and lewd Catholic libels, texts also highly dependent on oral transmission, are directed straight at the writers of those texts, who have entered the polemical arena voluntarily and on their own behalf, with the basic equipment and training to conduct a fight. In general no answer is solicited, either from the superstitious peasant or the libeller; the pretence of the polemicist is invariably that his arguments are unanswerable, and when they are answered, he declares outrage. But in stressing this unanswerability, the implications are differently slanted: the peasant is unfit to fight, whereas the libeller has had all his arguments refuted.

Nevertheless, refutations were sometimes refuted in turn, and much of this chapter deals with the polemical exchanges between Catholic and Protestant, as they found their way into verse. In some ways these are not very different from their prose counterparts, especially since the longer verses could practise point-by-point refutation to almost the same level of detail as a short controversial pamphlet. But even though prose controversy sometimes tilts at the opponent's metaphor rather than his doctrine, this tendency becomes foregrounded in verse. Metrical controversy, too, stresses at all times the interface between mnemonics and live theological argument, and was often intended to provide its users with portable points for use in oral debate.[3] In this context the ballad's uses were wide, ranging from versifications of Catholic apologetic to laments or libels, all couched in metres which were already familiar, aided memorisation and could be sung. Theological grievances need not always be voiced in theological terms, and as with the Catholic contribution to the popular genre of conservative lament, an answer can simply be a matter of articulating discontent; though the sentiments are simply reactive, the act of voicing them – on paper, in recitation or in song – is one of defiance, and of what we would now call consciousness-raising.

CONTROVERSIAL DIALOGUES

Like the controversial pamphlets which they supplement, the verses in this chapter are interventions and skirmishes in the great Reformation contest; and like these, they can bear a remarkably close relationship to spoken dialogue. Within both pamphlets and poems, structure is often determined by the need to disprove the other writer as one goes: an evocation of dialogic exchange which often demanded substantial quotation from one's opponent. The type of controversial publication where a text is printed together with its refutation has the effect of recalling the original, while making the difference between the two voices clear – often by the alternation of italic and roman types. This high level of quotation was intended above all to be embarrassing, first setting up one's opponent, then emasculating him by one's authoritative response. The Reformation debate is one in which closure was constantly promised – even if it has never been achieved to this day – and it was important for both sides to lay claim to the advantages of having spoken last.[4]

By Protestants, this could be undertaken in various typographical ways. One typical passage-by-passage refutation is undertaken by Francis Bunny in *An Answer to a Popish Libel . . . Lately Spread Abroad in the North Partes* (1607), while in *The Supplication of Certaine Masse-Priests Falsely Called Catholikes* (1604) Matthew Sutcliffe reprints a printed Catholic libel with marginal glosses. Sutcliffe even reproduces the title page of the Catholic pamphlet he answers, annotated with sardonic comments demonstrating both his disapproval of Catholic discipline and his awareness of Catholics' frequent bibliographical subterfuges: against the year of publication a note runs 'Where and by whom was this geare Printed?' (f. A4a). This was an authority borne out of antistrophic rhetorical convention, turning an opponent's plea against him; and it mimicks a reader's habit of annotating texts, in a way that is enormously enhanced by print. Though English Catholic controversial writing quoted and refuted its opponents just as enthusiastically, typographical sophistication of this kind was more difficult for their authors and publishers to achieve: certainly on clandestine presses at home, and often abroad too, because of the problems posed by non-English-speaking printers – which stands as paradigmatic of how an untroubled access to printing technology weighted the scales towards the Protestant side. Yet since even marginal annotation could not wholly direct reader response, Catholic ideas probably benefited from this kind of mainstream distribution.[5]

This illustrates how, even at its most condemnatory, controversy cannot avoid giving platform-time to opposing points of view. This could turn into something more; the presence of Catholics in post-Reformation England posed insistent questions about freedom and toleration, and as Phebe Jensen has commented, 'alongside increasingly draconian attempts to control both theological and political Catholic writings [there existed] a cultural ideology that championed . . . the principle that open disputation and debate was the best way to arrive at religious truth'.[6] But despite this, and despite the many controversial rejoinders from Catholic pens distributed via both print and manuscript, the inequality is plain, and suggests the importance to Catholics of ballads, libels and other orally transmissible genres. Catholics had an underdog's interest in exploiting oral methods of communication, methods which were versatile, labile and difficult to censor. Among these methods must be included the printed and manuscript ballad, as a type of printed material often intended for a quick release into oral circulation. Spoken and sung verse was accessible to illiterates, and because oral transmission tended towards anonymity and was far less easy to control than print, it had strong associations with the illicit. Hence,

Protestant polemicists accused Catholics of courting those too ignorant to know any better, and of winning souls by underhand stratagems because they were afraid to engage in open fight – which conveniently ignores the fact that, while disputations between Catholic and Protestant did take place, it would often have been difficult for a Catholic writer to identify himself or appear in public.[7]

Oral transmission was not, of course, the only way that debates between Catholic and Protestant could take place at one remove or more from their originators, and exchanges in manuscript and print have a similarly important role as standing in for formal oral disputation. Yet at innumerable points in these pamphlet-wars, one is forcibly reminded of oral analogues – not least because of their bellicose character. Walter Ong has commented that 'many, if not all, oral or residually oral cultures strike literates as extraordinarily agonistic in their verbal performance and indeed in their lifestyle', and that 'writing fosters abstractions that disengage knowledge from the arena where human beings struggle with one another'.[8] Read onto theology, this is at least paradoxical – the history of Christianity is marked by disputes over high theological abstractions, which until recently have been governed by oral conventions to an unusual degree – but his point about the agonistic nature of early print culture is well taken. In early modern England, the sequential replies of the controversial pamphlet approximated much more closely to a conversation – at times a shouting match – than anything else in contemporary print culture. Within those pamphlets, as within most early modern writing, argumentation was governed by rhetorical conventions originally evolved for oral exchanges rather than written or printed ones.[9] Yet perhaps the conversational nature of the medium is most obvious of all at the points where formal rhetoric degenerates. Long-running pamphlet controversies developed increasingly allusive referential patterns, while all pamphleteering demonstrates unpredictable switches between reasoned argument and personal abuse, and interventions by third parties.

CONTROVERSY AND POPULAR VERSE

Religious debates could not be confined to a scholarly audience. On both sides, the battle for souls needed to enlist literates, complete illiterates and the enormous category of those from a residually oral background; thus, universally accessible genres like ballads would have had an obvious utility.[10] Ballads have attracted much recent interest among historians of popular culture, but in two of the most authoritative recent studies of the early modern English ballad, Catholic ballads have been nearly invisible.

Natascha Würzbach's *The Rise of the English Street Ballad, 1550–1650* (1st edn 1981) works from collections compiled in the nineteenth and early twentieth centuries; some of these include Catholic ballads, but the study, primarily concerned with a structural analysis of the ballad's subject matter, does not consider the political and religious differences between one martyr-ballad and another, or distinguish between printed and manuscript sources.[11] Tessa Watt's *Cheap Print and Popular Piety* (1991), as the title suggests, is primarily interested in printed material: in particular, broadside ballads before 1640. Her methodology has rightly been influential, yet with regard to Catholic material it has obvious limitations, screening out texts which only survive in manuscript, and which – because of their Catholic content – may never have been printed at all.

Surviving evidence of Catholic balladry is frequently from manuscript sources, and this in itself is suggestive.[12] Manuscript miscellanies, by definition, were compiled by the educated: at the very least, by those whose ability to write elevated them above the unlettered and the partially literate. Often, where enough evidence of ownership survives, they seem to have been written by those whose education had progressed considerably further. Elite disapproval of the form, contemptuous or satirical, existed in abundance;[13] but this must not obscure the fact that educated authors could use the ballad form for propagandist purposes, and that an educated audience could sing ballads, disseminate them and copy them into miscellanies for further reference. Some of the material discussed below, while responding to ballads, is generically distinct from them and obviously intended for an elite audience, while other elite texts were rewritten as ballads. Tessa Watt has commented that the buyers of cheap print were 'socially variegated';[14] the material discussed below comes from both print and manuscript sources, but bears her conclusions out. From the manner of their preservation and from what they say – sometimes even from the languages in which they say it – one can conclude that they were not addressed exclusively to a semi-literate audience, but to a wide audience which included the unlettered.

Where a text only survives in manuscript, how useful is it to call it a ballad? There are certainly difficulties, not least because identifying a printed ballad is easier than establishing whether a given poem in manuscript approaches ballad form or not. An ideal model of the ballad would be flexible enough to accommodate the ballads that never made it to print, yet helpful enough not to include every poem that has a popular pedigree or seems intended to have been sung.[15] Models of this kind are, of course, notoriously difficult to construct.[16] But metre gives some indication; so, if not invariably, does syntactical straightforwardness; and so, most of all, does a punchy, emotional, populist tone comparable to that found in printed ballads. Writing a ballad was a generic choice like any other, and it is certainly possible to envisage situations in which one would adopt a low style for an elite audience; homely metres could imply that the message deserved broad distribution, even if one was not minded to cast it abroad oneself, or they could show an author's modesty in the face of important subject matter.[17] Whether or not a particular ballad was written for the masses in the first instance, the genre itself would have ensured that it spoke to the masses.

CONSERVATIVE LAMENTS, REVERSIBLE WORLDS

A concern to attract popular sympathy was, of course, not restricted to Catholics. At the very beginning of the English Reformation, Henry VIII's propagandists made ruthless use of many popular media to stigmatise popery.[18] Their activities have often been discussed by scholars, but the Catholic response is less easy to find in literary history – in part because there is not as much of it as there might be.[19] Eamon Duffy has commented of the period after Thomas More's death that 'there was never enough security to permit the emergence of a consistent conservative public rhetoric, or the formation of a recognizable conservative voice'.[20] Certainly, while specific events like the Pilgrimage of Grace called forth defiant expressions of Catholicism, confusions and cross-currents also characterise sympathy for the old order in these early years.[21] A poem in a manuscript attributed to Thomas Langdon castigates the greed of priors and abbots, but laments the socio-economic consequences of the Reformation and asks Christ 'w[i]t[h] thy mother mary / [to] save thys our Dowry':

> We Englisshemen beholde
> Our aunciect customs bolde
> more p[re]ciouser then golde
> be clene cast away.
> And other new be fownd
> the which ye may understand
> that causethe all your land
> so gretly to decay . . .[22]

Does one call this the complaint of a committed Catholic, or merely of a religious and social conservative? Though the distinction can be a highly problematic one at this date, it is useful in Langdon's particular case, since his social discontent has an explicitly religious motivation. Expressions of Catholic doctrine figure in the manuscript, and there is enough external evidence to prove that Langdon – formerly a monk at Westminster Abbey – was a Catholic at the time of writing, and for many years afterwards: indeed, a sufficiently overt one to declare to a Crown informer in 1561 that 'this Religion was not the true Religion but the olde Religion was'.[23]

Even in less easy cases one may be right to suspect Catholic sympathies behind conservative laments, especially where they are found side-by-side with other material of post-Reformation Catholic origin, as in the case of the following poem:

> So longe may a droppe fall
> that it may perse a stone
> So longe trewthe may thrall
> that it shall scarce be knowen . . .
>
> So longe Errore may Raigne
> And untruthe soo increase
> that it shalbe mutche payne
> the same agayne to cease
>
> So longe lies may be cryed
> unto the peoples eares
> that whan truthe shalbe tried
> ytt may be with sume teares . . .[24]

While any period is too long for truth to remain in thrall, and perceptions of error's duration are bound to be subjective, the writer's impatience suggests that the cause of complaint is a familiar and long-standing one; and it finds an echo in another ballad first recorded several decades later and unequivocally identified as subversive. In 1594 the Catholic gentleman Thomas Hale was indicted before the Essex Assizes for possession of a Catholic ballad which he had copied eight years before. Like the above ballad it identifies a continued grievance, which suggests that it dates from a time when Protestantism was widespread. It is not merely lamentation which is described and enjoined within it, but persistent lamentation.

> Weepe, weepe, and still I weepe,
> For who can chuse but weepe,
> To thyncke how England styll
> In synne and heresey doth sleepe.
>
> The Christian faythe and Catholick
> Is everywhere detested,

> In holy servyce, and such like,
> Of all degrees neglected.
>
> The Sacramentes are taken awaye
> The holy order all,
> Religious men do begg astraye,
> To ground their howses fall.
>
> The Byshoppes and our pastors gone,
> our Abbottes all be deade,
> Deade (alas), alyve not one,
> Nor other in their steede . . .[25]

Broadly speaking, the authorship and collection of conservative laments may be more likely to betray positive Catholic sympathies from the latter half of the sixteenth century onwards. Though the lingering patterns of conservatism invite chronological imprecision by their nature, the prolonged confessional stability of Elizabeth's reign would have done something to soothe poets whose adverse reactions were prompted merely by unaccustomed or continuous upheaval, rather than confessional disaffection.[26] But the connection between conservatism and Catholicism could be either tight or loose, since Catholicism was primarily a consequence of belief, not of preference for a vanishing societal order. Historically, England had plainly been Catholic before it was Protestant; confessionally, Catholics' conception of orthodoxy stemmed from their notion of the church as unitary and unchanging, in which custom could be seen as hallowed by divine institution.[27] Social conservatism could follow from that, but did not have to: Elizabeth's reign bred Catholics who had known nothing but a Protestant status quo, and Robert Persons's *Memorial* demonstrated that it was possible to re-imagine a Catholic England along lines which were far from medieval.[28]

As this study has already commented, there was no necessary correspondence in early modern England between Catholicism and nostalgia for medievalism. Nevertheless, Catholic writers often give literary expression to outrage felt at the dismantling of the medieval world, and nowhere is this achieved more powerfully than in the anonymous ballad 'Walsingham', probably written for the ballad tune which shares its name. The Norfolk village of Walsingham is associated above all with a shrine to the Virgin Mary, one of England's most popular pilgrimage sites before the Reformation, but destroyed in 1538.[29] The Fitzwilliam Virginal Book provides evidence that, well into the seventeenth century, the tune of 'Walsingham' was a popular one among Catholic musicians.[30] While it would have evoked Catholic complaint and threnody simply by being played, it would also have been a potential vehicle for polemical words of this kind:

> In the wrackes of walsingam
> Whom should I chuse,
> But the Queene of walsingam,
> to be guide to my muse
> Then thou Prince of walsingam
> graunt me to frame,
> Bitter plaintes to rewe thy wronge,
> bitter wo for thy name . . .
> Bitter bitter oh to behould,
> the grasse to growe
> Where the walles of walsingam
> so statly did sheue . . .
> Levell Levell with the ground
> the towres doe lye
> Which with their golden glitteringe tops
> Pearsed once to the skye . . .[31]

The lines on the 'Prince of Walsingham' permit two opposed but equally satisfying readings.[32] In the first the 'Prince' is Christ, permitting the speaker to complain on his behalf at the wrongs he has suffered, while in the second he is Henry VIII, who has committed the wrong, and whom the speaker ironically asks for permission to lament; woe is experienced by Christ, but predicted for Henry. This reinforces Helen Hackett's suggestion that the ballad was composed in the late 1530s or early 1540s, and certainly a number of the lines use Isaiah's prophetic writings to evoke the indignation of an eyewitness:

> Bitter was it oh to see,
> The seely sheepe
> Murdred by the raveninge wolves
> While the sheephardes did sleep . . .
> Oules do scrike wher the sweetest himnes
> lately weer songe
> Toades and serpentes hold ther dennes,
> Wher the Palmers did thronge . . .[33]

While the image of the sleeping shepherd does convey a sense that somnolent Catholic clerics were partly to blame for the depredations of the Reformation, this is only fleeting; however familiar anticlericalism was to late medieval churchmen, it would have been letting the side down for Catholics to make sustained use of it later. Certainly, Catholic conservatism more often takes the form of lamenting churchmen's change in status. From the early 1560s there survives a miscellany of Catholic controversial material which includes a number of protest ballads, one of which explicitly equates the old societal order with the true religion:[34]

> In holy Churche of Xpistys foundacion
> were thre estatys by no[m]i[n]ation
> as aunciente volumys make relation
> In towne a in towne a
> wch maye not be layde downe a
> Whoo lyste to revolve maye reade & se
> howe knytehod pr[ie]sthode & co[m]naltye
> weare sette uppe by the deitie
> In towne a in towne a
> Nev[er] to be pulled downe a . . .
>
> (f. 22a)

Catholicism and conservatism are indivisible in a number of the ballad writer's complaints: 'To god I take hyt no small transgression / the cure to procure the Curats suppression[35] / hys father gostly by waye of co[n]fession . . .' (f. 23b). Images of reversal, as the next section will discuss, feature commonly in ballads, and another ballad from the same manuscript gives an eschatological slant to them. It is an unusual, though not an unparalleled, example of Catholic apocalyptic, and some of its tropes may have come from Protestant texts as well as directly from the Book of Revelation. But it demonstrates how evocation of the earth's last days could just as easily be conservative as radical. Old Testament types of injustice and irreligion jostle with 'meretrix babylon', the ten-horned *bellua maris*, and other apocalyptic references.

> baasa (sic) hathe baale auntorousely founded
> Achab hathe Nabothis vine take
> Jeroboam false godds hathe grounded
> Salomon for lecherye hys god did forsake
> Nowe fleeyth aboute the greate drake[36]
> hys tayle hathe towched owre affiaunce
> the churchys of Asia be all to shake
> So gogg hathe geven hys governaunce . . .
>
> (f. 18a–b)

This opens up the possibility that Catholics and Protestants could both sing the same apocalyptic ballad while positing different meanings for it; but other verses within this particular ballad stamp it as a Catholic production. Protestants spoke of popery as a novelty, but not as a suddenness; and even without the names of countries where Protestantism was posing a threat, the word 'rysythe' in the lines quoted below would have come oddly from a Protestant writer.

> Nowe rysythe the foule abusion
> in beome (sic). germanye. Inglande & fraunce
> me thynkythe therfore by thys co[n]clusion
> that gogg hathe geven the \<hys\> governaunce . . .
> (f. 18a)

Aaron's priestly beard and ceremonial clothing, typifying the splendour of God, are used as a reproach to those who have plundered the church.

> lette god be berded after the olde gyese [i.e. 'guise']
> hys golden mantell ys no grevaunce
> Catche hyt notte a waye for covetouse
> thoughe googg hathe geven hys governaunce . . .
> (f. 19b)

The percussive refrain forges connections between the Old Testament and the terrible new order: Gog appears in Ezekiel's vision of the last days as the enemy of Israel, and again in Revelation as Satan's second-in-command.[37] More deftly, by pushing the disasters of the present onto a cosmic scale, the Crown is exonerated from local responsibility; in fact, the ballad ends with an impeccable tribute to Elizabeth as Britain's Daniel, and the writer's gloomy prediction that 'under googg maye [be] another Jack Strawe' reminds us of the supposed connection between irreligion and rebellion.[38]

Fears of violent protest from below could certainly accompany alarm at heresy; conversely, characters from traditions of popular complaint, so often utilised by Protestant radicals, could also be given a Catholic script. For instance, a written pamphlet-libel of 1582, arguing that England has separated itself from the universal church, has the title 'Peers plowghman hys answer to the doctours Interrogatoryes & Scrybes of the lawe, in stede of an Apology for the late martyrs of noble memory', and asks that readers should 'take no dysdayne of any further encounter in a clowted shoe'.[39] An evocation of Piers Plowman, that famous spokesman for the common sort, may seem surprising in this context; yet it usefully problematises what can be an automatic association of Catholics with reactionary social mores, and is not the only occasion on which Catholics appropriated images from popular culture to express a desire for reversal. As James C. Scott has remarked, a longing for reversal is frequently expressed by oppressed or subordinate groups; common to most of those he discusses, whether German peasants or nineteenth-century American slaves, is a fierce jubilation at the prospect.[40] Justice will be done, and the iniquitous will have cause to quail; in the words of two frequently used biblical texts, the mighty will be put down from their seat, and the valleys exalted.[41] Among early Protestants, who had a vested interest in pitting themselves against the powerful, the trope could be linked to visualisations of the pope as Antichrist, Christ's opposite.[42] But evidence of popular complaint from a group once powerful, and now suppressed, is a rarer commodity. For Catholics operating in this idiom – which sometimes seems a world away from Counter-Reformation ideals – reversal had already occurred, and was to be feared unless it took the form of turning the clock back. David Kunzle comments that the trope of reversal could be used both by those satisfied with the status quo and those with an interest in changing it, but does not make the further deduction, crucial for understanding Catholic use, that it could also be used by those yearning after a past order.[43]

Scott distinguishes between three kinds of reversal: explicit social critiques, in which a lord may serve a peasant at table; the beast-fable such as two geese turning a human on a spit over the fire, where a subversive meaning resides in the analogy with human relations; and violations of natural law with no obvious social content, like fish flying in the air or birds under water. It is the third type, frequently incorporated into apocalyptic imagery as portents, which Catholics most often evoke; and of the third, Scott suggests only that it is 'obviously harmless material' to divert attention from inflammatory political ideas.[44] However, this is to underestimate the huge implications of the fantasy, since illustrations from natural law demonstrate a continuum with moral law. If the one is out of joint, so is the other: as suggested by the beginning of a poem from one of the most important manuscripts of Catholic verse, which compares the outlawing of priests to climatic disorder.

> Winter could into summer hoate
> well changed now may bee
> for thinges as strange doe come to passe
> as wee may plainlie see
> England priests which honourd hath
> soe manie hundred yeares
> doth hange them up as Traytors now
> which causeth manie teares.
>
> (f. 33b)[45]

This demonstrates how Catholic images of reversal typically comment on the disruption of old hierarchies, harking back to the conservative laments described earlier. A manuscript poem copied and probably written by William Blundell, 'The Tyme hath been wee hadd one faith', focuses on the beast analogy to describe pastoral anarchy:

> The tyme hath been that sheepe obaide
> Their pastors, doinge as they saide;
> The tym is nowe each sheepe will preach.
> And th'ancient pastors seeme to teach . . .[46]

Suspicions of moral reversal widen the meaning of this upside-down world, letting it be read as a metaphor for other oppositions: unity against anarchy, timeless truths against ephemeral proclamations, and – almost always – the past against the present:

> The Tyme hath been[47] wee hadd one faith
> and trode aright one ancient path
> the thym is now that each man may
> See newe Religions coynd eich day . . .

The Golden Age – not that of the pagans, but of an undivided and hospitable Christendom – replaces the Land of Cockayne in the collective fantasy of another Catholic ballad.[48]

> In dayes of yore: when wordes did passe for bandes
> before deceit: was bread or fraud was seene
> when tounges did signe: and seale with clappe of handes,
> before the pure: gainst Christians tooke their spleene
> The maister paid: and pleased was the man
> and then unborne was anie *Puritane*
>
> In those good daies: lived hospitalitie
> men hoarded not. nor did they hyde their pelfe
> Then lived resident kynd Charitie
> and then plaine dealinge. bouldlie showd himselfe
> The blacke Jacke us'd. noe pewter nor noe canne
> nor men neare heard. of anie *Puritanne*[49]

The demise of liberality was a complaint frequent among Catholic writers, and an understandable one, given what could often be pronounced differences between Catholic and Protestant notions of charity. Felicity Heal has commented that 'Catholics did not have any scruples about indiscriminate charity or about the traditional cycle of feast and fast' and that, 'at least by the later years of Elizabeth's reign, they were motivated by a conscious desire to maintain customary social patterns as a means of consolidating communal behaviours . . . there are a number of individual examples of

Catholic families who were thought by their contemporaries to be unusually assiduous in the maintenance of hospitality'.[50] Ballads like this, by lamenting the passing of a golden age, exhort their audience to recover it – and may, indeed, even have been sung at hospitable gatherings. Catholics made heavy use of elegy, and as the above quotation and many others in this chapter suggest, the elegiac mode often found its way into Catholic ballads – perhaps it flavoured Catholic drinking songs too.[51]

'I PRAY THEE PROTESTANT': ALLEN'S *ARTICLES* IN VERSE

Though popular verse had an obvious role as a means of voicing discontent, it could also be used to influence the beliefs of Englishmen whose mental world was still largely or totally oral. Christians' use of simple verse to acquaint the unlearned with the rudiments of their faith and equip them for controversial debate dates back as far as St Augustine of Hippo's *Psalmus Abecedarius*, and at the time of the Reformation, it remained a highly practical device exploited by both sides.[52] For English Catholics, forced as they were into a defensive position, it had particular usefulness. Trials were only the most conspicuous of the countless cross-examinations that Catholics underwent in public and in private, and catechistical verses setting out the main points of difference between the denominations would have been a useful supplement to guides which – to quote the subtitle to one such – 'sett downe a Method to instruct, how a Catholike (though but competently learned) may defend his Fayth against the most learned Protestant'.[53] The most famous set of Catholic verses within this genre accosts the reader from the beginning,

> I Pray thee Protestant beare with mee,
> to aske thee questions two or three:
> And if an answere thou canst make,
> more of thy counsaile I will take.
> (f. C3b)

with the speaker going on to deliver several reasons why Protestantism is false.

In its first appearance in print, as an appendix to Gregory Martin's *The Love of the Soule* [1602?], the poem's argument is summarised under six headings, 'Catholike; Continuance; Visible; Unitie; Holy; Heretickes': in other words, the 'marks of the true church' which it was in the Catholic interest to stress.[54] A more detailed description of the content could read as follows. Christ committed the church to his apostles; they preserved the

Bible and separated true Scripture from spurious; the Church has remained, though rival conventicles have decayed; it has instituted ceremonies to God's glory and formulated canon law; no martyrs, confessors or saints have been other than Catholic; there has been a continued succession of ecclesiastical offices, unlike any other church; Protestants cannot explain when the primitive church changed to popery; there are no non-Catholic liturgies; Catholics recognise no Protestant appointments; Protestants have built no churches and set up no pious foundations; the Catholic church can demonstrate unity, while it is unclear whether the various Protestant sects are of one congregation or not; those sects bear the name of their founders, not of Catholics or Christians; the Protestant cannot say whether professors of Christ were saved during the period of unchallenged Catholic hegemony, and has no way of proving that his hidden church is Christ's spouse; the Catholic church is the only visible one; morality is clearly demonstrable within the Catholic church, just as immorality is among Protestants; and a Protestant church can neither be Catholic nor apostolic. Such an inclusive series of points, as well as arguing a comprehensive knowledge of polemic among the ballad's intended audience, shows an anxiety that the Catholic's polemical armoury should be well-stocked; and the catenation of a ballad's verses ensured, in turn, that, when any particular controversial issue was randomly accessed within conversation, interlinking points could also be retrieved by those who had memorised it.

When dealing with religious controversy, the prevailing tendency among scholars is to consider one topic at a time, extracting it from the totality of the argument. But early modern historians, concerned with a period of heavy cross-fertilisation between oral, manuscript and printed transmission, should perhaps pay more attention to the history of arguments: how individual assemblages and catenations of points can be passed on from text to text, and how some can be suppressed, others emphasised or ramified. Allen's *Articles*, the polemical assemblage which 'I pray thee protestant' versifies, has a complicated pedigree and an equally confusing capacity to mutate: the summary above comes from the second printed prose version,[55] and should not be taken as inclusive. But its long survival within oral conversation, manuscript and print, via texts directed at very different audiences, illustrates how an argument can go through a number of metamorphoses while retaining an identity. The importance of such a retention is indicative to some degree of the charisma surrounding Allen's name, but it also reflects the portmanteau quality of its conception. Like the Credo, it summarised articles of belief, and its authority rested on the notion of completeness; but its articles were polemically defined, consisting only of points of dissent between Catholic and Protestant. Just as the relative importance of these points varied from decade to decade, and from person to person, it too had to vary; yet for many individuals it remained not simply *a* Catholic argument, but *the* Catholic argument.[56]

Richard Bristow, one of the teachers in William Allen's seminary at Douai, tells us that Allen drew up the original summary in the late 1560s: round about the time the college itself was founded, and for somewhat similar reasons. Allen used a brief sojourn in England to 'deale . . . with many Gentlemen, confirming some, and setting up agayne others, by most evident and undouted rules of truth, which were always common for the most part among Catholikes, but the weight of them deeply considered of very few, and the number of them as yet neither by him nor by any other bound up together'. But despite their semi-improvised quality, the *Articles* seem to have fulfilled a need from the beginning. Allen was begged for written copies, and when Bristow's own copy was requested by a friend travelling to England, 'affirming that he saw how medicinable it would be to many soules', Bristow himself was commissioned by Allen to put together a version for print.[57] It was published in 1574 under the title of *A Briefe Treatise of Diverse Plaine and Sure Wayes to Finde Out the Truthe in This . . . Time of Heresie*, usually referred to as 'Bristow's Motives', while another, shorter version appeared in the appendix to Jean Albin de Valsergues's *A Notable Discourse . . . Discussing, Who Are the Right Ministers of the Catholike Church*, published the next year in 1575.[58]

The rhymed *Articles* seem to have been derived from the second of these versions.[59] But as already suggested, there is no especial reason to suppose this version authoritative. The *Articles* mutated endlessly in number, content and order, as can be seen by the considerable degree of variation both among the surviving versions and among their answers; and rhyme did little to fix them. Spoken argument brings an iterative capaciousness to a text, even when that text has been designed to be easily memorable, and interpolation certainly affected the *Articles* as they spread. As opponents were happy to point out, they can appear distinctly unstructured on the page. Samuel Hieron, for instance, complained that 'it hath come through the hands of a very homely and sluttish Cooke, by whom it is neyther seasoned with wit or argument, no, nor yet set forth after any good ordinary fashion: But it is even a very Gally-mawfrey, of certayne naked and indigested Allegations . . . without eyther order or proofe, as though every Papist were a Pope, and every word of his mouth an Oracle. Belike the Sloven thought it good enough for those, for whom it was provided.'[60] Hieron's complaint that the ballad presents assertions without evidence points to one obvious limitation of popular verse, while his splenetic commentary identifies a very important characteristic of vernacular controversial rhyme; since an orally transmitted text is open to modification by everyone who repeats it, every papist is indeed a pope.

The last printed refutation of the *Articles* seems to date from 1640, suggesting that they had a lifespan of approximately seventy years: successful, by any standards.[61] This success may have been precisely because of the cross-fertilisation between orality and print, and the mutation, or updating, which was thereby encouraged; despite being reshaped many times, the original argument retained its identity. This is a phenomenon easy enough to recognise in a generalised sense, and yet, when it comes to particularities, the nature of this identity can seem astonishingly slim. It even bypasses authoritative devices found elsewhere in oral culture: for instance – as with the attribution of proverbial wisdom to legendary sages – Allen's name might have had a continuous use as a means of validation, yet within the various versions of the rhymed *Articles* as we have them, this is not apparent. Even the name of the argument varied: it could be called 'Challenges', 'Articles', 'Reasons', 'Demands', 'Motives', 'Questions' or 'Offers'.[62]

As Hieron saw, the structure of the argument is loose: loose because accretion is endemic to oral texts, and because controversial points are interconnected and not linear, so where a structure is fluid, one point can either go in one of several different places or be iterated. There are few constants. One is the initial premise of a Catholic asserting to a Protestant that he is willing to be convinced if the arguments are sufficiently weighty, 'more of thy counsaile I will take . . .'. Another is simply the mnemonic tag of the opening lines. With this *incipit*, the speaker defines himself as speaking in a tradition, and once that is established, he is free to use the current received text or to extemporise from material within the memory bank of orthodoxy. It would have been more important, perhaps, to adhere to the rhyme scheme than to any rigorously defined argumentative structure.

In small compass, the history of the *Articles* is that of all controversial discourse between Catholic and Protestant. Such discourse was on a restricted variety of topics from which all authors selected, whether they were augmenting a ballad or writing a pamphlet. Both of these genres privilege the temporary emphases of an individual author, since ballads as we have them are often arrested at some arbitrary point in transmission. But the differences are equally obvious. Two printed prose-pamphlets might be more similar to each other than two rhymed versions of Allen's *Articles*, in assemblage of topics and even in diction, but in the second case it is appropriate to speak of a version of an original, and in the first – though one might suspect influence or plagiarism – it is not. The claims of individual authorship have more meaning within cultures depending on writing, more still when print comes into play. After the bibliographical evolution of title pages, pamphlets tended to parade their authorship, while within ballad culture, even where the original author's name is preserved, the names and contributions of intermediary authors are usually irrecoverable. Moreover, difference is easier to identify in a written or printed text than in an oral; consequently arguments emanating from literate sources were able to be more static. Print – and even manuscript – had the effect of arresting the flux of connection; the oral controversies of the literate were much more tailored to occasion than could be the case among those who relied only on orality.

Hieron's answer to the *Articles* was only the second to be printed. The first answer, by the Protestant ballad-writer John Rhodes, had appeared two years earlier in 1602. Rhodes's account of how he discovered the text reveals how widely this version had permeated popular literature, in written, in printed and – by implication – in oral versions:

We found there amo[n]g other things also, a Toy in Rime, entituled, A proper new Ballad, wherein are certaine Catholike questions . . . to the Protestant. [This], with an other note booke, written of like argument, I keep by me . . . A Minister . . . told me of the same Ballad, before I met with this, and desired me to undertake the answering of it, & he would helpe me to it, but could not: and therefore till now . . . I thought no more of it; although I am perswaded, there are many such Pa[m]phlets, together with other like Romish wares, that are sent abroad among the common people, both Protestants and Papists in London and in the countrey, & that, by certaine women Brokers and Pedlers (as of late in Staffordshire there was) who with baskets on their armes, shal come and offer you other wares under a colour, and so sell you these, where they see and know any likelyhood to utter them.[63]

Rhodes had earlier published a book of alternative carols tied to the Church's year, *The Countrie Man's Comfort* (1588), and here too his intention was to pre-empt popish singing.[64] The *Articles* and the answer are alternated, ten lines at a time. Rhodes rewrites the original, partly in order to improve the verse: '. . . the Authour of this Ballad, his skill seemed to me, to be as bad in Poetry, as in Divinity, and therefore I am herein driven sometimes to adde and abbreviate the Authours particular words, but I faile him not an iote for his owne sense and false meaning . . .' (f. A2b). This magnanimity is, in fact, an extremely practical mnemonic concern; if the propositions were rendered difficult to remember through false rhyming and scansion, the answer too would prove less memorable. After the *Articles*' 'Amen', Rhodes adds: 'Amend, Papists, amend.' Benefiting still further from having the last word, he added an epilogue and a derisory song on popery, and referred the reader to a prose answer to the *Articles*, Robert Crowley's *A Deliberate Answer Made to a Rash Offer* (1588).[65]

The *Articles* were next answered in Patrick Forbes's *Eubulus*,[66] *or a Dialogue, Where-in a Rugged Romish Ryme . . . Is Confuted*. Though his book was published in 1627, Forbes says in the Epistle to the Reader that his initial stimulus occurred about thirteen years ago, when 'ignorant Souls' were 'vaynlie glorying of this their Ballad, which numbers of them had continuallie in their mouthes, who never had eyther read, or gotten by heart, anie one Psalme of David . . .' (f. A3a).[67] But unlike Rhodes, he chooses to answer the ballad by means of another genre entirely. *Eubulus* consists of a series of dialogues between the Protestants Philadelphus, Eubulus and Theriomachus, and the papists Philomathes and Eriphilus, based on the premise that a lady has been seduced by the ballad. It is enlivened by occasional rhymes, including the one quoted at the beginning of this chapter. According to his own explanation, Forbes was commissioned by a nobleman to write an answer, gave out a few manuscripts of it, then put it aside until the ballad's recurrence. But despite the residual orality of the dialogue form, the piece is essentially one for reading and not for reciting and memorising. A limited manuscript circulation would not have penetrated to the illiterate; and so, if it was indeed directed at the ignorant souls of the preface, both genre and manner of publication would be very off-target.

But the seeming mismatch between problem and answer can perhaps be explained another way. Here, the idea that a *lady* has become pro-Catholic is suggestive. A dialogue of this kind would have been an attractive piece of reading for elite women, as the dedication to Anna, Lady Gordon suggests. Combined with the fact that a nobleman did the commissioning, this implies that the initial audience was not ignorant souls but aristocratic women; and since Lady Gordon was the dedicatee of the manuscript version too, possibly one aristocratic woman in particular.[68] The dialogue begins with Philadelphus soliciting Eubulus's services, and Forbes's prefatory verse 'To Philadelphus' further implies that the name is a thin disguise for his patron:

> Loe, Philadelphus how Thy love hath led mee,
> To penning of this PAMPHLET, for Thy pleasure:
> Where-of, with Reason, well I could have fred mee,
> If this I durst, with Thy Contentment measure.
> It may seeme strange, that of my little leasure,
> I anie part waste on such Wares, so vaynlie:
> Where-in, all-bee-it weake Women place a Treasure;

> Yet hath their Poët playde the Foole so playnlie,
> As, if my Motives bee not well esteemed,
> For answering, I shall a Foole bee deemeed (*sic*).
>   (f. A4a)

Within the actual dedication Forbes is more tactful, while still strongly implying that the piece had originally been written to save Lady Gordon's soul. The verse is 'for satisfying some Godlie Myndes, and obviating the insolencie of some ignorant, and ydle Humours' (f. A2a); the latter have been importunate again, and so he solicits Lady Gordon's renewed patronage. 'Receive, then, that which is Your owne; as a poore, but an upright Token, how farre the Author, and all of his Calling, account them-selves obliedged, to give Your Honour, all Heartening, and Encowragement, for cleaving, so constantlie, (agaynst manyfolde assaultes and temptations) to that Trueth, which, heerein, is defended' (f. A2b). As the problem stands, this is at least further evidence that the audience of controversial ballads was not restricted to the poor.

If Forbes's concerns were elsewhere, this invites one to probe his ostensible complaint about the prevalence of the ballad among the uneducated. His venture into print more than a decade after manuscript publication could have been prompted by the ballad's continuance among the illiterate, or the continued religious perversions of the aristocracy, or a mixture of factors.[69] If the former, it is easier to imagine his piece being appropriated for print in the hopes of it penetrating further down the social scale, than to suggest that it was initially written in the hopes of pervading oral culture. But whatever his actual readership, it is very much in Forbes's interests to downgrade the ballad's supposed audience. Any individual who could read the dedication would wish to distance himself from those who could not, while an aristocratic woman might well be alienated still further from the verses if she thought that they were principally intended to convert the poor.

Eubulus is a prose work which only occasionally breaks into rhyme, and Forbes seems to have thought it necessary to dismiss any idea that the side writing wholly in rhyme somehow had a better claim to truth. In reply to a comment that 'Syllogismes' are needed, not 'invective Sonnets', Eubulus says: 'By a Sonnet one may verie convenientlie give sentence of a Song ... wee are not so farre borne in despite of all the Muses, but that wee could render you as compact Verses, as anie your proper Ballad hath in it' (p. 20). Conversely, because it carried the double implication of theological irresponsibility and poor literary craftsmanship, it was also useful to be able to dismiss the points of an opponent as advanced merely for stylistic reasons. In response to Eubulus's objection that a difference of opinion is not the same as sectarianism, Philadelphus interjects: 'You miss-take the matter . . . it is not maliciouslie done of him, but for Metres sake, to make up his Verses, which, other-wayes, would not have runne well' (pp. 22–3).

But the usefulness of verse was primarily for summary attention-grabbing. Once it had elicited a response from the other side, which needed in its turn to be refuted, the limitations of metre became increasingly clear. Samuel Hieron complained of how the rules of cadence and number straitened the unaccustomed practitioner to such a degree that he was often in danger of obscuring the sense or the meaning.[70] This frustration also dominates a preface to another Catholic intervention in the debate, answering an answer to the original verses.[71]

> My Frend if soe thou dost desyre to be
> If not but please thy selfe thou pleasest me.
> When I beheld this old worne stuffe of thyne
> Soe fully answered by Bellarmine
> And many learned authors moe beside
> I thought to slay my Muse: yet fearinge pride
> Might make thee thinke thou hadst perform'd the art (*sic*)
> Of some Divine in Poetasters art
> I thought if fitting to plucke off thy maske
> And soe invite thee to a greater taske.
> At sight here of if thou dar'st undertake
> In any point thy partie good to make
> Chose what thou best can'st prove, or best defend
> And at thine elbow ready I'le attend
> In prose, or verse, or both or how thou please
> By schollers weapons lett us make our peace.
>
> (f. 1a)

Though the writer goes on to use the 'Poetasters art' as a vehicle for the arguments of divines – exactly what he accuses the other side of doing – he has still secured the rhetorical high ground; by throwing doubt on the medium, he prepares the way to invalidate the message. His diatribe acknowledges the limited versatility of metre; verse may be appropriate for evangelisation, but 'schollers weapons' are best once the original text has run up against controversy individually tailored to itself. Nevertheless, the writer continues within metre's confines and exploits its peculiarities to advantage. The preface goes on:

> But lett me now crave pardon at this tyme
> By cause I follow not thy curt-tal'd ryme

> Though he yt. first these quaestions did propose
> Thought it more correspondent to thy nose
> Yet I'le none of your too much used balmes
> They smel of Ballads and Geneva psalmes . . .
>
> (f. 1a)

Sure enough, the Catholic then proceeds to answer the Protestant's shambling four-stressed lines in dignified iambic pentameter. With superb cheek, the metre originally chosen by the Catholic side was imputed to the low tastes of Protestants, once its unsuitability for detailed controversy had become clear. John Rhodes, who had clearly not seen this piece – an omission which may help to date it – returned to the attack in 1606:

> Some three yeares since, your questions put in rime,
> Were answered all, according to the time.
> Since then we heard of no reply at all,
> Nor yet of Popish Poets greate or small:
> But now of late one stole out of his denne,
> And shamefully abuz'd both tongue and penne.
> That is to say at Enborne in Barkeshire,
> They delt as if they would set all on fire,[72]
> The Church doore they brake open with strong ha[n]d
> Which is plaine sacriledge in every land.
> They cut one Booke, and did disprayse the rest,
> Scattering the leaves, to shew how they detest:
> Our bookes and us, with all the power they have,
> Our Ministers and all things they deprave.[73]

Rhodes is alluding to an incident of 1601/2 where a rhymed Catholic libel was scattered around the parish church at Enborne.[74] It has nothing especially to do with Allen's *Articles*, other than the fact that both are popish, both are in rhyme and both refer to common controversial issues; so again, this depends on rhyme being seen as a different kind of discourse from prose. Transparently alluding to himself as the answerer of Allen's *Articles*, Rhodes assumes a continuum between controversies conducted in verse, on which prose polemic does not impinge. Rhodes's pamphlet, despite the fact that its author was one of the most skilful Protestant exploiters of ballad-metre in this period, also plays on the common prejudice against the medium of popular verse; Rhodes sneers at his balladeering opponents within the verse quoted above as 'Ballad Mungers' and 'merry Beggars' (f. D3b). Though polemic is necessarily undiscriminating, this would not have been a possible insult unless the medium itself were a little suspect.

SWEETENING THE MESSAGE

While it might at first seem an arbitrary decision to separate controversial exchanges in verse from their counterparts in prose, as this chapter does, the above exchange demonstrates how early modern writers instinctively made a distinction between the two.[75] A printed answer to a rhymed Catholic libel, which attacks the offending text on several generic fronts, advises the reader: 'You shall perseave both libell and answere the better, if you confer proes wyth proes & miter wyth miter.'[76] The reason that verse was perceived as different may have been hierarchical in part: despite the fact that ballads had a very heterogeneous audience, they were usually referred to as disreputable. But all verse was more governed than prose by demands of form, and where a piece of polemic is written in verse, this reflects a decision that for this particular purpose the advantages of metre outweigh metre's limitations. It was not always an easy decision to make. In a reply to Allen's *Articles*, discussed above, Samuel Hieron declared, 'I have even forced my selfe to this straiter course of Verse-making, though I know, that for mine own case (having to deale in such a distempered and unruly Subject) that lesse-limited & freer kind of discourse, which Prose alloweth, had bene more convenient: Because the rules of Cadence, & number (to which our English poetry especially in [*sic*] co[n]fined) do many times so straiten an unaccustomed Practitioner, that he is in hazard, either of obscuring the sence (which in a matter of this nature were something dangerous) or of marring the Verse (which to the apprehensions of every common conceit were very ridiculous).'[77]

Verse also tended more towards imaginative suffusion. Though metre is not imaginative in itself, it is used within popular moralism in a manner similar to allegory and other imaginative devices. Both are conceived as sweeteners, useful for rendering doctrinal and moral lessons more attractive, and especially fit for a non-scholarly audience. Riddles are allegorical by their very nature, inviting an active interpretive response from their reader or hearer, and metrical riddles would have been especially memorable. In *Tessaradelphus* (1616), Thomas Harrab bases a whole pamphlet around what is described in the subtitle as an 'old Riddle':

> Foure bretheren were bred at once
> Without flesh, bloud, or bones.
> One with a beard, but two had none,
> The fourth had but halfe one.
>
> (Title page)

In this tiny allegory with a twist at the end, the four brothers stand for the heretical churches, and beards for the religious ceremonial which Lutheranism has retained, while Calvinists and Anabaptists are clean-shaven, and the Church of England has half a beard. Harrab is well known as the coiner of the term 'Anglicanism', and this may be the first ever joke about Anglican compromise.[78]

In his book of anti-Protestant epigrams, I. B. confessed: 'I know an Epigramme should be brief and acute: the first rule I acknowledge my self to have sometimes transgressed . . . but howsoever, it is not upon such exact lawes that I have stood; al my study was how I might best frame the[m] to doe the most good' (p. 7).[79] Other Catholic epigrammatists might have seen brevity as even more efficacious than content. Epigrams, like riddles, were typically short, surprising and infectiously easy to remember; characterised by unpredictable reversals of argument in a compact space, they had portability and shock value for a polemicist.[80] One of the most famous pro-Catholic epigrams of the early seventeenth century is utilised by Henry Fitzsimon in a controversial pamphlet, *The Justification and Exposition of the Divine Sacrifice of the Masse* (1611).

> In Elder times an ancient custume t'was,
> to sweare in weightie maters by the Masse.
> But when Masse was put down, as Ould men note,
> They swore then by the Crosse of this graye grote.
> And when the Crosse was held like wise in scorne
> Then Faith, and trowth, for common oathes weare sworne.
> But now men banisht have both faith & trouth,
> So that God damne me, is the common oath.
> So custome keeps Decorum, by gradation,
> Loosing masse, Crosse, Faith, trouth, followth damnation.
> (pp. 130–1)

Like Harrab, Fitzsimon presents himself as merely passing on the rhyme he uses.[81] Introducing it, he observes of the Reformers: 'They love rime, and poetrie, in al things, even in their psalmes (& why should not a light religion love a light stile?) . . . Therfor I wil in their affected stile, present them this Epigram[m]e. What may wante in the rime, shalbe recompensed in the maters pithines.' As usual, the opponent is blamed for the necessity of a low style, but this should not mislead one into thinking that the advantages of verse have not been calculated.

Sweeteners such as rhyme, allegory and wit, whenever they are superimposed on plain meaning and blatantly intended to make persuasion an easier task, could evoke anti-rhetorical prejudice in an opponent. To accuse the other side, one needed only to point to these devices and swear that they concealed poison – though, as Fitzsimon shows, this did not necessarily mean having to eschew rhyme oneself. In *Eubulus*, Patrick Forbes described how the pleasures of metre, like rhetoric itself, enhanced the flavour of good doctrine but disguised the bitterness of error.

> Reason and Ryme, if sweetlie they bee sembled,
> Implant in Men the pleasanter Impression:
> Quicke Arguments, with Eloquence enæmbled,
> Draw contrare Myndes, more quicklie to Confession.
> But, of true Fayth, if under false Profession,
> Songs bee made Syropes, but to sweeten Errours,
> Prudence will spye, and keepe of Trueth possession,
> Unsnar'd with Syrens, or yet tost with Terrours . . .
>   (p. 20)[82]

Sometimes, the whole discourse of opponents could be condemned by calling attention to their methods of persuasion. In a libel criticising detractors of Edmund Bonner, the Marian bishop who refused to take the Oath of Supremacy and died in prison, the writer deftly demonstrates the superiority of Catholic works over a pulpit-based Protestantism which makes no reference to truth outside its own rhetorical constructions.

> We see how thou in Rethoricke roollest,
> as one in Schemes and Tropes expert.
> Frequenting of this figure rare,
> which some men call sauce malipert.
> What truth in preaching thou declarest,
> I am content that other try.
> In this thy worke I can affirme,
> that every line contaynes a lie.[83]

This attention to rhetoric is not merely ornamental; as with other moments where texts discussed in this chapter show their workings, it incites an awareness of the mechanics of controversy. Beginning by casting suspicion on the rhetorical devices of schemes, tropes and figures, the verse mounts to an arraignment of all Protestant suasive technique, accusing its proponents of saucing their fare so cunningly that the audience cannot taste how rotten it is.

CATHOLIC LIBELS AND THEIR AUDIENCE

Rhetoric was not always employed to sweeten: particularly not in libels, a genre which this chapter will now consider more closely.[84] Adam Fox has recently described the circumstances of a libel's distribution. Multiple copies were made, and drawn upon walls; some of the techniques of print were alluded to, with pen-men and artists substituting for print and woodcuts; and the progenitors took pains to 'caste abrode, devulge, publishe, and singe the same in dyverse and sonderye open and publicke places, and dyd sett upp and fix the same uppon dyverse and sundry doors, walls and posts'.[85] Just as this uncontrollable diffusion excited fear, descriptions of it lent themselves to metaphorical fancifulness. In an answer to libellous threats against his person, Robert Cecil complained of 'many contumelious Papers and Pasquils, dispersed abroad in divers parts of the Citie, without any Author, and yet continually comming upon me . . . like the messengers of Job . . .' (f. B1a) and 'Shewells[86] or dead papers, which move with the winde . . .' (f. E4a).[87] Authors too showed intense awareness of textuality: for instance, a Catholic rhymed polemic of 1579 against clerical marriage has a rhymed injunction at the end where, in the pasquinade tradition, the text itself speaks:

> Obscurelye to conuaye me hence that Labour were in vayne
> For I haue me abrode good frynd I tell the playne
> who means therefore to take me dont let him observe this ordre
> Tho carye me unto ye mayour orels (*sic*) to ye madde Recorder.[88]

Paper has a life of its own, the writer implies, and rhymes are broadcast on the innumerable tongues of gossip. Though the same would be true of any libel, Catholic or non-Catholic, the threat has an especial edge where theological errors and sedition are in question.

Like other insults, libels had a particular importance for those with no access to official censure, even if Catholic libels would not have gone down well with all co-religionists.[89] As insult in formal dress, they were only one part of the Catholic's polemical wardrobe, but they are premeditated, recoverable evidence of how Catholics and Protestants would have traded insults of all kinds in day-to-day intercourse: Edward Slegg, for instance, trained his daughters to shout 'preests chits, preests bastardes . . . preestes dingdongs' at the children of the minor canons of St Paul's Cathedral, part of a long-standing local quarrel which also involved the production of libels.[90] This type of behaviour forms a continuum with other occasions of public dissent: some church-papists' unruly behaviour during divine service, or the Catholic plumber who was apprehended because 'in mending of a church he did not cease knocking while the service was singing'.[91] More generally, it would have threaded through the day-to-day business of gathering news, spreading rumour and formulating opinion within conversation.[92]

But if not all libellous abuse was written or printed, not all written or printed activity described as libellous by contemporaries was abusive. The examples given in the *Oxford English Dictionary* show that the term 'libel' acquired defamatory overtones during the sixteenth century – surely in part as a consequence of the Reformation. While it could still be used in its neutral medieval sense, to denote a small book or written document, it more often carries the insinuation that a text has been distributed by secret methods to ensure maximum publicity: a paradox encapsulated in the complaint on the title page of Matthew Sutcliffe's *The Supplication of Certaine Masse-Priests* (1604) which describes libels as being 'scattered in corners'. Thus, Catholic texts aimed at an elite audience, or documents with an apologist rather than a strictly libellous or deliberately offensive content, could be referred to as libels whenever they were distributed in manners similar to rhyming insults with a Catholic flavour, the main topic covered within this section.[93] The term certainly has additional implications of low abuse, but this is sometimes no more than an opportunity given to Protestant polemicists, and gladly taken. William Charke's answer to Campion's *Challenge* was written when the author found 'the letters to be more and more spred as Libels, abusing the name and holy authoritie of the Counsell . . .'.[94] The term could also be applied to other papers which were scattered abroad: anonymous petitions like that of 1606 asking how Catholics might resort to church services without sin, or threats to specific individuals, such as the Catholic Admonition of 1605–6 warning Robert Cecil that his life would be in danger if he did not moderate measures against Catholics.[95] To the early modern controversialist, then, Catholic libels – like other libels – were not necessarily popular, imaginative, or rude; all the same, those in rhyme do tend to fulfil these conditions.

The same libeller could write in prose or verse: the Star Chamber's judgment against the Catholic Stephen Vallenger in 1582, for writing several libels against Elizabeth and her government, specifically designates one as being in rhyme.[96] One factor which would have governed the initial choice between prose and verse was the intended level of audience. Prose – in theory at least – gave an unrestricted opportunity to present sophisticated ideas, while verse had mnemonic advantages which were of particular importance to the illiterate or semi-literate. Prose, too, had a more obvious initial association with seriousness and rhyme with ridicule. Both would have had their uses: ridicule, for instance, gives particular opportunities for imaginative excursus on the part of both prosecutor and defender. Composing a retort to a Catholic's 'namelesse, shamelesse loose lewde Libell',

Stephen Jerome describes it in Juvenalian terms which may be responding in kind to the original.

> A confused Chaos or a lumpe of sinne,
> *Pandoraes* box, diseas'd without, within . . .
> A messe, a masse of malice, sincke of evill,
> A false-tun'd Black-bird, feathered from the divell:
> A hellish brand inflam'd from Cainish ire,
> His pen the taper, and his paper fire.
> A silly sottish song from rurall Straines,
> Or blood impostumed, burst from Popish vaines . . .[97]

The term 'lewd', so often applied alliteratively and casually to libels, carries the convenient double implication of an uneducated audience and coarse subject matter. Authors of libels must have been conscious that this was often fair comment, and indeed that the two kinds of lewdness had a symbiotic relationship; just because a coarse jest would have helped most audience members to remember what they were hearing, it would have been an unusually effective way of making one's point to illiterates. Within the field of anti-Protestant polemic, some points of controversy were much better suited than others to this treatment; it is no coincidence that so many libels in this section and the next take clerical marriage as a topic, with all the possibilities it gave for specific character-attacks and generalised sneers about parsonical lust. One such, attacking the puritan clergyman Percival Wiburn, was distributed around the streets of Northampton in 1570. Wiburn was apparently married,[98] but there is a striking discrepancy between the generalised abuse of married clergy and the one offence of which Wiburn is actually accused: how he 'sought by all the meanes he coulde, / The Easter[99] to plucke downe'. This suggests how such abuse was a near-ubiquitous component of libels against Protestant clergy: as standardised as a cheap woodcut on a broadside, and sometimes with as little relevance to the ostensible purpose of the text.

As with some others, we have access to the text because it was printed together with a point-by-point refutation. Unusually there survive two different answers, one in a broadside and one in a pamphlet, separately conceived to target different markets and varying levels of literacy.[100] Both counter the original accusations by accusing Catholic clergy of sodomy and of condoning prostitution, but they do so in markedly different styles. The answers are of different lengths, with Verse 1 being given an eighty-six-line refutation in the pamphlet, compared to four lines in the broadside. In the pamphlet, considerable play is made with the riposte to the Latin pay-off in the Catholic original, 'FINIS. Non est inventus' (Not found):

> *Non est inventus* made this sclaunder so bolde,
> But *Est inventus* tooke in hand it to unfold.
> *Veritas non quærit angulos*, Shew thy face:
> *Non audeo dixit*, For my deedes deserve no grace.
> *Tunc desine*, Thou Foole, leave off thy works, dispatch
> *Aut prode mendax* That straight the gallows may thee catch.[101]

This piece of macaronic verse, which makes no sense unless the reader understands both English and Latin, is playing to the likelihood that the pamphlet would have had a more upmarket readership than the broadside. Even so, it is striking that even the broadside assumes that basic Latin tags will be meaningful to some of its audience.[102] To the same concluding phrase, the broadside *Answer* responds 'FINIS Coronat opus, Exitus acta probat' (The end crowns the work; the end justifies the means). But its incorporation is tactful; while those with basic Latin or better would have appreciated the retort, the eye of a non-Latinist could have skipped over it. While more research on the vocabulary and referential range of ephemeral popular literature would be highly desirable, one can at least remark that the denominational subject matter of Catholic and anti-Catholic libels would have ensured them an audience at many social levels, and that this is very likely to have affected their composition and sometimes their targeting.[103] But conversely, the Wiburn broadside also shows that varying levels of learning could be catered for in a single text – and, incidentally, how those who never went to grammar school could have been exposed to Latin vocabulary through cheap print or manuscript distribution. This mirrors the level of familiarity with rhetorical technicality assumed elsewhere in the libels discussed in this chapter; in particular, given that rhyme enforces economy on a writer, there is a notable degree of overt attention paid to the rhetorical structure of the argument in both libels and refutations. In the pamphlet *Answer* defending Wiburn, for instance, the writer scornfully counters the 'Epithite' (epithet) of 'preaching knave', and later, arguing against Verse 3, observes, 'Of proposition false, proceedes / Conclusion most vile . . .'

LIBELS, BALLADS AND THEIR OCCASIONS

The exchanges over Wiburn and the disturbance at Enborne, referred to above, both show the intensity with which libellers could respond to specific local circumstances.[104] The individuals responsible for the Enborne demonstration appear to have been specifically objecting to the incumbent's removal of a cross from the church: 'hollie cross then disgrace not but bring it in renoume / for up shall ye crosse, and you shall go downe'. They expressed their disapproval by scattering pages from the Bible, the Prayer Book and the post-Reformation portion of the parish register around the church; as the libel explains, this was a way of doing away with heretical documentation.

> The service booke here scattered all
> is not divine but hereticall
> so is the bible of false translacon
> to cutt it, and mangle it is no damnation
> The Register also if so we do serve
> from right (sure) we shall never a whitt swerve
> for why should new heritiques thus be inrold
> Inroll good catholiques long dead & ould
> Out w[i]th new heretiques here lett them go
> register catholiques & register no mo
> for Catholiques onely are worthie record
> & into ye Church register to be restord.[105]

Another Catholic libel, making a more pointed use of the physical space of a church, dates from the years of the Edwardian Reformation. This rhyme, affixed to a pulpit, is objecting to the King's preachers who visited the church, and was probably intended to rally support against others.

> This pulpit was not here set,
> For knaves to prate in and rayl.
> But if no man may them let,
> Mischef wil come of them, no fail.
>
> If God do permit them for a tyme
> To brabble and ly at their wyl,
> Yet I trust or that be prime.
> At their fal to laughe my fill.
> Two of the knaves already we had,
> The third is comyng as I understand . . .

It attracted an answer describing how papists sow the seeds of sedition in spreading libels, neatly combining this familiar metaphor with a jibe at the doctrine of purgatory.

> A rope is a fytt reward for such rysshe[106] repers,
> As have strowed this Church ageinst the Kings prechers . . .
> When such as with you trust shal al ly in the dust,

> And ryse thereout agayne unto perpetual payne,
> With them that laugh and scorne eyther at hye or lowe,
> Had better not been borne such evil seeds to sowe . . .
> . . . Ye are like for to be taken, and quartered like a baken,[107]
> And of your frends forsaken, for these sedis ye have sowen . . .[108]

But though libels are characterised by an occasional quality, ballads too were often written to commemorate an execution or other event, and particular occasions of discontent could call forth general laments. Among the poems preserved by William Blundell is a 'Dittie . . . upo[n] the p[er]secution made in Sefton parishe especially by Vahon [Vaughan] Bishop of Chester, & Nutter parson of Sefton & Deane of Chester' which deliberately addresses a public audience from the beginning, 'Youe that p[re]sent are, take of us some pitie, who in dolefull wyse shew our grieffs in songe . . .', and continues:

> Husbands and their wyves parted are a sunder
> parents severde are from their children deare,
> servants men and mayds forced are a number
> service newe to seeke, god, not they knowes wheare
> suckinge babes do crye
> which at home do lye
> in the cradle for the pappe
> mothers do bewayle
> lyinge fast in Jayle
> their sweet Babies heavie happe,
> all the countrie talketh
> everie way one walketh
> what in Sefton wee endure,
> for no strange opinion
> But that ould Religion
> Austin planted here most sure.[109]

Though the reflections are deliberately generalised, the composition exploits autobiographical pathos: for instance, the reference to mothers in jail probably alludes to an occasion during the Sefton persecution when Blundell's wife was imprisoned. If Blundell wrote the ballad – as seems likely – his self-presentation as confessor would have been obvious to anyone who knew its author, which suggests how this often impersonal form could take on autobiographical significance.

But if Blundell's verse looks forward to the confessor- and martyr-ballads which form the subject of the next chapter, this chapter ought to end by remarking how fiercely contested the martyr-ideal was. As the introduction to this study commented, Catholic and Protestant word-choice was polemicised to a high degree, and one of the fiercest terminological battles of all was over the term 'martyr'.[110] The notion that the cause and not the punishment made the martyr – to use St Augustine's formulation – could inspire comparisons of heretical martyrs to suicides, undertaken in everything from sophisticated polemical treatises like John Donne's *Pseudo-Martyr* (1610) to crude individual character assassinations and blanket condemnations.[111] 'Com forthe fond ffox, w[i]th all [th]e rable rowte / of monstruouse Martyres, in thi brainsicke booke', declared one Catholic versifier, 'compare them to, this gloriowse Martir stowte / and thou shalte see, how lothly fowle [th]ei looke.'[112] The quarrel over martyrdom could extend to other kinds of Catholic exemplarity, and a spat over whether Bishop Bonner achieved a good death or not called forth epitaphs and libels from both sides.[113] Halfway through the last Catholic intervention in the argument, anti-heretical abuse becomes a declared willingness to die for the faith, and libel and martyr-ballad – close relations at the best of times – finally merge.

> Turne over the chaine, good Jacke an ape,
> But keepe well cut behind thee,
> Least Smithfield fyre doe burne thine arse:
> If Hereticke it finde thee.
> God graunt her highnesse, long to raigne,
> Not onely here but evermore:
> Yet must we not foresake our fayth,
> Though we be martred therefore . . .
> Our Martridomes we see you meane,
> Yet Martirs names, you do envie us:
> And therefore dunghils be devised,
> with toyes to make you fooles, defye us.
> Well shameles marchants play your parts,
> As impudently as you will:
> We thrist (*sic*) for that which you do threat,
> Let come the cup, and then be still . . .[114]

Genre can oscillate outrageously in these controversial productions, and bravery is often less stately than hagiographers could wish – which is why, when the cup came, it could be accompanied by repentance for one's more unguarded utterances. Perhaps the most fitting end of all is the Catholic schoolmaster Richard White's: accused at his trial of making rhymes against married priests and ministers, he was to ask God's forgiveness before his execution for his songs and jests.[115]

4

Martyrs and confessors in oral culture

To acclaim martyrs is to align oneself with them and their cause. To do so publicly near the time and place of their death is something confessors do, since the notion of confessorship associates proclamation of one's faith with the willingness to remain steadfast in it, risking danger and sacrifice. The Catholic martyr-ballads of late Tudor and Stuart England, with their associated oral culture, yield intimate links between the representation of martyrs and the practice of confessorship: not surprisingly, given the immediacy of oral declaration and its inseparability from public religious and ethical commitment.[1] The practice of making public or semi-public oral statements about Catholic martyrs could have had a threefold effect: commemorating the individuals in question; committing the speaker to follow their example till death; and stimulating zeal in like-minded hearers and viewers. Thus, preservation of a martyr's memory could inspire exemplary behaviour in the public arena – which makes it ironic that the legacy of martyr scholarship has been such an ethically mixed one.

Over the centuries, remembering martyrs of one's own camp has sometimes involved denouncing those of rival beliefs, but more often ignoring them; many Christian denominations have had good reason to forget about those who died exemplary deaths at their hands. Within the academy, at least among post-medievalists, hagiography has usually been seen as the business of denominational scholars – or even, at times, as what mainstream historians are there to prevent. Nor can one underestimate the sheer visceral unpleasantness of the topic, for generations not accustomed to improving their piety by meditating on godly exemplars or the mutilated flesh of saints. New historicism on the one hand, and shifts in taste on the other, have jointly facilitated a rediscovery of martyr-narratives in recent years among mainstream historians and literary critics. After a grim period when practitioners of sub-Foucauldian body-scholarship tried their best to dehumanise the martyrs of the Reformation – and conference papers dealing with them were not infrequently played for laughs – commentary has progressed past anatomising and hysteria. More humane scholars such as Sarah Covington, Brad Gregory and Susannah Breitz Monta have taken the obvious but radical step of considering martyrs and martyrologies from different denominations side-by-side, unostentatiously reversing St Augustine's notion that the cause and not the punishment makes a martyr. In an age uncomfortable with the idea of saints except as media creations, Anne Dillon has given clear-headed and respectful attention to how the post-Reformation Catholic martyrological ideal was constructed, in a way that only serves to confirm how the English Catholic martyrs – like martyrs from all denominations – tended to behave in an exemplary manner.[2] Thomas M. McCoog has discussed the international interest they evoked, while Arthur F. Marotti has explored the key role of manuscript transmission in disseminating accounts of martyrdom.[3] This chapter attempts to supplement and continue the work that these scholars have begun, by showing how the memory of Catholic confessors and martyrs, and a consciousness of the pattern they gave to other Catholics, survives not only in texts circulated via print and manuscript but in a wide range of material intended for oral transmission.

One of this chapter's aims is to examine the relationship between celebrating martyrs and making confessors, present in all martyrology but perhaps at its most intense in orally transmissible material. Another is to survey the sophisticated and astonishingly various techniques by which the memory of Tudor and Stuart Catholic martyrs and confessors could be retained in the popular consciousness. Sometimes instigated by the martyrs themselves, sometimes contrived in their memory, these range from ballads, psalm-singing and motets to rebuses, punning on names, the erection of architectural features and the exploitation of local memories. Some of these techniques, like the Latin motet, were characteristically Catholic; others, like popular verse, can be paralleled in the English Protestant martyrology of this period.[4] Though material designed for oral transmission can be easily identified, it is more difficult to measure its success or otherwise, but some evidence of reception does survive. The chapter ends with two strikingly contrasting instances of Catholic martyrology finding a long-term place in local tradition: firstly the cult of Nicholas Postgate in the Yorkshire villages of Ugthorpe and Egton, which continues to the present day; and secondly, stories surrounding the relics of Ambrose Barlow preserved at Wardley Hall, Lancashire. Though one should not underestimate the degree to which memories of martyrs may be accurate and specific, one must also be sensitive to the more unorthodox imaginative reverberations they could excite. Secrecy was more often an imperative for the

Catholic community than speaking out, and the story of the skull of Wardley Hall shows how the combination of shouting and whispering could have remarkably unpredictable effects on popular remembrance.

HISTORICAL RECORD AND THE RECENT SAINT

The Catholic conception of sainthood is based on a highly interactive model of the traffic between living and dead, and mnemonic responses to the English martyrs are perhaps most denominationally specific in the relationship they play to between saint and audience. While both Catholic and Protestant reminiscences of contemporary martyrs were an exhortation to the living, Catholics had the additional comfort that their saints held out a promise of practical succour, and an undertaking that intercourse between faithful souls did not end with death – a consciousness which would, in many cases, have been enhanced by personal memories of recent martyrs. Thus, the evocation of a recently departed Catholic saint interrogates the audience in a manner which could not have been replicated in Protestant popular hagiography; saints are, as it were, listening in on their own history, and personally inviting the audience to join them. Catholic ballads constantly pivot between polemic, the subject of the last chapter, and an optimistic popular martyrology of this kind.

The effect of this would have been particularly intense when ballads describing martyrs in the third person were juxtaposed with ballads authored or voiced by them. In one of the most important surviving manuscripts of Catholic verse, BL Add. MS 15,225, a ballad attributed to the martyr John Thewlis is copied next to one on his death, which may reflect the sequencing of the two in oral performance.[5] The ballad voiced by Thewlis, 'True Christian harts, cease to lament', reads as anticipating the martyrdom which he is said to have foretold for himself before he was sent to England.[6] The ballad's affective techniques are those of face-to-face exhortation, playing off present immediacy against the future certainty of absence.

> Marke well my ghostlie victorie
> my frendes both great and smale
> Bee firme of faith remember me
> and dread not of your fale . . .
> The saints also did suffer death
> and marters as you heare
> And I my selfe am now at hande
> but death I doe not feare . . .

> Thus I your frend Iohn Thuelis
> have made my latest end
> Desyreinge god when his will is[7]
> us all to heaven send . . .
>
> (stanzas 4, 17, 19)[8]

The ballad includes a catalogue of martyred saints, St Andrew, St James, St Bartholomew, St Stephen and others: a standard feature of martyr-ballads which has the effect both of invoking tradition and of arousing devotion. If Thewlis was indeed its author, he would have included them as exemplars to himself, though the effect on the audience would have been very similar if, instead, the ballad was written as a prosopopoeia voiced by Thewlis. In either case, once Thewlis had been executed, its audience would have placed Thewlis himself as the latest of the line.[9] The text exploits the cultic authority given its speaker by the prolonged moment between condemnation and death, which is also the moment of writing; Thewlis is the medium and the messenger, blazing a connection between his fellow-prisoners and the saints in heaven.

> As for my selfe I'am not affraid
> to suffer constantlie
> For why due debt must neede be paid
> unto sweete god on hye
> St: Paule he being firme of faith
> hopinge with saintes to singe
> Most patientlie did suffer death
> lord send us happie ryseinge . . .
>
> (stanza 3)

In the ballad of his death, 'O God above relent', Thewlis's exemplary behaviour blends with individuation on the part of the storyteller.[10]

> When Thewles was unbarde
> a vision there was seene
> out of his mouth appeard
> of couller bright and sheene
>
> Most lyke the glorious sunne
> shyninge in clearest skye
> downe over his bodie ranne
> and vanish from their eye . . .
>
> (Part 2, stanzas 23–4)

It is simplistic to dismiss this as pious myth, more helpful to try and recover the ways that piety could have brought about the anecdote, since the miracle described is – as so frequently – specific in a way that suggests phenomenological observation. Thewlis's mouth-haemorrhage 'of couller bright and sheene / Most lyke the glorious sunne' was perhaps nothing more than vomit; but the Catholic witnesses of a priest's execution would have been alert for signs from heaven, and, interpreted as a providential sign, it would have testified to the orthodoxy of his verbal witness, his prophetic authority, and his exhortation of his audience in the ballad he wrote.[11] As described in the ballad, it gives authority to oral anecdote and newsgathering.

The ballad continues, relating another miracle:

> Then were his quarters set
> upon the Castell hye
> Where hapt as strang a thinge
> as ever man did see
>
> A flight of Ravens came,
> and pyked flesh from bones
> In the Church yarde ye did light
> & scraped there deepe holes
>
> O Christian hartes, relent
> prepare your soules to save
> When fethered foules shall help
> for us to make a grave!
>
> (Part 2, stanzas 27–9)

Stories of this kind often derive from environmental quiddities observed on the day. One famous example of this is the unusually high tide in London on the day Edmund Campion was executed, which was incorporated into his hagiography, and interpreted as a violation of the natural order in a manner which makes it very hard to distinguish between literary conceit and providentialist observation.[12] Here, the behaviour of ravens is accorded a similar importance. This anecdote may be based on an actual observation – after all, there is nothing intrinsically improbable about ravens pecking at flesh and then flying off to a nearby churchyard.[13] But the very exemplarity of martyrdom invites the imposition of universal tropes onto particular occasions. Here, the report of the ravens' behaviour both invokes and reverses standard lamentations about how the bodies of martyrs are thrown to the birds and beasts. A near-contemporary analogy, using the trope in a more straightforward manner, would be the motet 'Deus venerunt gentes' by the recusant composer William Byrd, which has been linked by scholars to the Catholic community's shock at the death of Edmund Campion: this sets the biblical text *Posuerunt morticina servorum tuorum escas volatilibus coeli, carnes sanctorum bestiis terrae* (They have laid out the dead bodies of thy servants as food for the birds of the air, the flesh of thy saints for the beasts of the earth).[14] Lighting in the graveyard, and appearing to pick holes in the soil, Thewlis's ravens normalise a world where the remains of martyrs are not buried, but publicly dishonoured – indeed, one where there could be difficulties about burying any Catholic in the graveyard of the parish church.[15] Ravens suggest the miraculous feeding of Elijah by these birds in 1 Kings 17, itself interpretable as a type of the Eucharist; and as with the Eucharist, disgrace is here turned into vindication through the process of eating.[16] Every time pious local Catholics passed the graveyard, this symbolically resonant story would have reminded them of Thewlis.

There is no necessary connection between the use of metre and poetic licence, and the fact that a report was metrical did not necessarily invalidate it as evidence for historians of subsequent generations. The early eighteenth-century antiquary John Knaresborough, making his collections on post-Reformation Catholic history within living memory of the last Catholic martyrs in England, gives 'an Old Copy of verses' – probably those discussed above – as his authority for John Thewlis's head and parts of his body being fixed on the walls at Lancaster, and used a ballad as the main source for his manuscript biography of the martyr Edward Reading or Bamber.[17] The account given by Knaresborough of the materials he has used reminds one that though ballads were highly suitable for oral transmission, they would also have been written down, and thus have had greater authority among historians who regarded oral reminiscence as a second-class source of evidence.

The short Account inserted here concerning the Two Priests of the Secular Clergy, is very imperfect, being grounded upon, the Information of some ancient Catholicks of Lancashire now living who either remember'd the Martyrs themselves, or heard the few particulars hereafter mention'd, from such as had been present at their Tryal and Execution. The rest I have transcribed from a Manuscript penn'd by an Ancient Priest,[18] who Stiles himself their Fellow Prisoner in Lancaster Goal (*sic*); where he was even 'till their Execution. (p. 406)

Bamber's last moments, in which he exhorts some Protestants who are exhorting him, are summarised from it: 'But . . . The (*sic*) Sheriff call'd out hastily to the Executioner to Dispatch him. And so turn'd off he was that moment. But then either the Sheriff or the Hangsman were a little too Expeditious in their Dispatches; for the poor Gentleman was but permitted to hang a very short time, when the Rope was cut, the Confessor yet alive;

and thus was He Butcherd in a most cruel and Savage manner, as my Author, a Priest and Confessor then actually prisoner at Lancaster, has avowed, in the paper above mention'd, which he drew up upon that Subject, and which is yet carefully preserv'd' (p. 414). This rewords and expands upon two verses from the ballad itself, sadly the only two which Knaresborough quotes verbatim:

> Few words He Spoke they Stop'd his mouth
> And Choak'd him with a Cord;
> And least He shou'd be dead too Soon
> No Mercy they afford.
>
> But quick and live they cut him Down
> And butcher him full Soon
> Behead tear and Dismember Straight
> And laugh when all was done.

CONFESSORSHIP: IDEALS IN PRACTICE

Bamber's is not the only case in which martyrs were hymned by other prisoners. Another topical poem, on the martyrdom of Peter Elcius, has been attributed to Thomas Pounde, a confessor renowned for having been imprisoned over a period of more than three decades.[19] This ambitious piece, clocking in at eighty-five stanzas, is in no sense a ballad, but does suggest why ballads, over and above the ease with which they could be memorised, would have been considered an appropriate kind of verse for those wishing to spread the martyrological message. Despite the fact that ballads and other popular verse often make sophisticated use of metaphor, allusion and other literary devices, they were still thought of as an unpretentious literary genre by both writers and audience; and the conclusion of this poem has an affectation of homeliness, using the trope of authorial incapacity to suggest that literary flourishes would be inappropriate to the subject matter, even a handicap to veneration. In a context of this kind, a Catholic was just as capable of invoking the plain style as a Puritan.[20]

> So these no dowbte, w[hi]ch seased have the skyes
> and rest in peace, w[i]thin the porte of blisse
> p[re]sent your prayeres, your teares, your groanes & cryes
> to him of helpes, the only helpe w[hi]ch ys
> and yf yow worke, they labour all theire beste
> to bring yow lykewyse to the land of reste . . .
> Heare w[i]th our Saviours speeche I will co[n]clude

> & yow renoumed co[n]fessors, do requeste
> in humble sorte, my homely meeteres rude
> To take in gree,[21] and conster [i.e. 'construe'] to the beste
> for zeale, not skill, did make me take my pen[ne]
> to stirre my selfe by stirring other men
>
> ffor as the tru[m]peter whose lym[m]es be lame
> to battailes broyles, encouraging the knighte
> som comforte, takes, pertaking of the fame
> yf foes be foyle, & gans [i.e. 'gains'?] the spoyle by fighte
> So I in hope, that yow of pray(?) righte sure
> will helpe w[i]th, prayeres, my lamed lymes to cure
>   (fols. 108a, 110b)

A poet, while he remains a poet, is only capable of exhorting rather than acting, and must necessarily rank lower than a martyr. This has an impact both on the genre he chooses, and on the reader-response he seeks to elicit. He is at his most honest about the limitations of his calling when he is most unpolished; one can speculate that popular verse may sometimes have been employed not only as an effective means of publicity, but as a way of ensuring humility for the author. Besides, his task is not accomplished until he has successfully affected the behaviour of others: a process which involves them in construing and improving the verses, supplying the author's deficiencies but also legitimising what he does.

Even if a poet is less praiseworthy than a martyr, his proclamations enable him to partake in the martyr's fame and stir up well-affected members of his audience. If Puritans dubbed themselves saints, Catholics – as here – often used the term of confessors to describe their own kind. The title of confessor, technically one who suffers privations for the Catholic faith without becoming a martyr, was attainable by more people than the martyr's crown. Everyone who laid themselves open to privation by committing an illegal act for the sake of Catholicism was, in one sense, a potential confessor; but in the passage above, the poet is exploiting an ambiguity in the term, since it is often also used to denote someone who makes a public acknowledgement of his or her religion. Conscious that his subject matter is dangerous, the poet acknowledges that all those who willingly read or listen to his poem are confessors. Since the whole intention of the poem is to have an impact on everyday speech and behaviour, this is both an honour and a responsibility for the audience. *Parrhesia*, the notion of public declaration, is the ideal that Catholic moralists are setting out in texts of this kind; and these heightened acknowledgements, arrived at in the context of the martyrs' trials and executions, need to be read against a time when – as both writers and audiences would have been aware – most early modern English Catholics would have made constant compromises with the ideal of confessorship in day-to-day conversational interchange.[22] Yet ideal behaviour occurred in real life, quite often; the martyr-ballad is an obvious example of its reportage, and one which stirs the audience to quieter feats.

All Catholic oral commonality – listening, speaking, singing and interpreting – refers to an ideal which, above all, is liturgical and collective. But texts of this kind blur the distinction not only between audience and congregation, but between earth and heaven, powerfully reminding the listeners that their prayers and praises should be united with those of the saints. The most famous martyr-ballad of all from this period, written to commemorate the death of Edmund Campion, can be read as a sustained meditation on the united remembrance of martyrs both in heaven and on earth.[23] As we saw in the previous poem, this goes along with an admission of authorial incapacity. The opening of the ballad stresses the limitations of writing as a medium for commemoration:

> Why doe I use my paper ynke and pen,
> and call my wyttes to counsell what to say?
> such memoryes weare made for mortall men,
> I speake of sayntes whose names shall not decay.
> An angells Trumpe weare fytter for to sound
> theyre glorious deathe yf suche on earthe wear founde.
>
> Pardon my want: I offer noughte but will,
> theyre register remaynethe safe above.
> Campion exceeds the compasse of my skyll.
> Yet let mee use the measure of my love,
> And geve me leave in lowe and homelie vearse
> His highe attemptes in England to reherse.
>
> (1–12)

Trumpets, a common iconographical attribute of fame, are as indispensable to the self-definition of the panegyrist as oaten reeds to the pastoral poet. This poet is making a very different statement from that contained in the poem on Peter Elcius's martyrdom, even though both connect trumpets with the idea of authorial incapacity; here, trumpets are the instruments of angels, and illustrate how the kind of fanfare that Campion deserves cannot be achieved on earth. Missing from most accounts of early modern rumour and news-dissemination is an awareness of the perceived supernatural dimension of communication. But here, the ballad-writer presents himself, in a way that one is obliged to take literally, as only supplementing what heaven has to say about Campion. In the company of all who spread Campion's fame on earth, his overriding concern is to participate in the corrective processes of heaven. In keeping with the fact that Catholics were dissidents, his notion of fame is both angelic and disorderly:

> Yee thought perhapps, when learned Campion dyes,
> his pen must cease, his sugred townge be still.
> But yow forget how lowd his deathe yt cryes,
> how farre beyond the sownd of tounge or quill.
> yow did not know how rare and great a good
> yt was to write those precious guiftes in bloode.
>
> Lyvyng he spake to them that present weare,
> his wrytinges took theyre censure of the vew.
> now fame reportes his lerninge far and neere,
> and now his deathe confirmes theyre doctryne trew,
> his vyrtues now are written in the skyes,
> and often red with hollye inward eyes.
>
> (109–20)

Saints' virtues are both written and declared in heaven, sustaining Campion's own use of both oral and written media – 'With tounge and pen the truthe he tawghte and wrote' (l.31) – but the relationship between heavenly fame and earthly rumour is particularly close. Popular report is perceived as part of the judicial process, where a cloud of witnesses has the chance to correct earthly injustice by declaring Campion's virtues and quashing adverse criticism. Hence, when the poet condemns the Protestant ballad-writer William Elderton along with the judge and jury at Campion's trial, it is no mere commentary on his literary skills to jeer 'thy scurrill ballads are too bad to sell' (l.98). In this unusually self-reflexive ballad, the line 'On every gate his martyrdome wee fynde' (l.130), as well as reminding the audience of how Campion's remains were displayed, could also be interpreted as referring to the public posting of illicit Catholic ballads – and if so, would be a rare piece of evidence about their distribution.[24] It occurs in the following passage, which by describing how rumour subverts the intentions of those who wish to obscure Campion's memory, provides an almost schematic description of the Catholic oral challenge. Particularly striking is the use of prosopopoeia to describe a real-life devotional activity: within a culture where – as the introduction to this book describes – local topography was so often consciously exploited as a mnemonic aid to the veneration of saints, to describe the London streets and the Tower of London as speaking in Campion's defence was not just a figure of speech:

> All Europe wonders at so rare a man.
> England was filled with rumore of his end.
> And London most for yt was present then,
> When constantly three sayntes theyre lyves did spend
> The streates, the steppes, the stones yow hallde them by,
> Proclaymes the cawse, whearfore thease martyrs dye.
> The Tower dothe tell the trewthe he did defend,
> the barre beares witnesse of his giltlesse mynde.
> Tyburne did try he made a pacient end.
> On every gate his martyrdome wee fynde.
> In vayne ye wrought that would obscure his name,
> for heaven and Erthe will still record the same.
>
> (121–32)

MOTTOES, MOTETS AND MARTYRDOM[25]

Whatever Foxe and his disciples might have assumed, the Marian martyrs had no monopoly on quoting Scripture. Biblical verses frequently came to be associated with particular Catholic heroes, in cases where those individuals had quoted them at trials, executions or other public events. Making his scaffold-speech, Campion took as his text 'We are made a spectacle, or a sight, unto God, unto his Angels, and unto men', a reference which was taken up by ballad writers on both sides of the religious divide.[26] As shown in a ballad preserved by William Blundell on the martyrdom of Robert Anderton, the Psalms were an especially popular source for appropriate verses. In this passage, the martyr quotes twice from the Psalms:

> When that his Judgment passed was
> hee spoke theise words most sweete
> [O holy lord of Saboth god
> with whom I nowe shall meete].
> And senge this verse; [no honoure lord
> no honour give to us
> But to thy sacred name shewe it];
> & then in prose spoke thus;
> [Againste me strangers risen are
> the stronge my soule have sought
> not settinge god before theire sight
> who dearly hath them bought.
> Behould how god my helper is
> & safegard of my soule

A sheeld most suer at all assayes].
In spiritte hee spake this whoule . . .²⁷

If the ballad preserves anecdotal evidence as to what actually happened at the trial, this would give us a fascinating glimpse of a prospective martyr deliberately choosing the medium of song to express joy at his death sentence. Either way, the ballad makes suggestive distinctions between singing and speaking, verse and prose. Giving voice to his delight at the sentence of death, Anderton sings a portion of the first verse of Psalm 115: 'Not unto us, O Lord, not unto us, but unto thy name give glory'; then, immediately afterwards, recites two verses from Psalm 54: 'For strangers are risen up against me, and oppressors seek after my soul: they have not set God before them . . . Behold, God is mine helper: the Lord is with them that uphold my soul' (v.3–4). While the accusation is described as spoken in prose, Anderton's thanksgiving is sung: a point which, given the fact that a ballad has to be written in metre, the ballad writer is obliged to spell out.²⁸ Exploiting their ready-made context, both quotations are carefully selected as points of entry to a polemical lesson which both sympathetic and unsympathetic observers would have understood: Psalm 115 goes on to condemn the worshippers of idols who 'have mouths, but they speak not; eyes have they, but they see not' (v.5), while Psalm 54 continues both to indict Anderton's accusers, '[God] shall reward evil unto mine enemies; cut them off in thy truth', and to anticipate the reflections of an incipient martyr, 'I will freely sacrifice unto thee: . . . For he hath delivered me out of all trouble; and mine eye hath seen his desire upon mine enemies' (v.5–7). But the action of singing when sentenced to death is most important of all; Anderton anticipates heaven in his disclaimer of personal glory, raising himself into an angelic register where prayer is all song.

There is evidence that Catholic composers chose texts for motets on the basis of anecdotal association. A theological collection in the Bodleian Library, compiled by one 'Thomas Jollett', preserves a four-part setting attributed to William Byrd – though probably not by him – of the psalm verse chanted by Mark Barkworth on his way to execution in 1601, 'Haec est dies quam fecit Dominus exultemus et laetamur in ea.'²⁹ According to this account, Barkworth sang a version of the verse over and over again, 'Haec est dies: haec est dies, hec est dies domini, gaudiamus, gaudiamus, gaudiamus et letaemur in ea', with another priest, Roger Fieldcock, chiming in, 'Et letaemur in ea.'³⁰ In addition, after an account of Henry Garnet's life and death, there is a setting by Jollett himself of words said by Garnet at his execution, 'Adoramus te Christe.'³¹ Both settings would have possessed a powerful occasional force to coexist with the revealed content of Scripture.[32] Jollett's chosen text, 'We adore you, O Christ, and we bless you; because by your cross you have redeemed the world', operates on two levels of specific reference.[33] Firstly, it attributes christological devotion to Garnet, explaining his heroic death; secondly, it is Jollett's chosen prayer to a God who is praised through the deeds of his martyrs. In the case of the other motet, the initial choice of text was Barkworth's;[34] but as Anderton's use of *Non Nobis Domine* might suggest, the language of rewriting and adaptation, so often used to explain how text was appropriated to occasion in early modern literary culture, is inappropriate to a martyr's declarative singing. Personal use of the psalms and liturgy on the way to execution proclaims an identification with Christ and his followers, and therefore an ecstatic relinquishing of any claim to individuality. More appropriate is the idea of selection, stressing the individual as chooser but not as originator. Even outside the immediate context of a religious service, this is essentially a liturgical choice, where one selects portions from a sacred text because of their appropriateness to a particular day, season or historical occasion. To the implied audience, the text would have operated – like the words of any other devotional motet – as an inspiration for personal reflection, which would have been steered by how much they knew of the reasons for Jollett's choice.

Motets were often – to use the contemporary term – private music.[35] The ability to second-guess the responses of a coterie audience might have affected the musical setting of biblical texts, as well as their choice and adaptation. Musicologists have long emphasised the affective qualities of Byrd, and his concern to maximise his chosen texts' semantic expressiveness is explicitly set out in his dedication to Book I of his *Gradualia*. Here, he describes sacred words as having 'such a profound and hidden power ... that to one thinking upon things divine and diligently and earnestly pondering them, the most suitable of all musical measures occur (I know not how) as of themselves and suggest themselves spontaneously to the mind that is not indolent and inert'.[36] For instance, there may – as Joseph Kerman has suggested – be a direct relation between Byrd's religious nonconformity and his pioneering use of dissonance; musical harmony was a commonplace metaphor for concord, while disharmony could be used to express political jars.[37]

This illustrates how motets could be used to voice general discontent as well as commenting on a specific occasion.[38] The words for motets tended to be biblical, but because the choice was subject to less liturgical prescriptiveness, it was easier to select those most susceptible to a contemporary application.[39] Psalm-texts figured largely, and in a well-known exchange of motets between Byrd and Philippe de Monte, Kapellmeister to the Holy Roman Emperor, both composers take their texts from the most famous psalm of Israel's captivity, Psalm 137.[40] The analogy of English Catholicism – or other religious minorities – with Israel in Egypt is a commonplace; and here, the reference to suppressed songs can be read as alluding to banned worship. Textual selection and textual rearrangement point up the allusion. De Monte initiated the conversation as follows:

Super flumina Babylonis illic sedimus et flevimus dum recordaremur tui Sion. Illic interrogaverunt nos, qui captivos abduxerunt nos, verba cantionum. Quomodo cantabimus canticum Domini in terra aliena? In salicibus in medio eius suspendimus organa nostra. (Ps.137, v.1,3,4,2)[41]

The verses are rearranged to allow Verse 2 to come at the end, pointing up the personal allusion to Byrd, and even rendering eloquent the silence at the end of the piece when the instruments have been hung up. But in his answer, Byrd reverts to the original order of the verses within the psalm, allowing the Scriptures to guide his formal expression of hope.

Quomodo cantabimus canticum Domini in terra aliena? Si oblitus fuero tui, Hierusalem, oblivioni detur dextra mea; adhaeret lingua mea faucibus meis, si non meminero tui. (*2a pars*) Si non proposuero Hierusalem in principio laetitiae meae. Memor esto, Domine, filiorum Edom in die Hierusalem. (Ps.137, v.4–7a)[42]

Psalms were sung across denominational divides as lyrical expressions of sectarian defiance; and because of its greater musical eloquence, the motet extended the idea further. Remarking on the large number of penitential texts which Byrd set to music, Joseph Kerman sees these as commenting on the contemporary Catholic plight; certainly, these and many other texts quoted in this chapter would have been readily interpretable by contemporaries as relevant to English Catholicism, because references to Babylon and Jerusalem, or lamentation and persecution, are so common in the community's polemical literature.[43] But if the story of Barkworth had not survived, one would not guess that the more joyful text of 'Haec est dies' had a specific relevance to one of the English martyrs; and one wonders how many other motets by Catholic composers might have been derived from similar occasions.

Both martyr-ballads and motets would have encouraged people towards exemplarity, perhaps even acting as a means by which members of an audience could keep one another up to the mark in future. An active, even a critical, interaction of this kind can sometimes be traced in the texts. One ballad, on the deaths of Nicholas Garlick, Robert Ludlam and Robert

Simpson, includes a response to previous versions of the story that, if left unaddressed, would have undermined Simpson's exemplarity. Narration of the episode serves a double function: Simpson's momentary lapse of courage is made to conduce to his eventual triumph, but ideally, it would also have taught the audience how not to act. The ballad's author knew how performativity worked:[44]

> And what tho SIMSON seem'd to yeeld
> for doubt and dreede to dye:
> He rose againe, and woone the field,
> and dyed most constantly.
> His watching, fasting, shirt of haire;
> his speech his death and all
> Do record give, and witnesse beare,
> he wail'd his former fall.[45]

BLESSED CONSCIENCES

Ballads could also foreground the role of the confessor in ways that involved both veneration and role playing. Some describe a particular heroic episode and praise the steadfastness of its protagonist, while others play out a process of exhortation, often by employing two different voices. The ballad 'The Blessèd Conscience' has as its hero Thomas Hoghton, who fled from England around 1570 when recusants began being harassed in Lancashire, and lived in France and the Low Countries until his death in 1580.[46] Of the version of this ballad printed in *Ancient Ballads and Songs of Lancashire* (1st edn 1865), the compiler John Harland says that it was taken from the recitation of a Lancashire fiddler.[47] What we have is a modified text, and the degree of alteration must remain speculative.[48] The original ballad could date from any time after Hoghton's death, and even while admitting the difficulty of disentangling genuine oral tradition from later antiquarian speculation, one needs to bear in mind that the biographical details it gives could be correct.[49] The story begins in an outdoor 'private place', where Hoghton is accosted by an unnamed visitor who warns him to depart. He makes preparations and leaves:

> Oh! Hoghton high, which is a bower
> Of sports and lordly pleasure,
> I wept, and left that lofty tower
> Which was my chiefest treasure.
> To save my soul and lose the rest,
> It was my true pretence:

> Like frighted bird, I left my nest,
> To keep my conscièncé . . .
>
> Thus merry England have I left,
> And cut the raging sea,
> Whereof the waves have me bereft
> Of my so dear country.
> With sturdy storms and blustering blast
> We were in great suspense;
> Full sixteen days and nights they last
> And all for my conscience.
>
> (stanzas 9, 11)

From the continent he asks his relatives to compensate the servants that have accompanied him, and his brother Richard obliges. This stress on Hoghton's concern for the welfare of his subordinates, lasting – as we have the text – for nine stanzas out of a total of twenty-two, may be designed to appeal to a popular audience and anticipate criticism that Hoghton had not fulfilled his seigneurial role.[50] Philip V. Bohlman has commented on the way in which oral tradition can act as a repository for a community's shared values, and determine 'the social acceptability . . . of these values through a continuous process of sifting and winnowing'; but one should also acknowledge how those values can be endorsed by adding ethical glosses to a story.[51]

The ballad needs to have two voices: that imputed to Hoghton, and the commentator's, who frames Hoghton's testimony and voices the praise necessary to the poem's existence as a moral artefact, which it would be improper for Hoghton himself to voice. The end of the poem sees these voices juxtaposed. Dying, Hoghton gives his audience a last injunction – 'Farewell, farewell! good people all, / And learn experiènce; / Love not too much the golden ball,[52] / But keep your consciènce!' (stanza 21) – which is immediately followed by the voice of the commentator, exhorting the listeners to behave like Hoghton. But though the epithet 'confessor' consigns Hoghton to heaven, it is also something of a pre-emptive strike, emphasising the degree of self-sacrifice involved in fleeing – an action which could, after all, easily be seen as unheroic:

> All you who now this song shall hear,
> Help me for to bewail
> The wight, who scarcely had his peer,
> Till death did him assail.
> His life a mirror was to all,
> His death without offence;

> 'Confessor', then, let us him call,
> O blessed consciènce!
>   (stanza 22)

Another Catholic ballad of banishment is voiced alternately by two lovers. The male lover explains why he must go abroad: 'Tis long of Englands strang division / and the altering of religion / that I am exposd to danger / and to travell like a stranger . . .'[53] In the second half of the ballad, his mistress sets out her determination to follow him:

> If to the Sea thou make thy venture
> I in the Ship will allsoe enter
> or if thou one the Shore wilt tarry,
> I the selfe same mind doe carry.
> soe thou vowchsafe to take me to thee
> speake but the word and ile goe with t[hee] . . .
>
> Since thou standest firme to the old religion
> my selfe am of the same condition
> England weel leave and march togeathe[r]
> noe earthly creature shall know whether[54]
> conscience moves mee to come to thee
> now thou hast spoke Love Ile goe with thee[.]

The obligations of gender, which could potentially work against confessorship, here result in a new recruit to the old faith. The attitude of this speaker is summed up in her promise 'I will stately [i.e. 'stoutly'] fight thy quarrell': conscientious demands are real, but resolve into a matter of standing by one's man.

CONFESSORSHIP, MARTYRDOM AND THE POWER OF NAMES

The theme of exile in these ballads shows how religious constancy can have two contrasting topographical effects, obliging one either to flee, or to stand one's ground with an unambiguous proclamation of allegiance. Post-Reformation Catholics often acted in the latter way by erecting denominationally specific signs and inscriptions on houses and other sites. Theirs was an age in which it was natural to do so. Historians and literary scholars have long been sensitive to the interplay between word and image in the Renaissance, and in recent years this has been supplemented by an awareness of how inscriptions at this period tend to exploit the location of words in a space, and on a physical surface.[55] As with any text, inscriptions depend crucially on their audience for meaning; and since they are more static than most texts, their physical location dictates that audience in the first instance. But if this is a limitation, oral transmission can compensate for it, and amplify an inscription's effect. Though an inscription, like any conversation piece, can only suggest oral occasions and not respond to them, this can be an advantage. At their most successful, inscriptions can associate a particular building or site ineluctably with Catholicism, accepting and capitalising upon the element of inflexibility in the medium: after all, inflexibility can signify constancy when carved in stone, and serve as an emblem of confessorship. In 1674, for instance, two spinster sisters living at Aldcliffe Hall near Lancaster placed a stone on the house reading 'Catholicae virgines nos sumus: mutare vel tempore spernimus' (We are Catholic virgins who scorn to change with the times), and their house became known locally as 'The Catholic Virgins'.[56] The best-known building erected by an Elizabethan Catholic, Thomas Tresham's Triangular Lodge at Rushton in Northamptonshire, is the most sophisticated example of this trend which remains to us. Simultaneously punning on Tresham's own name and notions of the Holy Trinity, it exhibits a combination of blatancy and enigma that commentators have found exceptionally provocative.[57]

Though Tresham took it to exaggerated lengths, it was not unusual for confessors and martyrs to pun on their own names. Examples survive in conversational exchanges which went on hagiographical record; a retort of the martyr John Boast[58] during his trial, for instance, survives among the material drawn upon by Challoner in his *Memoirs of Missionary Priests*:

the Lord President . . . made . . . a prolix speech concerning the long search that had been made for him . . . but that now, to his great satisfaction, he had taken him at last. To which speech Mr. Bost in the end replied with a smiling countenance: *And after all this, my Lord, you have but gotten Boast,* – alluding to the Earl's boast in having used such diligence for his apprehension.[59]

Jokes of this kind were an effective means for an incipient martyr to turn the tables on his accusers, demonstrating a recollected and cheerful spirit in the face of death; moreover, they were an effective trigger for anecdote. Stories taking their bearings from a martyr's name, as this does, were a striking way of rendering someone memorable; and they would also have played to the strong Renaissance interest in onomastic theory – the theory of naming – which so often drew correspondences between nomenclature, character and destiny.[60] These could operate on several levels, from the literary to the pseudo-scientific; and even those most sceptical about the idea that names were always appropriate to natures would have been sensitive to the value of having, as William Camden put it, 'good, hopefull, and luckie significations, that accordingly we do carrie and conforme our selves; so that wee faile not to be answerable to them, but be *Nostri nominis homines*'.[61]

The ideal of a cheerful martyr crossed denominational boundaries, and for martyrs and confessors to pun on their names was not an especially Catholic activity in itself.[62] However, those Catholic priests who had to operate under pseudonyms when ministering in England had a distinctive opportunity for testifying to the exemplary value of particular names, often to a degree that must have worked against the need to keep one's religion inconspicuous: for instance, the surname 'Campion' was taken as a pseudonym by several priests on the English mission.[63] While descriptive names in literature emblematise personality as it is, a pseudonym often shows one's aspiration towards certain characteristics and ideals, and so is not dissimilar to the process – again Catholic – of taking a name in religion; unlike the process of naming a baby, one names oneself, and there is no gap between the choosing of a name and having to prove oneself answerable to it.[64] Inventors of pseudonyms would have found themselves rediscovering the first purpose of names, since aliases were often chosen because they figured a direct relationship between designation and user, perhaps alluding metaphorically to the holder's occupation. Arriving in England, the priest William Freeman, 'fallinge into acquaintaunce with a goode ould man, was demaunded by the same how he would be called. "Call me," quoth he . . . "how you will, you shall geive me my name." "Why then," said the other, "you shall be called Mason, for that yow are to be a workman & layer of stones in the buildinge of God's Church."'[65] Puns were an alternative to other common sources for aliases, like distant family names, names indicating place of origin, or names taken when priests entered on the religious life; and like these, they helped to soothe the casuistical anxiety that aliases should be true in some sense.[66]

In this context, it is hardly surprising that martyr-narratives so often point up the power of names; one can guess that conversation around the scaffold would often have centred round the anecdotal correspondences between the martyr's name and his life and death.[67] These would sometimes have been very easy to identify: 'Campion is a champion', the first line of one of the ballads on Edmund Campion's martyrdom, does no more than point to the felicitous correspondence between his name and his heroism, since 'Campion' was a variant form of 'champion' in the late sixteenth century.[68] Another, less immediately obvious onomastic pun of this kind is preserved within the ballad on John Thewlis quoted earlier. Thewlis's limbs are damaged by those who bear him to execution:

> In wrastinge of[f] his bondes
> somwhat too hastilie
> they hurt his tender leggs
> whereat they seemd sorie
>
> Then smylinglie he said
> forbeare to mourne for mee
> smale hurts doe little greeve
> when great on[e]s are soe nye
>
> I thanke my saviour sweete
> from these bonds I am free
> soe soone I hope I shalle
> from all extremitie
> (Part 1, stanzas 23–5)

This is a conversational exchange sufficiently distinctive for a factual basis to be likely; but at first it seems odd that the author should have recorded it in so much detail, given that martyr-ballads tend to concentrate on praise and economise on factual reportage. The reason is that, perhaps deliberately on Thewlis's part, the conversation draws attention to a correspondence between his confessorship and his name. 'Thewlis' connotes 'thew', which in early modern English had two main meanings: a man's bodily powers, as when Falstaff says in *2 Hen. IV*, 'Care I for the limb, the thews, the stature, bulk and big assemblance of a man?',[69] or more generally a man's distinctive characteristics, particularly his good qualities. The meaning of bodily ability is the stronger in the ballad, which sets out by conceptualising execution as an enforced disability, or condition of thewlessness: the writer laments, 'Thy lambes their lyms[70] have lost / through Tyrants Cruelltie / One Thewlis is the man / which makes me call & cry . . .' (stanzas 2–3). But as the words attributed to Thewlis make clear, a martyr thinks of the body only as a form of bondage which he longs to escape: a meaning which is accentuated by the double meaning of 'extremitie', referring both to Thewlis's limbs and to the fate he is about to suffer. The way in which damaged limbs are made to signify Thewlis's bravery suggests one direction that onomastic interpretation should take, and rules out another, pre-empting what is actually the more common meaning of 'thewless', weak or cowardly. Instead, the damage to Thewlis's legs is made proleptic of his death and triumph.[71]

This way of using the onomastic pun is a vernacular counterpart to the international language of rebus, the enigmatical representation of a name, word or phrase by figures or pictures suggesting the syllables from which it was made up.[72] Some of the better-known English Catholic martyrs were celebrated in rebuses from the first: famously, Thomas More – *Morus* or mulberry in Latin – became a bleeding mulberry tree.[73] Another can be seen in a description of how patches of grass started sprouting in the shape of a crown in front of the house where the Jesuit Edward Oldcorne was captured.[74] On one level, this is a typical providentialist anecdote of the kind recently identified by Alexandra Walsham, seeking out supernatural messages in unusual features of a landscape;[75] but its original inspiration seems likely to have been the *corona graminea* described by Pliny in his *Natural History*.[76] Made of grass or wild flowers, the *corona graminea* was presented by a beleaguered army to the general who rescued them. The link between the *corona graminea*, notions of spiritual generalship and Oldcorne's gramineous name would have been irresistible to the more learned among Oldcorne's supporters, while the idea of a grassy martyr's crown was an imaginatively delightful one at every level.[77]

Similarly, the referential ripples extending outwards from names could determine the form and meaning of relics: a way in which Catholic popular onomastics would certainly have been different from Protestant. The miracle at the execution of the martyr Henry Garnet, celebrated across Europe at the time, is still well known: a piece of straw near the scaffold was said to have been splashed with blood in such a way as to give a likeness of Garnet's face.[78] John Gerard gives an account of the miracle, explaining how it was found by a young man hoping to secure a drop of the martyr's blood, who was standing by the basket where the martyr's head was cast:

Out of this basket did leap a straw, or ear void of corn, in strange manner, into the hand of this young man, which he beholding, and seeing some blood upon it . . . carried it away safely, and delivered it unto a Catholic gentlewoman of his acquaintance . . . after three or four days, a devout Catholic gentleman coming thither, she showed him the bloody straw . . . beholding the same more curiously than the others had done, he saw a perfect face, as if it had been painted, upon one of the husks of the empty ear, and showed the same unto the company, which they all did plainly behold, and . . . did acknowledge the mighty hand of God, Who . . . is able both out of stones and straws to raise a sufficient defence for His faithful servants.[79]

Straws were quite commonly gathered up for relics at executions, but it is only of Garnet that a tale of this nature survives.[80] To the twentieth-century scholar, the name of Garnet suggests the semi-precious red stone – and not inappropriately for a martyr, given the equation of jewels with blood in baroque poetics. The introduction of the idea of straw seems arbitrary enough to suggest, at first, that the story is simply an eyewitness account of a bizarre phenomenon. But this is not a record of arbitrariness, or even an attempt at mimesis; instead, it is a revelation of meanings already inscribed in Garnet's name.

At the time, a second meaning of 'Garnet' would have been as apparent as that with which we are now familiar.[81] A garneter was the overseer of a granary, and the idea of priests reaping the English harvest of souls was a commonplace metaphor which Garnet himself used. A letter of Richard Verstegan's, which partly quotes another of Garnet's, illustrates this. Both men, as usual in missionary correspondence of this date, are employing codes for priestly activity, and using 'corn' as a code for conversion, Garnet writes: 'Concerning our marchandise . . . We are lyke to have heare a very plentifull yeare, so that we may make great comoditie of corne, yf we be secret in our course.'[82] When it came to his martyrdom, his audience took up the conceit in both hagiographical and unsympathetic contexts. The best-known contemporary reference to the execution, alluding to the fact that one of Garnet's aliases was 'Farmer', comes from the porter in *Macbeth*, who describes Garnet as 'a farmer that hanged himself on th'expectation of plenty'.[83] But reinterpreted in terms of a sacred onomastic pun, Garnet ensured the fullness of the granary by being cut down, sacrificing himself and inspiring others: an image common within imaginative depictions of the persecution in England, and one which, as Anne Dillon has recently commented, lends itself well to an eucharistic interpretation.[84] To adapt Tertullian's famous saying, the blood of the martyr Garnet literally became the Church's seed by springing onto the husk of corn and rendering it fertile again.[85] None of this discounts the possibility that, on the day of Garnet's execution, his spattered blood actually did create the likeness of a face. Contemporary Catholics hailed the straw as a miracle, contemporary Protestants assumed that it had been faked, and even a twenty-first-century sceptic has to allow the possibility of a freakish accident, of a kind which the popular press still enjoys. We may never know what happened, especially since the straw itself has been lost, but the referential field of Garnet's name does, perhaps, help to explain why Catholics should have been looking at straw so attentively in the first place.

In the letter quoted above, Verstegan also gives news of a fellow priest, exploiting the idea of the clergy as fishers of men: 'Mr. Garlyke the fishmonger was oute of towne, but he saith he will very shortly be there and

3. Garnet's straw: a contemporary engraving, reproduced in Henry Foley, *Records of the English Province of the Society of Jesus* (1878), vol. 4 (ninth, tenth and eleventh series), plate opposite p. 133.

give order for our affaires.'[86] As this demonstrates, harvesting souls and fishing for men are interchangeable metaphors in this or any other evangelical context. Just as with Garnet and farming, a priest's name could generate metaphorical associations with fishing; and evidence of this survives in a cluster of stories about the priest and martyr Thomas Pilchard, given in John

Gerard's catalogue of martyrs.[87] Though substantial, the relevant passage deserves to be quoted at some length.

Thomas Pilchard Preist, quartered at Dorchester at Lent Assice. Most cruelly mangled, for beinge cut downe alive and layd on his backe the executioner beinge a cooke and unskilfull or careles first cut him over thwart the belly, withowt he offering to rise the executioner cut him all over the hand. Then the people cryinge owt upon him, he began to slit him up the belly and to pull owt his bowels. The Priest reised himself and putting owt his hands cast forward his owne bowells cryinge owt *Miserere mei* ... The officers retorninge home, many of them died presently crying out they were poisoned with the smell of his bowels. The chiefe keeper of the prison where he was kept, goinge into his gardaine somewhat late, saw one comminge towards him like Mr. Pilchard, and being astonied asked him what he did there. '[I] goe in to Mr. Jesoppe (a gentleman Catholicke prisoner), and presently I will retorne to you.' The keeper went in and sickned, Mr. Jesop died, and the keeper alsoe, who refused the preachers when they offered to come to him. An old prest there in prison in his sleepe was sodenly wakened, and sawe his chamber full of light and a thinge like a fishe bigger then a man from which the light proceeded. There was a gentleman prisoner there then (who tould me all this) whose wife, alsoe prisoner for the cause, was greate with child & neere her tyme, she wakened one night suddeinly in greate fright, and beinge demanded of her husband what she ailed, she affirmed she had seene Mr. Pilchard whoe tould her she must come to him. She fell that night into her labour and died in childbirthe. A laye man was executed there some 4 years after ... whoe being asked at his deathe, [what] had moved him to that resolution, etc., he saide, 'Nothinge but the smell of a pilcharde.'[88]

Of the process of interpreting early modern history, Robert Darnton has said: 'We constantly need ... to be administered doses of culture shock ... Where we cannot get a proverb, or a joke, or a ritual, or a poem, we know we are on to something. By picking at the document where it is most opaque, we may be able to unravel an alien system of meaning.'[89] This passage is so very different from later, statelier conventions of martyr-narrative that it is immediately arresting.[90] This is not because punning itself is necessarily low or indecorous, but because, even at this date, comic references to a pilchard would seem more natural than tragic or exemplary ones. The manner of the passage's composition is also unusual, less a continuous narrative than a number of generically distinct anecdotes making up a continuum: the martyr-narrative with the miraculous punishment, the ghost story, the vision, the prophetic dream, the humorous scaffold-retort. But it is by far the longest of the entries in the catalogue, and it seems no coincidence that it relates to the martyr with the most distinctive name. Clearly, two of the stories would lose their point if Pilchard's name were changed. But it is the martyr-narrative, which seems on the surface like a straight piece of reportage, that may be the most careful typological construct of all, and the key to how one is to read those that come afterwards.

Pilchard, the fish, links one narrative with another, and the equation of Catholic with fish has a multiple significance. Fishing had been the profession of St Peter and other apostles, and Catholic priests routinely referred to themselves and each other in Biblical terms as fishers of men.[91] Fish also had an association with Friday fasting, as well as being the secret sign of the early Christians: a symbol which had again become appropriate for those who had to worship in secret. The image was used by Protestants of Catholics, both priest and lay: Spenser, for instance, uses it to mount an attack on the marriage negotiations between Elizabeth and the Duc d'Alençon, while the Jesuitical Mal-engin in *The Faerie Queene* spreads a net to 'fish for fooles'.[92] But despite this, it was still used within Catholic codes. Robert Southwell, writing to Alphonsus Agazario in 1586 about some quarrels between Catholics in the colleges overseas, compares England's Catholic martyrs to fish. 'Be patient, dear Father, with our shortcomings, if occasionally the breath of storms ruffle your sea. You have "fishes" there greatly wanted here, which, "when disembowelled, are good for anointing to the eyes and drive the devils away," while, if they live, "they are necessary for useful medicines".'[93]

Southwell is alluding to the Book of Tobit in the Apocrypha.[94] Here, Tobias is commanded by the archangel Raphael to catch and disembowel a fish, and to save the heart, liver and gall. Asking why, he is told that the heart and liver drive away evil spirits when burnt, while the gall will cure a blind man when it is used for an ointment.[95] Tobie Mathew, picking up on a correspondence suggested by his own name, used the incident in a sonnet 'To St. Michaell Th'archangell', where the orthodox plea to be delivered from sin has intimations of a request for conversion:

> And since that glorious feather of thie winge
> the Angell Raphaell cured an ould mans eyes
> Behold another of that name who lies,
> blind in beliefe, bid him like succor bringe
> and cure this hart more blind, then that blinde face
> not with the gall of fish; but oyle of grace[96]

The reference to disembowelling also alerts one to the potential connection of this story with the hanging, drawing and quartering of Catholic priests, and the narrative presentation of Pilchard's execution is, like Southwell's letter, in dialogue with the story of Tobias throughout. Pilchard is the fish who allows himself to be caught, and to be gutted on the slab of martyrdom. The circumstance of the executioner being a cook or butcher must have strengthened the connection between man and beast.[97] When slit up the belly like a fish, Pilchard even casts forth his own bowels. Reversing the topos of saints' exhumations, where perfume emanating from the corpse is a sign of sanctity, it is the stench of Pilchard's viscera that bears disease to the ungodly: that the prison officers are overcome by the smell of his bowels signals that one is to read them as equivalent to the demons in the Tobias story. But Pilchard's disembowelling also, in contrast, confirms the faith of the man who is converted by the 'smell of a pilchard'. Other subsidiary narratives demonstrate how blind men's eyes are opened: they realise the truth of Catholicism, or see visions, dream dreams and have their deaths revealed to them. The configuration of anecdotes, which seems random at first, is instead a deliberate means of harking back to biblical precedent. Like all pious early modern Englishmen, John Gerard and his readers would have thought in biblical types and been anxious to discern the patterns drawn by the hand of providence; but Pilchard's name gives them a broad hint about where to begin.

One needs to remember how very differently Catholic and Protestant popular onomastics would have been received, given how radically the conception of saints differed between the two denominations. The layman who describes his confessorship and martyrdom as being moved by the 'smell of a pilchard' is expressing admiration for Pilchard's example in a manner at once reverent and jocular, but in a Catholic context the phrase also carries connotations of a belief in Pilchard's saintly intercession. In addition, the Catholic convention of pseudonyms for priests meant that metaphors and anecdotes of this kind could be incited by a deliberately chosen or adapted name, and this seems to have happened here. According to Pilchard's biographer, his subject was born Thomas Pylcher but served the West Country area of his apostolate under the name of Pilchard – a decision made easier, no doubt, by the fluidity of early modern spelling.[98] While any name connected with fish could have strengthened a Catholic priest's connection with the Apostles, and thus his pastoral utility, Pilchard's name is that of a fish rather than a fisherman, and therefore takes on its full appropriateness at the martyrdom that Pilchard must always have known was a possible fate. Finally, Pilchard is employed in a manner specific to his breed, and with a striking local relevance to the area of his ministry, since pilchards were used as bait by West Country fishermen to catch other fish; thus, they are a remarkably neat metaphor for the fisher of men who sacrifices himself in the process.[99] In this context, Dorchester Catholics would have seen the apparitions of Pilchard as showing how, having been fished himself, he came to fetch others to heaven or to hell.

LOCAL SANCTITY AND POSTHUMOUS REPUTATION: NICHOLAS POSTGATE

Pilchard's local ministry resulted in a posthumous cult that was also largely local, and Nicholas Postgate, a martyr who suffered later in the century as a result of the Popish Plot, can serve as a point of comparison here.[100] Postgate spent most of his long life as a priest on the Yorkshire moors, and his close identification with this locality was signalled, as with Pilchard, by an alias: 'Whitmore', alluding to Blackamor, a Yorkshire village that fell within the area covered by his ministry. His association with this area, both during his lifetime and after his death, is strikingly brought out in Thomas Ward's poem *Englands Reformation* (1st edn 1710). This poem, written in hudibrastic verse and popular throughout the eighteenth century, tells the story of Catholicism in England from the time of the break with Rome through to Ward's own times. The jogtrot metre and clownish satire of hudibrastic verse, in Ward's poem and elsewhere, demonstrate a kinship with the vernacular tradition of English versifying; but just as with ballads, one needs to be aware that these features need not get in the way of factual reportage. Though Ward is certainly exploiting burlesque as a comment on the comic horror of the English Reformation, his choice of hudibrastic verse is not intended to diminish the seriousness of the subject matter or the documentary value of his reminiscences; it is both for ornamentation and factual content that Ward's account is quoted by Challoner.

Ward gives Postgate more space than any other Popish Plot martyr, claiming in a side-note, 'I knew him well',[101] and chooses to describe Postgate's neighbourhood in as much detail as Postgate's character, showing how much the priest's ministry, and hence his sanctity, was defined in topographical terms. The humility of the one is embodied in the roughness of the other, and Ward's characterisation of Postgate as a contemplative and his house as a hermitage has the effect of connecting his life and example to those of medieval English saints:

> Nor Spar'd they Father *Poskets* Blood,
> A Reverend Priest, Devout and Good,
> Whose Spotless Life in length was spun
> To Eigty Years, and three times one.
> *Sweet* his Behaviour, *Grave* his Speach
> He did by good Example Teach.

> His *Love right bent*, his Will *Resign'd*,
> *Serene* his Look, and *Calm* his Mind,
> His *Sanctity* to that degree
> As *Angels* live, so lived he.
>
> *A Thatched Cottage* was the Cell
> Where this Contemplative did dwell,
> Two Miles from *Mulgrave Castle't* stood,
> Shelter'd by Snow-drifts, not by Wood;
> Tho' there he liv'd to that great Age,
> It was a dismal *Hermitage*,
> But God plac'd there the Saints abode
> For *Blakamor's* greater Good.[102]

Postgate's name is also associated with a locally popular hymn. As this has come down to us, it is a free adaptation – by Postgate himself, if the tradition is to be believed – of 'O blessed God, O Saviour sweet', a Catholic ballad first recorded in early seventeenth-century sources.[103] Given that its original author – like so many other writers of early modern English Catholic verse – will probably always remain unknown, there is an irony in how Postgate's name has become attached to what is not entirely an original composition; but the attribution confirms that, though Postgate did not initiate the poem, his was the life and death that informed people's reading of it. The hymn may have been transmitted orally by Catholics in the district throughout the eighteenth century, though it was consciously revived in the nineteenth century, and its use thereafter probably had a strong element of invented tradition. Bede Camm describes it as having been revived by Nicholas Rigby, a nineteenth-century priest at Ugthorpe, a parish near the site of Postgate's ministry, who recited it with his congregation every day after Mass.[104] However, the beginning of the hymn's use as a part of self-conscious Catholic revival dates instead from a few years earlier, and its inclusion in George Leo Haydock's *A Collection of Catholic Hymns*. First published in 1805, this collection was prepared for the press by Nicholas Alain Gilbert, a French émigré priest living in Whitby whose distinctive brand of missionary spirituality was, as Dom Aidan Bellenger has remarked, much welcomed by English Catholics in the North-East. According to the introduction of the third edition, it was Postgate's hymn which gave the editors the idea of forming a collection.[105] Certainly, in a hymnal where most verses are anonymously presented, both Postgate's name and biographical details are flagged up: in the first edition, the verse is headed 'Hymn, By the Rev. N. Posket, of Ugthorpe: Who, after having fought a good fight and kept the Faith, finished his course at York on the 7th of August, 1679.' As the hymnbook's patron saint, Postgate gives a local flavour to a locally printed collection.

Postgate's apprehension was the result of a betrayal by local people, and inevitably, his fate and its effect on the neighbourhood invited providentialist interpretation at a local level and beyond. John Danby, corresponding with John Knaresborough nearly three decades after Postgate's death, supplies an account of it and the subsequent history of three witnesses against him, Elizabeth Wood, Elizabeth Baxter and Richard Morrice. Morrice 'is dead some time since, while he lived very poor abused by every one with ye odious name of Hang-Priest'; Wood's husband, Ralph, was paralysed for several years, though is now better; Baxter is still living, 'of whom I hear of noe misfortune excepting poverty, & yt which is common to them all, & ye greatest of misfortunes, obduracy and impenitence'. Reeves, the exciseman who apprehended Postgate, was found drowned in a small brook, 'where I can not learn, my neighbours differing in ye particular place but all agreeing yt soe he dyed'. Before his death he suffered from terrible pain in all his joints, 'as he himself complained in ye hearing of a sensible, credible old man now living'.[106] This attentiveness to oral testimony as revealing God's judgment on the betrayers of martyrs proved remarkably resilient in the locality, in a way that was surely helped by the nineteenth-century revival of the cult. Bede Camm, writing in the early twentieth century, relates the traditional belief that Reeves had drowned himself, and been found in a pool called The Devil's Hole, where no fish had ever again been caught. Showing that a pious providentialist interpretation of local landmarks was by no means dead in his own time, Camm writes: 'The good old priest at Egton Bridge told the present writer that a colleague of his had desired to test the truth of the tradition, and had fished at Devil's Hole for a whole day, but without seeing a single fish rise.'[107]

Providential legends were not the only trace which – at the turn of the twentieth century, and over two hundred years after Postgate's martyrdom – Camm found of the martyr's continued remembrance and veneration in the district. A local Catholic church, St Hedda's, had acquired some architectural and other relics, including a pyx-bag that had been preserved by descendants of Postgate's housekeeper, showing how relics could be preserved in humble families just as effectively as in aristocratic ones.[108] When Postgate's cottage was pulled down, a beam was made into small wooden crosses, preserved by Catholics in the district. Still later than Camm, Elizabeth Hamilton recorded an oral reminiscence about these crosses in her biography of Postgate, published in 1980, with the same informant remarking how 'Father Postgate . . . was still spoken of by the ordinary folk all over the area'. The Postgate cult extended to a variety of objects which had been preserved as relics. 'When [the church at Sleights] was first opened . . . people from the moors, mostly non-Catholics, came to the priest, Fr Gannon, bringing all sorts of things, candle-sticks, cloths, and so on. "These," they would say, "belonged to Father Postgate."'[109] A legend that Postgate had been the first to bring the daffodil to the area may have had its basis in the daffodils which grew for many years on the site of the martyr's garden[110] – though in the earliest years of the Catholic Revival, a contributor to the *Catholic Magazine* visited the garden at Ugthorpe, and reported: 'A few daffodils had long survived the rest, but the mistaken reverence of some visitors had led them to transplant those perennial relics into their own gardens.'[111]

Oral and material culture cannot be considered in isolation from each other. As this chapter has argued, hymnody and anecdote are both means of preserving a martyr's memory within oral discourse, while the high incidence of Postgate relics preserved locally points to an especially strong association of the martyr with the traditions of the district. All suggest a genuinely popular, locally based hagiographical tradition, enhanced and rendered self-aware by the Catholic Revival, which Camm – the Cecil Sharp of recusant history – recorded at a period when antiquarians from all subject areas had become very conscious of the urgent need to preserve oral tradition.[112] In the 1950s the Postgate cult was still active, and one Laurence Canter described how the martyr was still being invoked by local petitioners, who wrote petitions to Postgate to put on the altar of the English Martyrs church in Sleights, North Yorkshire; when the altar was being repaired in 1959, quantities of these petitions were found inside it.[113] In more recent years, the Postgate cult has metamorphosed into the Postgate Society, which still flourishes at the start of the twenty-first century.

Because the local veneration of Postgate was pursued on so many fronts and is so well-documented and long-lived, it may be deceptive as a general guide to how martyrs were remembered. But the various accounts add up, at least, to an illuminating case study – not least because it is rare to have such strong evidence of lay participation. Nicholas Gilbert and Postgate's other priestly successors in the locality had an obvious interest in stimulating the cult, and some might even have employed local landmarks as a teaching aid; but the preservation of Postgate relics in humble homes, and the high degree of quiddity in the legend, combine to suggest an active, imaginative participation in the cult by the local Catholic population in general. Antiquarian testimonies, on which the above account has drawn, show the cult being periodically rediscovered; and while educated interest could only have helped its continuance at a humbler level, it is striking how many of these antiquaries make explicit use of their contemporaries' oral evidence, rather than copying earlier written sources. Yet at the same time, this should not surprise one. Both Challoner's and Camm's historical collections, and those of many other Catholic scholars, were motivated in part by an attempt to gain official recognition at Rome for the English martyrs, and for this, all evidence of a strong and continuing cult was grist to the mill.[114]

The history of gaining official recognition for the English martyrs was, one has to admit, very protracted. As early as the 1580s, Pope Gregory XIII agreed that a Te Deum might be sung on the news of an Englishman's martyrdom, that relics of them could be used to consecrate altars and that their pictures might be placed in the chapel of the English College in Rome. Systematic enquiry into their causes was begun in 1642 under Pope Urban VIII, and though progress was seriously hindered by the Civil Wars in England, Richard Smith, Bishop of Chalcedon, drew up a list which was later to form the basis of Challoner's historical investigations. However, it was only in the late nineteenth century that the lobbying became seriously effective. Some groups of martyrs, including Postgate himself, were beatified then; another cohort was to follow in 1929; and finally, forty English and Welsh martyrs were canonised in 1970 under Pope Paul VI.[115] But even though the story is a long one, this testifies to how the individuals in question could, finally, not be ignored. Since this chapter has largely been dedicated to chronicling how martyr-cults began, one needs to remember that, as far as the Catholic church is concerned, many of them are now official.

THE SKULL OF WARDLEY HALL: SECRECY AND FICTIONAL MISINTERPRETATION

If the story ended there, it would be triumphant, but also misleadingly straightforward. Given that this chapter has also dealt with the interplay between declaration and secrecy, it is bound to contain some mixed messages: anonymous authors who stoutly declare their faith; pseudonymous individuals who conceal their real name and flaunt their Catholic allegiance; exiles who make sacrifices, but escape. In this context, it is no wonder that English Catholic priests operating during penal times should have been such a powerful focus for imaginative attitudes towards concealment, both in their own use of aliases, as this chapter has shown, and in the anecdotes inspired by their activity. At one level, there was no problem about this. Even Christ had had to hide himself at times, and there was no contradiction between a Catholic priest acting secretly or discreetly when going about his business and performing admirably when caught.[116] The reckless courting of martyrdom was consistently frowned upon, and successive Jesuit generals of the Elizabethan era, Everard Mercurian and Claudio Acquaviva, were nervous of English Jesuits behaving too dangerously, thus making caution simply a matter of obedience for their underlings.[117] But to manifest confessorship through the act of hiding is at least a paradox, and one which gives an edge to Protestant commentators' contempt for Catholic disguise and equivocation.[118]

Nevertheless, it remained part of priestly practice and Catholic self-representation. The Jesuit John Gerard gives a well-known account of hiding in a priest-hole, and a scene where a priest is discovered in hiding was dramatised in a Catholic play surviving in the archives of the English College, Rome.[119] In one scene, a character is discovered hiding under a bed by a group of pursuivants, one of whom comments:

> For I have known some justices of the peace
> Inspired with zeal; among the rest a knight
> So punctual in searching of an house,
> And forward to undo the Papists . . .
> That he hath brought in engineers by art,
> With mathematic and instruments to sound
> The depth, the breadth, and length of ev'ry room,
> To see what close conveyance may be found,
> Or secret place that might conceal a priest . . .
> (3503–5, 3512–16)[120]

The paradox is visible in celebratory Catholic scholarship of all eras, and well summed up in Bede Camm's *Forgotten Shrines*. For a scholar who, like Camm, wanted to identify a living, popular and visible tradition of heroic recusancy, Postgate was perhaps the ideal saint to prove a case; certainly, Camm takes issue with Newman over the famous picture set out in Newman's sermon 'The Second Spring', of pre-Emancipation Catholics barricaded within gothic houses:

An old fashioned house of gloomy appearance, closed in with high walls, with an iron gate, and yews, and the report attaching to it that 'Roman Catholics' lived there; but who they were, or what they did, or what was meant by calling them Roman Catholics, no one could tell; – though it had an unpleasant sound, and told of form and superstition . . . Such was about the sort of knowledge possessed of Christianity by the heathens of old time, who persecuted its adherents from the face of the earth, and then called them a *gens lucifuga*, a people who shunned the light of day. Such were Catholics in England, found in corners, and alleys, and cellars, and the housetops, or in the recesses of the country; cut off from the populous world around them, and dimly seen as if through a mist or in twilight, as ghosts flitting to and fro, by the high Protestants, the lords of the earth.[121]

But while Camm politely distances himself from this picture of decay in his preface to *Forgotten Shrines*, the book as a whole has the effect of endorsing Newman's picture as well as correcting it.[122] Much of his fact-gathering focused on the great recusant houses and the oral traditions connected with them, often suggested by characteristically Catholic architectural features and objects, and many of these fit Newman's description very well.

The English Catholic culture of secrecy had various imaginative effects, some intended, others completely unpredictable. But much English Gothic fantasy takes its bearings from one empirical fact: that great houses owned by Catholics during penal times are more likely than most to have features which exacerbate a fear of the unknown, and inspire the kind of rumour that is a near relation to fiction. Priest-holes, private chapels and caches of relics all corroborate the common equation between Catholics and secrecy, and – by the same token – between Catholics and narrative speculation. John Bossy has argued that the servants in a Catholic house would have tended to be either Catholics themselves or pro-Catholic, but in a rural community, no great house could hope to operate independently of gossip and rumour generated by outsiders.[123] In any community where Catholicism was not completely accepted, secret rooms, uncertain comings and goings, and individuals who shunned visibility would have accompanied the provision of hospitality for itinerant priests, or having one as a permanent member of the household. A story related by Edmund Campion captures the type of moment where the potential relationship between fact, gossip and fiction becomes plain. When on the run in Ireland, he was put up at the great house of Turvey; and while he was working in an upper room, an old woman came in who was unaware of his presence. She took him for a ghost: 'The hair on her head stiffened, her colour left her, her mouth hung open in stupefaction. She didn't say a word, but rushed out of the room as fast as she could to warn the mistress that a hideous thing was writing in the upper room.'[124]

Even after martyrs met their end, and achieved a piecemeal afterlife in relics, they might continue to be hidden – like any other Catholic object. In one particularly well-documented case, this had the double effect of removing them from immediate local consciousness for generations, and encouraging fictional explanations of how their remains came to be hidden.

At Wardley Hall in Lancashire, a human skull hidden in the walls of the Hall and rediscovered in 1745 is preserved to this day, in a glazed niche of the staircase landing: a relic of the Benedictine monk Dom Edward Ambrose Barlow, apprehended and executed in 1641, who was connected with the Downes family of Wardley Hall during the period of his ministry.[125] However, another identification of the skull as the remains of Roger Downes, Earl of Wardley, was current in the nineteenth century, and may well have earlier antecedents. The story was that Downes, as legendary a local sinner as Barlow was a saint, was decapitated in a drunken brawl in 1676, and his head was sent back to Wardley to be buried. Nineteenth-century antiquarian accounts of the district relate the tradition of how Downes's head refused to stay interred, and moved to the niche accompanied by a great storm.[126] In his *Traditions of Lancashire*, John Roby even gave a semi-fictionalised account of the episode, drawing blatantly on Gothic stereotype:

... invariably [the skull] returned. No human power could drive it thence. It had been riven in pieces, burnt, and otherwise destroyed; but ever on the subsequent day it is seen filling its wonted place. Yet was it always observed that sore vengeance lighted on its persecutors ... Sometimes, if only displaced, a fearful storm would arise, so loud and terrible that the very elements indeed seemed to become the ministers of its wrath.[127]

However, Roby's account and similar ones were written long after the identification of the skull as Downes's had been effectively disproved. The antiquarian Thomas Barritt, writing around the 1780s, notes the story of the moving skull in his manuscript collections, remarking that it 'smells like a fireside tale on a winter's night', and records that the Downes family vault had been opened around 1779, showing Roger Downes's head *in situ*.[128] His writings also set out the alternative and more accurate local tradition that the skull belonged to a Catholic priest executed at Lancaster; but though Barritt is invariably cited as one of the sources for Wardley Hall lore, this story is either ignored or mentioned only in passing by those who draw on him.[129] The discontinuity must have been exacerbated by the fact that, at the time the skull was discovered, the ownership of the Hall had passed away from the Downes family.

As with the Roger Downes story, a storm is said to have arisen when Barlow's skull was moved.[130] This supernatural element suits both a ghost story and a piece of popular hagiography, and gives a clue as to how the two tales may have come to be linked; but the two opposing identifications of the Wardley Hall skull give the reader a choice of ways to interpret human remains, and two alternative reasons why they should provoke disturbances in the natural order. The antiquarians' identifications draw on, though inevitably tamper with, two orally conveyed anecdotal traditions inspired by opposed notions of the numinous: one at ease with the idea of relics, the other assuming that publicly displayed human remains must be there for a sinister reason. Out of context, bones can inspire either hagiography or Gothic horror, and explanations arrived at retrospectively are likely to be shaped by fictional tropes. Here, the character of the skull's supposed original owner suggests the literary genre: as Roby's story shows, the ghostly peripatetic skull of the reprobate Roger Downes slips quite happily into Gothic scaremongering. Roby is anti-Catholic to an extent that positively fends off alternative explanations of the skull involving an exemplary Catholic figure, even while capitalising on the supernatural traditions surrounding that figure. Outside the realms of fictionalisation, denominational allegiance continued to shape attitudes towards the material. The first serious piece of research into the story was written by the bibliographer of post-Reformation Catholics, Joseph Gillow – thus proving that the hermeneutics of suspicion, and even confessional agendas, do sometimes elicit accurate scholarship.[131]

As David Hufford has commented, memory slips, fabrication and simple misinterpretation of events have a part to play in the construction of ghost stories.[132] All these feature in the story of the Skull of Wardley Hall as re-told above; so, too, does a recognition of how antiquarians can blur the boundaries between fact and fiction as they collect and interpret oral traditions for the reading public. All this directs one back to the readings of Gothic romance featured in chapter 1 of this study. But in the context of the material discussed earlier in the present chapter, the story presents the other side of the coin to the tales of popular providentialism which surrounded Catholic martyrs. Even though Gothic and providentialist narratives make ample use of the supernatural, what is miraculous in one becomes sinister in the other – which is why reading the providentialist story of Ambrose Barlow after the Gothic story of Roger Downes has the effect of turning the lights up. Yet it also shows how oral tradition can get the remembrance of martyrs almost totally wrong.

Conclusion: orality, tradition and truth

To repeat Joseph Hall's challenge, '. . . as for oral Traditions, what certainty can there be in them?'[1] Whether one can prove the authenticity of oral tradition is not a question specific to religious discourse, in early modern England or at any other time. But the questions thrown up by the Reformation about its reliability show how, in the days before the academy was secularised, it was theological debate which often set the pace on questions of hermeneutics.[2] Religious polemic is an unsurpassed means of clarifying ideas, and these ideas, in turn, often develop well beyond their original impetus. If the notion of oral tradition began life as a deliberately partial definition, not least because the passage ignores the importance of non-scriptural written sources in Catholic concepts of tradition, it has become an entirely different endeavour since Hall's time. Hall would have been surprised to see how his contemptuous phrase has metamorphosed, both within common usage, and within the speech of a discipline concerned, where possible, with recovering truth through oral means.

Even so, the title of this book is partly a tribute to Hall for recognising the close relationship between Catholicism and ideas of oral tradition, and for posing a challenge with which any exponent of orally transmitted material has to engage – whether in a direct or an oblique manner. So far, this study has considered the many ways in which oral transmission and dissemination had an impact on the post-Reformation English Catholic experience, and in particular, the way it shaped so much of the literature. Oral traditions can be seen as oral transmissions that keep going; while it is hard to judge the impact and longevity of much of the material discussed above, one can see in some cases not merely a transmission, but a perpetuation of Catholic topics and Catholic ways of thinking, often in company with non-Catholic responses. Irrespective of subject matter, oral methods of transmission also played a crucial part in forming perceptions of Catholicism among both Catholics and non-Catholics. While all this material is at some remove from the main subject of Hall's criticism, the place of tradition within the official doctrine and discipline of the Catholic church, it poses many of the same methodological issues, and sometimes relates specifically back to it. Traditions relating to a local martyr, for instance, would have shored up Catholicism's traditional endorsement of praying to saints, which is not explicitly enjoined in Scripture.

Yet Hall's point, with regard to saints' lives as to much else, would have been that one cannot place traditions on a par with the Bible, because the Scriptures are divinely dispensed and orality is prone to error. While this book has certainly asked questions about authentication, accuracy and distortion in relation to individual pieces of evidence, it has not so far used Hall's suspicion of orality to survey the broader picture. When one does this, his view that oral tradition leads to distortion appears well-founded in many cases – notably the fragments of Catholic prayers within spells, and the tale of the Skull of Wardley Hall told at the end of the last chapter. But if this evidence would need to be treated with extreme caution if one wanted to reconstruct the Sarum Missal or write up Ambrose Barlow for the *Dictionary of National Biography*, it is very revealing indeed on other counts. One scholar's distortion is another scholar's reception history, and a key preoccupation of this book has been the imaginative, often wayward operations of antiquarian and popular remembrance. Truth is not necessarily absent from the equation either, if one broadens one's definition of it into considerations of diversity and emotional authenticity: an area where minority groups, Catholics and others, have special demands on a compassionate reader's attention, and where oral historians researching more recent periods have often made large claims, in their attempt to recover the voices of those whom previous generations of educated commentators have tended to sideline or despise.[3]

To leave it there, though, would imply that Hall was right: that oral tradition can only ever have a tenuous and unhelpful relationship to factual certainty, whatever the ethical reasons for studying it might be. Written evidence has certainly tended to be seen as more trustworthy than oral, especially in subject areas where both oral and written sources are available, while Ronald Hutton, a historian whose work is deeply engaged with oral tradition, has admitted to personal experiences of disillusion with it: 'Against . . . droplets [of fact] must be set an ocean of misinformation.'[4] But the argument that there can be no certainty in oral tradition is answered by every historian who identifies occasions when oral and non-oral sources concur, and problematised by everyone who asks why one should regard data probable in itself as necessarily unreliable, just because it has been preserved by oral transmission. D. R. Woolf, one of the most illuminating scholars to have written on the relationship between history and oral tradition in early modern England, has described the increasing preference for written tradition over oral as the seventeenth century progressed, attributing it to the widening division between learned and popular cultures during this period; commenting that the Tudor and early Stuart antiquaries have often been condemned for their reliance on both written and oral sources, he argues that they should have a better press: 'They helped to keep open not one road to the past, but two.'[5] His comment is typical of the move towards affirming oral tradition which has taken place in recent years: not, perhaps, because the relationship between orality and fact has begun to be seen as less problematic, but because post-structuralism has ensured that scholars' suspicions are now more thinly spread.[6] It is no coincidence that interest in oral tradition has burgeoned in early modern studies at a time when attention, here and elsewhere, has increasingly focused on the instability of written and printed evidence – as foreshadowed by many Catholic apologists for tradition who pointed to the problems with interpreting Scripture.[7]

This study has also pointed to two further issues: how both educated and uneducated individuals could use oral transmission as a means of deliberate, responsible factual dissemination, and how this in time created new traditions which could be seen as authoritative. We have seen missionary priests using orally transmissible ballads to educate unlearned Catholics about their faith, and antiquarians treating orally transmissible martyr-narratives as good evidence: the interplay between orality, manuscript and print in both these cases illustrates how oral traditions are not divorced from other media, rendering it very problematic to single them out for condemnation. The use made of orally transmissible material by educated Catholics is not, of course, without parallel among other denominations, yet Catholics might well have felt it ratified to some degree by their church's high doctrine of tradition, and its affirmation of non-scriptural ways to instruct Christians.[8] Even the highly local, highly specific material in this book is shaped by general notions of tradition and refers insistently back to them, begging the question: where does church tradition stop?

What has been said so far, in both this conclusion and the book in general, has tended to confirm Hall's suspicion that oral tradition is a highly imperfect means of transmitting factual detail. But questions of truth are not always the same thing as questions of accuracy. Since the truth-claims of religion are bolder than those attached to any other area of knowledge, the claims made for church tradition can evoke, at their most far-reaching, a lived religious authenticity guided by the Holy Spirit – at times going well past what can be checked in Scripture, since Scripture is seen as a second source of truth rather than as a final appeal. This was an empowering vision for some early modern thinkers, but a highly dubious one for others. Hence, perhaps the most appropriate response this book can give to Hall comes from the mouths of his immediate forebears, contemporaries and successors, both Catholic and Protestant, as they consider the whole question of church tradition. The brief survey of Reformation attitudes to this topic given below is a way of setting Hall in context, since he was intervening in an international debate, not writing specifically about the afterlife of the old religion in his own country. But because of the strong connection between unofficial or suppressed religious practices and oral culture, material from English sources does throw up some suggestive connections between Catholics, oral tradition and questions of truth: nowhere more so than among the Blackloists, a group of secular priests politically dominant in 1650s and 1660s England, who held that the Catholic rule of faith was to be identified with oral transmission of the Christian message between generations.[9] In response to questions like Hall's, Catholics typically stressed the uncertainty of the written word and the reliability of tradition, and this was nowhere more strikingly set out than by the most radical of the Blackloists, John Sergeant. His adaptation of the rule-of-faith debate was tailor-made for the unique conditions prevailing in England, and this book will conclude by discussing it.

TRADITION, THE RULE OF FAITH AND THE ENGLISH CHURCH

Though ideas of tradition and orality are so often linked, tradition in the wider theological arena has implications far beyond oral instruction. First and foremost in the early modern period, it related to any authoritative but non-Scriptural material, particularly the Church Fathers, church councils, liturgies and sacramental practice, though it could also be used as a way of endorsing traditions surrounding particular saints or cults. In general, Catholic theologians have always tended to accord greater importance to the role of church tradition than their Reformed counterparts, partly because it is so basic to notions of the visible church.[10] For pre-Reformation Catholics as for their Counter-Reformation successors, Christian tradition was embodied in the church's belief and practice. Texts such as 2 Thessalonians 2:15, 'Therefore, brethren, stand fast, and hold the traditions which ye have been taught, whether by word, or our epistle', gave this idea biblical warrant, in a manner which itself illustrates the symbiotic relationship between Scripture and tradition; most traditions could, after all, be argued back to

Scripture by interested parties. But how exactly to formulate the relationship between Scripture and tradition, already a problematic issue in the medieval church, was to emerge as one of the main points in dispute between Catholics and reformers, with polemicists on both sides fostering an artificially clear distinction between the two; and the controversial rhetoric of the early Reformation sometimes suggests how much the Catholic church – like other venerable institutions since – resented justifying its traditions and management practices to upstarts demanding mission statements.[11]

This was as true in England as on the Continent. Edmund Bonner, as reported by Alexander Alane, is reiterating a party line rather than engaging with the Protestant argument when he states: 'the tradicions and ceremonyes wherof the old ecclesiastical writers do make mencyon / were received of the apostles and geven us of the fathers from hand to hand and therfor thei may be laufully called the word of god unwritto[n]'.[12] Alane is particularly offended by this epitome, commenting that defenders of tradition '[i]magyne god to be lyke some ignorant poete which hath given us a patched and an unperfight worke' (f. E5a). His metaphor, consciously blasphemous in comparing God to an imaginative writer, demonstrates typical Protestant unease at the idea that tradition should ever be thought of as supplementing written revelation from God; like so many of the other writers in this study, Alane demonstrates how close the relationship is between the repudiation of church tradition and a fear of the human imagination. Sir Thomas More was a more sophisticated contemporary apologist for the Catholic cause than Bonner, and keeping a sharply paradoxical eye on his own deployment of proof-texts, he reminds the reader in his *Dialogue Concerning Heresies* that Christianity was founded not on Scripture but the verbal promises of Christ.[13]

A more comprehensive Catholic response to the *sola scriptura* argument was to come in the long term. At their most convincing, Counter-Reformation ripostes come across as attentive to Protestant demands for reliability and accountability, making a case for tradition as capable of both qualities and stressing its normative bias. Opening up the argument to broader questions of hermeneutics, they stress that Scriptural interpretation is unavoidable, whether orally conveyed or not:[14] an approach more congenial to most twenty-first-century commentators than the typical Protestant gambit of dismissing all arguments which appeared to represent a dilution of biblical authority. Serenus Cressy mocked the *sola scriptura* argument by an anecdote illustrating the stupidity of those who expect the Scriptures to comment explicitly on everything: 'As for these men they seem not unlike an honest Northern tenant of the late Earle of Cumberland . . . who when another his companion had in discourse imputed treason to some of the said Lords Ancestours, replyed: I am sure that is false: for I have read all the Bookes of histories both in the old and new Testament, and I defie any man to shew me that ever any Clifford has been a Traytour.'[15] A typical mainstream Catholic idea of the relationship between Scripture and tradition compared it to that between a law-book and a judge, with the Scripture essential for salvation not 'folded up in Characters; or letters, figured with inck, painted, or impressed on paper', but 'ingrafted, and preserved, in conservatives that are more noble (viz. the heart of man, the mouth of the Church, the lips of her Priests, the fiery tongues of her Apostles)'.[16] Law-book and judge are equally necessary for keeping order, which is why post-Reformation Catholicism in general, whatever its respect for tradition, can hardly be described as downplaying Holy Scripture.

The Council of Trent has been described as moving from a 'rough-and-ready arrangement whereby Tradition . . . introduced a believer to the doctrines of the faith, while Scripture was used at a later stage to test, to amplify and to collate those doctrines', by more carefully delimiting the spheres of Scripture and tradition, arriving at a formulation which called for the books of Holy Scripture to be venerated equally with divine and apostolic traditions concerning faith and morals:[17]

> The council clearly perceives that this truth and rule are contained in written books and in unwritten traditions which were received by the apostles from the mouth of Christ himself, or else have come down to us, handed on as it were from the apostles themselves at the inspiration of the holy Spirit. Following the example of the orthodox fathers, the council accepts and venerates with a like feeling of piety and reverence all the books of both the old and the new Testament . . . as well as the traditions concerning both faith and conduct, as either directly spoken by Christ or dictated by the holy Spirit, which have been preserved in unbroken sequence in the Catholic church.[18]

Here, the explicit veneration of Scripture responds to Protestant accusations that Catholics ignored the Bible when it suited them, and is just as striking, in its way, as the endorsement of tradition; towards the end of the seventeenth century, as discussed below, the Catholic scholar Richard Simon was to find himself in trouble with his fellow Catholics not for ignoring tradition, but – if anything – overemphasising it.[19]

Nor should one underestimate the place of tradition in Protestant thought, since most major Protestant denominations at the time of the Reformation would have endorsed patristic and conciliar witness up to a point, and the principle of historical continuity in general. Though the idea of tradition often did function as a catch-all for what Protestants disliked about Catholicism, their use of the term is certainly not always pejorative.[20] Nevertheless, suspicion of tradition was perhaps a more formative influence for them. Luther, for instance, declared that he saw Scripture as counting for more than all church councils and fathers, while Calvin's stress on a hidden church worked against the idea that tradition could be endorsed by collective witness. While Philip Melanchthon's stress on the notion of handing down doctrine and sacraments has broad affinities with Catholic thought, he too condemned tradition as soon as it obscured the gospel.[21] As Hans Frei has commented, the view that tradition was dangerously hard to monitor and likely to engender departure from the Bible affected Protestant conceptions of authority, and led to an intensified concentration on Scriptural hermeneutics.[22] For the Church of England, a key statement of the limits of tradition came in Richard Hooker's *Of the Laws of Ecclesiastical Polity*. In a chapter headed 'The benefit of having divine laws written', he writes: 'When the question therefore is, whether we be now to seek for any revealed law of God otherwise than only in the sacred scripture, whether we do now stand bound in the sight of God to yield to traditions urged by the Church of *Rome* the same obedience and reverence we do to his written law, honouring equally and adoring both as Divine: our answer is, no.'[23] Hooker continues, 'What hazard the truth is in when it passeth through the hands of report, how maimed and deformed it becometh; they are not, they cannot possibly be ignorant'; the word 'hazard', also used by Hall, testifies to the element of chance involved in any process of transmission, but also to the sense of personal danger felt by Protestants when venturing beyond Scripture.

Catholic and Protestant concepts of tradition were regularly opposed at a polemical level.[24] In the hands of some Protestant commentators, this abstract concept received vivid satirical pictorialisation: the preface to William L'Isle's translation of Aelfric depicts the Catholic 'hood-winked with his implicite faith, as with a bumble on his head, [who] thinkes he goes forth-right, when he windles in a mill: aske him how he beleeves, and he will say as the church beleeves; aske him how the Church beleeves, and he will say as he beleeves: and out of this compasse can he not goe . . .'.[25] This patently circular argument illustrates the suspicion that tradition might be a way of keeping the unlearned in intellectual subjection, unable to reason their way out of popery or to gain access to the Scriptures: a topic which, not surprisingly, found its way into popular anti-Catholicism. In a woodcut illustration to the ballad 'A new-yeeres-gift forthe (*sic*) Pope' (c.1625), God is depicted with a pair of scales, proving the Bible to be more weighty than 'Masses and Dirges, with such superstitions, / Decrees and Decretals, with other Traditions, / The golden Legend with late new additions'.[26] Conversely, the concept of tradition figured in the libel which formed part of the Catholic demonstration in Enborne church, discussed in chapter 3:

> ... many a miracle holie crosse hath wraught
> all w[hi]ch by tradition to light Churche hath brought
> Wherfore holie worshipp holie churche doth giue
> & so will wee as long as we liue
> thoughe thou saiest idolatry & vaine sup[er]stition
> yet we know it is holie church tradition ... [27]

ORAL DELIVERY AND THE ENGLISH CHURCH

Catholic and Protestant self-definition in this type of text has a kind of parodic relationship to the rule of faith or *regula fidei*, one of the names used in the early church to describe outline statements of orthodox Christian belief. Intended to serve as guides in scriptural exegesis, they comprised the basic minimum of what one needed to know to be saved, though unlike creeds, which came later, they varied in wording. Even after creeds came into existence and catechisms became widely used, the rule of faith continued a useful notion for church educators, though in the debates on the topic in post-Reformation England, it is seen less as a practical teaching aid and more as a way of defining the curriculum. Not surprisingly, it became an embattled term as a result: so much so that definitions of it are inextricably bound up with the emergence of scepticism.[28] Catholic commentators could turn this trend to advantage, using it to maximise the role of the church as providing a continuous revelation to override intellectual doubts. Conversely, some Protestant writers went so far as to suppress all the phrase's connotations of church tradition, applying it instead only to the Scriptures.[29] At all times, it posed a challenge to zealous clerics of all denominations: just how uneducated could you be and still call yourself a Christian? Few Protestants would have denied that the rule of faith could be instilled into an illiterate congregation by godly preachers, but the puritan stress on direct access to the Bible could still imply that an illiterate Christian – or, at the very least, one without detailed command of God's word – was an inadequate Christian.[30] In a dialogue written by the puritan George Gifford, the popish 'Atheos' cries 'GOD forbidde that all those shoulde bee awry which are not learned', and the admirable 'Zelotes' asserts in response that 'man can not be lead by Gods spirite, and refuse to knowe the Scriptures: . . . he teacheth onlie in his worde'.[31] Thus, debates about the place of orality in tradition were at their most heightened when they touched on the rule of faith, since then they addressed the whole question of how salvation could be achieved.

In England, the rule-of-faith controversy reached its zenith in a period stretching from the 1650s to the 1680s. One of the best-known Catholic converts from this date, John Dryden, wrote about the topic twice: once before his conversion and once after. *Religio Laici* (1682), Dryden's versified apologia for Anglicanism, contains a critique of Richard Simon: a Catholic theologian controversial in his time, and without many immediate heirs, who is now seen as pioneering modern-day biblical criticism.[32] His work on the Scriptures stressed the error inherent in the process of Scriptural transmission, raising the kind of textual problems which, when explored by more heterodox writers, were to inspire such radical shifts away from organised religion during the Enlightenment. To distance himself from the more radical thought of his time and counteract the implications of his findings for a church already nervously aware of sceptical and deistic trends among the European intelligentsia, Simon laid heavy stress on church tradition as a guarantor of faith – though in a post-Tridentine climate, even this was not enough to save him from his co-religionists' opprobrium, and his books were banned in his native France.[33] Dryden's tactically brilliant response to Simon's thought is to argue that Simon cannot possibly mean us to take this seriously, and that his real aim must be not to reinforce the church, but to undermine both Scripture and tradition:[34]

> For some who have his secret meaning guessed
> Have found our author not too much a priest:
> For fashion sake he seems to have recourse
> To Pope and councils, and tradition's force,
> But he that old traditions could subdue
> Could not but find the weakness of the new:
> If scripture, though derived from heavenly birth,
> Has been but carelessly preserved on earth,
> If God's own people (who of God before
> Knew what we know, and had been promised more,
> In fuller terms, of heaven's assisting care,
> And who did neither time, nor study spare
> To keep this book untainted, unperplexed)
> Let in gross errors to corrupt the text,
> Omitted paragraphs, embroiled the sense,
> With vain traditions stopped the gaping fence,
> Which every common hand pulled up with ease,
> What safety from such brushwood helps as these?
> If written words from time are not secured,

> How can we think have oral sounds endured?
> Which thus transmitted, if one mouth has failed,
> Immortal lies on ages are entailed;
> And that some such have been is proved too plain,
> If we consider interest, church, and gain.
>
> (252–75)[35]

However, *The Hind and the Panther*, written in 1687 after Dryden converted to Catholicism, contains a no less eloquent argument in favour of tradition. While the notion of tradition encompassed all non-scriptural matter endorsed by the church, the two poems illustrate how notions of oral transmission were never far from the debate. Dryden is, for instance, either misunderstanding or taking a polemicist's liberty when he attacks Simon on the grounds that oral tradition is unstable; Simon's conception of tradition, like that of Counter-Reformation Catholicism in general, is geared towards such written matter as the works of the Church Fathers and conciliar decrees.[36] Still, it was an ambiguity inherent in the topic, especially in the standard phrase *non scripta*, used to describe 'unwritten' doctrines and implying only that these were doctrines not originally written down by their authors; both Catholic and Protestants commonly went one step further, and equated these unwritten traditions with oral ones.[37]

Paradoxically, even while it was useful to Protestants to play up orality in debunking Catholic notions of tradition, Catholic writers could use orality to reinforce the claims of tradition as a guide. Writing as Protestant and then as Catholic, Dryden illustrates this well; the following passage from *The Hind and the Panther* is one of the many moments in the poem when the Catholic Hind seems to be answering not only the Anglican Panther but Dryden's earlier self:

> 'If not by scriptures, how can we be sure',
> Replied the Panther, 'what tradition's pure?' . . .
> 'How but by following her', replied the dame,
> 'To whom derived from sire to son they came;
> Where every age does on another move,
> And trusts no farther than the next above;
> Where all the rounds like Jacob's ladder rise,
> The lowest hid in earth, the topmost in the skies?'[38]

When the Panther retorts that 'Succeeding times such dreadful gaps have made / 'Tis dangerous climbing' (225–6) the Hind goes on the offensive: 'You must evince tradition to be forged, / Produce plain proofs, unblemished authors use, / As ancient as those ages they accuse' (233–5).

This passage is not simply reversing the arguments advanced in *Religio Laici*. In the passage from this poem quoted above, Dryden certainly stresses the possible knock-on effects of one orally transmitted mistake, 'Which thus transmitted, if one mouth has failed, / Immortal lies on ages are entailed';[39] but the Hind's picture of church tradition as a series of short transmissions between generations is one which is not counteracted or even addressed, perhaps because its stress on collective authority would weaken the point being made. In employing it in his later poem, Dryden is bringing the question of oral transmission into the foreground, drawing especially on the work of some seventeenth-century English Catholic theologians whose thought on the topic of oral tradition had taken a distinctive turn.[40]

To explain why it was distinctive, one needs first to sketch in the background from which it diverged. Catholics would all have agreed that the church was the sum total of orthodox Christian believers and acted as a means of conveying tradition, which was in turn essential to the rule of faith; but in practice, formulations varied widely about which elements of the church were actively responsible for the preservation of the faith. Most writers were concerned with the inter-relationship of three elements in particular: the ordained ministry, the writings of orthodox theologians, especially the Church Fathers, and the decrees of church councils.[41] Ideas of the rule of faith brought lay people and the uneducated into the picture, since it was a shorthand means of saying that even those of modest formal education could be good Christians, and that oral means of transmission were catechetically effective. Conversely, it could be used as a defence against humanist and Protestant claims that church tradition was esoteric.[42] As Serenus Cressy argued, oral or practical traditions were 'obvious to all me[n]s eyes, and sou[n]d aloud in all me[n]'s eares shining in the publique visible practise and profession of the Church';[43] and as John Sergeant proved, the idea could have even more demotic implications.

Sergeant was one of the Blackloists, a group of English secular priests and laymen who engaged in radical political and philosophical experimentation in the middle and latter decades of the seventeenth century, and dominated the Chapter of the English Secular Clergy during the 1650s and early 1660s.[44] Nicknamed after the pseudonym 'Blacklo' used by their dominant figure, Thomas White, the Blackloists also included William Rushworth, whose work on the rule of faith stimulated Sergeant's own. The Blackloists' interpretation of the rule, central to their theoretical distinctiveness, made a fundamental distinction between believers in God's word as delivered orally and as set down on paper, and was most influentially set out in *Rushworth's Dialogues* (1st edn 1640), which seems to have been a joint production by Rushworth and Thomas White.⁴⁵ For their time, the Blackloists have a remarkable ability to imagine themselves into the position of the unlearned, which in turn accounts for the importance they attach to tradition. In the *Dialogues*, for instance, a scholarly and an ordinary, common-sensical way of reading Scripture are distinguished, and the latter is identified as sufficient to explain the Catholic faith. Like tradition, it is seen as conveying its sense not just to scholars but to the wider church, and in the words of George Tavard, 'cannot be imposed by a minority on a majority'.⁴⁶ Sergeant goes even further than Rushworth and White along the demotic road, and sympathetic readers of his *Sure-Footing in Christianity* (1665) would have found themselves admitting that tradition could be seen not as a supplement of Scripture or partner of it, but a guide which, for the average believer, was surer than Scripture by far.⁴⁷ As John Tillotson pointed out when writing an Anglican response, Sergeant's preference for tradition over Scripture goes well beyond the Council of Trent's demand that they be held in 'equal pious affection and reverence'.⁴⁸

The emphasis, while striking, is by no means unprecedented among Catholics. Writing in the early years of the Reformation, the theologian Richard Smith declared that oral traditions were 'delyvered and taught the churche by mouth, and by the lyvely voices of the teachers, which is a stronger instrument to teach both the fayth and good manners also, than is the wryters hand'.⁴⁹ Besides, the Blackloists would have argued that, since orally delivered material was acknowledged by all denominations to have preceded the written Scriptures, they were only acting in accordance with a pattern set by the earliest Christians:⁵⁰

> the Apostles and their Successors went not with Books in their hands to preach and deliver Christ's Doctrin, but Words in their mouths; and . . . Primitive Antiquity learn't their Faith by another Method a long time before many of those Books were universally spread amongst the vulgar, much less the Catalogue collected and acknowledg'd . . . (p. 40)

Sure-Footing in Christianity, from which this quotation is taken, was the most consciously scientific attempt by any of the group to employ the rule of faith as a systematic means of authorising oral tradition. Evident throughout the book is the Blackloists' tactic of endorsing the spoken word by setting out the reasons why one should radically suspect the written. While Sergeant is not arguing for a purely oral tradition, he maintains that Scripture is hard to interpret unless one is a scholar, and that the meaning of the Bible is damagingly hard to pin down: 'as for the Certainty of the Scripture's Significativeness, . . . nothing is more evident than that this is quite lost to all in the Uncertainty of the Letter' (p. 38).[51] The possibility that its meaning might have been obscured by misinterpretation and scribal error can act as a weapon for deists.[52] Moreover, the canon of Scripture is itself acknowledged to be a matter of tradition.[53] Thus far, the Blackloists' dissociation from mainstream Catholic commentary on the topic should not be overemphasised: the practices of the first apostles, the obscurity of Scripture and the need to establish a scriptural canon were standard ways of justifying the role of the hierarchy, and Sergeant is at pains to stress how he means no disrespect to the Catholic church in saying that Scripture was never designed to convey the rule of faith. But his comments anticipate the higher-profile controversy on textual difficulties which Simon and others were to undertake in the 1670s and 1680s, and which Dryden addressed in *Religio Laici*; like Simon, the Blackloists found themselves in trouble with their co-religionists for arguments which were intended to consolidate the church's position rather than undermine it.

Setting out why oral tradition was to be preferred to Scripture as a rule of faith, Sergeant's conception of orality encompasses both words and acts. His description of tradition uses a pre-existent formula, 'oral or practical', to stress the indivisibility of the two. Tradition is 'a Delivery down from hand to hand (by words, and a constant course of frequent and visible Actions conformable to those Words) of the Sence and Faith of Forefathers' (p. 41).[54] The Christian learns just as children learn, from a combination of sense-impressions and deliberate education. Thus, so far from being lost in antiquity, tradition can be seen as an 'immediate Delivery' (p. 43), a continuous series of exchanges over very short chronological periods, as endorsed by Dryden in *The Hind and the Panther*. Taking a more polemical stance, Sergeant points out how Protestants hardly seem to realise that they benefit from tradition themselves, in so far as they adhere to the Christian faith because of their own upbringing: 'So hard it is to beat down Nature by Designe, or not to follow Tradition in practice, though at the same time they write and talk never so vehemently and loud against it' (p. 46). Here, he identifies a recurrent problem for early modern Protestants: how does one reconcile respect for one's forefathers with the notion of a corrupt church and a Pauline model of personal conversion?[55]

Sergeant is at pains to stress that oral tradition is not esoteric, as Protestants would imply, but a transparent and 'open conveyance down of Practical Doctrines by our best senses of Discipline, that is, our Eyes and Ears' (p. 47), perpetuated by the common testimony of all Christians.[56] In effect, it is a form of witnessing, a 'vast Testification' (p. 54), the more effective because parents have an interest in ensuring that their children be brought up in the way of salvation. Sergeant's friend John Austin put the same idea more emotively in one of his original psalms, where he asked:

> Tell me, can any reason considerately think; that so many witnesses should conspire in a falsehood?
> Such as must necessarily damn themselvs; and desperately endanger all their posterity:
> Such as by every Ey may easily be discern'd; and the credit of the forgers confounded with shame.
> Stay till a thousand Mothers freely agree, to poyson themselvs and their beloved Children . . .[57]

In the second of his two extensive surveys of Scripture and tradition in early modern Europe, George Tavard discusses how White, Sergeant and other English Catholic theologians of this date develop a 'sort of pedagogical concept of Tradition . . . which, extended not simply to one family, but to the entire family of nations, becomes a philosophy of culture: Christian Tradition is a religious form of a phenomenon which already accounts for the education of children and for the transmission of human lore among all the peoples of the world'.[58] As this implies, Sergeant's argument operates on two levels: pointing towards how traditions are routinely transmitted in non-religious contexts, but constantly asserting the uniqueness of sacred tradition. The idea of transmission within a family is intended to be taken both literally and metaphorically, as referring to the family of the church. But Sergeant's concept of oral or practical tradition goes well beyond catechetical instructions administered to younger members of a church by their elders, or homilies delivered to laymen by clerics: partly because he sees tradition as governing behaviour both inside and outside formal contexts, partly because he presents an unusually positive picture of the ordinary Christian, who is seen as not merely capable of orthodoxy when taught, but as a repository and guarantee of it.[59]

This is where Sergeant is more radical than Rushworth and White, and the Blackloists in general more radical than many of their co-religionists. A bias towards grass-roots practice is uncommon among Catholic writers on the rule of faith, while some of them were positively hostile towards the phenomenon of popular transmission. From around Sergeant's time, Edward Sheldon's English translation of François Véron's *Règle Générale de la Foi Catholique* promised in its subtitle a rule of faith 'sever'd from the opinions of the schools, mistakes of the ignorant, and abuses of the vulgar'.[60] Even *Rushworth's Dialogues*, so very attentive to how children and ignorant persons can be saved by signing up to Christian tradition, argue that priests are important for purveying tradition because it should not be subjected to the 'weak and wavering judgment of the Laitie'.[61] Though the *Dialogues* speak of the faith being passed from father to son, they are written as a conversation between an uncle – possibly a priest – and a nephew, suggesting that Rushworth and White are thinking more about spiritual fathers than biological ones. Sergeant, in contrast, takes the church-family metaphor in another direction; and because his conception of tradition makes so little distinction between priests and laity, his model of instruction within a family has the effect of de-centring a celibate priesthood.[62] From a twenty-first-century perspective, Sergeant seems astonishingly free of clericalism, and unusually imaginative in his consciousness of what it means to be a Christian who is not a churchman – at times, he comes close to arguing Catholic priests out of a job. It is a remarkable gambit, especially for a member of a party which could be very clericalist indeed in other ways, while using ideas of tradition to underpin this clericalism: during the Commonwealth, the Blackloists campaigned for a Catholic episcopacy directly answerable to the government, explicitly as a means of keeping the Catholic laity under control.[63] Yet, contradictory as they might seem, both moves arise out of a pragmatic concern that the English Catholic church should survive, and were shaped by the specificities of the English experience.[64]

John Bossy has argued that the survival of the old faith in post-Reformation England rested largely in the hands of lay people.[65] In any case, in a country where priests had to act underground and were often in short supply, it would have been entirely prudent to affirm the role of the laity in transmitting Catholicism – as well as to downplay the importance of the sacraments, as Sergeant's argument has the effect of doing here.[66] There are local implications too in how Sergeant's idea of tradition compares to the idea of an invisible church, often used by Protestants to explain how true doctrine survived through periods when it was at odds with what the hierarchy was saying. The Protestant invisible church is anything but universal, predicated as it is against a corrupt visible church. Post-Reformation English Catholics, in contrast, would have had to see themselves as members of a universal church which was invisible in England; and in an environment where members of the clerical hierarchy had to keep a very low profile indeed, a stress on the sustained witness of lay Catholics would have had the effect of maximising visible continuity. The lay Catholic is not, of course, the same as the uneducated or illiterate Catholic; but in arguing that the rule of faith is passed on by behaviour rather than written texts, Sergeant is affirming the position of the unlearned in the economy of salvation.[67] Here again, his argument has a specific relevance to the English situation:

women, for instance, were less likely than men to be literate at all levels of society, but were crucial as conduits for the faith because of their role in running households and educating children, and had a large part to play in sustaining Catholicism within post-Reformation England.[68] Anticipating the notions of socialisation and enculturation, now such crucial tools within anthropological and sociological thought, Sergeant's has to rank as one of the most ingenious and prophetic answers to the reformers' perennial accusation that the Catholic church exploited its more ignorant followers.[69] In terms of this book, his argument asks us to problematise the common dichotomy between oral tradition as preserved by the lower orders, and conscious elite intervention in oral culture.

THE AFFIRMATION OF POPULAR RELIGION

Ironically for thinkers who depended so much on the notion of tradition, the Blackloists had few immediate successors. Both within the Catholic and Anglican mainstream, their short-term importance can be seen as largely provocative. As described above, their interpretation of the rule of faith aroused the ire of such high-profile Anglican controversialists as John Tillotson and Edward Stillingfleet, while in the context of mainstream contemporary Catholic thought, their theories appeared eccentric bordering on heretical. Sergeant was, in fact, denounced to the Inquisition and investigated by the Holy Office, though eventually cleared with an admonition to make his meaning more evident.[70] While the Blackloists' penchant for intellectual experiment was likely in itself to leave them on the fringes of contemporary thought, their political dominance among the Catholics of mid-seventeenth-century England may, ironically, have helped to limit their influence still further. Unsparing in both intellectual debate and political jockeying, they made too many enemies among the Catholic clerisy to retain even their political influence for long; in 1667, two years after *Sure-Footing in Christianity* came out, Sergeant was forced to resign the secretaryship of the Chapter.[71]

If the Blackloists' thought had been more influential outside their own circle, it might have been possible to see it as a theoretical underpinning to the oral challenge that the two previous chapters have discussed. But though it would be difficult to read it back onto what has gone before, one can recognise in their work the same pragmatic recognition of the usefulness of popular culture that one finds in a controversial rhyme or martyr-ballad; and even if their distinctive advocacy of oral tradition fell mostly on deaf ears at the time, they would have felt vindicated by several hermeneutical trends since. The post-structuralist assertion that texts are open to endless interpretive possibilities – something which still makes advocates of *sola scriptura* feel queasy – is explicitly anticipated in most Catholic writing on the rule of faith, and works especially in favour of a rule which, like Sergeant's, is based on speech and action rather than written words. Sociologists of religion interested in how sects perpetuate themselves present a picture remarkably similar to Sergeant's, reinforcing the idea that Sergeant's theoretical formulations were inspired by Catholic sectarian practice in England.[72] More generally, if one leaves aside Sergeant's claims that the Catholic tradition is uniquely sacred, his model of oral tradition – a series of short relays undertaken by people who have an interest in ensuring accuracy – would appeal to historians, anthropologists and others who know nothing about Reformation polemic, but whose apologias for their own topic have evolved along parallel lines.[73]

The demotic emphasis of Sergeant's argument also looks remarkably up-to-date now, though in terms of its time, its progressiveness is more questionable. Catholic polemic attacking the Protestant stress on Bible-reading tends to ignore or sideline the question of whether greater literacy among the faithful is a good thing; and Sergeant too has a reluctance to address this issue directly.[74] Like many subsequent celebrators of popular culture, he could be accused of cultural conservatism precisely because he does affirm the position of the uneducated. In an early modern context, though, this contrasts attractively with the disdain towards the illiterate felt by many educated commentators, both Catholic and Protestant, and in particular with the attitude which England's Protestant dissenters so often adopted towards the unlearned. Because the puritan ideal of a Scripture-reading populace was such a powerful stimulus towards the spread of literacy at the lower levels of society, its adherents sometimes equated illiteracy with culpable ignorance: a model which in the short term might well have encouraged the separatism of which puritans were accused, and which, even at its least divisive, could do no more than look towards the future. Even catechisms, liturgies and sermons, more mainstream responses to instructing the unlearned, needed to be written or delivered, and thus required clerical mediation between the scriptural text and the unlearned believer.

It is no surprise that Sergeant's rule of faith, responding as it was to the shortage of Catholic clergy in England, de-emphasised sermons and all forms of sacramental instruction. More radically still, and more unpredictably – after all, catechisms were much used by English Catholics – it erased the distinction between formal and informal catechetical occasions, seeing the rule of faith as preserved by the day-to-day activity of all members within the body of the faithful.[75] The idea of the Catholic rule of faith as rooted less in Scripture, patristics, the deliberations of church councils or the example and ministrations of the clergy, and more in a common way of life, points to a world which, in English terms, is at once medieval and post-Reformation: one where religion pervades all facets of experience, but where the visible church comprises the sum of orthodox believers rather than being manifest in sacred space or the visible authority of the clerisy. One could almost call it a priesthood of all believers.

Certainly, there has never been a larger claim made for the importance of oral transmission within popular culture: which, according to Peter Burke in a formulation which has stood the test of time, is cultural activity in which everyone can participate, whatever their level of education.[76] If this assertion involves a shift away from the festival bias of most recent studies on popular culture, this may be useful in itself. The festivals of early modern England were routinely condemned as popish by puritans and could certainly take on a Catholic flavour, while specifically Catholic festivals – such as the feast of St Winifred – existed too.[77] The latter type of festival, especially, could have been a bonding experience almost on a par with the Mass. But ideally – and no doubt to a great extent in real life – the Catholic community in post-Reformation England would have expressed its beliefs and its differences through cotidiurnal action: not just the sacraments, not just prayer, but by a coherent and distinctive cast to everything said and done. Sergeant gives us a vision, but also a pragmatic acknowledgement of a *de facto* church: flexible, resilient and impossible to stamp out, grounded less in clandestine masses than the day-to-day words and actions of the ordinary believer.

How, if at all, does Sergeant's picture differ from puritan ideals of the godly community? Sergeant certainly manifests more awareness than his puritan counterparts of how performativity works – as our generation would put it. Perhaps this is hardly surprising. If God's saving grace is seen as necessarily preceding any good action performed by an individual, the logic of Calvinist theology is to deny all efficacy to the performative – though one can certainly identify a tension between theory and practice, given the puritans' constant anxiety to bring up their children in the way they should go. Even John Bunyan, after all, was to modify his vision of Christianity between Parts I and II of *The Pilgrim's Progress*, playing down a Christian's stout individualism and emphasising instead the educative function of a church.[78] But while there are bound to be points of similarity between one sect and another, the same notion of enculturation is true in a weaker way for any Christian whose beliefs have been derived from the practice of the community in which he or she lives. One answer that could have been given to Hall's question, 'as for oral Traditions, what certainty can there be in them?', is that Hall himself, a product of a Christian society, would have been steeped in Christian notions before he read a word of the Bible. Sergeant's notion of oral tradition is hardly convincing as a mechanism for ensuring accurate word-for-word transmission, but then, Hall's concern is with textual accuracy and Sergeant's is not. It is, though, a compelling description of how a church defines itself; and thus far, he succeeds in problematising arguments like Hall's to an extent that both Catholic and Protestant opponents, arguing in the same vein as Hall, are unwilling to admit. More widely still, Sergeant can be seen as describing any community's process of collective witness, whereby oral transmission acts as a means of determining shared values through sifting and winnowing.[79]

Even if this is moving beyond what Sergeant himself would have endorsed, Sergeant's claims perhaps make most sense if one shifts the debate onto questions of emotional authenticity rather than factual. In an age when truth-claims are routinely contested, it is hardly surprising that present-day historians' definitions of truth are so often less concerned with what actually happened than with how the participants felt about it. Oral historians, with their traditional concern to recover minority voices, have a large part to play here, which should also influence the work of scholars operating without recording equipment.[80] Certainly, while this book has asked at times how far one can recover the factual truth of orally reported events, it has been more concerned to discuss orally transmissible material as a rich source of views held about Catholicism in early modern England, and as a key means of Catholic self-definition. One of the most remarkable features of Sergeant's argument, though, is the implication that one need not always separate these two authenticities. Sergeant saw Catholicism as a lived tradition, authenticable through the day-to-day behaviour of the faithful: a context in which English Catholic statements of self-definition, orally delivered and otherwise, can be seen as not only edifying but authoritative – perhaps even as a kind of recusant Scripture.

If so, then he was prophetic. The idea of the church as a community deriving its strength from a counter-cultural stance and distinctive behavioural patterns has remarkable similarities to the thought of Stanley Hauerwas, currently one of the highest-profile, most provocative theologians in the Anglo-American academy.[81] Hauerwas and his various collaborators identify a move in their own time, dateable around the 1960s, from a Constantinian model of the church as accommodated to the world to the church as counter-cultural. Similarly, those who remained Catholics during England's Reformation would have begun by seeing the church as indivisible from society, and ended up by setting it in opposition to society. Believing that the church was never intended to be in collusion with worldly hierarchies, Hauerwas and his followers acclaim this dissociation as a positive move – something which it is easier to do in a time and place where, though Christians are sometimes despised and often misunderstood, they are unlikely to suffer for their faith financially or physically. Yet, while no post-Reformation Catholic would have done other than look towards a time when Catholicism was recognised and tolerated by the government, Catholics' celebration of martyrdom and confessorship can certainly be seen as an elevation of the counter-cultural. Their very real nostalgia for medieval times, which this study began by identifying, would be misleading if considered on its own.

The church, according to Hauerwas and his followers, is comprised of people who act in a distinctive manner inspired by shared patterns of worship, preserving and even celebrating their difference from the rest of society, as epitomised in the title of the movement's best-known book, *Resident Aliens*.[82] If one sees masses, rosaries and all other expressions of Catholic difference as assimilable to this theory, it helps to explain why post-Reformation Catholics held these things dear at a time when attendance at a mass, or possession of a rosary, could be severely punished. But the shared experience of the Eucharist, so central to Hauerwas's model of how a Christian community should behave, presumes in turn an environment of relative toleration where the sacraments are widely available. This is something which most Catholics in post-Reformation England did not enjoy: which is why, though the Catholic hierarchy in England would have liked all Catholics to be counter-cultural, this never happened. And this in turn is why, knowing the practical difficulties of servicing England's church, Sergeant's brilliance was to maximise the possible occasions of Catholic cohesion and Catholic difference within his theory of oral tradition.

In searching for Catholic interests, allegiances and beliefs within England's post-Reformation oral culture, this book has cast a wider net even than Sergeant's. His transmitters of oral tradition are very ordinary citizens, but they are still self-defined as Catholic believers; their occasions of illegal Catholic activity might be few and far between, but that does not make them any the less counter-cultural. Wherever the individuals who figure in this study synthesise elements of Catholicism and Protestantism, or tread the Tom Tiddler's Ground between religion and superstition, Sergeant would have had little time for them. Over three centuries later, we can recognise how they, too, reinforce the contention running throughout this book: that oral traditions were a crucial means of preserving Catholic matter in post-Reformation England. But it is surely more in Sergeant's own spirit to end with Hauerwas's twenty-first-century Christians: luckier than many of their forebears, but sharing with some of the Catholics who inhabit the pages of this book a sense of being at odds with the times, and a stubborn desire to talk themselves, sing themselves and act themselves into recusancy.

Notes

PREFACE

1. 'The Turn to Religion in Early Modern English Studies', *Criticism*, 46:1 (2004), pp. 167–90.
2. E.g. Peter Lake's essays on early modern English drama in *The Antichrist's Lewd Hat* (New Haven: Yale University Press, 2002).
3. Robert S. Miola (ed.), *Early Modern Catholicism: An Anthology of Primary Sources* (Oxford: Oxford University Press, 2007).
4. A judicious recent summary of the debate can be found in John D. Cox, 'Was Shakespeare a Christian, And If So, What Kind of Christian Was He?' *Christianity and Literature*, 55:4 (2006), pp. 539–66. See also Jean-Christophe Mayer, *Shakespeare's Hybrid Faith* (Basingstoke: Palgrave Macmillan, 2006).
5. Richard Dutton, Alison Findlay and Richard Wilson (eds.), *Region, Religion and Patronage* and *Theatre and Religion* (Manchester: Manchester University Press, 2004). Both volumes have the subtitle 'Lancastrian Shakespeare'.
6. Scott R. Pilarz, *Robert Southwell and the Mission of Literature, 1561–1595* (Aldershot: Ashgate, 2004); Peter Davidson and Anne Sweeney (eds.), *The Collected Poems of S. Robert Southwell* (Manchester: Carcanet, 2007); Anne Sweeney, *Robert Southwell* (Manchester: Manchester University Press, 2007).
7. Donna B. Hamilton, *Anthony Munday and the Catholics, 1560–1633* (Aldershot: Ashgate, 2005).
8. Heather Wolfe (ed.), *The Literary Career and Legacy of Elizabeth Cary, 1613–1680* (Basingstoke: Palgrave Macmillan, 2007).
9. *The Universal Baroque* (Manchester: Manchester University Press, forthcoming).
10. *Edmund Campion, Memory and Transcription* (Aldershot: Ashgate, 2005).
11. *Religious Ideology and Cultural Fantasy* (Notre Dame: University of Notre Dame Press, 2005).

INTRODUCTION

1. *The Old Religion* (1st edn 1628: 1686 edn used), p. 179 (see also p. 113). Cf. Richard Hooker, *Of the Lawes of Ecclesiastical Polity (I, VIII)*, ed. Arthur Stephen McGrade (Cambridge: Cambridge University Press, 1989),

pp. 110–11. Hall's is the first instance given for the phrase's use in the third edition of the *OED*.
2. Nearer our own time the term 'the old religion' has often been applied to post-Reformation English Catholicism, though as Eamon Duffy points out, there are limits to its usefulness: 'The Conservative Voice in the English Reformation', chapter 6 in Simon Ditchfield (ed.), *Christianity and Community in the West* (Aldershot: Ashgate, 2001), reference p. 105. For an early modern Catholic use of the phrase, see *ARCR* II, no. 490 (title).
3. See conclusion for a discussion of oral tradition vis-à-vis tradition in general.
4. *Catholicism, Controversy and the English Literary Imagination, 1558–1660* (Cambridge: Cambridge University Press, 1999).
5. See especially Adam Fox, *Oral and Literate Culture in England 1500–1700* (Oxford: Clarendon, 2000); D. R. Woolf, 'Speech, Text and Time: The Sense of Hearing and the Sense of the Past in Renaissance England', *Albion*, 18:2 (1986), pp. 159–93, and *The Social Circulation of the Past* (Oxford: Oxford University Press, 2003); Bruce R. Smith, *The Acoustic World of Early Modern England* (Chicago: University of Chicago Press, 1999). Of the wider literature on orality, the following books were especially useful in the writing of this study: Walter J. Ong, SJ, *Orality and Literacy* (1967: this edn London: Routledge, 2002), critiqued in D. R. Olson and Nancy Torrance (eds.), *Literacy and Orality* (Cambridge: Cambridge University Press, 1991) and chapter 1 of Joyce Coleman, *Public Reading and the Reading Public in Late Medieval England and France* (Cambridge: Cambridge University Press, 1996); Jan Vansina, *Oral Tradition as History* (Madison: University of Wisconsin Press, 1985); Ruth Finnegan, *Oral Poetry* (Cambridge: Cambridge University Press, 1977). See also Jack Goody, *The Domestication of the Savage Mind* (Cambridge: Cambridge University Press, 1977), pp. 36–51, on the differences in human thought between oral and literate cultures; Michel de Certeau, *The Practice of Everyday Life*, trans. Steven Rendall (Berkeley: University of California Press, 1984), chapter 10, on the mediated nature of orality; and on the orality/literacy interface, Eric A. Havelock, *The Muse Learns to Write* (New Haven: Yale University Press, 1986). Henri-Jean Martin, *The History and Power of Writing*, trans. Lydia G. Cochrane (Chicago: University of Chicago Press, 1994), p. 87, warns against a binary opposition of orality and literacy.
6. 'The Meaning of Literacy in Early Modern England', in Gerd Baumann (ed.), *The Written Word* (Oxford: Clarendon, 1986), pp. 97–131 (quotation p. 98). See also Fox, *Oral and Literate Culture*; David Cressy, 'Literacy in Context: Meaning and Measurement in Early Modern England', chapter 15 in John Brewer and Roy Porter (eds.), *Consumption and the World of Goods* (London: Routledge, 1993), esp. p. 311; Smith, *Acoustic World*, esp. pp. 12–13. On literacy in early modern England, see David Cressy, *Literacy and the Social Order* (Cambridge: Cambridge University Press, 1980); Margaret Spufford, *Small Books and Pleasant Histories* (1st edn London: Methuen, 1981), and 'First Steps in Literacy: The Reading and Writing Experiences of the Humblest 17th-Century Autobiographers', *Social History*, 4 (1979), pp. 407–35; Tessa Watt, *Cheap Print and Popular*

Piety, 1550–1640 (Cambridge: Cambridge University Press, 1991); Jonathan Barry, 'Literacy and Literature in Popular Culture: Reading and Writing in Historical Perspective', chapter 4 in Tim Harris (ed.), *Popular Culture in England, c.1500–1850* (Basingstoke: Macmillan, 1995); R. A. Houston, *Literacy in Early Modern Europe* (London: Longman, 1988); and Wyn Ford, 'The Problem of Literacy in Early Modern England', *History*, 78 (1993), pp. 22–34. The inseparable topic of illiteracy is emphasised by David Cressy in 'Levels of Illiteracy in England, 1530–1730', reproduced as chapter 6 in Harvey J. Graff (ed.), *Literacy and Social Development in the West* (Cambridge: Cambridge University Press, 1981).

7. M. T. Clanchy, *From Memory to Written Record* (1979: rev. edn Oxford: Blackwell, 1993) performs a similar task for an earlier era.
8. The sociohistorical implications of this are discussed in Smith, *Acoustic World*, p. 25.
9. *Lyrics from English Airs, 1596–1622*, ed. Edward Doughtie (Cambridge, Mass.: Harvard University Press, 1970), p. 36. Walter J. Ong has commented that 'it is to be expected that the oral residue in Tudor literature is, by contrast with most writing in comparable genres today, heavy in the extreme': 'Oral Residue in Tudor Prose Style', *PMLA*, 80:3 (1965), pp. 145–54 (quotation p. 146). For how verse forms developed in written cultures can subsequently be used orally, see Jack Goody, *The Interface between the Written and the Oral* (Cambridge: Cambridge University Press, 1987), p. 106.
10. For the issues thrown up by the term 'oral literature', see the introduction to Joseph Harris (ed.), *The Ballad and Oral Literature* (Cambridge, Mass.: Harvard University Press, 1991).
11. See footnote 69 below.
12. On the historical memory, see D. R. Woolf, '"The Common Voice": History, Folklore and Oral Tradition in Early Modern England', *P & P*, 120 (1988), pp. 26–52, a revised version of which appears in *Social Circulation*, chapter 10; Fox, *Oral and Literate Culture*, esp. chapters 5–6. On consciousness of change, see Woolf, *Social Circulation*, chapter 1.
13. *A Goodly Gallery* (1st edn 1563), f. 40b, 'Of beames or streames of light appearing through a cloude.'
14. On imagery in churches still surviving at the time of the Civil Wars, see Trevor Cooper (ed.), *The Journal of William Dowsing* (Woodbridge: Boydell & Brewer, 2001).
15. See Margaret Aston, 'English Ruins and English History: The Dissolution and the Sense of the Past', *Journal of the Warburg and Courtauld Institutes*, 36 (1973), pp. 231–55; Woolf, *Social Circulation*, pp. 310–15; and chapter 1 of this study.
16. Eamon Duffy, 'Bare Ruined Choirs: Remembering Catholicism in Shakespeare's England', chapter 2 in Richard Dutton, Alison Findlay and Richard Wilson (eds.), *Theatre and Religion* (Manchester: Manchester University Press, 2003), and 'Conservative Voice', pp. 103–4.
17. *Antiquitie Triumphing Over Noveltie* (1619), p. 8. I owe this reference to Arnold Hunt. See his *Art of Hearing* (forthcoming from Cambridge University Press),

chapter 7; Ronald Hutton, *The Rise and Fall of Merry England* (Oxford: Oxford University Press, 1994), p. 89; and below, pp. 94, 211.

18. Cf. John Selden: 'There was never a merry world since the ffairyes left danceing, & the parson left conjuring. The opinion of the Latter kept theeves in awe, & did as much good in a Country as a Justice of Peace' (*Table Talk*, ed. Sir Frederick Pollock (London: Quaritch, 1927), p. 91). *Table Talk* was compiled between the 1630s and 1650s (p. xi) and this ballad suggests that Selden was deliberately – and probably ironically – exploiting a pro-Catholic proverbial formula. See also Francis Trigge's comment that 'Many do lament the pulling downe of abbayes, they say it was never merie world since . . .' (*Apologie* (1589), p. 7; quoted in A. G. Dickens (ed.), *Tudor Treatises* (Yorkshire Archaeological Society Record Series, 125 (1959), p. 38)) and Woolf, *Social Circulation*, chapter 1. Diane Purkiss, *Troublesome Things* (London: Penguin, 2000), links the saying with the pastness of the faery kingdom (pp. 106, 184): see chapter 2, pp. 75–81.

19. Quoted from Thomas Deloney, *The Garland of Good Will* (1631 edn), fols. F2b–3b. Though the first surviving edition dates from 1628, this collection was entered at Stationers' Hall in 1593: see *STC* 6553.5. See also Timothy Scott McGinnis, *George Gifford and the Reformation of the Common Sort* (Kirksville: Truman State University Press, 2004).

20. 'Conservative Voice', p. 104.

21. On Catholic antiquarians, see Patrick Collinson, 'John Stow and Nostalgic Antiquarianism', in J. F. Merritt (ed.), *Imagining Early Modern London* (Cambridge: Cambridge University Press, 2001), chapter 1; D. R. Woolf, 'Little Crosby and the Horizons of Early Modern Historical Culture', chapter 5 in Donald R. Kelley and David Harris Sacks (eds.), *The Historical Imagination in Early Modern Britain* (Cambridge: Cambridge University Press/Woodrow Wilson Center Press, 1997) and *Social Circulation*, pp. 156, 186–7, 246–55; Donna B. Hamilton, 'Richard Verstegan's *A Restitution of Decayed Intelligence* (1605): A Catholic Antiquarian Replies to John Foxe, Thomas Cooper, and Jean Bodin', *Prose Studies*, 22:2 (1999), pp. 1–38; Graham Parry, *The Trophies of Time* (Oxford: Oxford University Press, 1995), esp. chapter 2; Theo Bongaerts (ed.), *The Correspondence of Thomas Blount (1618–1679), a Recusant Antiquary* (Amsterdam: APA-Holland University Press, 1978); Richard Cust, 'Catholicism, Antiquarianism and Gentry Honour: The Writings of Sir Thomas Shirley', *Midland History*, 23 (1998), pp. 40–70; Joseph Donatelli, 'The Percy Folio Manuscript: A 17th-Century Context for Medieval Poetry', *English Manuscript Studies*, 4, ed. Peter Beal and Jeremy Griffiths (London: British Library, 1993), pp. 114–33, esp. p. 129; Paul Arblaster, *Antwerp and the World* (Leuven: Leuven University Press, 2004), chapter 5 (on Richard Verstegan); and, on recusant historiography more generally, W. B. Patterson, 'The Recusant View of the English Past', in Derek Baker (ed.), *Studies in Church History*, 11 (1975), pp. 49–262. On Catholic antiquarianism and the Gothic Revival, see Rosemary Hill, '"The Ivi'd Ruins of Folorn (*sic*) Grace Dieu": Catholics, Romantics and Late Georgian Gothic', in Michael Hall (ed.), *Gothic Architecture and its Meanings 1550–1830* (Reading: Spire Books/

Georgian Group, 2002), pp. 159–84. I am grateful to Eileen Harris for the latter reference.
22. Hutton, *Rise and Fall*, esp. chapter 3.
23. Charles Jackson (ed.), 'The Life of Master John Shaw', in *Yorkshire Diaries and Autobiographies in the Seventeenth and Eighteenth Centuries*, Surtees Society, vol. 65 (Durham: for the Society, 1877), pp. 138–9. See (most recently) Anne C. Parkinson, 'Religious Drama in Kendal: The Corpus Christi Play in the Reign of James I', *Recusant History*, 25:4 (2001), pp. 604–12. I am grateful to the author for letting me see a copy of this piece before publication. See also below, p. 67.
24. On the move from medieval to post-Reformation drama, see (most recently) Michael O'Connell, *The Idolatrous Eye* (New York: Oxford University Press, 2000), chapters 1, 3 and 4. See also H. C. Gardiner, *Mysteries' End*, Yale Studies in English 103 (New Haven: Yale University Press, 1946); Paul Whitfield White, *Theatre and Reformation* (Cambridge: Cambridge University Press, 1993). For a wide-ranging assessment of the influence of medieval drama on Shakespeare's early plays, see Beatrice Groves, *Texts and Traditions* (Oxford: Oxford University Press, 2007).
25. On the beginnings of licensing, see Richard Dutton, *Mastering the Revels* (Basingstoke: Macmillan, 1991), chapter 1.
26. For two examples of carols with medieval roots, respectively containing extra-Scriptural religious material and Marian-centred devotion, which survived via a combination of oral tradition and popular print till the nineteenth century, see Hugh Keyte and Andrew Parrott (eds.), *The New Oxford Book of Carols* (Oxford: Oxford University Press, 1992), items 128 (Cherry Tree Carol) and 131 (Seven Joys of Mary). For two recent accounts of carolling in post-Reformation England, see Keyte and Parrott (eds.), *New Oxford Book of Carols*, pp. xviii–xix, and Ian Bradley (ed.), *The Penguin Book of Carols* (London: Penguin, 1999), pp. xii–xv. On popular festivity, see also Leah Marcus, *The Politics of Mirth* (Chicago: University of Chicago Press, 1986); David Cressy, *Bonfires and Bells* (London: Weidenfeld & Nicolson, 1989); Hutton, *Rise and Fall*, esp. chapters 5 and 7, and pp. 206–17 (the latter relating to carol singing); David Underdown, *Revel, Riot and Rebellion* (Oxford: Oxford University Press, 1985: paperback edn 1987), chapter 3; A. B. Chambers, 'Christmas, the Liturgy of the Church and English Verse of the Renaissance', *Literary Monographs*, 6 (1975), pp. 109–53. For the celebration of Christmas during the Interregnum, see John Spurr, *The Restoration Church of England, 1646–1689* (New Haven: Yale University Press, 1991), chapter 1.
27. Richard James, *Poems*, ed. Alexander B. Grosart (n.p.: printed for private circulation, 1880), pp. 249–53, is one example among many of a Christmas carol written by a Protestant. Ian Bradley has observed, though, that 'they tended to be the work of those distanced from the political and religious establishment' (p. xiv).
28. E.g. H. E. Rollins, 'Ballads from Additional MS 38599', *PMLA*, 38 (1923), pp. 133–52; Peter J. Seng (ed.), *Tudor Songs and Ballads from MS Cotton Vespasian*

A-25 (Cambridge, Mass.: Harvard University Press, 1978); *Epitaphs* (1604) (see description in *ARCR* II, no. 914); *A Smale Garland, of Pious and Godly Songs* (1684); Bod MS Eng.poet.b.5 (Southwell's verse in a collection otherwise centring around carols). The latter manuscript is associated with the Fairfax family: see *Bodleian Library Record*, 3 (1950–1), p. 50, under 'Notable Accessions'; Deborah Aldrich Larson (ed.), *The Verse Miscellany of Constance Aston Fowler: A Diplomatic Edition* (Tempe: Renaissance English Text Society, 2000), and the review of this by Marie-Louise Coolahan in *Early Modern Literary Studies*, 7:2 (2001), e-journal; and Cedric C. Brown, 'Recusant Community and Jesuit Mission in Parliament Days: Bodleian MS Eng. poet. b. 5', *Yearbook of English Studies*, 33 (2003), pp. 290–315.

29. On early nineteenth-century folk-song collectors, see Bradley (ed.), *Penguin Book of Carols*, p. xv.
30. An interplay of script and print is the more usual model; in *Early English Carols*, 2nd edn (Oxford: Clarendon, 1977), p. cxxxii, Richard Leighton Greene identifies only two medieval carols that appear to have survived to the twentieth century in outright oral tradition (or, at least, for which no printed analogues survive).
31. Nicholas Temperley, *The Music of the English Parish Church*, vol. I (Cambridge: Cambridge University Press, 1979: this edn 1983), p. 339. On carols within the liturgy of the late medieval church, see Bradley (ed.), *Penguin Book of Carols*, pp. xi–xii.
32. See Eamon Duffy, *The Stripping of the Altars* (New Haven: Yale University Press, 1992), chapters 11–13.
33. *The Idea of the Holy*, trans. John W. Harvey (London: Oxford University Press, 1928), p. 67.
34. Alexandra Walsham, 'Unclasping the Book? Post-Reformation English Catholicism and the Vernacular Bible', *Journal of British Studies*, 42:2 (2003), pp. 141–66. England was the one major country in Europe to be without a vernacular translation of the Bible by 1520: David Daniell, *William Tyndale: A Biography* (New Haven: Yale University Press, 1994), pp. 92–5. For a recent account of biblical scholarship across Europe at the Reformation, see Christopher de Hamel, *The Book: A History of the Bible* (London: Phaidon, 2001), chapter 9. The Council of Trent, while reaffirming the pre-eminence of the Vulgate, recognised that needs for a vernacular bible might differ from country to country: see F. J. Crehan, 'The Bible in the Roman Catholic Church from Trent to the Present Day', *The Cambridge History of the Bible*, vol. III, ed. S. L. Greenslade (Cambridge: Cambridge University Press, 1963), chapter 6, esp. pp. 202–5. On the Douai/Rheims Bible, see Lynne Long, *Translating the Bible from the 7th to the 17th Century* (Aldershot: Ashgate, 2001), pp. 176–81; Evelyn Tribble, *Margins and Marginality* (Charlottesville: Virginia University Press, 1993), pp. 44–50; Crehan, 'The Bible in the Roman Catholic Church', pp. 161–3, and S. L. Greenslade, 'English Versions of the Bible, 1525–1611', chapter 4 in *The Cambridge History of the Bible*, vol. III, ed. Greenslade. For English Catholic arguments against the use of the vernacular for Scripture, see Richard

Foster Jones, *The Triumph of the English Language* (Stanford: Stanford University Press, 1953), pp. 62–6. For an epigram by the religious conservative John Heywood, describing a countryman who tries to learn his Pater Noster in English but only ends up forgetting it in Latin, see his *Woorkes* (1562), fols. O2b–3a (discussed in John N. King, *English Reformation Literature* (Princeton: Princeton University Press, 1982), p. 251).

35. For lay knowledge of Latin in the late medieval period, see Duffy, *Stripping of the Altars*, chapter 6.
36. 'A Religious Trage-Comedy': BL Add. MS. 64124, dated c.1660–85 by the cataloguers (quotations fols. 103a–4a). For an example of an Elizabethan layman praying out loud in Latin, see Augustine Baker's reminiscences of his father: Dom Justin McCann and Dom Hugh Connolly (eds.), *Memorials of Fr. Augustine Baker*, Catholic Record Society, vol. 33 (London: CRS, 1933), p. 18. Interestingly, Baker comments that 'his manner in this kind . . . [was] imitated by none, no, not by his own children'.
37. 'Little John Nobody', from Thomas Percy, *Reliques of Ancient English Poetry*, ed. Henry B. Wheatley, 3 vols. (repr. New York: Dover, 1966), vol. II, pp. 135–7. The libel is dated to c.1550. See the comments on the ballad in Woolf, *Social Circulation*, p. 63. On the background to the satirical characters 'Nobody' and 'Somebody', see Charles Mitchell (ed.), *Hogarth's Peregrination* (Oxford: Clarendon, 1952), pp. xxiv–xxxi.
38. The word 'synagogue' comes into hostile controversial use in English as early as 1464 (*OED*), though more commonly in an anti-Catholic context.
39. See Marcy L. North, *The Anonymous Renaissance* (Chicago: University of Chicago Press, 2003), chapter 4.
40. William Allen to Alphonsus Agazzari SJ, July 1580 (no day given): *Miscellanea*, VII, Catholic Record Society, vol. 9 (London: Aberdeen University Press for CRS, 1911), p. 27.
41. Diego de Yepes, *Historia Particular de la Persecución en Inglaterra* (1599), quoted in Pierre Janelle, *Robert Southwell the Writer* (London: Sheed & Ward, 1935), p. 32. See also *The Poems of Robert Southwell*, ed. James H. Macdonald and Nancy Pollard Brown (Oxford: Clarendon, 1967), pp. xix–xx.
42. *History of His Own Times* (London: [s.n.], 1883), p. 423: quoted in *Dominicana*, Catholic Record Society, vol. 25 (London: CRS, 1925), p. 3. For the association of Catholicism with foreignness, see G. K. Hunter, 'English Folly and Italian Vice', chapter 4 in his *Dramatic Identities and Cultural Traditions* (Liverpool: Liverpool University Press, 1978).
43. *Liber Ordinacionum et Depositionum*, Colchester (1562–72), Essex Record Office: examinations of William Blackman and Margaret Sander, fols. 33a, 34b. Quoted by M. S. Byford, 'The Price of Protestantism: Assessing the Impact of Religious Change in Elizabethan Essex: The Cases of Heydon and Colchester, 1558–94' (Oxford D. Phil., 1988), pp. 158–62.
44. See R. W. Scribner, *For the Sake of Simple Folk* (Cambridge: Cambridge University Press, 1981); and Andrew Pettegree, *Reformation and the Culture of Persuasion* (Cambridge: Cambridge University Press, 2005).

45. See Hunt, *Art of Hearing*; Patrick Collinson, 'Elizabethan and Jacobean Puritanism as Forms of Popular Religious Culture', chapter 1 in Christopher Durston and Jacqueline Eales (eds.), *The Culture of English Puritanism, 1560–1700* (Basingstoke: Macmillan, 1996), section 3; Bryan Crockett, *The Play of Paradox* (Philadelphia: University of Pennsylvania Press, 1995); Cressy, 'Literacy in Context', p. 310.
46. Pettegree, *Reformation*, esp. p. 41.
47. *A Pittilesse Mother* (1616), a tale of a Catholic wife married to a Protestant who murdered her children so that they might not be brought up heretics, shows how popular literature not explicitly religious in genre could still convey anti-Catholic messages. See Betty S. Travitsky, '"A Pittilesse Mother"? Reports of a Seventeenth-Century English Filicide', *Mosaic*, 27:4 (1994), pp. 55–76. Conversely, ballads can also preserve a pre-Reformation referential field: *Robin Hood and the Bishop*, of which several editions survive (dated by *ESTC* between 1650 and 1700), has Robin tying up the bishop and getting him to sing Mass. Cf. 'Robin Hood and Queen Katherine' (in Francis James Child (ed.), *The English and Scottish Popular Ballads* (this edn New York: Dover, 1965), vol. III, pp. 196–205) which, as Peter Davidson suggests, appears to respond to Reformation issues (personal communication). For a discussion of conservative religious material in secular ballads, see Mary Diana McCabe, 'A Critical Study of Some Traditional Religious Ballads' (Durham MA thesis, 1980), pp. 7, 12, 301. See also Helen Phillips (ed.), *Robin Hood* (Dublin: Four Courts Press, 2005); Stephen Knight, *Robin Hood: A Complete Study of the English Outlaw* (Oxford: Blackwell, 1994); and Knight's *Robin Hood: An Anthology of Scholarship and Criticism* (Woodbridge: D. S. Brewer, 1999).
48. See Robert Scribner, 'Oral Culture and the Diffusion of Reformation Ideas', *History of European Ideas*, 5:3 (1984), pp. 237–56.
49. *The Literary Culture of the Reformation* (Oxford: Oxford University Press, 2002). For differences between medieval and Reformation oral experiences of Scripture, see Walter J. Ong, SJ, *On the Presence of the Word* (New Haven: Yale University Press, 1967), chapter 5. Ceri Sullivan has argued for recusant writers' distinctive use of rhetorical tropes: *Dismembered Rhetoric* (London: Associated University Presses, 1995).
50. Staffordshire Record Office, D(W) 1734/4/3/11. For a conformist treatment of the same topic in verse, see Richard Crashaw's 'On a Treatise of Charity', first published as part of the prefatory material to Robert Shelford's anti-puritan *Five Pious and Learned Discourses* (1635) f. A1a–b. Crashaw had not converted to Catholicism at the time of writing.
51. 'Catholikes must abhorre from hereticall phrases and wordes', Staffordshire Record Office, D641/3/P/4/13/1 (unpaginated), 13 leaves from end. Conversely, William Loe was hostile to foreign and popish elements in the language: *An Hymne or Song* (1620), f. A3, quoted by Woolf, 'Speech, Text and Time', p. 182.
52. See Long, *Translating the Bible*, p. 123. Edmund Bunny's *A Treatise Tending to Pacification*, appended to his edition of Robert Persons's *A Booke of*

Christian Exercise (1584), comments on the question of denominational word-choice (p. 66).
53. This describes a Protestant–Catholic debate held on 27 June 1623. On disputations in general, see Ann Hughes, 'The Pulpit Guarded: Confrontations Between Orthodox and Radical in Revolutionary England', in Anne Laurence, W. R. Owens and Stuart Sim (eds.), *John Bunyan and his England, 1628–88* (London: Hambledon, 1990), pp. 31–50.
54. 'An Additionall Appendix' to *Rusticus ad Academicos* (1660), p. 47. Fisher himself was a Quaker.
55. *Conversion, Politics and Religion in England, 1580–1625* (Cambridge: Cambridge University Press, 1996).
56. J. A. Sharpe, '"Last Dying Speeches": Religion, Ideology and Public Execution in 17th-Century England', *P & P*, 107 (1985), pp. 144–67; Peter Lake and Michael Questier, 'Agency and Appropriation at the Foot of the Gallows: Catholics (and Puritans) Confront (and Constitute) the English State', chapter 7 in *The Antichrist's Lewd Hat* (New Haven: Yale University Press, 2002); and the discussion of martyr-narratives in chapter 4 below.
57. '[I]n *parrhesia* the danger always comes from the fact that the . . . truth is capable of hurting or angering the interlocutor': Michael Foucault, *Fearless Speech*, ed. Joseph Pearson (Los Angeles: Semiotext(e), 2001), p. 17.
58. See under 'equivocation' in *OED*. On these and related issues, see Perez Zagorin, *Ways of Lying* (Cambridge, Mass.: Harvard University Press, 1990); Lowell Gallagher, *Medusa's Gaze* (Stanford: Stanford University Press, 1991), pp. 96–7; John Morrill and Paul Slack (eds.), *Public Duty and Private Conscience in 17th-Century England* (Oxford: Oxford University Press, 1993); Steven Mullaney, '"Lying Like Truth": Riddle, Representation and Treason in Renaissance England', *ELH*, 47:1 (1980), pp. 32–47; Camille Wells Slights, *The Casuistical Tradition in Shakespeare, Donne, Herbert and Milton* (Princeton: Princeton University Press, 1981); Johann P. Sommerville, 'The "New Art of Lying": Equivocation, Mental Reservation and Casuistry', chapter 5 in Edmund Leites (ed.), *Conscience and Casuistry in Early Modern Europe* (Cambridge/ Paris: Cambridge University Press, 1988); P. J. Holmes, *Elizabethan Casuistry*, Catholic Record Society vol. 67 (London: CRS, 1981); and Arthur F. Marotti, *Religious Ideology and Cultural Fantasy* (Notre Dame: University of Notre Dame Press, 2005), pp. 51, 235.
59. See Conclusion, pp. 159–61. On Catholics and equivocation, see Elliot Rose, *Cases of Conscience* (Cambridge: Cambridge University Press, 1975), pp. 72–3, 83–5, 89–93, and Ronald J. Corthell, '"The Secrecy of Man": Recusant Discourse and the Elizabethan Subject', *ELR*, 19 (1989), pp. 272–90. On the perceived association between equivocation and the Jesuit order, see Garry Wills, *Witches and Jesuits* (Oxford/New York: Oxford University Press/New York Public Library, 1995). Though Shakespeare's *Macbeth*, discussed by Wills, is the first text cited by the *OED* which uses the word 'equivocation' in a negative sense, earlier pejorative associations, some anti-Catholic, can be found for words from the same stem from the 1590s.

60. The distinction between medium and message is most strongly associated with the thought of Marshall McLuhan: see Phillip Marchand, *Marshall McLuhan* (this edn Cambridge, Mass.: MIT Press, 1998).
61. Foley, vol. III, pp. 676–7.
62. Quoted from third edition (1630), f. A4b. The poem is signed 'E. W.'.
63. Carl Lindhal has called for scholars to 'stop assuming that folk culture is in every way opposed to elite and is always that which is lost in the translation from speech to writing': 'The Oral Undertones of Late Medieval Romance', in W. F. H. Nicolaisen (ed.), *Oral Tradition in the Middle Ages*, Medieval and Renaissance Texts and Studies, 112 (New York: SUNY, 1995), p. 60.
64. See Fox, *Oral and Literate Culture*, p. 19. Cressy, *Literacy*, accounts for the discrepancy between reading and writing skills.
65. For prejudices against illiteracy, see Cressy, *Literacy*, chapter 1.
66. 'Text as Interpretation: Mark and After', in John Miles Foley (ed.), *Oral Tradition in Literature* (Columbia: University of Missouri Press, 1986), p. 161. Ong is quoting Brian Stock's *The Implications of Literacy: Written Language and Models of Interpretation in the Eleventh and Twelfth Centuries* (Princeton: Princeton University Press, 1983), p. 31; Stock's comment is equally valid in an early modern context. For a later period, David Vincent has commented that the 'vocabulary of aspiration' towards literacy 'was derived directly or indirectly from the Church': *Literacy and Popular Culture: England 1750–1914* (Cambridge: Cambridge University Press, 1989), p. 5.
67. See Harvey J. Graff, introduction to *Literacy and Social Development in the West: A Reader*, Cambridge Studies in Oral and Literate Culture, 3 (Cambridge: Cambridge University Press, 1981). For the stimulus towards education brought about across Europe both by the Reformation and the Counter-Reformation, see Houston, *Literacy*, pp. 35–7. On how a suspicion of illiterates operated interdenominationally, see chapter 2, pp. 56, 81. A nuanced restatement of the association between Protestantism and greater levels of literacy can be found in R. A. Houston, *Scottish Literacy and the Scottish Identity* (Cambridge: Cambridge University Press, 1985), pp. 148–58.
68. Quotation from David Cressy, 'The Environment for Literacy: Accomplishment and Context in Seventeenth-Century England', chapter 3 in Daniel P. Resnick (ed.), *Literacy in Historical Perspective* (Washington: Library of Congress, 1983), p. 28. See also Hunt, *Art of Hearing*.
69. 'Puritans and the Dark Corners of the Land', *Transactions of the Royal Historical Society*, 5th ser., vol. 13 (1963), pp. 77–102.
70. See Adam Fox, 'Aspects of Oral Culture and its Development in Early Modern England', Cambridge PhD thesis, 1993, chapter 6. Aubrey's comment on the perceived supplanting of oral fictions by printed matter is well known: 'many good Bookes, and variety of Turnes of Affaires, have put all the old Fables out of dores: and the divine art of Printing and Gunpowder have frighted away Robin-good-fellow and the Fayries' (p. 290). All Aubrey quotations are taken from *John Aubrey. Three Prose Works*, ed. John Buchanan-Brown (Fontwell: Centaur Press, 1972). Cf. Reginald Scot, *The Discoverie of Witchcraft*, ed. Brinsley

Nicholson (London: Elliot Stock, 1986): 'But Robin goodfellowe ceaseth now to be much feared, and poperie is sufficientlie discovered' (p. xx). See chapter 2 below, pp. 75–80.
71. For a classic discussion of the relationship between religion and secret oral tradition, see Max Weber, *The Sociology of Religion*, trans. Ephraim Fischoff (London: Methuen, 1922), p. 67.
72. See Conclusion, pp. 164–6.
73. Foley, vol. VII:2, pp. 1109–10: discussed in Patrick Collinson, Arnold Hunt and Alexandra Walsham, 'Religious Publishing in England, 1557–1640', chapter 1 in *The Cambridge History of the Book in Britain*, vol. IV (1557–1695), ed. John Barnard and D. F. McKenzie with Maureen Bell (Cambridge: Cambridge University Press, 2002), p. 54.
74. 'Clown' at this date could imply either a rustic or a jester (*OED*). For another anecdote in which a country Catholic worsts a learned Protestant, see 'A Religious Trage-Comedy', [c.1660–85], BL Add. MS 64124, fols. 36a–40a. On the 'almost ritual enquiry after news' typical of printed dialogues, see Dagmar Freist, *Governed by Opinion* (London: I. B. Tauris, 1997), p. 250.
75. Coleman, *Public Reading*; Cressy, 'Literacy in Context'.
76. Phebe Jensen, 'Ballads and Brags: Free Speech and Recusant Culture in Elizabethan England', *Criticism*, 40:3 (1998), pp. 333–54. Thomas M. McCoog, SJ, 'Playing the Champion: The Role of Disputation in the Jesuit Mission', chapter 7 in Thomas M. McCoog, SJ (ed.), *The Reckoned Expense* (Woodbridge: Boydell, 1996).
77. E.g. Elizabeth Eisenstein, *The Printing Press as an Agent of Change* (1st edn, 2 vols. (Cambridge: Cambridge University Press, 1979).
78. However, as Eamon Duffy reminds us, 'we should not underestimate the extent to which [Huggarde's] writing [represents] a wider recovery of conservative confidence in the later 1550s': 'Conservative Voice', p. 97. A more negative view can be found in (e.g.) David Loades, *Politics, Censorship and the English Reformation* (London: Pinter, 1991), pp. 7, 140–2. See also J. W. Martin, *Religious Radicals in Tudor England* (London: Hambledon, 1989), chapter 5. On the Catholic ballads of the Northern Rising, see Dom Bede Camm, *Forgotten Shrines* (London: Macdonald & Evans, 1910), pp. 109, 125; and Daniela Busse, 'Anti-Catholic Polemical Writing on the "Rising in the North" (1569) and the Catholic Reaction', *Recusant History*, 27:1 (2004), pp. 11–30, esp. pp. 21–3. I am grateful to Dr Busse for letting me consult a copy of her paper prior to its publication.
79. Christopher Haigh, *English Reformations* (Oxford: Clarendon, 1993). On the progressive strategies of Marian Catholicism, see (most recently) Alexandra Walsham, 'Translating Trent? English Catholicism and the Counter-Reformation', *Historical Research*, 78 (2005), pp. 288–310. Cf. chapter 3, p. 89.
80. See Abbreviations for full bibliographical details of A. F. Allison and D. M. Rogers's magisterial two-volume bibliography, *The Contemporary Printed Literature of the English Counter-Reformation*. Volume II is a revised edition of *A Catalogue of Catholic Books in English Printed Abroad or Secretly in England,*

1558–1640 (1st edn 1956). Allison and Rogers's work has been carried forward by Thomas H. Clancy, SJ, *English Catholic Books, 1641–1700* (revised edition, Aldershot: Scolar, 1996), F. Blom, J. Blom, F. Korsten and G. Scott, *English Catholic Books, 1701–1800* (Aldershot: Scolar, 1996). In '"Domme Preachers": Post-Reformation English Catholicism and the Culture of Print', *P & P*, 168 (2000), pp. 72–123, Alexandra Walsham draws especially on Allison and Rogers to refute common historiographical assumptions. Barry in Harris (ed.), *Popular Culture*, p. 70, claims that a shift to the religion of the word was facilitated by both the Reformation and the Counter-Reformation; Alexandra Walsham's 'Reformed Folklore? Cautionary Tales and Oral Tradition in Early Modern England', chapter 6 in Adam Fox and Daniel Woolf (eds.), *The Spoken Word* (Manchester: Manchester University Press, 2002), argues that Protestantism's part in the eclipse of the spoken word was equivocal (p. 173).

81. For two recent extended considerations of Catholic manuscript circulation, see Gerard Kilroy, *Edmund Campion, Memory and Transcription* (Aldershot: Ashgate, 2005), and Marotti, *Religious Ideology*. See also Henry Woudhuysen, *Sir Philip Sidney and the Circulation of Manuscripts, 1558–1640* (Oxford: Clarendon, 1996), pp. 12, 18, 49, 52–3, 82, 151, 257, 283; and Nancy Pollard Brown, 'Paperchase: The Dissemination of Catholic Texts in Elizabethan England', *English Manuscript Studies*, 1 (1989), pp. 120–43.
82. For a helpful discussion of the interpenetration of oral culture with popular print culture, see Barry, in Harris (ed.), *Popular Culture*, p. 82.
83. On the phenomenon of Catholic 'seepage', see my *Catholicism, Controversy*, chapter 2, and 'What is a Catholic Poem? Explicitness and Censorship in Tudor and Stuart Religious Verse', chapter 6 in Andrew Hadfield (ed.), *Literature and Censorship in Renaissance England* (Basingstoke: Macmillan, 2001).
84. Tessa Watt, *Cheap Print and Popular Piety, 1550–1640* (Cambridge: Cambridge University Press, 1991). However, see her Appendix C; STC 23884a.6 and 23884a.8, noted by Watt in her Appendix D; and *ARCR* II, no. 525 (a popular poem on Mary, Queen of Scots in broadside format).
85. See John Hinks, '"Dyvers Papisticall Books...": A Preliminary Note on Pedlars of Recusant Literature in 17th-Century Leicester', *Quadrat*, 13 (2001), pp. 22–5, and his PhD thesis for Loughborough University, 'The History of the Book Trade in Leicester to c.1850' (2002). I am grateful to Dr Hinks for discussions on the topic. See also Adam Fox's account of messengers who carried letters between Catholics: *Oral and Literate Culture*, pp. 371–2. Julie Van Vuuren is currently writing a doctoral thesis on Catholic ballads at Reading University.
86. On the complementarity of oral and manuscript dissemination, see Harold Love, 'Oral and Scribal Texts in Early Modern England', chapter 3 in John Barnard and D. F. McKenzie with Maureen Bell (eds.), *The Cambridge History of the Book in Britain, vol. IV, 1557–1695* (Cambridge: Cambridge University Press, 2002).
87. Fox, *Oral and Literate Culture*, p. 5. See also Thomas, 'Meaning of Literacy', p. 121; Woolf, *Social Circulation*, p. 184. On newsgathering, see Love, 'Oral and Scribal Texts'; Freist, *Governed by Opinion*, chapter 5.

88. For the relationship between manuscript culture and subversive discourse at a later period, see Harold Love, *The Culture and Commerce of Texts* (this edn Amherst: University of Massachusetts Press, 1993), esp. chapter 5.
89. Barry in Harris (ed.), *Popular Culture*, distinguishes between the two (esp. pp. 69–72). This volume also includes a recent bibliography of the extensive literature on popular culture. For the early modern period, the study of oral culture has often been used as a means of interrogating the various distinctions drawn by social historians between elite and popular culture: see Woolf, "'Common Voice'", pp. 48–50. See also Christopher Marsh, *Popular Religion in 16th-Century England* (Basingstoke: Macmillan, 1998), p. 10 *et passim*, for a critique of the term as applied to religious activity. For the replacement of the bipolar model of elite/popular culture by a stress on diversity and multiplicity, see Barry Reay, *Popular Culture in England, 1550–1750* (London: Longman, 1998), chapter 7 (though as he comments (p. 198) most bipolar accounts have allowed for an element of 'overlap and interaction' between the spheres).
90. Ethan Shagan, 'Rumour and Popular Politics in the Reign of Henry VIII', chapter 2 in Tim Harris (ed.), *The Politics of the Excluded, c.1500–1800* (Basingstoke: Palgrave, 2001), quotation p. 31. See also M. Lindsay Kaplan, *The Culture of Slander in Early Modern England* (Cambridge: Cambridge University Press, 1997); G. R. Elton, *Policy and Police* (Cambridge: Cambridge University Press, 1972), chapter 2.
91. Habermas's most influential book has been *Strukturwandel der Öffentlichkeit* (1962), translated into English as *The Structural Transformation of the Public Sphere* (1st edn London: Polity/Blackwell, 1989). On newsgathering among Catholics and other minorities, see Margaret Sena, 'William Blundell and the Networks of Catholic Dissent in Post-Reformation England', chapter 4 in Alexandra Shepard and Phil Withington (eds.), *Communities in Early Modern England* (Manchester: Manchester University Press, 2000); Paul Arblaster, *Antwerp and the World*; and Harris (ed.), *Politics of the Excluded*.
92. 'How Myths are Made', chapter 1 in *Witches, Druids and King Arthur* (London: Hambledon, 2003), quotation p. 19.
93. Paul Thompson, *The Voice of the Past* (2nd edn Oxford: Oxford University Press, 1988).
94. On siding with those of different social status but the same religious affiliations, see Tim Harris, 'Problematising Popular Culture', chapter 1 in Harris (ed.), *Popular Culture* (esp. pp. 19, 26). On Catholic 'feudalism', see Bossy, *English Catholic Community*, chapter 7.
95. On the mediated nature of the 'popular' voice, see Barry, 'Literacy and Literature', in Harris (ed.), *Popular Culture*.
96. For an example of how the similar material could be differently targeted for different audiences, see chapter 3, pp. 109–10.
97. But for a case study of what appears to have been a genuinely popular and successful intervention in oral culture, see the discussion of the versified version of Allen's 'Articles' in chapter 3.

98. *Pious Instructions in Meter Fitted to the Weaker Capacities* (1693), fol. *3a. Parlor was a Franciscan, whose name in religion was Leo of St Mary Magdalen. In *Early English Carols*, 2nd edn (Oxford: Clarendon, 1977), p. cxxxii, Richard Leighton Greene comments on the Franciscan tradition of working with popular song (pp. clv–clvi); cf. Luke Wadding, *A Smale Garland, of Pious and Godly Songs* (1684).
99. However, Freist, *Governed by Opinion*, comments on the relationship between orality and figurative language (pp. 20, 184) and the use of mnemonic aids within collective memory (pp. 240–1).
100. Review article in *HJ*, 45:2 (2002), pp. 481–94 (quotation p. 493). Marie B. Rowlands (ed.), *English Catholics of Parish and Town, 1558–1778* (London: CRS, 1999) is a pioneering exploration of the world of 'ordinary' Catholics.
101. For the proverb as a source of wisdom, see Woolf, *Social Circulation*, p. 381; as an orally transmissible 'community resource', see Juliet Fleming, *Graffiti and the Writing Arts of Early Modern England* (London: Reaktion, 2001), pp. 46–7; and as a mechanism of oral recall, see Laurie Maguire, *Shakespearean Suspect Texts* (Cambridge: Cambridge University Press, 1996), p. 115. On music, see Bennett Zon, *The English Plainchant Revival* (Oxford: Oxford University Press, 1998); Philip Brett, 'Edward Paston (1550–1630): A Norfolk Gentleman and his Musical Collection', *Transactions of the Cambridge Bibliographical Society*, 4 (1964), pp. 51–69; and the discussion of Byrd in chapter 4 of this study. On drama, see Phebe Jensen, 'Recusancy and Community in Recusant Yorkshire: The Simpsons at Gowlthwaite Hall', *Reformation*, 6 (2002), pp. 75–102; Dutton, Findlay and Wilson (eds.), *Region, Religion and Patronage* and *Theatre and Religion*. On prison, see Peter Lake and Michael Questier, 'Prisons, Priests and "the People" in Post-Reformation England', chapter 6 in *The Antichrist's Lewd Hat* (New Haven: Yale University Press, 2002). On the theatre of death, see p. 12 above.
102. For the disastrous upshot of one Catholic sermon, see Alexandra Walsham, '"The Fatall Vesper": Providentialism and Anti-Popery in Late Jacobean London', *P & P*, 144 (1994), pp. 36–87.
103. However, see D. M. Rogers, '"Popishe Thackwell" and Early Catholic Printing in Wales', *Biographical Studies, 1534–1829* (later *Recusant History*), 2:1 (1953), pp. 37–54 (on *Y Druch Christianogawl*, the first ever book printed in Wales); and Michael A. Mullett, *The Catholic Reformation* (London: Routledge, 1999), p. 179, on how Catholicism in Scotland associated itself with the Gaelic language. This is in keeping with other Counter-Reformation missionary methods, for which see David Gentilcore, '"Adapt Yourself to People's Capabilities": Missionary Strategies, Methods and Impact in the Kingdom of Naples, 1600–1800', *JEH*, 45 (1994), pp. 269–96; and John W. O'Malley et al. (eds.), *The Jesuits* (Toronto: University of Toronto Press, 1999), parts 3–4. Calvinism too adapted to 'oral literate' methods of cultural transmission in the Gaelic-speaking Scottish Highlands and Islands: see Collinson, Hunt and Walsham, 'Religious Publishing', p. 55, citing Jane Dawson, 'Calvinism

and the Gaidhealtachd in Scotland', pp. 231–53 in Andrew Pettegree, Alastair Duke and Gillian Lewis, *Calvinism in Europe, 1540–1620* (Cambridge: Cambridge University Press, 1994). See also Walsham, 'Domme Preachers?', pp. 113–14, and chapter 2 of the present study.

104. On the historical memory, see (most recently) Fox, *Oral and Literate Culture*, esp. chapters 5–6, and Woolf, *Social Circulation*.
105. See chapter 4, p. 144.
106. Influential studies in these areas include Pierre Nora (director), *Les Lieux de Mémoire*, 7 vols. (Paris: Gallimard, 1984–92), translated, revised and abridged as *Realms of Memory* (New York: Columbia University Press, 1996); and 'Between Memory and History: *Les Lieux de Mémoire*', trans. Marc Roudebush, *Representations*, 26 (1989), pp. 7–24; Maurice Halbwachs, *Les Cadres Sociaux de la Mémoire* (1st edn Paris: Librarie Félix Alcan, 1925), *La Topographie Légendaire des Evangiles en Terre Sainte* (1st edn Paris: Presses Universitaires de France, 1941) and *La Mémoire Collective*, ed. Jeanne Alexandre (Paris: Presses Universitaires de France, 1950), translated by Francis J. Ditter and Vida Yazdy Ditter as *The Collective Memory* (New York: Harper & Row, 1980); and Jacques Le Goff, *History and Memory*, trans. Steven Rendall and Elizabeth Claman (New York: Columbia University Press, 1992). See also Woolf, *Social Circulation*, pp. 271–4, 298. On the metamorphosis of Halbwachs's term 'collective memory' into 'cultural memory', see Dan Ben-Amos and Liliana Weissberg (eds.), *Cultural Memory and the Construction of Identity* (Detroit: Wayne State University Press, 1999), pp. 13–16, which also includes a comprehensive bibliography. On historical trauma, see Dominick LaCapra, *Writing History, Writing Trauma* (Baltimore: Johns Hopkins University Press, 2000), and Roger I. Simon, Sharon Rosenberg and Claudia Eppert (eds.), *Between Hope and Despair* (Lanham: Rowman & Littlefield, 2000).
107. *State Repression and the Labors of Memory*, trans. Judy Rein and Marcial Godoy-Anativia, in *Contradictions*, vol. 18 (Minneapolis: University of Minnesota Press, 2003) p. 2.
108. Quoted from the second quarto of *Hamlet*, ed. Ann Thompson and Neil Taylor, Arden Shakespeare, third series (London: Thomson, 2006), 4:5, lines 23–6 and 191–2.
109. *A Cleer Looking-Glass for All Wandring Sinners* (1654), p. 177. Not in Clancy.
110. Cf. the principle on which the post-Reformation *Rites of Durham* were compiled: 'the work [is] constructed on a curious geographical principle, going methodically around the cathedral and recording the decorations in and rituals connected with each place within and around it': John McKinnell, 'The Sequence of the Sacrament at Durham', *Papers in North-Eastern History*, 8 (Middlesbrough: NEEHI/Teesside University Press, 1998), p. 9. McKinnell further comments that 'much of the work represents the oral reminiscences of older people with catholic sympathies who remembered the ceremonies of the pre-reformation church more clearly than the compiler would have done' (p. 9). The *Rites of Durham* was probably written during the 1590s, and has been attributed to William Claxton (c.1530–97): see A. I. Doyle, 'William

Claxton and the Durham Chronicles', in James P. Carley and Colin G. C. Tite (eds.), *Books and Collectors, 1200–1700* (London: British Library, 1997), pp. 335–55, and the edition of the *Rites* by J. T. Fowler, Surtees Society, vol. 107 (Durham/London: Andrews/Quaritch, 1903, repr. 1964). I am grateful to Professor McKinnell for these references. R. A. Houston has suggested of Catholic culture in general in this era that the importance it ascribed to visual culture, custom and collective memory contributed to its relatively lower literacy rates (*Literacy*, p. 115). For medieval and Renaissance theories concerning the interplay of memory and place, see Mary J. Carruthers, *The Book of Memory* (Cambridge: Cambridge University Press, 1990) and Frances Yates, *The Art of Memory* (1st edn London: Routledge & Kegan Paul, 1966).

1. ABBEY RUINS, SACRILEGE NARRATIVES AND THE GOTHIC IMAGINATION

1. 'A Little Monument', in *The History and Antiquities of Glastonbury* (1722), quotation p. 104 (see also pp. 74–5). For the attribution to Eyston, see *ESTC*, n017974; Hearne was the publisher of the book and his name appears on the title page, while Eyston's contribution is anonymous. For biographical details on Eyston, see *ODNB*. William Stukeley, *Itinerarium Curiosum*, 2nd edn (1776), p. 152, describes a 'presbyterian tenant' selling stone from the Abbey: 'I observed frequent instances of the townsmen being generally afraid to make such purchase, as thinking an unlucky fate attends the family where these materials are used; and they told me many stories and particular instances of it: others, that are but half religious, will venture to build stables and out-houses therewith, but by no means any part of the dwelling-house.'
2. *Funerall Monuments* (1631), p. 47 (see also pp. 51–4).
3. See Introduction, p. 22.
4. During the reign of Queen Mary, Sir William Petre of Ingatestone obtained absolution from the Pope for receiving property at the Dissolution: Maurice Howard, *The Early Tudor Country House* (London: George Philip, 1987), p. 139. Urban VIII wrote to Viscount Montague of Cowdray in 1625 absolving him from any previous excommunication because of his pious action in building a household chapel: Julia Roundell (Mrs Charles Roundell), *Cowdray* (London: Bickers & Son, 1884), p. 74. However, the impropriations were remembered as late as the eighteenth and early nineteenth centuries, when a fire devastated Cowdray House in 1793, and the family line died out in a series of accidents involving fire and drowning. See Roundell, *Cowdray*, pp. 13–14, 108–9, chapter 10 and appendix, 'The Story of a Curse'; *Notes and Queries*, first ser., vol. 3 (1851), pp. 66, 194, 307: 'The old villagers, the servants, and the descendants of servants of the family, point to the ruins of the hall, and religiously cling to the belief that its destruction and that of its lords resulted from the curse' (p. 194); and most recently, Michael C. Questier, *Catholicism and Community in Early Modern England* (Cambridge: Cambridge University Press, 2006), p. 10.

5. Keith Thomas, *Religion and the Decline of Magic* (London: Penguin, 1973, repr. 1984), pp. 112–13.
6. Howard, *Early Tudor Country House*, chapter 7. A discussion of whether curses should restrain Parliament from disposing of church land, written in 1646, is published in Richard Steward, *A Discourse of Episcopacy and Sacrilege* (1683), pp. 28–9. See also Howard Colvin, 'Recycling the Monasteries: Demolition and Reuse by the Tudor Government, 1536–1547', in his *Essays in English Architectural History* (New Haven: Yale University Press for Paul Mellon Centre, 1999), pp. 52–66. Fears about sacrilege could extend to other stones once used for sacred purposes: see Nicholas Orme (ed.), *Nicholas Roscarrock's Lives of the Saints: Cornwall and Devon* (Exeter: Devon and Cornwall Record Society, 1992), pp. 94, 160 (discussed by Eamon Duffy, 'Bare Ruin'd Choirs: Remembering Catholicism in Shakespeare's England', in *Theatre and Religion*, ed. Richard Dutton, Richard Wilson and Alison Findlay (Manchester: Manchester University Press, 2003), p. 47).
7. This text forms part of the Ten Commandments, extending the warning against idolatry in Exodus 20:4–5: 'for I the LORD thy God am a jealous God, visiting the iniquity of the fathers upon the children unto the third and fourth generation of them that hate me' (Exodus 20:5). It is quoted at other points in the Old Testament (Exodus 34:7, Numbers 14:18, Deuteronomy 5:9), while the story of Ananias and Sapphira in Acts 5 was also widely drawn upon. Thomas, *Religion*, p. 114, believes this specific idea was not current till the later years of Elizabeth I's reign.
8. See Nicholas Tyacke (ed.), *England's Long Reformation, 1500–1800* (London: UCL, 1998), introduction.
9. E.g. in Maggie Kilgour, *The Rise of the Gothic Novel* (London: Routledge, 1995), p. 4.
10. Michael Charlesworth is the only critic I know of who recognises Spelman's importance to the genre, in his brief but suggestive comments within the introduction to *The Gothic Revival*, 3 vols. (Mountfield: Helm Information, 2002), vol. I, pp. 10–12.
11. See Preface, fols. n3b–4a, for Eyston's justification of his citation practices. Cf. another Catholic antiquary, Anselm Touchet, who quotes a number of sacrilege narratives from the conformist William Dugdale's *Antiquities of Warwickshire: Historical Collections out of Several Grave Protestant Historians, Concerning the Changes of Religion, and the Strange Confusions Following* (1686), appendix. For another Catholic condemnation of sacrilege, see William Forbes Leith, *Memoirs of Scottish Catholics during the XVIIth and XVIIIth Centuries*, 2 vols. (London: Longman, 1909), vol. II, pp. 92, 101–2 (also pp. 74–6), giving two stories from the Scottish Mission's Annual Letters for 1663: one of a nobleman who used the stones of a ruined chapel to build a house and who suffered hauntings thereafter, the other of how attempts to knock down a chapel to the Virgin Mary were foiled by a violent gust of wind.
12. *History of Sacrilege*, pp. 5, 7 (see also p. 259); Graham Parry, *The Trophies of Time* (Oxford: Oxford University Press, 1995), pp. 159–66.

13. For an instance of the manuscript circulation of the *History of Sacrilege* previous to its publication, see BL Add. MS 40160 (the commonplace-book of William Lloyd, Bishop of Norwich), item 14, headed 'S[i]r Henry Spelman's papers found among [the] papers of his Amanuensis Mr [Jeremiah] Stephens of [Quinton,] Northamptonshire'. Writing in 1643, the Catholic author Serenus Cressy seems to know the work (*Exomologesis*, pp. 9–10: I am grateful to Anne Barbeau Gardiner for this reference). An extended study of the manuscript circulation of the *History of Sacrilege* would be a rewarding topic; F. M. Powicke, 'Sir Henry Spelman and the "Concilia"', reprinted in Lucy Sutherland (ed.), *Studies in History: British Academy Lectures* (London: Oxford University Press, 1966), pp. 204–37, has the most authoritative conspectus of Spelman manuscripts to date. (I am grateful to Arnold Hunt for this reference.)
14. It has been postulated that the delay to publication in the 1660s may have been due to deliberate obstruction: see Parry, *Trophies*, p. 164, and the edition of the *History of Sacrilege* by J. M. Neale and J. Haskell (1st edn 1846, 4th edn used: London: John Hodges, 1895).
15. However, the preface by Clement Spelman to *De Non Temerandis* summarises many of the ideas in the *History of Sacrilege*, and deplores that committed at the Reformation (pp. ix–xxvi).
16. Quoting Gibson's preface to Spelman's collected works, this editor writes: 'in *him* there might be prudential Reasons to exclude this Treatise from the Volume of *Reliquiae Spelmanniae*. But it has happen'd, that a true Copy of the Manuscript is now fall'n into the hands of (it seems) a less discreet Person, who will e'en let the World make what Use of it they please' (fols. A4a–b). See Parry, *Trophies*, p. 164; Philip Styles, 'Politics and Historical Research in the Early 17th Century', in Levi Fox (ed.), *English Historical Scholarship in the 16th and 17th Centuries* (London: Oxford University Press for Dugdale Society, 1956), chapter 4.
17. Spelman, ed. Gibson, *Works*, pp. vi–viii. White Kennett – interestingly, given his frequent conflicts with the High Church party – also gives examples of people shamed by Spelman into restoring tithes and glebe land: *The Case of Impropriations* (1704), pp. 226–37, and (for Kennett's churchmanship) his biography in *ODNB*.
18. 'Elegie. On the Death of Sir Henry Spelman', *Men-Miracles* (1646), p. 115.
19. *The Church-History of Britain* (1655), Book 6, p. 371.
20. 'Essays', item 14 in *Miscellaneous Tracts* (1707), p. 30.
21. Anthony Milton, *Catholic and Reformed* (Cambridge: Cambridge University Press, 1995), points out that attacks on Henry VIII and the alienation of church lands was not an exclusively Laudian phenomenon, 'even if the Laudians' emphasis upon the perils of sacrilege was shriller than most' (p. 334). On Isaac Watts Senior cautioning against sacrilege, see below, p. 41; on his religious affiliations, see the entry for his son in *ODNB*.
22. Thomas, *Religion*, pp. 113–14. It could be argued that, by diverting property from churches to religious houses, the Pope had been 'the *first founder* of all our impropriations': Gryffith Williams, *The Chariot of Truth* (1663), p. 102. Milton

has commented on Laudian literature's 'de-emphasis on the issue of idolatry as such, and its replacement at the centre of religious concerns by the problem of profanity and sacrilege': *Catholic and Reformed*, p. 196 (see also pp. 208, 312, 331–4, 500–2). A typical High Church tract is Lancelot Andrewes's *Sacrilege a Sinne* (1646). For the stimulus given to the debate by the appropriations of Church property in the Civil Wars, see Martin Dzelzainis, '"Undouted Realities": Clarendon on Sacrilege', *HJ*, 33:3 (1990), pp. 515–40. See also the comments on Spelman in Graham Parry, *The Arts of the Anglican Counter-Reformation* (Woodbridge: Boydell, 2006), pp. 172–9.

23. A key discussion of topics relating to sacrilege can be found in Richard Hooker's *Of the Laws of Ecclesiastical Polity*, vol. 5: see *The Folger Library Edition of the Works of Richard Hooker*, vol. 2, ed. W. Speed Hill (Cambridge, Mass.: Belknap/Harvard University Press, 1977), pp. 448–63.
24. On ghost stories, see John Newton, 'An Examination of Interpretations of Ghosts from the Reformation to the Close of the 17th Century', PhD thesis, University of Durham, 2004.
25. Spelman, *Sacrilege*, p. 238. Some newspaper reports and commentaries on the fire at York Minster in 1984 made a connection between it and the recent consecration in the Minster of the controversial then Bishop of Durham, David Jenkins, while not (in most cases) explicitly invoking ideas of sacrilege: http://www.bbc.co.uk/northyorkshire/iloveny/minster/fire/what_happened.shtml (accessed 8 May 2006); Humphrey Carpenter, *Robert Runcie* (London: Hodder & Stoughton, 1996), p. 272; and the neo-conservative tract by Charles Moore, Gavin Stamp and A. N. Wilson, *The Church in Crisis* (London: Hodder & Stoughton, 1986), p. 64. I am grateful to the Revd Dr Michael Brydon for the latter references.
26. Spelman, *Sacrilege*, p. 279; cf. Roger Gostwyke, *The Anatomie of Ananias* (1616), pp. 65–6, 74–5.
27. Quoted from *The Complete Angler and Lives of Donne, Wotton, Hooker, Herbert and Sanderson*, ed. Alfred W. Pollard (London: Macmillan & Co., 1906), 'Life of Hooker', p. 323. Whitgift's speech to Elizabeth on the topic of the Church's rights is being quoted.
28. 'The nest is fired with embers, by which there perishes the offspring of an impious mother.' Udall explains the significance of the eagle in the main text: the sacrilegious 'are like the Eagles Feathers, by which the Ægyptians in their Hieroglyphicks signifie, *pernitiosa potentia*; for they are said to consume all Feathers among which they are mingled . . .' (pp. 32–3). For this trope, see also Humfrey Brown, *The Ox Muzzled* (1649), p. 6; and Fulke Robartes, *The Revenue of the Gospel is Tythes* (1613), Latin/English verses and ornament on title page.
29. 'Touch me not, lest I destroy you and yours' (containing an allusion to Christ's words to Mary Magdalene, John 20:17).
30. See above, note 6.
31. 'Casta fides superest, velatae tecta sorores / Ista relegatae desurere [i.e. defuerunt?] licet? / Nam venerandus Hymen hic vota iugalia seruat / Vestalemque focum mente fouere studet' (Weever, *Funerall Monuments*, p. 430).

32. 'Upon Appleton House', stanzas 11–35: quoted from the edition in Andrew Marvell, *Poems*, ed. Nigel Smith (Harlow: Longman, 2003), pp. 210–41. Smith calls this interpolated story a 'small gothic fiction' (p. 213). Patsy Griffin suggests that it may be a deliberate riposte to notions of sacrilege: '"'Twas No Religious House Till Now": Marvell's "Upon Appleton House"', *Studies in English Literature, 1500–1900*, 28:1 (1988), pp. 61–76, esp. 62–7.
33. The nunnery was dissolved in 1539 (Marvell, ed. Smith, *ibid.*).
34. I.e. the first nun to have corrupted the convent.
35. However, the collection in which this poem appears is dateable to around the time that Cary renounced Catholicism: see *The Poems of Patrick Cary*, ed. Sister Veronica Delany (Oxford: Clarendon, 1978), pp. lviii–lix, lxxxiii (poem p. 64, discussion of poem on pp. 99–101, 110–11). The poem is emblematic, illustrated by a wine-press with the motto 'EXPRIMATUR', translated by Delany as 'To the last drop'.
36. See (most recently) *A Tribute to Horace Walpole and Strawberry Hill House*, Borough of Twickenham Local History Society, Paper No. 74 (June 1997), pp. 12, 19.
37. See *The Yale Edition of Horace Walpole's Correspondence*, ed. W. S. Lewis, 48 vols. (London/New Haven: Oxford University Press/Yale University Press, 1937–83), vol. 35, p. 153 (to Richard Bentley, September 1753). Earlier in the same letter, he writes: '. . . my love of abbeys shall not make me hate the Reformation till that makes me grow a Jacobite like the rest of my antiquarian predecessors . . .' (p. 146). For Walpole's association of the Gothic style with liberty and the English church, shared by some earlier and contemporary antiquarians and following elements of the current Whig ideology, see David D. McKinney, 'Horace Walpole and Strawberry Hill: A Study in 18th-Century Associative Thought' (MA thesis, University of Virginia, 1983), p. 68; and McKinney's 'History and Revivalism: Horace Walpole's Promotion of the Gothic Style of Architecture' (PhD thesis, University of Virginia, 1992), chapter 6; for Whig attitudes to the Gothic, see also Samuel Kliger, *The Goths in England* (Cambridge, Mass.: Harvard University Press, 1952). The most recent biography, Tim Mowl's *Horace Walpole* (London: John Murray, 1996) briefly discusses Walpole's ambivalence towards Catholicism (p. 32). There was a strong anti-Catholic slant to some of the material by other authors produced at Walpole's private press, e.g. Hannah More, *Bishop Bonner's Ghost* (1789). On Sir Robert Walpole's harassment of Catholics, see J. H. Plumb, *Sir Robert Walpole, Vol.II. The King's Minister* (1st edn 1960: London: Penguin, 1972), p. 98.
38. *The Castle of Otranto*, ed. W. S. Lewis, rev. E. J. Clery (Oxford: World's Classics, this edn 1998), p. 5. All quotations are taken from this edition. Fred Botting, *Gothic* (London: Routledge, 1996), pp. 48–54, highlights questions of authorial disavowal. Fiona Robertson, *Legitimate Histories* (Oxford: Clarendon, 1994), discusses the medieval manuscript as authentication strategy. However, on Walpole's desire to confuse the reader in the *Otranto* prefaces, see James Watt, *Contesting the Gothic* (Cambridge: Cambridge University Press, 1999), pp. 25–8.
39. 'Afterword: Some Remarks on Gothic Origins', in Kenneth W. Graham (ed.), *Gothic Fictions*, (New York: AMS, 1989) pp. 259–68 (quotation p. 259). Robert

Miles has argued that Horace Walpole is defending his father Sir Robert's claims to be seen as the legitimate inheritor of Whig traditions: 'Europhobia: The Catholic Other in Horace Walpole and Charles Maturin', chapter 5 in Avril Horner (ed.), *European Gothic* (Manchester: Manchester University Press, 2002), p. 94.

40. This also owes something to the common folktale motif of giants in castles, ubiquitous in England as elsewhere in Europe: *Castle of Otranto*, eds. Lewis and Clery, p. xxiv.
41. Elizabeth Napier's discussion of *The Castle of Otranto* in *The Failure of Gothic* (Oxford: Clarendon, 1987) emphasises how discord and incongruity co-exist with Walpole's own contention that the work has a clear retributive scheme (pp. 75–8).
42. See Robert Miles, *Gothic Writing, 1750–1820* (London: Routledge, 1993), p. 106.
43. Walpole has often been seen as exploiting his own unconscious for imaginative purposes: see (e.g.) Betsy Perteit Harfst, *Horace Walpole and the Unconscious* (New York: Arno, 1980); and *Castle of Otranto* Lewis and Clery (eds.), pp. vii–ix. In the context of this study, the dreamlike near-parallels between Manfred's intended divorce from Hippolita and the events surrounding England's break with Rome may be worth another scholar's attention.
44. For Joseph Mede's similar enterprise, see Dzelzainis, '"Undouted Realities"'.
45. Chapter 8 of the *History of Sacrilege* describes the experiment; the Walpoles are cited on p. 246.
46. For references to Spelman, see *Correspondence*, vol. 16, p. 46 (Henry Zouch to Walpole, 15 March 1762), and vol. 41, p. 222 (Bishop Garnett to Walpole, c. March 1772). Spelman's *English Works* figure as no. 2065 in Allen T. Hazen, *A Catalogue of Horace Walpole's Library*, vol. II (New Haven: Yale University Press, 1969). See also Mowl, *Horace Walpole*, p. 32.
47. *Correspondence*, vol. 15, p. 149 (to Sir David Dalrymple, 1 January 1781); vol. 17, pp. 84–5 (to Sir Horace Mann, 5 July 1741); vol. 35, p. 497 (to Lord Harcourt, [no day], October 1779).
48. Bertrand Evans, *Gothic Drama from Walpole to Shelley* (Berkeley: University of California Press, 1947), p. 11.
49. *The Nebuly Coat*, ed. Christopher Hawtree (Oxford: World's Classics, 1988), p. 79.
50. All the stories referred to can be found in M. R. James, *Casting the Runes and Other Ghost Stories*, ed. Michael Cox (Oxford: World's Classics, 1995).
51. See the suggestive discussion of James in Victor Sage, *Horror Fiction in the Protestant Tradition* (London: Macmillan, 1988), pp. 61–8.
52. Adam Fox, *Oral and Literate Culture in England, 1500–1700* (Oxford: Clarendon, 2000), pp. 35, 216, 219, 240, 256–7; Daniel Woolf, *The Social Circulation of the Past* (Oxford: Oxford University Press, 2003), p. 290 (on ruined abbeys as *lieux de mémoire*).
53. Reproduced and described in Susan B. Matheson and Derek D. Churchill's exhibition catalogue, *Modern Gothic* (New Haven: Yale University Art Gallery, 2000), item 4.
54. On the pleasure of ruins, see Botting, *Gothic*, pp. 32–8; and Christopher Woodward, *In Ruins* (London: Chatto & Windus, 2001).

55. Francis Grose, *Antiquities of England* (1783–7 edn), vol. II, pp. 213–14. Subterranean passages became a common trope in Gothic fiction: see (e.g.) Elizabeth Helme, *St Margaret's Cave* (1801), Frank 174; and Ann Ker, *Adeline St Julian* (1800), Frank 217. R. H. Barham makes a jocular reference to it in 'Netley Abbey', first printed in 1842: 'But deep beneath the basement floor / A dungeon dark and drear! / And there was an ugly hole in the wall – / For an oven too big, – for a cellar too small! / And mortar and bricks / All ready to fix, / And I said, "Here's a Nun has been playing some tricks! – / That horrible hole! – it seems to say, / "I'm a Grave that gapes for a living prey!"' (Quoted from *The Ingoldsby Legends*, ed. D. C. Browning (London: Everyman, 1960), second series, p. 173.)
56. See Jenny McAuley, 'Representations of Gothic Abbey Architecture in the Works of Four Romantic-Period Authors: Radcliffe, Wordsworth, Scott, Byron', PhD thesis, Durham University, 2007.
57. Gray to Nicholls, 19 November 1764: quoted from *Correspondence of Thomas Gray*, ed. Paget Toynbee and Leonard Whibley, 3 vols. (Oxford: Clarendon, 1935), vol. II, pp. 852–3 (for another report of the incident, see Gray's letter to James Brown, [Oct. 1764], p. 843).
58. Cf. William Lisle Bowles's later verses on Netley Abbey: 'Fall'n pile! I ask not what has been thy fate; / But when the winds, slow wafted from the main, / Through each rent arch, like spirits that complain, / Come hollow to my ear, I meditate . . .' (*The Poetical Works*, ed. George Gilfillian, 2 vols. (Edinburgh: James Nichol, 1855), vol. I, p. 21).
59. Walpole to Lady Ossory: *Correspondence*, vol. 33, pp. 42–3. See also vol. XI, p. 80 (to Mary Berry, 3 July 1790), vol. 14, p. 83 (from Thomas Gray, 22 July 1755), vol. 35, pp. 249–51 (to Richard Bentley, 18 September 1755).
60. See John Hare, 'Netley Abbey: Monastery, Mansion and Ruin', *Proceedings of the Hampshire Field Club Archaeological Society*, 49 (1993), pp. 207–27.
61. Hare uses 'Lewis', but the surname is sometimes given as 'Lucy' elsewhere.
62. Cf. Thomas's discussion of Aubrey in *Religion*, p. 113.
63. William Gilpin, *Observations on the Western Parts of England* (1798), pp. 350–1.
64. *Beauties of England and Wales* (1801–15), vol. 6 (1805), pp. 149–51, referring to Skelton's *Southampton Guide*, of which the 18th edition was published in 1805 (T. Skelton is the bookseller/printer). The anonymous editor of the *Guide* quotes Browne Willis (pp. 67–8) and comments: 'The editor was desirous to authenticate the preceding narrative, by enquiring of Mr. Taylor's family the particular circumstance. This trouble a gentleman of Southampton most condescendingly undertook, and obligingly communicated the result to the editor, without which, this work had been very imperfect' (pp. 68–9). Brayley's account is quoted in the highly derivative *Antiquarian and Topographical Cabinet*, vol. 6 (1809), and copied, unattributed, by Henry Moody, *Antiquarian and Topographical Sketches of Hampshire* (1846), pp. 299–300.
65. *The Stranger's Guide and Pleasure Visitor's Companion to Southampton* (3rd edn Southampton: W. Sharland, 1851), pp. 33–4, 38, 90, 95–6. 1st edn undated.
66. For a general account, see Simon Bradley, 'The Englishness of Gothic: Theories and Interpretations from William Gilpin to J. H. Parker', *Architectural History*,

45 (2002), pp. 325–46. On Milner, see also Bridget Patten, *Catholicism and the Gothic Revival*, Hampshire Papers 21 (Winchester: Hampshire County Council, 2001). On Pugin, see, most recently, Paul Atterbury and Clive Wainwright (eds.), *Pugin: A Gothic Passion* (New Haven: Yale University Press/Victoria & Albert Museum, 1994); and Paul Atterbury (ed.), *A. W. N. Pugin, Master of Gothic Revival* (New Haven: Yale University Press, 1995). Also on the Catholic imaginative antecedents of the Gothic Revival, see Rosemary Hill, '"The Ivi'd Ruins of Folorn (*sic*) Grace Dieu": Catholics, Romantics and Late Georgian Gothic', in Michael Hall (ed.), *Gothic Architecture and its Meanings, 1550–1830* (Reading: Spire Books/Georgian Group, 2002), pp. 158–84.

67. Neale believed that Spelman's *History of Sacrilege* had been deliberately withheld from publication, and that 'the Devil has used, and will use, all his strength to prevent the republication of Spelman': Eleanor A. Towle, *John Mason Neale, D. D.* (London: Longmans, Green & Co., 1906), pp. 126–9 (quotation p. 129). Sacrilege is used as a theme by the High Church novelist Charlotte M. Yonge in her novels *Heartsease* (1st edn 1854) and *Pillars of the House* (1st edn 1873). I am grateful to Arnold Hunt and Jean Shell for these references.

68. *The Greater Abbeys of England* (London: Chatto & Windus, 1908), pp. 144–51. The story is given at more length, also in a manner which does not impel the reader to take sides about sacrilege, in Ralph Adams Crum, *The Ruined Abbeys of Great Britain* (London: Gay & Bird, 1906), pp. 88–9. The *Victoria County History* quotes Browne Willis ironically: *VCH, Hampshire*, vol. III (1908: repr. London: University of London Institute of Historical Research, 1973), p. 476.

69. *Netley Abbey. An Elegy*, 2nd edn (1769). This is much revised from the first edition of 1764, which is shorter and contains no allusion to sacrilege. Imitations of Gray's 'Elegy' were a not uncommon means of exploring Catholic subject matter from a variety of ideological stances, e.g. 'The Nunnery', by Edward Jerningham, himself a convert from Catholicism, in *Poems on Various Subjects* (1767), pp. [1]–11; Joseph Jefferson, *The Ruins of a Temple . . . To Which Is Prefixed, an Account of . . . the . . . Holy-Ghost-Chapel, Basingstoke* (1793); Byron, 'Elegy on Newstead Abbey', pp. 31–3 in *Poetical Works*, ed. Frederick Page and John D. Jump (Oxford: Oxford University Press, 1970, repr. 1984). For Byron at Newstead, see Haidee Jackson (ed.), *Ruinous Perfection* (exhibition catalogue, Newstead Abbey, 1998).

70. *The Ruins of Netley Abby* (*sic*) (1765), pp. [5]–7, 10.

71. Though if so, manuscript circulation of the revised version would have had to start very soon after the first version was printed (see above, note 69).

72. Paul Ranger, *'Terror and Pity Reign in Every Breast'* (London: Society for Theatre Research, 1991), pp. 64, 156: also (p. 7) commenting on the scene-painter Michael 'Angelo' Rooker's use of Netley Abbey.

73. Ranger, *'Terror and Pity . . .'*, p. 64.

74. See above, note 55.

75. Quotation from first edition (Southampton, 1795), vol. I, p. 134. The book was reissued the same year in London and reprinted the following year, when an anonymous reprint was also issued in Philadelphia. Plot summaries are given

in Ann B. Tracy, *The Gothic Novel, 1790–1830* (Lexington: Kentucky University Press, 1981), pp. 184–5; and Frank, no. 468 (who comments 'The location of the major portion of the story in and around Netley Abbey . . . must have evoked an immediate shudder from the Gothic readership. . . . [Warner] had the good sense to situate his Gothic materials in an environment already steeped in Gothic legend').

76. *Poems* (1811): 'Stanzas Written Near a Ruined Farm', lines 5–12.
77. 'Weston Grove', Part III, lines 58–65, 73–4, from *Dramatic Scenes, Sonnets, and Other Poems* (1827).
78. *Poems: Consisting of a Tour Through Parts of North and South Wales* (1790), p. 75. Sotheby's footnote actually reads: 'This alludes to a circumstance recorded in *Grose's Antiquities*, and still believed in the neighbourhood'; Francis Grose's illustrated antiquarian study *The Antiquities of England and Wales*, to which Sotheby is referring (see note 55), cites Browne Willis. Sotheby was living near Southampton at the time he wrote this verse (*ODNB*).
79. Jan Vansina, *Oral Tradition as History* (Madison: University of Wisconsin Press, 1985), p. 7. On antiquarian interest in Gothic architecture after the Reformation, see (most recently) Rosemary Sweet, *Antiquaries* (London: Hambledon, 2004), p. 241.
80. *Gentleman's Magazine*, August 1805, p. 710. The piece is serialised from June 1805 onwards; the author is given only as B. T.
81. See E. J. Clery, 'The Genesis of Gothic Fiction' and Robert Miles, 'The Effulgence of Gothic', chapters 2–3 in Jerrold E. Hogle (ed.), *The Cambridge Companion to Gothic Fiction* (Cambridge: Cambridge University Press, 2002).
82. See Thomas, *Religion*, chapter 19; and Peter Marshall, 'Old Mother Leakey and the Golden Chain: Context and Meaning in an Early Stuart Haunting', pp. 92–105 in John Newton (ed.), *Early Modern Ghosts* (Durham: Centre for Seventeenth-Century Studies, 2002). I am grateful to Professor Marshall for letting me see a draft of this before publication.
83. Michael Sherbrook's 'The Fall of Religious Houses' is an often-cited example of how a conformist regretted the fall of the monasteries, which includes an imaginative account of how they were seized: ed. in A. G. Dickens, *Tudor Treatises*, Yorkshire Archaeological Society, vol. 125 (1959), p. 123. For how regrets about the Dissolution affected England's historical consciousness, see Margaret Aston's pioneering 'English Ruins and English History: The Dissolution and the Sense of the Past', *Journal of the Warburg and Courtauld Institutes*, 36 (1973), pp. 231–55.
84. Theo Brown, *The Fate of the Dead* (Cambridge: D. S. Brewer for Folklore Society, 1979), p. 41: see also the response to Brown's work by Ronald Hutton in 'The English Reformation and the Evidence of Folklore', *P & P*, 148 (1995), pp. 89–116.
85. Hutton, 'English Reformation', has commented on how, while some stories associated with ruined monasteries assume anti-Catholic anticlericalism, others contain elements of Catholic doctrinal presumptions. In 'Beyond Etiology: Interpreting Local Legends', *Fabula*, 24:3/4 (1983), pp. 223–32, Jacqueline

Simpson discusses topographical legends in which a place becomes unlucky because of an injustice committed there in the past.
86. On ghosts in early modern England, see Peter Marshall, *Beliefs and the Dead in Reformation England* (Oxford: Oxford University Press, 2002); Bruce Gordon and Peter Marshall (eds.), *The Place of the Dead* (Cambridge: Cambridge University Press, 2000); Newton, 'Examination'; and on the literary front, Stephen Greenblatt, *Hamlet in Purgatory* (Princeton: Princeton University Press, 2001).
87. See Chris Brooks, *The Gothic Revival* (London: Phaidon, 1999), pp. 41–2.
88. The classic study is Evans, *Gothic Drama*.
89. Edith Birkhead, *The Tale of Terror* (London: Constable, 1921), pp. 1–15, points out that, though the supernatural was effectively absent from the early eighteenth-century novel, it was visible elsewhere in the form of chapbooks and translated tales (p. 12).
90. See Chris Brooks, *The Gothic Revival* (London: Phaidon, 1999), p. 20; and Giles Worsley, 'The Origins of the Gothic Revival: A Reappraisal', *Transactions of the Royal Historical Society*, 6th ser., 3 (1993), pp. 105–50, who remarks 'one could question the very concept of the Gothic Revival and argue that one should instead be talking of the continuing tradition' (p. 106). In harking back to pioneering studies such as C. L. Eastlake, *A History of the Gothic Revival in England* (1st edn London: Longmans, Green & Co., 1872), Brooks and Worsley are consciously presenting an alternative to such interim studies as Kenneth Clark's *The Gothic Revival* (1st edn 1928: 3rd edn London: John Murray, 1962), where the emphasis is on shifts in taste from the mid-eighteenth century onwards: see Michael Hall's introduction to *Gothic Architecture and its Meanings, 1550–1830* (Reading: Spire Books in association with Georgian Group, 2002). Michael McCarthy, *The Origins of the Gothic Revival* (New Haven: Yale University Press, 1987), pp. 15–26, also briefly discusses antiquarian efforts prior to the mid-eighteenth century.
91. For instance, James Hogg's *Confessions of a Justified Sinner* (1st edn 1824) is a Gothic exercise which draws its terrors from Protestant antinomianism. The presence of anti-Catholicism in the Gothic novel is routinely acknowledged, seldom addressed in detail; but see the entries under 'Catholicism: Attacked in Gothic Fiction' in the index to Hogle (ed.), *Cambridge Companion to Gothic Fiction*, and Sister Mary Muriel Tarr, *Catholicism in Gothic Fiction* (PhD dissertation, Catholic University of America, Washington DC, 1946).
92. There are two recent editions of *A Simple Story* in Oxford World's Classics (ed. Jane Spencer) and Penguin (ed. Pamela Clemit). I am grateful to Professor Clemit for advice on Inchbald.
93. *The Recess*, 3 vols. (1783–5). A chronology of Gothic novels can be found in Frederick S. Frank, *The First Gothics* (New York: Garland, 1987), appendix 3.
94. I am grateful to Nicola Watson for this reference. The plot is summarised in Frank, *First Gothics*, no. 18.
95. Miles, *Gothic Writing*, chapter 5.
96. Miles, *Gothic Writing*, p. 3.
97. 'It is conspicuously anachronistic that, since the scenes are usually set in, or shortly after, the medieval period, the edifices of Gothic literature are almost

invariably in an advanced state of decay': Evans, *Gothic Drama*, p. 8 (see also pp. 210–11).

98. For instance, Anna Barbauld's essay 'On Monastic Institutions' begins with an admission of 'secret triumph' at seeing abbey ruins, but modulates into a more sympathetic assessment: *Works*, 2 vols. (London: Longman, 1825), vol. II, quotation p. 195. The essay is discussed in Botting, *Gothic*, p. 31.
99. Evans, *Gothic Drama*, has estimated that England had a 'full ten-year lead' over Germany 'in the development of mystery, gloom, and terror materials' (chapter 7, quotation p. 252). Montague Summers, *The Gothic Quest* (London: Fortune Press, n.d.), chapter 3, is still useful in this context. More recently, see Horner (ed.), *European Gothic*, and Terry Hale, 'French and German Gothic: The Beginnings', chapter 4 in Hogle (ed.), *Cambridge Companion to Gothic Fiction*. For the popularity of the English Gothic novel in France during the 1790s, see also Maurice Lévy, 'English Gothic and the French Imagination: A Calendar of Translations, 1767–1828', in G. R. Thompson (ed.), *The Gothic Imagination* (Pullman, Wash.: Washington State University Press, 1974), pp. 150–76.
100. Sade's observation is commented upon by, among others, Kenneth W. Graham in 'Emily's Demon-Lover: Gothic Revolution and *The Mysteries of Udolpho*', in Graham (ed.), *Gothic Fictions*, pp. 163–71. Graham comments in the same volume (p. 260) that revolution would have been a preoccupation earlier in England than in France.
101. Commenting on William Henry Ireland's *The Catholic* (no. 202) Frederick Frank has argued that popular ideas of Catholicism allowed 'a union to be made between pleasure and pain of the sublime degree that Burke had called for' (p. 171).
102. Discussed in Sage, *Horror Fiction*.
103. *The Literature of Terror* (1980: rev. edn London: Longman, 1996).
104. Robert Miles, *Gothic Writing*, p. 3: 'theoretical approaches are always in danger of dehistoricising the Gothic through retrospective reading'. Sage, *Horror Fiction*, p. xii, critiques assumptions of a 'timeless' unconscious unmediated by cultural and ideological factors.
105. Cf. Ronald Paulson's discussion of Goya in *Representations of Revolution (1789–1820)* (New Haven: Yale University Press, 1983): 'Entail and primogeniture, the oppressive structures of the closed society, were at the bottom of the imagery of the French Revolution. They were also available to Goya in the English gothic novel, where the repressive family had become the prison-like monastery . . .' (p. 301).
106. *Gothic Fiction/Gothic Form* (University Park: Pennsylvania State University Press, 1989), p. 8.
107. 'Das Unheimliche' (1919): trans. James Strachey, in the Pelican Freud Library, 15 vols. (Harmondsworth: Penguin, 1973–86), vol. 14 (1985), pp. 339–76.
108. *The Female Thermometer* (New York: Oxford University Press, 1995), introduction. See also Valdine Clemens, *The Return of the Repressed* (New York: State University of New York Press, 1999), which argues that horror can be societally therapeutic.

109. The theme of live burial in Eve Kosofsky Sedgwick, *The Coherence of Gothic Conventions* (New York: Methuen, 1986 edn), is interesting in this context. See also Nicholas Royle, *The Uncanny* (Manchester: Manchester University Press, 2003), chapter 10. David Salter's forthcoming monograph on representations of the Franciscan order contains analogous arguments, and I am grateful to Dr Salter for allowing me to herald it here.
110. In *Horror Fiction*, one of the most suggestive considerations to date of the relationship between religion and Gothic fiction, Victor Sage discusses the relationship between horror fiction and 'theological uncertainties' (p. xvii) and reads Freud's essay in the light of the *memento mori* tradition (chapter 1).
111. See Colin Haydon, *Anti-Catholicism in 18th-Century England, c.1714–80* (Manchester: Manchester University Press, 1993), esp. chapters 6–7; John Bossy, *The English Catholic Community 1570–1850* (1975: this edn. London: Darton, Longman and Todd, 1979), part 3.
112. Cf. David Punter's Kleinian analysis of Gothic fiction, relating it to the fear of change engendered by the Industrial Revolution: 'Narrative and Psychology in Gothic Fiction', in Graham (ed.), *Gothic Fictions*, pp. 1–27; and Robert Miles, 'Europhobia', chapter 5 in Horner (ed.), *European Gothic*.
113. 'Miss' Pilkington's *The Accusing Spirit* (1802) has been recognised as a novel of ideas where 'the Protestant champion of Calvinistic principles ... liberates the mind of his beloved ... from its prison of Catholic beliefs' (Frank 332).
114. *The Romantic Novel in England* (Cambridge, Mass.: Harvard University Press, 1972), p. 32.
115. Joel Porte, 'In the Hands of an Angry God: Religious Terror in Gothic Fiction', in G. R. Thompson (ed.), *The Gothic Imagination* (Pullman, Wash.: Washington State University Press, 1974), pp. 42–64.
116. Cf. Tarr, *Catholicism in Gothic Fiction*, pp. 21–2, 30, 53.
117. Ed Ingebretsen's *Maps of Heaven, Maps of Hell* (New York: M. A. Sharpe, 1996), discusses American Gothic as 'unspeakable' religious discourse. Recounting an exchange with a Christian student on ideas of the Gothic, Nicholas Royle comments on the present-day incompatibility of religious discourse with academic, and remarks: 'No doubt from different perspectives religion may be uncanny for a so-called non-believer (such as Freud claimed to be) just as non-belief may be uncanny for a so-called believer': *The Uncanny*, p. 36 (see also pp. 20–2, 35).

2. ANTI-POPERY AND THE SUPERNATURAL

1. I am grateful to Alexandra Walsham for her detailed and insightful comments on an earlier, unpublished version of this chapter, and for engaging in creative dialogue with it in her article 'Reformed Folklore? Cautionary Tales and Oral Tradition in Early Modern England', chapter 6 in Adam Fox and Daniel Woolf (eds.), *The Spoken Word* (Manchester: Manchester University Press, 2002).
2. 'The English Reformation and the Evidence of Folklore', *P & P*, 148 (1995), pp. 89–116.

3. On common problems with the folkloric approach, see Daniel Woolf, *The Social Circulation of the Past* (Oxford: Oxford University Press, 2003), chapter 9.
4. For a recent reconsideration of 'superstition' in early modern Europe, see Helen Parish and William G. Naphy (eds.), *Religion and Superstition in Reformation Europe* (Manchester: Manchester University Press, 2002); for the view that Catholic and Protestant attempts to dissuade people from superstition were differently implemented, see Euan Cameron, 'For Reasoned Faith or Embattled Creed? Religion for the People in Early Modern Europe', *Transactions of the Royal Historical Society*, 6th ser., 8 (1998), pp. 165–87. See also Natalie Zemon Davis, 'Some Tasks and Themes in the Study of Popular Religion', in Charles Trinkaus and Heiko A. Oberman (eds.), *The Pursuit of Holiness in Late Medieval and Renaissance Religion* (Leiden: E. J. Brill, 1974), pp. 307–36, and William Monter, *Ritual, Myth and Magic in Early Modern Europe* (Brighton: Harvester, 1983), chapter 7. Cameron and Davis critique the view of a magical peasant culture impervious to religious reform, articulated by Jean Delumeau in *Le Catholicisme Entre Luther et Voltaire* (Paris: Presses Universitaires de France, 1971), and the related tendency to define popular religion primarily in terms of deviation. On Counter-Reformation missionary attempts to meet the unlearned half-way, see David Gentilcore, '"Adapt Yourself to the People's Capabilities": Missionary Strategies, Methods and Impact in the Kingdom of Naples, 1600–1800', *JEH*, 45:2 (1994), pp. 269–96, and Trevor Johnson, 'Blood, Tears and Xavier-Water: Jesuit Missionaries and Popular Religion in the 18th-Century Upper Palatinate', chapter 9 in Bob Scribner and Trevor Johnson (eds.), *Popular Religion in Germany and Central Europe, 1400–1800* (Basingstoke: Macmillan, 1996). On rural missions more generally, see Louis Chatellier, *The Religion of the Poor* (1993: trans. Brian Pearce, Cambridge: Cambridge University Press, 1997), and R. Po-Chia Hsia, *The World of Catholic Renewal 1540–1770* (Cambridge: Cambridge University Press, 1998), pp. 200–1.
5. See below, p. 69.
6. Edmund Campion, *Two Bokes of the Histories of Ireland*, ed. A. F. Vossen (Assen: Van Gorcum, 1963), pp. 46–50; and A. C. Southern, *Elizabethan Recusant Prose* (this edn London: Sands & Co., 1950), pp. 294–7 (quotation p. 296).
7. Camden, *Britain* (1610 edn), section on Ireland, p. 116. Occasionally this could be complicated by mythological interpolation from an elite source. Still describing St Patrick's Purgatory, Camden complained that it was 'much spoken of, by reason of, I wot not what fearefull walking spirits, and dreadfull apparitions, or rather some religious horrour: Which cave, as some dream ridiculously, was digged by Ulisses, when hee went downe to parlee with those in hell' (p. 116). See Robert Easting (ed.), *St. Patrick's Purgatory. Two Versions*, EETS 298 (Oxford: Oxford University Press, 1991), introduction.
8. Cf. D. R. Woolf, '"The Common Voice": History, Folklore and Oral Tradition in Early Modern England', *P & P*, 120 (1988), pp. 26–52, revised as chapter 10 in *The Social Circulation of the Past* (Oxford: Oxford University Press, 2003). Woolf identifies a growing division between learned and popular views of the past during the seventeenth century in England.

9. *Satans Invisible World Discovered* (1685), pp. 22–3.
10. See Gillian Bennett, *Traditions of Belief* (Harmondsworth: Penguin, 1987), p. 149.
11. As Diane Purkiss comments, this type of appropriation supported the reformers' assertion that the Mass was nothing but hocus-pocus: *Troublesome Things* (London: Penguin, 2000), pp. 130–1.
12. *The Stripping of the Altars* (New Haven: Yale University Press, 1992), pp. 278 (quotation), 283, 285 (on the distinction made in the *Malleus Maleficarum* between legitimate and illegitimate uses of charms). On folk healers and magical cures in medieval and early modern Europe, see also Stephen Wilson, *The Magical Universe* (London: Hambledon, 2000), chapter 13. On charms, see Jonathan Roper (ed.), *Charms and Charming in Europe* (Basingstoke: Palgrave, 2004), and Thomas A. Forbes, 'Verbal Charms in British Folk Medicine', *Proceedings of the American Philosophical Society*, 115:4 (1971), pp. 293–316.
13. See Valerie Flint, *The Rise of Magic in Medieval Europe* (Oxford: Clarendon, 1991), chapter 11; and (for a slightly unsympathetic view) Thomas, *Religion*, chapter 2.
14. Valerie Flint has argued that the church conducted prolonged negotiations with the proponents of pagan cults to bring about an 'enduring fusion of religious sensibilities' and consolidate its position: *Rise of Magic*, p. 407.
15. See Robert W. Scribner, 'The Reformation, Popular Magic and the "Disenchantment of the World"', reprinted as chapter 9 in Scott Dixon (ed.), *The German Reformation* (Oxford: Blackwell, 1999); Cameron, 'For Reasoned Faith?', p. 171.
16. Cf. the introduction to Elizabeth Mazzola, *The Pathology of the English Renaissance* (Leiden: E. J. Brill, 1998).
17. See Introduction, pp. 3–7, and Eamon Duffy, *The Voices of Morebath* (New Haven: Yale University Press, 2001), on the retention of traditional ritual.
18. Hutton, 'English Reformation', pp. 96–8.
19. J. C. H. Aveling comments that there is no clear connection between Catholicism and offenders presented for casting spells, crossing, bell-ringing and rush-bearing: 'Catholic Households in Yorkshire, 1580–1603', *Northern History*, 10 (1980), pp. 83–101 (esp. p. 95). On 'reformed' adaptations of earlier Catholic charms, see Scribner, 'Reformation'.
20. 'The Winnowing of White Witchcraft', [early seventeenth century], BL, MS Sloane 1954, pp. 3–4. I am grateful to Arnold Hunt for this reference.
21. Anthony Kenny (ed.), *The Responsa Scholarum of the English College, Rome. Part I: 1598–1621*, Catholic Record Society, vol. 54 (London: CRS, 1962), under 16 October 1607.
22. Cf. Richard Leighton Greene, *The Early English Carols* (2nd edn Oxford: Clarendon, 1977), p. cxxxi.
23. On contemporary representations of the Black Mass, see Stuart Clark, *Thinking With Demons* (Oxford: Clarendon, 1997), pp. 14–15, 18, 89, 139–41, 352, 426–7.

24. On the devil's abuse of pious prayers, see Clark, *Thinking*, p. 86.
25. From the definition of 'charm' in Rossell Hope Robbins, *The Encyclopaedia of Witchcraft and Demonology* (London: Peter Nevill, 1959).
26. From the examination of Anne Whittle, alias Chattox, in Thomas Potts, *The Wonderfull Discoverie of Witches in the County of Lancaster* (1613), fols. E2b–3a. See also Margo Todd, *The Culture of Protestantism in Early Modern Scotland* (New Haven: Yale University Press, 2002), p. 356.
27. See Thomas, *Religion*, pp. 31–2, 58–67. On Catholic sacramentalia, see also Cameron, 'For Reasoned Faith?', p. 173.
28. Cf. Ronald Hutton, *The Pagan Religions of the Ancient British Isles* (Oxford: Blackwell, 1991), p. 290: '. . . magic did a lot of the work later taken over by pharmaceutical medicine, fertilisers, insurance schemes and advertisement columns. Those practising it were generally devout Christians and saw charms and rituals in the same functional sense as these modern commodities and services.'
29. John Aubrey, *Three Prose Works*, ed. John Buchanan-Brown (Fontwell: Centaur Press, 1972), p. 86.
30. On the altar-controversy, see Anthony Milton, *Catholic and Reformed* (Cambridge: Cambridge University Press, 1995), esp. pp. 204–5.
31. This has been intensively discussed. See (e.g.) David Underdown, *Revel, Riot and Rebellion* (Oxford: Oxford University Press: this edn 1987); Leah Marcus, *The Politics of Mirth* (Chicago: University of Chicago Press, 1986).
32. Marcus, *Politics*, p. 14.
33. For details of when Herrick wrote his verse and of his probable audience, see the introduction to L. C. Martin's edition (Oxford: Clarendon, 1956). Herrick's most recent scholarly editor has said that 'his reputation before 1648 [the publication date of *Hesperides*] rested almost entirely on manuscripts' (*The Complete Poetry of Robert Herrick*, ed. J. Max Patrick (New York: New York University Press, 1963), p. xi). Martin points to the fact that, in the early nineteenth century, Herrick's verse had become part of oral tradition around his Devonshire parish (p. xix). Marcus, *Politics*, chapter 5, links Herrick's views on the efficacy of traditional pastimes to the struggle to preserve feudalism. In that she argues for Herrick's elision of the cultural boundaries between paganism and Christianity, and the medieval and post-Reformation churches (p. 158), her emphasis differs from my own; though, as Achsah Guibbory has commented, 'the pagan shares space with the Christian' in *Hesperides* (*Ceremony and Community from Herbert to Milton* (Cambridge: Cambridge University Press, 1998), p. 83).
34. Transcription taken from Jane Stevenson and Peter Davidson (eds.), *Early Modern Women Poets* (Oxford: Oxford University Press, 2001), no. 91 (from BL, MS Lansdowne 231, in John Aubrey's autograph). As they comment, the survival of later versions suggests that it remained in oral circulation long after the early seventeenth century. Another edition of the Dirge can be found in 'Remaines' (in John Buchanan-Brown (ed.), *John Aubrey. Three Prose Works* (Fontwell: Centaur Press, 1972), pp. 177–8). For commentary on it, see Peter Marshall,

Beliefs and the Dead in Reformation England (Oxford: Oxford University Press, 2002), pp. 138–9.
35. See Marcus, *Politics*, p. 289.
36. I am grateful to Kate Bennett for making this point. However, on Aubrey's positive views about medieval England and general distrust of religious controversy, see Michael Hunter, *John Aubrey and the Realm of Learning* (London: Duckworth, 1975), pp. 40, 176, 215–17 (also chapter 4 for an account of Aubrey's methods of recording). Aubrey confessed that his antiquarian interests had been partly stimulated by old people's reminiscences of the Catholic past: 'I was always enquiring of my grandfather of the old time, the rood-loft, etc., ceremonies, of the priory, etc.' (*Brief Lives*, ed. Andrew Clark, 2 vols. (Oxford: Clarendon, 1898), vol. I, p. 36).
37. Subsequently re-edited by John Brand (1777), Sir Henry Ellis (1st edn 1813) and W. C. Hazlitt (1st edn 1870). See David Vincent, *Literacy and Popular Culture* (Cambridge: Cambridge University Press, 1989), p. 6; Richard M. Dorson, *The British Folklorists* (London: Routledge, 1968), chapter 1.
38. Cf. Ronald Hutton's discussion of Bourne's preface, which comments that, if Bourne's attitude was typical of an earlier generation of reformers, they should be congratulated for displaying a 'canny sense of priorities': 'English Reformation' (quotation p. 116). This may be a difficult argument to pursue: partly because it underplays the high level of generalised suspicion expressed in polemicists' writing, partly because the eighteenth century tended to be more eirenical than the centuries preceding.
39. One possible rival, Sir Thomas Browne's *Pseudodoxia Epidemica*, includes criticism of idolatry 'in some Christian Churches, wherein is presumed an irreproveable truth, if all be true that is suspected, or halfe what is related, there have not wanted, many strange deceptions, and some thereof are still confessed by the name of Pious frauds' (quoted from the edition of Browne's *Works* by Robin Robbins, 2 vols. (Oxford: Clarendon, 1981), vol. I, p. 19). See Walsham, 'Reformed Folklore?'.
40. For the latter, see Thomas Ady, *A Candle in the Dark* (1656: collection of charms on pp. 55–9).
41. For Catholic prophecy in early modern England, see Alexandra Walsham, *Providence in Early Modern England* (Oxford: Oxford University Press, 1999), chapter 4; Howard Dobin, *Merlin's Disciples* (Stanford: Stanford University Press, 1990), pp. 39–41, 52, 108–10; Janet Cooper, 'A Royal Imposter (*sic*) in Elizabethan Essex', in Kenneth Neale (ed.), *Essex 'Full of Profitable Thinges'* (Oxford: Leopard's Head Press, 1996), pp. 137–48. For a specific example of an Elizabethan Catholic prophecy, see *CSPD*, Addenda (1580–1625), vol. 28, item 58. For Sir John Harington's comment that Catholics were thought to be more credulous about prophecies than Protestants, see Jason Scott-Warren, *Sir John Harington and the Book as Gift* (Oxford: Oxford University Press, 2001), p. 169; for an example of the polemical link between Catholics and prophesying, see Edward Topsell, *Times Lamentation* (1st edn 1599), p. 63. For general studies

of the early modern prophecy, see also Rupert Taylor, *The Political Prophecy in England* (New York: Columbia University Press, 1911); Thomas, *Religion*, esp. chapters 5, 13.
42. *Policy and Police* (Cambridge: Cambridge University Press, 1972), p. 46 (and chapter 2 generally).
43. On post-Reformation English Catholic prophets and visionaries, see Alexandra Walsham, 'Miracles and the Counter-Reformation Mission to England', *HJ*, 46:4 (2003), pp. 779–815, esp. 805–9.
44. On moldwarps, see Dobin, *Merlin's Disciples*, p. 40; Elton, *Policy and Police*, pp. 59–60, 72; Taylor, *Political Prophecy*, p. 50. On prophecy in the 1530s, see Ethan H. Shagan, 'Rumours and Popular Politics in the Reign of Henry VIII', in Tim Harris (ed.), *The Politics of the Excluded, ca. 1500–1850* (Basingstoke: Palgrave, 2001), chapter 1 (esp. pp. 41–2, 63).
45. *Merlin's Disciples*, p. 41.
46. Garrett Mattingley, *The Defeat of the Spanish Armada* (London: Jonathan Cape, 1959), chapter 15; Dobin, *Merlin's Disciples*, pp. 107–10.
47. BL MS Lansdowne 50, item 77, printed in *The Reliquary*, II (1861), pp. 198–9. For the 'Cock of the North', see Taylor, *Political Prophecy*, pp. 56–8, 109, 111–12. For another example of how possessing prophecies could be incorporated into charges of subversive Catholic activity, see *CSPD* Elizabeth (1581–90), vol. 151, item 44 (the Earl of Oxford's accusations concerning Charles Arundel and Arundel's answers).
48. BL MS Lansdowne 96, item 44: printed in Douglas Gray, *Themes and Images in the Medieval English Religious Lyric* (London: Routledge & Kegan Paul, 1972), p. 164. The transcription below is based on Gray's. A version of the spell is quoted at the trial of James Device: see Potts, *Wonderfull Discoverie*, fols. K1b–2a. For a pre-Reformation occurrence, see W. Sparrow-Simpson, 'On a Magical Roll Preserved at the British Museum', *Journal of the British Archaeological Association*, 48 (1892), pp. 38–54.
49. Another version is quoted in J. Harland and T. T. Wilkinson, *Lancashire Folk-Lore* (London: Heywood, 1882), p. 73, as 'a charm to get drink within one hour'. The word 'spell', which seems so obviously occult to the twenty-first-century reader, is the victim of a semantic shift, though one which occurred for reasons that must have included the polemical. The primary medieval sense of 'spell' is that of discourse, only secondarily with the sense of idle talk. Of the examples given in the online *Oxford English Dictionary* (accessed May 2006), there are none between the 1500s and 1579. Its first post-Reformation quotation is also the first where the word clearly refers to a formula possessing magical powers: suggestively enough, in the modernised medievalism of E. K.'s glosses to *The Shepheardes Calender*. 'Spell is a kinde of verse or charme, that in elder tymes they used often to say over every thing, that they would have preserved ... And herehence I thinke is named the gospell, as it were Gods spell or worde' (quoted from Edmund Spenser, *Shorter Poems*, ed. William A. Oram *et al.* (New Haven: Yale University Press, 1989), pp. 63–4 (March, gloss to line 54)).

The examples of the earlier meaning of 'spell' given for 1612, 1617 and 1653 all prefix 'good' or 'holy' to it, suggesting that by this stage the pejorative meaning was primary.

50. Cf. Miles Mosse, *Justifying and Saving Faith* (1614), p. 14: 'My selfe did once know an aged and impotent woman, so silly as she was not able to give any reasonable account of her faith, and therefore no likelihood that she should be indued with a miraculous faith: who notwithstanding only with a cleane linnen cloth, and a short praier in the form of a riming spell, by blessing the sore part, cured manifold diseases, creeples, lazers, ulcers, fistulaes, numnes, lamenes, and what not? The whole countrie sought to her as a pettie God: but I verily beleeve, that though the cures were temporarily good to those that enjoyed the[m], yet they were all wrought by the power of the Devill.'

51. Quoted from John Bale, *Complete Plays*, ed. Peter Happé, 2 vols. (Cambridge: D. S. Brewer, 1986), vol. II, 'Three Laws of Nature', lines 409–24.

52. *The Tavistocke Naboth proved Nabal* (1658), p. 40; see Mrs G. H. Radford, 'Thomas Larkham', *Transactions of the Devonshire Association*, 24 (1892), pp. 96–146, esp. pp. 132–3. On Larkham's career, see his entry in *ODNB*.

53. Cf. John Holloway (ed.), *The Oxford Book of Local Verse* (Oxford: Oxford University Press, 1987), no. 144.

54. *Tavistocke Naboth*, pp. 40–1. For a contrasting – and more mainstream – puritan attack on the idea that words had an intrinsic power, see William Perkins, *A Discourse of the Damned Art of Witchcraft* (1st edn 1608), pp. 134–8.

55. *Anatomie of Abuses* (1583), ff. M3b–4a; see Marcus, *Politics*, p. 151, and Patrick Collinson, 'Elizabethan and Jacobean Puritanism as Forms of Popular Culture', pp. 32–57 in Christopher Durston and Jacqueline Eales (eds.), *The Culture of English Puritanism, 1560–1700* (Basingstoke: Macmillan, 1996), pp. 35–6, 57.

56. It was available to Lambarde only from oral sources: he comments, 'Althoughe I have not hytherto at any time, read any memorable thing recorded in hystorie, touching Chetham it self yet . . . I have often heard (and that consta[n]tly) reported, a Popish illusion done at the place . . .' (p. 286), and again, 'This tale, receaved by tradition from the Elders, was (long since) both commonly reported & faithfully credited of the vulgar sort: which although happely you shal not at this day learne at every mans mouth (the Image being now many yeres sithe[n]ce defaced) yet many of the aged number remember it well, and in the time of darkeness, *Hæc erat in toto notissima fabula mundo*' (p. 287). Cf. Walsham, 'Reformed Folklore?'; Margaret Aston, *England's Iconoclasts*, vol. I (Oxford: Oxford University Press, 1988), pp. 234, 247–8; and Woolf, '"Common Voice"', p. 34, who discusses Lambarde's recording of popish impieties.

57. In *The Natural History of Staffordshire* (1686) Robert Plot concludes – probably ironically – that if there is any truth in the tradition that fairy rings are caused by the dances of witches and supernatural beings, it can be so only where the grass is worn away, rather than where it is green (pp. 9–14).

58. Woolf, '"Common Voice"', p. 31. See also Keith Thomas, *The Perception of the Past in Early Modern England* (London: University of London Press, 1983), pp. 3–9; Jacqueline Simpson, 'Beyond Etiology: Interpreting Local Legends',

Fabula, 24:3/4 (1983), pp. 223–32; Vincent, *Literacy*, pp. 180–1; Flint, *Rise of Magic*, pp. 204–9; and Kent C. Ryden, *Mapping the Invisible Landscape* (Iowa City: University of Iowa Press, 1993), p. 26 and chapter 2.

59. Cf. Jacqueline Simpson, 'God's Visible Judgements: The Christian Dimension to Landscape Legends', *Landscape History*, 8 (1986), pp. 53–7, and 'The Local Legend: A Product of Popular Culture', *Rural History*, 2:1 (1991), pp. 25–35.

60. On attitudes towards holy wells, see Alexandra Walsham, 'Reforming the Waters: Holy Wells and Healing Springs in Protestant England', in Diana Wood (ed.), *Life and Thought in the Northern Church, c.1100–c.1700* (Woodbridge: Boydell/Ecclesiastical History Society, 1999), pp. 227–55, and 'Holywell: Contesting Sacred Space in Post-Reformation Wales', chapter 11 in Will Coster and Andrew Spicer (eds.), *Sacred Space in Early Modern Europe* (Cambridge: Cambridge University Press, 2005). Professor Walsham is currently engaged on a full-length study of holy wells. James Rattue, *The Living Stream* (Woodbridge: Boydell, 1995), chapter 7, suggests that, though there was a decline in many well-cults after the Reformation, they tended to be ignored by puritan reformers (cf. note 38 above). However, other natural features could be mutilated by puritans: for the story of the Glastonbury Thorn, see John Collinson, *The History and Antiquities of the County of Somerset*, 3 vols. (1791), vol. I, p. 265, and Alexandra Walsham, 'The Holy Thorn of Glastonbury: The Evolution of a Legend in Post-Reformation England', *Parergon*, 21 (2004), pp. 1–26.

61. Sir John Maclean (ed.), *The Berkeley Manuscripts . . . With a Description of the Hundred of Berkeley*, 3 vols. (Gloucester: John Bellows, 1883–5), vol. III, pp. 371–2. Smyth's MS was finished in 1605. Rattue, *Living Stream*, gives the correct derivation of 'Wanswell' (p. 41). Woden is a god, not a goddess; though this seems to be a genuine confusion rather than an attempt to tap into anti-Marian prejudice, a female dedicatee would have reminded the reader of the many wells throughout Britain which carried dedications to Mary or female saints.

62. See Conclusion, esp. pp. 154–5.

63. *The Bible and Reason* (Philadelphia: University of Pennsylvania Press, 1985), pp. 41–2.

64. This is to be distinguished from using the notion of tradition to assert that illiterates can be saved: see Conclusion, esp. p. 165.

65. On Jackson, see S. Mutchow Towers, *Control of Religious Printing in Early Stuart England*, Studies in Early Modern British History, vol. 8 (Woodbridge: Boydell, 2003), chapter 2; and Sarah Hutton, 'Thomas Jackson, Oxford Platonist, and William Twisse, Aristotelean', *Journal of the History of Ideas*, 39:4 (1978), pp. 635–52. I am grateful to the late Jeremy Maule for the latter reference, and to Professor Hutton for discussions about Jackson's *Treatise*; the following paragraphs incorporate several of her insights. On Jackson and idolatry, see also Reid Barbour, *Literature and Religious Culture in Seventeenth-Century England* (Cambridge: Cambridge University Press, 2002), p. 185.

66. Numbers 22–3 (text quoted, 23:27).

67. See also Richard Bovet, *Pandaemonium* (1684), pp. 37–8, 41.

68. On Herbert Spencer's notion of 'indwelling souls' as a phase in elementary religious development, see Malcolm Hamilton, *The Sociology of Religion* (London: Routledge, 1995), pp. 23–4. Much of the debate described above and below anticipates notions of animism, a term first used in 1886 (*OED*).
69. The marigold was one of many flowers linked to late-medieval cults of Mary: see Jack Goody, *The Culture of Flowers* (Cambridge: Cambridge University Press, 1993), p. 156. Jackson's definition problematises commonplace definitions such as that in Robert Turner, *Botanologia* (1687 edn), f. a2a, which compares the heliotrope turning with the sun to subjects obeying their sovereign. The heliotrope might have been seen as especially popish after its popularisation as an emblem for free will in Jeremias Drexelius's *Heliotropium seu Conformatio Humanae Voluntatis cum Divina* (1st edn 1627).
70. See (e.g.) Thomas Adams, *Works* (1630), fols. 15a–b.
71. Henry Vaughan's hieroglyphic perception of nature had the effect of privileging the learned: see Marcus, *Politics*, pp. 222, 226 (discussing his poem 'Regeneration'). One of the greatest losses which mankind sustained through Adam's fall was thought to be a loss of knowledge of the herbal world: see William Coles, *Adam in Eden* (1657), introduction, and John Parkinson, *Paradisi in Sole* (1629), p. 3. A distinction is sometimes made between similitudes, which were of moral usefulness, and signatures, which were held to explain plants' physical efficacy; but more often, the two appear to be used interchangeably. For a definition of signatures, see Coles, *ibid.*, f. a4a: 'Books out of which the Ancients first learned the Vertues of Herbes; Nature or rather the God of nature, having stamped on divers of them legible characters to discover their uses.'
72. Goody, *Culture of Flowers*, esp. p. 156. In a review of the book, James Fenton makes some important qualifications to Goody's argument (*Times Literary Supplement*, 17 September 1993).
73. Grigson further comments how pious names could be used as an alternative to occult ones: *The Englishman's Flora* (London: Hart-Davis, 1958; this edn 1975), pp. 146–9. These flower names probably owe something to the invention of tradition, but can nevertheless be paralleled in the usage of early modern botanists such as Nicholas Culpeper (see below, p. 73).
74. See 'St John's Wort', in Roy Vickery, *A Dictionary of Plant Lore* (Oxford: Oxford University Press, 1995). The plant flowers around the midsummer feast of St John the Baptist.
75. *The English Physitian Enlarged* (1656), p. 134.
76. Keith Thomas, *Man and the Natural World* (London: Allen Lane, 1983), pp. 78–82.
77. See Charlotte F. Otten, 'Milton's Haemony', *ELR*, 5 (1975), pp. 81–95.
78. *English Physitian Enlarged*, pp. 11–12. Culpeper is rewriting a more positive description in John Parkinson, *Theatrum Botanicum* (1640): 'This herbe hath gained many worthy names from sundry worthy persons: . . . but all in generall call it Angellica from the Angell-like properties therein. All these sorts are so

called by most Authors as their titles beare, . . . All Christian nations likewise in their appellations hereof follow the Latine name as neare as their Dialect will permit . . .' (p. 941). Cf. also Culpeper's *Pharmacopia Londiniensis* (1653 edn), p. 2.

79. *The History of the Royal Society*, ed. J. I. Cope and H. W. Jones (St Louis: Washington University Press, 1966), pp. 369–78 (quotation p. 371). The supposed association between Protestantism and empirical enquiry has often been challenged: for a recent contribution to the debate focusing on Catholic members of the Royal Society, see Leo Gooch, 'The Religion for a Gentleman: The Northern Catholic Gentry in the 18th Century', *Recusant History*, 23:4 (1997), pp. 543–68. For the shift away from tradition to empirical knowledge, see Thomas, *Religion*, pp. 509–14, 771–2, 793–4.

80. *The Printing Press as an Agent of Change*, 2 vols. (Cambridge: Cambridge University Press: this edn 1980), chapters 4 and 8 generally, and vol. 2, pp. 668–9.

81. M. T. Clanchy, *From Memory to Written Record* (2nd edn Oxford: Blackwell, 1993), pp. 226–34, explores the question of literacy among the medieval laity.

82. For a recent census of flowers mentioned in Greek literary texts, see John Raven, 'Plants and Plant Lore in Ancient Greece', *Annales Musei Goulandris*, 8 (1990), pp. 129–80, esp. pp. 159 ff.

83. *Way to the True Church*, fols. **8a. For vervain, see also Grigson, *Englishman's Flora*, pp. 336–9.

84. Purkiss, *Troublesome Things* and Regina Buccola, *Fairies, Fractious Women and the Old Faith* (Selingrove: Susquehanna University Press, 2006) both give full accounts of the British faery mythology. See also K. M. Briggs, *The Fairies in Tradition and Literature* (London: Routledge & Kegan Paul, 1967). Floris Delattre, *English Fairy Poetry* (London: Frowde, 1912), pp. 66, 71–4, lists literary equations of fairies with nymphs. See also Thomas Nashe, *Terrors of the Night* (1594), in *Works*, ed. R. B. McKerrow, 5 vols. (London: A. H. Bullen/Sidgwick & Jackson, 1904–10), vol. I, p. 347.

85. In 'Herrick's Fairy State', *ELH*, 46:1 (1979), pp. 35–55, Peter Schwenger distinguishes between three possible approaches: collecting and classifying information, and using popular myth to illuminate the nature of certain English social structures; an anthropological analysis of the faery kingdom itself, with its hierarchies, moral codes, customs and taboos; and exploiting literary works on fairies as 'storehouses of information about individual folk beliefs and often as conscious articulations of the fairy kingdom's nature as a whole' (p. 35). A seventeenth-century anticipation of this method is Robert Kirk, *The Secret Commonwealth of Elves and Fairies* (1691–2), ed. Stewart Sanderson (Cambridge: D. S. Brewer for the Folklore Society, 1976); see also the discussion of Hobbes below. Schwenger's comment that faery lore deserves a thorough anthropological analysis still holds good, since Purkiss's *Troublesome Things* is more psychoanalytical than anthropological in approach, while Buccola's *Fairies, Fractious Women . . .* is literary in focus.

86. *Three Treatises Concerning Wales*, intro. David Williams (Cardiff: University of Wales Press, 1960), pp. 32–3.
87. Abbey-lubbers were minor devils who tempted monks to drunkenness, gluttony and lasciviousness. See Katherine Briggs, *A Dictionary of Fairies* (Harmondsworth: Penguin, 1977), p. 1.
88. *A Discorsive Probleme Concerning Prophesies* (1588), pp. 68–9, quoted by Adam Fox, 'Aspects of Oral Culture and its Development in Early Modern England', Cambridge PhD thesis, 1993, p. 332 (see also p. 333).
89. *The Discoverie of Witchcraft* (1st edn 1584), ed. Brinsley Nicholson (Wakefield: EP Publishing, 1973), heading to chapter 4.
90. On Renaissance faery literature, see Warren W. Wooden, *Children's Literature of the English Renaissance*, ed. Jeanie Watson (Lexington: Kentucky University Press, 1986), chapters 6–7, and Agnes W. Latham, *The Elizabethan Fairies* (1936: repr. New York: Octagon, 1972). On faery lore in *A Midsummer Night's Dream*, see Mary Ellen Lamb, 'Taken by the Fairies: Fairy Practices and the Production of Popular Culture in *A Midsummer Night's Dream*', *Shakespeare Quarterly*, 51:3 (2000), pp. 277–312.
91. *Albion's England* (1606: revised and enlarged edition, 1612). This seems the best explanation of the 'perverseness' which Sukanta Chaudhuri identifies in the poem: *Renaissance Pastoral and its English Developments* (Oxford: Clarendon, 1989), p. 405. On the anti-Catholic satirical use of fairies, see Reid Barbour, *English Epicures and Stoics* (Amherst: University of Massachussetts Press, 1998), pp. 45–6.
92. Quoted from Spenser, *Shorter Poems*, ed. Oram *et al.*, p. 115 (June, gloss to line 25). See Evelyn B. Tribble, *Margins and Marginality* (Charlottesville: University of Virginia Press, 1993), pp. 79–80. For a late seventeenth-century expression of similar sentiments, see John Oldham, *Poems*, ed. Harold F. Brooks and Raman Selden (Oxford: Clarendon, 1987), Satire 3, lines 327–32 (p. 35).
93. See definitions in *OED*.
94. At South Kyme, Lincolnshire, in 1601, an anticlerical dramatic presentation was held including an episode where a mock minister read from the Book of Mab, Queen of the Fairies: see Adam Fox, 'Religious Satire in English Towns, 1570–1640', chapter 13 in Patrick Collinson (ed.), *The Reformation in English Towns* (Basingstoke: Macmillan, 1998), pp. 226–7. Fairies often featured in subversive quasi-dramatic activity; for transvestite and other 'fairy' riots, see Natalie Zemon Davis, 'Women On Top: Sexual Inversion and Political Disorder in Early Modern Europe', chapter 5 in Barbara Babcock (ed.), *The Reversible World* (Ithaca: Cornell University Press, 1978).
95. Quoted from *The Poems of Richard Corbett*, ed. J. A. W. Bennett and H. R. Trevor-Roper (Oxford: Clarendon Press, 1955), pp. 49–52. Purkiss, *Troublesome Things*, pp. 183–5, discusses Herrick's and Corbett's use of Catholic fairies; Regina Buccola's *Fairies, Fractious Women . . .*, which appeared just as this book was about to go to press, undertakes a full-length exploration of the link between Catholics and fairies at this date. Thomas Percy notes the similarity

between Corbett's poem and Chaucer's 'Wife of Bath's Tale': see *Reliques of Ancient English Poetry*, 3 vols. (1886 edn, repr. New York: Dover, 1966), vol. 3, pp. 207–8. The most extensive discussion of the poem to date is M. E. Bradford, 'The Prescience of Richard Corbet: Observations on "The Fairies' Farewell"', *Sewanee Review*, 81:2 (1973), pp. 309–17; see also Philip J. Finkelpearl, 'The Fairies' Farewell: *The Masque at Coleorton* (1618)', *RES*, 46:183 (1995), pp. 333–51, which comments on how both masque and poem show fairies driven into hiding by Puritans, and points out that Corbett visited Coleorton (p. 339).

96. Quotations taken from *Leviathan*, ed. Richard Tuck (Cambridge: Cambridge University Press, 1991), pp. 481–2. The passage is discussed by Quentin Skinner in *Reason and Rhetoric in the Philosophy of Hobbes* (Cambridge: Cambridge University Press, 1996), pp. 399–400. Cf. Samuel Harsnet, *A Declaration of Egregious Popish Impostures* (1603 edn.), p. 134.
97. *Reliques of Ancient English Poetry*, 3 vols. (London, 1765), vol. III, p. 201.
98. *A True Relation* (1601), p. 18, cited by Ronald Hutton, *The Rise and Fall of Merry England* (Oxford: Oxford University Press, 1994), p. 128.
99. Aubrey, *Three Prose Works*, ed. Buchanan-Brown, preface to 'Remaines of Gentilisme and Judaisme', p. 132.
100. *Miracles Lately Wrought by the Intercession of the Glorious Virgin Marie, at Mont-aigu* (1606), f. C2a.
101. See Thomas Lodge, *The Divel Conjured* (1596), f. H1b; Colm Lennon, *Richard Stanihurst the Dubliner, 1547–1618* (Dublin: Irish Academic Press, 1981), pp. 77–8. On Campion's opinion, see above, p. 56.
102. Quoted from the edition of *The Hind and the Panther* in John Dryden, *Poems*, ed. Paul Hammond and David Hopkins (Harlow: Longman, 2000), vol. III, Part I, lines 212–18; Part 3, line 1053.
103. On old wives' tales, proverbially comparable with popery as demonstrating the weaknesses of oral tradition, see Adam Fox, *Oral and Literate Culture in England, 1500–1700* (Oxford: Clarendon, 2000), chapter 3.
104. All passages from *The Rape of the Lock* are quoted from *The Twickenham Edition of the Works of Alexander Pope*, general ed. John Butt, 11 vols. (London: this edn Routledge, 1993), vol. II (ed. Geoffrey Tillotson).
105. 27 August 1714: quoted from George Sherburn (ed.), *The Correspondence of Alexander Pope*, 5 vols. (Oxford: Clarendon, 1956), vol. I, pp. 246–7. See Twickenham edn, pp. 103–4, concerning the February–March publication dates of the 1714 edition of *The Rape of the Lock*.
106. The families concerned in the incident which inspired the poem, the Fermors, Petres and Carylls, formed part of the group of intermarried Catholic families in whose circle Pope moved. See Twickenham edn, vol. II, pp. 81–105.
107. *Literary Hours or Sketches Critical and Narrative* (1798), pp. 88–9.
108. See, most recently, Kristen Poole, *Radical Religion from Shakespeare to Milton* (Cambridge: Cambridge University Press, 2000), introduction.

3. ANSWERING BACK: ORALITY AND CONTROVERSY

1. Bod MS Rawl. D. 10, ff. 134b–135a: discussed and quoted on p. 340 of Phebe Jensen, 'Ballads and Brags: Free Speech and Recusant Culture in Elizabethan England', *Criticism*, 40:3 (1998), pp. 333–54.
2. See chapter 1 above. Thomas Larkham (discussed above, p. 67), with other preachers who condemned superstition in sermons, may be a partial exception to this rule.
3. On the use of metre as an aid to memorisation, see Daniel Woolf, 'Memory and Historical Culture in Early Modern England', *Journal of the Canadian Historical Association*, n.s. 2 (1991), pp. 283–308 (esp. p. 292), and his *The Social Circulation of the Past* (Oxford: Oxford University Press, 2003), p. 265.
4. See (e.g.) the discussion of William Fulke's annotations to the Rheims New Testament in Evelyn B. Tribble, *Margins and Marginality* (Charlottesville: Virginia University Press, 1993), chapter 1.
5. Tribble, *Margins*, introduction (esp. p. 6), emphasises the fluidity of marginalia in respect to the text proper.
6. 'Ballads and Brags', p. 333. On toleration, see (most recently) Alexandra Walsham, *A Charitable Hatred?* (Manchester: Manchester University Press, 2006). On the role of controversial interchange in conversion, see Michael Questier, *Conversion, Politics and Religion in England, 1580–1625* (Cambridge: Cambridge University Press, 1996), esp. chapter 2.
7. See Introduction, p. 12.
8. *Orality and Literacy*, pp. 43–4.
9. This point is expanded upon in Walter Ong, *The Presence of the Word* (New Haven: Yale University Press, 1967), esp. chapter 5 ('Polemic and the Word'), and 'Oral Residue in Tudor Prose Style', *PMLA*, 80 (1965), pp. 145–54.
10. Michael Questier has commented that patristic disputes were within laymen's capacities: *Conversion*, p. 14.
11. English translation, Cambridge University Press, Cambridge, 1990 (German original published by Wilhelm Fink, Munich, 1981).
12. Watt lists some manuscript ballads from Catholic collections in Appendix C to *Cheap Print*. For the relationship between manuscript culture and subversive discourse, see Harold Love, *The Culture and Commerce of Texts* (this edn Amherst: University of Massachusetts Press, 1993), esp. chapter 5.
13. Würzbach, *Rise*, appendix, gives an anthology of elite commentary on the form.
14. In *Cheap Print*, p. 3; not assumed in (e.g.) Würzbach, *Rise*, p. 234.
15. See Adam Fox, 'Popular Verses and their Readership in the Early 17th Century', chapter 7 in James Raven, Helen Small and Naomi Tadmor (eds.), *The Practice and Representation of Reading in England* (Cambridge: Cambridge University Press, 1996).
16. W. E. Richmond, *Ballad Scholarship* (New York: Garland, 1989), pp. xx–xxi, defines the genre as combining stanzaic form, frequently with refrains; light and heavy stresses within lines; for story-ballads, narrative concentration on a single episode (often *in medias res*); employment of dramatic conventions

17. See chapter 4, pp. 120–2.
18. E.g. John N. King, *English Reformation Literature* (Princeton: Princeton University Press, 1982); Alistair Fox, *Politics and Literature in the Court of Henry VII and Henry VIII* (Oxford: Basil Blackwell, 1989), chapter 12.
19. For Catholic ballads from the early years of the English Reformation, see Introduction, p. 16, and Adam Fox, 'Religious Satire in English Towns, 1570–1640', in Patrick Collinson and John Craig (eds.), *The Reformation in English Towns* (London: Macmillan, 1996), chapter 13.
20. 'The Conservative Voice in the English Reformation', chapter 6 in Simon Ditchfield (ed.), *Christianity and Community in the West* (Aldershot: Ashgate, 2001), quotation p. 90. Duffy identifies Mary I's reign as the time when a coherent public expression of opposition to the Reformation began to be forged. See also Introduction, p. 16.
21. Lucy Wooding sees the period between the 1530s and 1570s as characterised by uncertainty: *Rethinking Catholicism in Reformation England* (Oxford: Clarendon, 2000).
22. Lambeth Palace Library, MS 159, fols. 261–3. Partially quoted in Guiney, pp. 24–37 (quotation p. 33).
23. Guiney, *ibid.*; PRO, State Papers 12/16/49.1 (14 April 1561).
24. Transcription taken from Peter J. Seng (ed.), *Tudor Songs and Ballads from MS Cotton Vespasian A-25* (Cambridge, Mass.: Harvard University Press, 1978), item 4. This is a collection of manuscripts which came into the Cotton Library (and thence into the British Library) as an integral book in the early seventeenth century. Seng comments on the Catholic origins of much of its material, and identifies the poem as being copied in the same hand as another written 'perhaps as early as the end of the reign of Henry VIII' (pp. xiv–xv).
25. F. G. Emmison, *Elizabethan Life* (Chelmsford: Essex County Council, 1970), pp. 59–61, suggesting a date of composition in the 1570s. See the comments in Fox, 'Religious Satire', pp. 228–9, and Woolf, *Social Circulation*, p. 340.
26. On Catholicism in the first years of Elizabeth's reign, see Wooding, *Rethinking Catholicism*, chapter 6.
27. See Conclusion, p. 152.
28. Duffy, 'Conservative Voice', p. 103.
29. On early records of the tune, see Claude M. Simpson, *The British Broadside Ballad and its Music* (New Brunswick: Rutgers, 1966), pp. 741–3. On Sir Walter Ralegh's poem of the same name and metre, 'As you came from the holy land / Of Walsinghame', Helen Hackett comments that 'many scholars have reasonably assumed that [it] makes use of an established ballad dating from the years when the shrine was still in operation' and that the anonymous Catholic poem discussed above 'certainly' predates Ralegh's, which makes use of Catholic terminology to express allegiance to Elizabeth: *Virgin Mother, Maiden Queen* (Basingstoke: Macmillan, 1995), chapter 5, section vii (quotations pp. 156,

159). See also Sir Walter Ralegh, *Poems*, ed. Agnes M. C. Latham (London: Routledge, 1951), pp. 22–3, 120; Margaret Aston, *England's Iconoclasts*, vol. I (Oxford: Oxford University Press, 1988), p. 234.

30. The Fitzwilliam Virginal Book contains two sets of variations on the 'Walsingham' tune – one by Byrd, the other a series of variations by John Bull – as well as a number of other pieces by Byrd, and material betraying the compiler's close connections with English Catholic musicians on the Continent, such as Bull and Peter Phillips. See J. A. Fuller Maitland and W. Barclay Squire, rev. Blanche Winogron, *The Fitzwilliam Virginal Book*, 2 vols. (New York: Dover, 1979–80), vol. I, pp. 1–18 (Bull) and 267–73 (Byrd); and W. Gillies Whittaker, 'Byrd's and Bull's "Walsingham" Variations', *Music Review*, 3 (1942), pp. 270–9. Its traditional attribution to Francis Tregian has been effectively queried by Ruby Reid Thompson, 'The "Tregian" Manuscripts: A Study of Their Compilation', *British Library Journal*, 18:2 (1992), pp. 202–4; however, it does seem to have been compiled by a Catholic.
31. Bod Rawl. MS poet.219, f. 16a–b [compiled c.1600]; quoted from David Norbrook and H. R. Woudhuysen (eds.), *The Penguin Book of Renaissance Verse, 1509–1659* (London: Allen Lane, 1992), no. 250.
32. I am grateful to James Austen for his insightful comments on this passage.
33. The allusions are to Isaiah, chapter 13. Hackett observes that, though the manuscript miscellany in which the poem survives dates from c.1600, 'it must surely have been composed not long after the destruction of the shrine' (*Virgin Mother*, p. 159). See above, notes 29 and 31.
34. National Art Library, Victoria and Albert Museum, Dyce 25.F.40 (reproduced by kind permission of the Library trustees). I am grateful to Diane Spaul of the NAL for checking doubtful readings.
35. I.e. 'for laymen to suppress their priest'.
36. I.e. 'dragon'.
37. Ezekiel 38–9; Revelation 20:2, 7–8; cf. Amos 7:1.
38. Cf. the ballad at fols. 19b–21b of the same MS, which duplicates several of the references from this ballad and is probably by the same author. For the place of Jack Straw in popular cultural reference, see Dagmar Freist, *Governed by Opinion* (New York: I. B. Tauris, 1997), pp. 202–3.
39. Beinecke Library, Yale: MS Osborn a.18 (f. 12a). For the use of Piers Plowman as a spokesman for Wycliffite and puritan polemic, see David Norbrook, *Poetry and Politics in the English Renaissance* (London: Routledge, 1984), pp. 42–3, 46, 59–60, 292–3; for the polyvalent meanings of folk heroes, see Freist, *Governed by Opinion*, p. 210.
40. *Domination and the Arts of Resistance* (New Haven: Yale University Press, 1990). For twentieth-century analogues, see Alessandro Portelli, 'Uchronic Dreams: Working-Class Memory and Possible Worlds', chapter 10 in Raphael Samuel and Paul Thompson (eds.), *The Myths We Live By* (London: Routledge, 1990).
41. Isaiah 40:4; Luke 1:52.
42. See Robert Scribner, *For the Sake of Simple Folk* (Cambridge: Cambridge University Press, 1981), chapter 6.

43. David Kunzle, 'World Upside Down: The Iconography of an European Broadsheet Type', in Barbara A. Babcock (ed.), *The Reversible World* (Ithaca: Cornell University Press, 1978), pp. 39–94. Nevertheless, the first example of the motif he identifies in England is used by a conservative, John Taylor, in *Mad Fashions, Old Fashions* (1642), and it became commonplace in the royalist literature of the Civil Wars, which some of the Catholic ballads quoted below predate by several decades. On general notions of reversal in the Civil Wars, see Christopher Hill, *The World Turned Upside Down* (1st edn London: Maurice Temple Smith, 1972); and Nigel Smith, *Literature and Revolution in England, 1640–60* (New Haven: Yale University Press, 1994). Reversal has received its most extensive theoretical treatment in Mikhail Bakhtin's now familiar notion of 'carnival' and critical responses to it: see, for example, the special issues of *Critical Studies*, 3:2–4:1/2, on 'Bakhtin, Carnival and Other Subjects', ed. David Shepherd (Amsterdam: Rodopi, 1991).
44. Scott, *Domination*, pp. 169–71, drawing on Kunzle, 'World Upside Down'.
45. BL Add. MS 15,225 [described by the cataloguer as compiled during James I's reign but including earlier material].
46. 'The Great Hodge Podge', Lancashire Record Office, DDBL acc. 6121, fols. 137b–138a (quotations f. 137b). All quotations from 'The Great Hodge Podge' in this chapter and chapter 4 are reproduced by kind permission of the depositor and the County Archivist, Lancashire Record Office. Another contemporary text of the poem survives in BL Add. MS 6402, f. 120 (Cole collections). Margaret Sena discusses this ballad in 'William Blundell and the Networks of Catholic Dissent in Post-Reformation England', chapter 4 in Alexandra Shepard and Phil Withington (eds.), *Communities in Early Modern England* (Manchester: Manchester University Press, 2000), pp. 62–3. I am grateful to the author for sharing her transcriptions of Blundell's work with me, and have made extensive use of them. On the ballad, see also Woolf, *Social Circulation*, pp. 63, 339–40; on the Blundells, see also Frank Tymer, 'An Account of the Recusancy of the Blundell of Crosby Family, and the Inhabitants of Little Crosby in Lancashire', typescript, 3 vols., Lancashire Record Office, Preston (RCLa acc. 6361).
47. Cf. Richard Corbett's 'Fairies' Farewell': 'They never daunc'd on any heath / As when the Time hath bin' (*The Poems of Richard Corbett*, ed. J. A. W. Bennett and H. R. Trevor-Roper (Oxford: Clarendon Press, 1955), pp. 49–52, lines 31–2 quoted). See chapter 2, p. 77, and Sena, 'William Blundell', p. 63. Another possibility is that both Blundell and Corbett are employing a phrase commonly recognised as pro-Catholic.
48. On Catholic nostalgia, see Introduction, pp. 3–5.
49. BL Add. MS 15,225, f. 30a–b: the colons and full stops seem intended as caesuras. A poem in the same manuscript, 'Noe wight in this world that wealth can attaine . . .' (fols. 7b–9b), describes how the Golden Age was ruined by personal covetousness.
50. *Hospitality in Early Modern England* (Oxford: Clarendon, 1990), p. 169: see also Anna Bryson, *From Courtesy to Civility* (Oxford: Clarendon, 1998); Keith

Thomas, *The Perception of the Past in Early Modern England* (London: University of London Press, 1983), pp. 16–17; Woolf, *Social Circulation*, pp. 61–2; and, for another contemporary comment on Catholic liberality, Robert Southwell, *An Epistle of Comfort*, ed. Margaret Waugh (London: Burns & Oates, 1966), p. 106.

51. On the Catholic use of elegy, see my *Catholicism, Controversy and the English Literary Imagination, 1558–1660* (Cambridge: Cambridge University Press, 1999), pp. 175–81.
52. Gerald Bonner, *Saint Augustine of Hippo* (1963: 3rd edn Norwich: Canterbury Press, 2002), pp. 253–8. I am grateful to James Austen for this reference.
53. Anon., *Keepe Your Text* (1619), title page: discussed on p. 90 of Alexandra Walsham, '"Domme Preachers": Post-Reformation English Catholicism and the Culture of Print', *P & P*, 168 (2000), pp. 72–123. More imaginative work could also be used for this purpose: the sardonic annotations to the Catholic Piers Plowman text, quoted on p. 92, remark that it could be used as a means 'to instruct pap[is]ts how to answe[r] tratorooslye'.
54. The quotation above is taken from this edition. Allison and Rogers believe the verses are probably not by Martin (*ARCR* II, no. 516). See also Guiney, section XIV. On the headings to the poem's argument, cf. a similar Catholic polemical verse, in BL Add. MS 23,229 (fol. 82a–b), divided into sections headed 'Miracles', 'Antiquitie', 'Unitie', 'Univ[er]sall' and 'Succession'.
55. Jean Albin de Valsergues, *A Notable Discourse* (1575), appendix.
56. One rival is Richard White's Welsh versification of Robert Persons's *Brief Discourse Containing Certain Reasons Why Catholics Refuse To Go To Church*, transcribed in John Hungerford Pollen (ed.), *Unpublished Documents Relating to the English Martyrs, Vol. I, 1584–1603*, Catholic Record Society, vol. 5 (London: CRS, 1908), pp. 93–5.
57. *Reply to Fulke* (1580), f. A1a.
58. Previously attributed to Edward Rishton: see *ARCR* II, no. 877. For chronologies of the various versions of the *Articles*, Protestant answers and further responses from both sides, see A. C. Southern, *Elizabethan Recusant Prose* (this edn. London: Sands, [1950]), pp. 144–5, 519–23; Milward, pp. 40–1 (both addressing prose versions only). See also *ARCR* II, nos. 67–72 and 877 (the connection between prose and rhymed versions being made in the notes to the latter). The history of the manuscript circulation of the prose *Articles* deserves further study; Milward points out that, because of the diversity engendered by near-simultaneous printed versions circulating at the same time as an incalculable number of manuscript versions, not all printed answers can be taken as referring back to the same version of the *Articles*: a fact that should also be borne in mind when considering the rhymed versions. Different prose answers are also very differently targeted; for instance, the international scholarly audience is addressed for the first time only in 1608, with Thomas Worthington's two-volume edition of *Motiva Omnibus Catholicae Doctrinae . . . Pernecessaria*, a work which Bristow had left unfinished at his death in 1581. After his arrest, Campion may have been questioned on points drawn from Bristow's *Motives*:

see Richard Simpson, *Edmund Campion* (this edn London: John Hodges, 1896), p. 341.
59. See above, note 54.
60. *An Answere to a Popish Ryme, Lately Scattered Abroad in the West Parts* (1st edn 1604), f. A3a. This has the answer printed after the *Articles*, but the next edition of 1608 – presumably for greater ease of reference – alternates the text of the *Articles* with the answer in sections of two, three or more verses. Both editions rely heavily on marginal notes to emphasise or back up points made in the poem. Hieron's answer actually post-dates John Rhodes's (see below).
61. *Runne from Rome* (1640). This is the last given in *STC* (though Wing may contain others so far unidentified). The author is responding to the printed version: 'A Rayling pamphlet I have read, / In G. M. [i.e. Gregory Martin] his name abroad is spread . . .' (f. A3a).
62. See Milward, p. 41.
63. *An Answer to a Romish Rime Lately Printed* (1602), f. A2a. The title 'A Proper New Ballad . . .', not used in *The Love of the Soule*, may indicate a version aimed towards the cheap-print market which has not survived. For Catholic pedlars, see Introduction, pp. 16–17.
64. See Margaret Spufford, *Small Books and Pleasant Histories* (1st edn London: Methuen, 1981), pp. 10–11, and Alexandra Walsham, '"Domme Preachers": Post-Reformation English Catholicism and the Culture of Print', *P & P*, 168 (2000), pp. 72–123 (esp. pp. 113–14).
65. Cf. the Wiburn broadside below (pp. 109–10).
66. Greek for 'fertile'. Forbes signs himself P. A. (Patrick, Bishop of Aberdeen). Not noticed in *ARCR* II.
67. The year after *Eubulus* appeared, Forbes received a commission to suppress popery in the diocese of Aberdeen: see Louise B. Taylor (ed.), *Aberdeen Council Letters*, 6 vols. (Oxford: Oxford University Press, 1942–61), vol. 1 (1552–1633), pp. 290–2. The Jesuit Annual Letters of the Scottish Mission for 1628 suggest that a rumour that Forbes was a magician may have helped to inspire one intervention in the lively libelling culture of the Aberdonian Catholics: William Forbes Leith, SJ, *Memoirs of Scottish Catholics during the XVIIth and XVIIIth Centuries*, 2 vols. (London: Longmans, Green & Co., 1909), vol. I, pp. 13–40 (esp. pp. 20, 34).
68. See f. A2a. There are a number of early seventeenth-century Anne/Anna Gordons: see Robert Douglas, *Peerage of Scotland* (Edinburgh: Ramsay, 1813), and William Gordon, *History of the Ancient, Noble and Illustrious Family of Gordon* (Edinburgh: Ruddiman, 1726). One possible candidate would be the daughter of George, 5th Earl/1st Marquis of Huntly, as this was a religiously divided branch of the family. I am grateful to Jane Pirie of Aberdeen University Library for this suggestion.
69. If William Fulke is to be believed, the prose version of the *Articles* was deliberately circulated within elite circles in the 1570s: 'now of late . . . I have seen it in diverse godly Gentlemens handes, to whome it hath bene delivered by Papistes, be like to pervert them' (*Two Treatises* (1577), f. *iiib).

70. See below, p. 104.
71. BL Add. MS 10,420, 'A reply to an answere of a protestant to a ryme intitled Catholicke questions to the protestants'. It seems to be answering a version of Hieron's verse.
72. This line, pointing to the fact that paper may be used as kindling, may also be intended to recall the firing of the House of Commons in 1605.
73. *A Briefe Summe*, f. D3b. The pamphlet includes a copy of the libel (f. D2). Manuscript copies of the libel can be found in BL MS Egerton 2877, fols. 182b–183a (a dated copy from which the quotations are taken); BL MS Harley 677, fols. 50b–51a; and Edinburgh University Library, MS La II 69, f. 18a. The incident is briefly commented on by Pauline Croft, 'Libels, Popular Literacy and Public Opinion in Early Modern England', *Historical Research*, 68 (1995), pp. 266–85, on p. 281.
74. See below, pp. 110–11, 156.
75. The intention has also been to supplement the attention which Catholic–Protestant polemical interchanges in prose have received, e.g. from Peter Milward, *Religious Controversies of the Elizabethan (Jacobean) Age* (London: Scolar, 1977–8); Southern, *Elizabethan Recusant Prose*; Anthony Milton, *Catholic and Reformed* (Cambridge: Cambridge University Press, 1995); Michael C. Questier, *Conversion, Politics and Religion, 1580–1625* (Cambridge: Cambridge University Press, 1996).
76. *A Reply with the Occasion Thereof, to a Late Rayling, Lying, Reprochful and Blasphemous Libel* (1579), side-note to rhyming answer, fols. A4a–B1a.
77. *An Answere to a Popish Ryme* (1st edn 1604), f. A2a.
78. Strictly speaking, 'Anglianisme': see, most recently, Julian Davies, *The Caroline Captivity of the Church* (Clarendon: Oxford, 1992), pp. 5, 289, 294.
79. *The Mirrour of New Re-Formation* (1634), first published under the title *Epigrammes* c.1634. See *ARCR* II, nos. 36–7, for questions of attribution. One of the British Library copies of *Epigrammes* (C.175.d.20) preserves an epigram (supposedly voiced by a Protestant) where the original sense has been improved by a sympathetic reader:

> To cheat, calumniate, glosse, deceave, and raile
> Is our cheif practise: soe we may prevaile
> Gainst our Opponents, all things we avouch
> <But greatly care not, what: I think, nor much.>
> *but care not much what falshood there doth couch.*
> (Epigram VIII, 'On the fruits of Protestancie', f. B2a)

80. Lawrence Manley, *Literature and Culture in Early Modern London* (Cambridge: Cambridge University Press, 1995), comments on the epigram's 'illusion of definition, stability and authority' and how it overlapped with primarily oral forms like ballads, jests and proverbs (pp. 410–11).
81. The epigram is usually attributed to Sir John Harington, figuring as item 263 in his *Letters and Epigrams*, ed. Norman Egbert Maclure (Philadelphia: University of Pennsylvania Press, 1930), where it is entitled 'Against Swearing'. See also Gerard Kilroy, *Edmund Campion* (Aldershot: Ashgate, 2005), p. 107.

However, Guiney argues for Fitzsimon's authorship (pp. 324–5). I am grateful to Jason Scott-Warren for help on this point.
82. Patrick Forbes, *Eubulus* (1627), discussed above, pp. 100–1.
83. Printed in T. Broke, Jnr, *A Slaunderous Libell (Cast Abroad) Unto an Epitaph Set Forth Upon the Death of D. E. Boner, With a Reply* . . . [c.1569] (quotation f. A4a). For a similar exchange on Thomas Prideaux's elegy on Stephen Gardiner and its refutation, see Richard Warner, *Collections for the History of Hampshire*, 5 vols. in 6 (1795), vol. I, part 2, pp. 292–9; Guiney, pp. 109–14, gives other sources.
84. Libels, especially within Tudor and Stuart political culture, have attracted considerable scholarly attention in recent years. See Andrew Macrae, *Literature, Satire and the Early Stuart State* (Cambridge: Cambridge University Press, 2004); Alastair Bellany, 'Raylyng Rymes and Vaunting Verse: Libellous Politics in Early Stuart England', chapter 11 in Peter Lake and Kevin Sharpe (eds.), *Culture and Politics in Early Stuart England* (Basingstoke: Macmillan, 1994); Thomas Cogswell, 'Underground Verse and the Transformation of Early Stuart Political Culture', chapter 12 in Susan D. Amussen and Mark A. Kishlansky (eds.), *Political Culture and Cultural Politics in Early Modern England* (Manchester: Manchester University Press, 1995); Croft, 'Libels'; Adam Fox, 'Popular Verses', *Oral and Literate Culture in England, 1500–1700* (Oxford: Oxford University Press, 2000), and 'Ballads, Libels and Popular Ridicule in Jacobean England', *P & P*, 145 (1994), pp. 47–83; Martin Ingram, 'Ridings, Rough Music and Mocking Rhymes in Early Modern England', chapter 5 in Barry Reay (ed.), *Popular Culture in 17th-Century England* (London: Croom Helm, 1985), and 'Libels in Action: Ritual, Subversion and the English Literary Underground, 1603–42', chapter 4 in Tim Harris (ed.), *The Politics of the Excluded, c. 1500–1850* (Basingstoke: Palgrave, 2001). On broadsides, see Watt, *Cheap Print*, and 'Publisher, Pedlar, Pot Poet: The Changing Character of the Broadside Trade, 1550–1640', in Robin Myers and Michael Harris (eds.), *Spreading the Word* (Winchester: St Paul's Bibliographies, 1990), pp. 61–81.
85. Quoted from Adam Fox, 'Ballads, Libels and Popular Culture in Jacobean England', *P & P*, 145 (1994), pp. 47–83 (quotation p. 50).
86. *An Answere to Certaine Scandalous Papers, Scattered Abroad Under Colour of a Catholicke Admonition* (1606). A shewell was a paper or cloth hung up to prevent deer from going in a particular direction (*OED*).
87. On Cecil and libels, see below, note 95.
88. Folger Shakespeare Library, Loseley MSS, item 80 (L b 598): autograph of Sir William More, dated 24 September 1579, headed 'A Chatholyk to his muse' and endorsed 'A Raylyng rotten Ryme of a Rank papyste . . .'. I am grateful to Heather Wolfe for checking this transcript.
89. One Catholic at least is recorded as objecting to inflammatory Catholic material imported from the Continent on the grounds that it was unnecessarily combative: 'They be out of the re[a]ch themselves and therfore do not regard what we endure.' Sir Thomas Cornwallis to John Hobart, BL MS Tanner 285, f. 27a, quoted by Jason Scott-Warren in 'News, Sociability and Book-Buying in

Early Modern England: The Letters of Sir Thomas Cornwallis', *The Library*, 7th ser., 1:4 (2000), pp. 381–402 (quotation p. 392).
90. Reavley Gair, *The Children of Paul's* (Cambridge: Cambridge University Press, 1982), pp. 114–15.
91. John Bossy, *The English Catholic Community, 1570–1850* (1975; this edition London: Darton, Longman & Todd, 1979), p. 122; Foley IV, p. 492; Alexandra Walsham, *Church Papists* (Woodbridge: Boydell for Royal Historical Society, 1993), pp. 90–1.
92. See Sena, 'William Blundell'; Adam Fox, 'Rumour, News and Popular Political Opinion in Elizabethan and Early Stuart England', *HJ*, 40:3 (1997), pp. 597–620; and Richard Cust, 'News and Politics in Early 17th-Century England', *P & P*, 112 (1986), pp. 60–90.
93. For Catholic libels, see Jensen, 'Ballads and Brags', and Fox, 'Religious Satire'.
94. *An Answere to a Seditious Pamphlet . . . By a Jesuite* (1580), f. A3a. For the distribution of the *Challenge*, see Simpson, *Edmund Campion*, pp. 229–32. At the Commencement in Oxford on 27 June 1581 the benches of the University Church were strewn with copies of Campion's later publication, *Decem Rationes*, and they were also given as gifts to particular individuals (*ibid.*, p. 299).
95. See Francis Bunny, *An Answere to a Popish Libell* (1607), where he also calls Parsons's *Brief Apology* a libel (p. 113); Robert Cecil, Lord Salisbury, *An Answere to Certaine Scandalous Papers, Scattered Abroad* (1606); and Pauline Croft, 'The Reputation of Robert Cecil: Libels, Political Opinion and Popular Awareness in the Early Seventeenth Century', *Transactions of the Royal Historical Society*, 6th ser., 1 (1991), pp. 43–69. Thomas Cogswell describes manuscript verse as a means of conducting a 'steady, often violent political debate' at this period: 'Underground Verse', p. 287.
96. Folger Library, X d 338 (though Vallenger only confesses to the rhymed libel). See H. R. Plomer, 'Stephen Vallenger', *The Library*, n.s. 2 (1901), pp. 108–12.
97. *Origens Repentance* (1619), f. B1b.
98. For biographical material on Wiburn, see *ODNB*, and Patrick Collinson, *The Elizabethan Puritan Movement* (1st edn 1967: this edn Oxford: Clarendon, 1990), pp. 141–3.
99. I.e. the Easter sepulchre. See Godfrey Anstruther, *Vaux of Harrowden* (Newport: R. H. Johns, 1953), p. 84.
100. Thomas Knell, *An Answer to a Papisticall Byll* (1570: broadside); the other answer, probably published the same year, is in quarto format, *An Answer At Large, to a Most Hereticall, Trayterous, and Papisticall Byll* (*STC* 15030, 15030.5).
101. The Latin may be translated thus: (1) It is not discovered; (2) It is discovered; (3) Truth does not seek out corners; (4) He said, I do not dare; (5) Then leave off; (6) Or appear, liar.
102. Keith Thomas comments that a smattering of Latin would have been quite widely dispersed in areas where grammar schools were plentiful: 'The Meaning of Literacy in Early Modern England', pp. 97–131 in Gerd Baumann (ed.), *The Written Word* (Oxford: Clarendon, 1986), p. 101.

103. The libel 'Couvre le feu, ye Hugonots', allegedly written by Catholics after the Great Fire of 1666, may provide a point of comparison. It exists in two versions, one of which translates the French and Latin tags and glosses the sole classical allusion, 'Stygian Lake', as 'Hell'; however, it is not clear whether this is part of an original text or supplied for the copyists' audience. J. P. Kenyon, *The Popish Plot* (this edn Harmondsworth: Penguin, 1974), p. 13, believes this libel to be the work of an *agent provocateur*. Though he does not give his reasons, the date of its distribution – 5 November – and the tenor of the text itself (which begins by denying Catholics' involvement in the fire but ends with threats of a Catholic takeover and more anti-Protestant action) make the hypothesis likely. Copies of the libel can be found in *State Tracts*, 2 vols. (1689–92), vol. II, p. 43; Somerset Record Office, Oliver MS DD/PH 205; and the manuscript additions to Beinecke Library, Yale, Osborn pb.121 (which also preserves two answers to it).
104. See above, pp. 103, 109–10.
105. See above, note 73, on the text used. The Enborne parish registers survive only from 1665 (I am grateful to Berkshire Record Office for this information).
106. I.e. 'rush', alluding to the practice of strewing rooms with rushes (*OED*).
107. Baken = pig's carcass (*OED*).
108. John Strype, *Memorials of Thomas Cranmer* (1694), appendix, p. 137.
109. 'Great Hodge Podge', f. 141a–b. This is discussed and partially transcribed by Sena, 'William Blundell', pp. 59–60, and also transcribed in T. E. Gibson (ed.), *Crosby Records* (Manchester: Chetham Society, 1887), pp. 24–6. For the harassment of Catholics at Sefton, see T. E. Gibson, 'A Century of Recusancy', *Transactions of the Historic Society of Lancashire and Cheshire*, 3rd ser., vol. VII (1879), pp. 33–66. William Blundell's account of how he was apprehended in November 1592 by John Nutter, parson of Sefton, is reprinted on pp. 40–2. See also Christopher Haigh, *Reformation and Resistance in Tudor Lancashire* (London: Cambridge University Press, 1975), pp. 288–9, 329.
110. C.f. Introduction, pp. 11–12.
111. See chapter 4, pp. 114–15.
112. 'A challenge unto ffox the martirmonger written upon occasion of this miracoulouse martirdom of . . . Peter Elcius w[i]th a comforte unto all afflicted Catholyques', *CSPD* 12/157/48, ff. 105a–110b (quotation f. 105a). See chapter 4, pp. 120–1, for further discussion of this poem and the question of attribution.
113. Thomas Broke Jnr, *An Epitaphe Declaring the Life and End of D. Edm[und] Boner, &c. An Other Epitaphe Made By a Papist, With an Answere. Also a Reply to a Slau[n]derous Libel* (1570). This reprints two earlier items, *STC* 3817.4 and *STC* 3817.7. For Bonner's biography, see *ODNB*. See above, note 83.
114. *A Reply with the Occasion Thereof* (c.1579), f. A3a.
115. *The History of... Powys Fadog*, ed. J. Y. W. Lloyd, 6 vols. (London: T. Richards/Whiting & Co., 1881–7), vol. 3, pp. 144, 152. For White's polemical 'carols', see John Hungerford Pollen, SJ (ed.), *Unpublished Documents Relating to the English Martyrs*, vol. I (London: Catholic Record Society, 1908), pp. 90–9.

4. MARTYRS AND CONFESSORS IN ORAL CULTURE

1. On the interplay between religion and free speech, see Introduction, p. 12, and David Colclough, *Freedom of Speech in Early Stuart England* (Cambridge: Cambridge University Press, 2005), chapter 2. Susannah Breitz Monta has commented that 'the difficulties of testifying to inwardness in reliable, understandable and persuasive ways are at the heart of the task which martyrologists undertake': '"Thou Fall'st a Blessed Martyr": Shakespeare's *Henry VIII* and the Polemics of Conscience', *ELR*, 30:2 (2000), pp. 262–83 (quotation p. 263).
2. Sarah Covington, *The Trail of Martyrdom* (Notre Dame: University of Notre Dame Press, 2003); Anne Dillon, *The Construction of Martyrdom in the English Catholic Community, 1535–1603* (Aldershot: Ashgate, 2002); Brad S. Gregory, *Salvation at Stake* (Cambridge, Mass.: Harvard University Press, 1999); Susannah Breitz Monta, *Martyrdom and Literature in Early Modern England* (Cambridge: Cambridge University Press, 2005). On cross-confessional studies, see Thomas M. McCoog, SJ, 'Construing Martyrdom in the English Catholic Community, 1582–1602', chapter 5 in Ethan Shagan (ed.), *Catholics and the 'Protestant Nation'* (Manchester: Manchester University Press, 2005). Foucault's notion of the scaffold as theatre is expounded in *Surveiller et Punir* (1st edn 1975) (*Discipline and Punish*) and usefully inspires chapter 7 in Peter Lake and Michael Questier, *The Antichrist's Lewd Hat* (New Haven: Yale University Press, 2002).
3. McCoog, 'Construing Martyrdom'; Arthur F. Marotti, *Religious Ideology and Cultural Fantasy* (Notre Dame: Notre Dame University Press, 2005), chapter 3. McCoog identifies something of a time-lag before Elizabethan Catholic martyrs became significant propaganda weapons to their own countrymen; it is striking that much (though not all) of the material discussed below dates from the seventeenth century.
4. On Protestant martyrdom, see above, note 2; John R. Knott, *Discourses of Martyrdom in English Literature, 1563–1694* (Cambridge: Cambridge University Press, 1993); and the ongoing work of the British Academy John Foxe Project.
5. However, only the ballad on Thewlis's death is recorded in another contemporary manuscript, Bod MS Eng. poet. e. 121, fols. 31a–36a.
6. Thewlis was martyred at Lancaster, 18 March 1616: Foley VI, p. 181. See also Arthur Marotti, *Manuscript, Print and the English Renaissance Lyric* (Ithaca NY: Cornell University Press, 1995), pp. 4–7; Godfrey Anstruther, *The Seminary Priests* (Gateshead: St Edmund's College, Ware/Ushaw College, Durham, 1968), vol. I, pp. 354–5. Natascha Würzbach, *The Rise of the English Street Ballad 1550–1650* (1981: trans. Gayna Walls, Cambridge: Cambridge University Press, 1990), discusses martyr-ballads (pp. 224–5, 230), though seems to assume that all speakers in them are fictional.
7. The rhyme suggests a two- or three-syllable pronunciation of 'Thewlis', though the name is sometimes spelt 'Thules'.
8. BL Add. MS 15,225, fols. 23a–25a. Würzbach, *Rise*, discusses the ballad (pp. 58 (f/n 77), 122, 181).
9. Cf. Würzbach, *Rise*, p. 58, on how the listener participates in the invocation.

10. BL Add. MS 15,225, fols. 25a–27b. This is only one text to problematise the common dichotomy proposed in hagiographical texts between 'exemplary character' and 'subjective experience' (e.g. in Würzbach, *Rise*, p. 181).
11. On the use of popular providentialism among Catholics at this date, see Walsham, 'Miracles and the Counter-Reformation in England', *HJ*, 46:4 (2003), pp. 779–815.
12. See Richard Simpson, *Edmund Campion* (revised edn London: John Hodges, 1896), p. 459, quoting contemporary stanzas on the topic (which can be found in Thomas Alfield (attr.), *A True Reporte of the Death & Martyrdome of M. Campion Jesuite* [1582], f. F2a). Simpson attributes the poem to 'Poundes' (i.e. Thomas Pounde) but without giving his reasons. See also Walsham, 'Miracles', pp. 790–1. One literary commentary on Campion's death is actually titled 'Thamesis In Edmundi Campiani nece amnem sistit' (Beinecke Library, Yale, MS 45, fols. 72b–74b).
13. The high level of discrepancy between accounts necessitates caution, though. The ballad claims Thewlis's quarters were set 'upon the Castell hye'; Richard Challoner, quoting a printed account (apparently not surviving, but cf. *ARCR* I, no. 1070), says that Thewlis's four quarters were hung up at Lancaster, Preston, Wigan and Warrington (*Memoirs of Missionary Priests*, rev. John Hungerford Pollen (London: Burns, Oates & Washbourne, 1924), p. 344); and Archivum Romanum SJ, Ang. 32, f. 22v, refers to Thewlis's body and that of a companion as being cut up and thrown into the square together, so that it was impossible to distinguish one from another (I am grateful to Barbara Ravelhofer for supplying a translation of the latter document from the original Italian).
14. Byrd's motet sets texts from Psalm 78 (Vulgate numbering)/79 (King James Bible numbering). On Byrd's recusancy, see the biographical entry by Joseph Kerman in Stanley Sadie (ed.), *The New Grove Dictionary of Music and Musicians*, 2nd edn (London: Grove/Macmillan, 2001), vol. 4, pp. 714–31; and David Mateer, 'William Byrd's Middlesex Recusancy', *Music and Letters*, 78 (1997), pp. 1–14. On the motet's possible link with Campion's death, see Grove, p. 718; John Harley, *William Byrd, Gentleman of the Chapel Royal* (Aldershot: Ashgate, this edn 1999), pp. 224, 228–9; and Craig Monson, 'Byrd, the Catholics and the Motet: The Hearing Reopened', in *Hearing the Motet*, ed. Dolores Pesce (Oxford: Oxford University Press, 1997), pp. 348–74 (esp. pp. 354–62), who gives several analogies for the use of these texts from contemporary Catholic martyrology.
15. For controversy over Catholic burials in early seventeenth-century Lancashire, see D. R. Woolf, 'Little Crosby and the Horizons of Early Modern Historical Culture', chapter 5 in Donald R. Kelley and David Harris Sacks (eds.), *The Historical Imagination in Early Modern Britain*, Woodrow Wilson Center Series (Cambridge: Cambridge University Press, 1997), pp. 99–100.
16. However, for an account of a crow that died after feasting on a martyr's flesh, see Stonyhurst MS A.IV.7, no. 5, cited in Alexandra Walsham, *Providence in Early Modern England* (Oxford: Oxford University Press, 1999), p. 242 (note 84).

17. Knaresborough, 'Foule draughtes', Hull University Library, DDEV/67/3, p. 422 (Thewlis); 'An Ode or Sonnet upon three Catholick Priests put to Death at Lancaster on the same Day. Viz. the Seventh of August One thousand six hundred forty six', stanzas 27–8: John Knaresborough, 'Sufferings of the Catholicks', 5 vols., Hull University Library, DDEV/67/1, vol. IV, p. 416 (Reading/Bamber). Challoner knew and used Knaresborough's work for his *Memoirs of Missionary Priests*: see Challoner, ed. Pollen, index under name.
18. This refers to the ballad, references to which are cited in the margin of Knaresborough's account.
19. 'A challenge unto ffox the martirmonger written upon occasion of this miracoulouse martirdom of . . . Peter Elcius w[i]th a comforte unto all afflicted Catholyques', *CSPD*, 12/157/48, fols. 105a–110b; portions quoted in Guiney, p. 186, and Foley, vol. III, pp. 623–6. For Pounde's biography, see Thomas M. McCoog's article in *ODNB*; for the attribution to Pounde, see Guiney, pp. 182–5. This poem is also referred to in chapter 3 above, p. 113.
20. I explore Catholics' stylistic utilitarianism further in the section on religious prose in the *Oxford History of Literary Translation in English*, ed. Robert Cummings (forthcoming).
21. Weeping, mourning (*OED*).
22. See Introduction, pp. 8–10.
23. Transcription taken from the edition in Gerard Kilroy, *Edmund Campion* (Aldershot: Ashgate, 2005), pp. 199–204; see also the commentary to a version of the poem in Ruth Hughey (ed.), *The Arundel Harington Manuscript of Tudor Poetry*, 2 vols. (Columbus, OH: Ohio State University Press, 1960), vol. I, item 66. For William Byrd's setting of an adaptation of the poem (seemingly intended to reach an audience beyond the Catholic community), see Grove, pp. 718–19; Harley, *William Byrd*, pp. 78–9. For other elegies on Campion, see Guiney, section XVI, and W. R. Morfill (ed.), 'Ballads Relating Chiefly to the Reign of Queen Elizabeth', in *Ballads from Manuscripts*, vol. II (Hertford: Ballad Society, 1873), pp. 157–91.
24. Brief printed and manuscript accounts of the martyrdom, and sketches of it, are all possible means of dissemination – though given the stringencies of underground Catholic publication in England, printed images would be unlikely. Simpson, *Edmund Campion*, describes Campion's remains as having been nailed up on a gate (p. 466) so the ballad may also be alluding to this.
25. I am grateful to John Harley and John Milsom for help with this section.
26. This is an adaptation of 1 Corinthians 4:9. See my '"We Are Made a Spectacle": Campion's Dramas', in *The Reckoned Expense*, ed. Thomas M. McCoog, SJ (Woodbridge: Boydell, 1996), pp. 103–18.
27. 'Great Hodge Podge', Lancashire Record Office, DDBL acc. 6121, f. 145a–b (quotation f. 145b; square brackets marking off reported speech/song), with the Latin originals copied into the margin. See also T. B. Trappes-Lomax, 'The Birthplace of the Blessed Robert Anderton', *Biographical Studies*, 1:3 (1951), pp. 235–8. The author was a priest, whose alias is given as Malton. Here as

elsewhere, I am grateful to Margaret Sena for sharing with me her unpublished work on William Blundell.
28. Bruce R. Smith, *The Acoustic World of Early Modern England* (Chicago: University of Chicago Press, 1999), pp. 194–5, discusses how singing by condemned individuals was a common feature of executions.
29. Bod MS.Eng.th.b.1–2. Gerard Kilroy suggests that 'Jollett' is a pseudonym of Sir Thomas Tresham's: *Edmund Campion*, pp. 13, 15, 21. The text is quoted from the Latin/English online edition of the Catholic Bible at www.newadvent.org. The King James Bible translates the verse as 'This is the day which the Lord hath made: we will rejoice and be glad in it' (Psalm 118, v.24; the same psalm is numbered 117 in the Douai/Rheims Bible, on which the online edition cited above is based). The attribution to Byrd is rejected by John Morehen in 'Is Byrd's *Haec* a Faec?', *Early Music Review*, 24 (1996), pp. 8–9; the motet is transcribed in the 'Annual Byrd Newsletter', 2, pp. 6–7, part of *Early Music Review*, 21 (1996), and commented on there by John Harley and Richard Turbet (p. 16). Byrd did, in fact, set the same text in *Cantiones Sacrae* (1591); since the execution took place in 1601, Barkworth's singing might well have alluded to this. See Monson, 'Byrd, the Catholics and the Motet', p. 362, and, for Byrd's involvement in this world, see Kerry McCarthy, 'Byrd, Augustine and *Tribue, Domine*', *Early Music*, 32:4 (2004), pp. 569–76, and note 14 above.
30. Bod MS.Eng.th.b.1–2, vol. 2, pp. 114 (quotation), 116 (motet). Barkworth became a Benedictine shortly before his death and appeared clothed as such on the scaffold: see Michael Questier, *Conversion, Politics and Religion, 1580–1625* (Cambridge: Cambridge University Press, 1996), p. 196. On 'last words' motets, see Monson, 'Byrd, the Catholics and the Motet', pp. 355–8.
31. On Garnet, see Foley IV, pp. 117–18. Bod MS.Eng.th.b.1–2, vol. 2, pp. 132–7.
32. See above, note 14.
33. This is an acclamation used on the feast of the Triumph of the Cross, 14 September (translation quoted from the Lectionary of the Roman Missal, vol. I (London: Collins, 1981), p. 998); and also the versicle which introduces each station of the Stations of the Cross, thus evoking Calvary in the context of the martyr's progression. (I am grateful to John Morrill for the latter observation.) On the specific resonances of this text among English Catholics, see Monson, 'Byrd, the Catholics and the Motet', pp. 366–70.
34. Though possibly (as commented above, note 29) inspired by Byrd's setting.
35. On Catholic music-making in private houses, see John Milsom, 'Sacred Songs in the Chamber', chapter 7 in John Morehen (ed.), *English Choral Practice* (Cambridge: Cambridge University Press, 1995).
36. *Gradualia* (1610), f. A2a. The original is in Latin; the translation is taken from Joseph Kerman, *The Masses and Motets of William Byrd* (London: Faber & Faber, 1981), p. 54.
37. Kerman, *Masses*, pp. 248, 288–9. Diane Kelsey McColley also comments of Byrd's settings of the Magnificat, Te Deum and Benedictus that they may be intended to express the feelings of a persecuted church: *Poetry and Music in*

17th-Century England (Cambridge: Cambridge University Press, 1997), p. 87. For the political uses of the idea of harmony, see Robin Headlam Wells, *Elizabethan Mythologies* (Cambridge: Cambridge University Press, 1994), pp. 66–7. Byrd may also have felt it appropriate to use Counter-Reformation features, especially those inspired by Alfonso Ferrabosco the elder, in his more Catholic pieces: see David Wulstan, 'Byrd, Tallis and Ferrabosco', chapter 5 in *English Choral Practice*, ed. Morehen, esp. p. 125.

38. Harley, *William Byrd*, pp. 227–9, sees Byrd's *Cantiones Sacrae* as expressing the Catholic community's general discontent.
39. Kerman, *Masses*, p. 37, comments: 'Free choice of this kind is something new in the history of Latin sacred music in Britain . . . To make a personal choice of a motet text implies an interest in and respect for the actual quality of the text in itself, an attitude which sooner or later is bound to affect the musical setting.'
40. See Grove, p. 718; Harley, *William Byrd*, pp. 224–5. This psalm was used by both Catholics and Protestants to express the sorrows of disaffection: for Protestant uses, see Hannibal Hamlin, *Psalm Culture and Early Modern English Literature* (Cambridge: Cambridge University Press, 2004), chapter 7. For Catholic mockery of a Protestant's doing so, see John Floyd, *The Overthrow of the Protestants Pulpit-Babels* (1612), p. 81. For the use of this psalm elsewhere in English Catholic discourse, see Monson, 'Byrd, the Catholics and the Motet', p. 353.
41. 'By the rivers of Babylon, there we sat down, yea, we wept, when we remembered Zion. We hanged our harps upon the willows in the midst thereof. For there they that carried us away captive required of us a song; and they that wasted us *required of us* mirth, *saying*, Sing us *one* of the songs of Zion. How shall we sing the LORD's song in a strange land?' (Ps.137, v.1–4 in original order, King James Bible).
42. 'How shall we sing the LORD's song in a strange land? If I forget thee, O Jerusalem, let my right hand forget *her cunning*. If I do not remember thee, let my tongue cleave to the roof of my mouth; if I prefer not Jerusalem above my chief joy. Remember, O LORD, the children of Edom in the day of Jerusalem . . .' (Ps.137, v.4–7a, King James Bible).
43. *Masses*, pp. 26, 39–44.
44. On performativity as a way of inculcating ideal behaviour, see Bridget Nichols, *Liturgical Hermeneutics* (Frankfurt: Peter Lang, 1996), chapter 8.
45. 'An epitaph, upon the death of three most blessed marters', *Epitaphs* (1604), fols. A4–B2a.
46. The Catholicism of the Hoghton family has been intensively studied in connection with the theory that Shakespeare spent part of his early life at Hoghton Hall: see E. A. J. Honigmann, *Shakespeare: The 'Lost Years'* (1985: 2nd edn Manchester: Manchester University Press, 1998), chapter 2.
47. Transcription taken from 3rd edn (Manchester: John Heywood, 1882), pp. 32–43. Harland describes it as having been taken from the first printed copy by Peter Whittle (not found) and also cites variants taken from a mid-eighteenth-century copy owned by the antiquarian J. W. Bone. Another version, described

as taken from 'framed ... manuscript verses', is given in G. C. Miller, *Hoghton Tower in History and Romance* (1948: rev. edn Preston: Guardian Press, 1954), attributed (without giving source) to Roger Anderson, butler to Thomas Hoghton (pp. 29–32); another version still is given in Joseph Gillow, *The Haydock Papers* (London: Burns & Oates, 1888), pp. 10–15.

48. 'Mr Whittle appears to have made free with several of the stanzas' (Harland, *Ancient Ballads*, pp. 32–3). As we have it, the text may bear some signs of elite composition (the first verse, for instance, begins 'Apollo, with his radiant beams ...'); but cf. Würzbach, *Rise*, p. 210, about uses of well-known literary material in popular ballads.
49. A study of the oral traditions surrounding late-seventeenth-century highwaymen has found that many tales survived till the early twentieth century, preserving a level of detail both remarkably high and historically verifiable as accurate: Alan Macfarlane and Sarah Harrison, *The Justice and the Mare's Ale* (Oxford: Oxford University Press, 1981), pp. 168–72.
50. On Hoghton's care for his servants, see Robert Bearman, '"Was William Shakespeare William Shakeshafte?" Revisited', *Shakespeare Quarterly*, 53:1 (2002), pp. 83–94.
51. *The Study of Folk Music in the Modern World* (Bloomington: Indiana University Press, 1988), p. 14.
52. I.e. the monarch's orb, or (figuratively) worldliness.
53. 'Verses concerning lovers divided by religion': Somerset Record Office, DD_WO/56/9/10, dated by the cataloguer to the late sixteenth century. I am grateful to Somerset Record Office for permission to quote this manuscript. Cf. the ballad where a Catholic husband travels overseas, discussed in my *Catholicism, Controversy, and the English Literary Imagination 1558–1660* (Cambridge: Cambridge University Press, 1999), pp. 163–4.
54. Probably to be read 'whither'.
55. See Juliet Fleming, *Graffiti and the Writing Arts of Early Modern England* (London: Reaktion, 2001).
56. Sharon Lambert, *Monks, Martyrs and Mayors* [Lancaster, n.p., 1991], page headed 'Aldcliffe Hall'.
57. See G. A. Gotch, *The Buildings ... by Sir Thomas Tresham* (Northampton: Taylor, 1883), and, among recent commentators, Peter Davidson, 'The Inscribed House', in Michael Bath, Pedro F. Campi and Daniel S. Russell (eds.), 'Emblem Studies in Honour of Peter M. Daly', *Saecula Spiritalia*, 41 (2002), pp. 41–62, as well as his article, 'Recusant Catholic Spaces in Early Modern England', pp. 19–51 in Ronald Corthell, Frances E. Dolan, Christopher Highley and Arthur F. Marotti (eds.), *Catholic Culture in Early Modern England* (Notre Dame IN: Notre Dame University Press, forthcoming 2007). On Tresham's religious agenda more generally, see Sandeep Kaushik, 'Resistance, Loyalty and Recusant Politics: Sir Thomas Tresham and the Elizabethan State', *Midland History*, 21 (1996), pp. 37–72; Richard Williams, 'A Catholic Sculpture in Elizabethan England: Sir Thomas Tresham's Reredos at Rushton Hall', *Architectural History*, 44 (2001), pp. 221–7; and Kilroy, *Edmund Campion*.
58. Also recorded as Bost and Boste.

59. Challoner, ed. Pollen, p. 203.
60. On onomastic theory in early modern England, see Anne Barton, *Ben Jonson, Dramatist* (Cambridge: Cambridge University Press, 1984), chapter 8, and Scott Smith-Bannister, *Names and Naming Patterns in England, 1538–1700* (Oxford: Clarendon, 1997), introduction.
61. *Remaines* (1605 edn), p. 37.
62. For a Protestant example of a jocular martyr, see the discussion of John Frith in Jeffrey Knapp, *Shakespeare's Tribe* (Chicago: University of Chicago Press, 2002), pp. 169–73.
63. In '"We Are Made a Spectacle"', I argue that, given the suspicious quality of the name after Campion's martyrdom, this was less a disguise than a proclamation of allegiance, and a claim on the martyr himself to be afforded special protection (p. 111).
64. On pseudonyms and names in religion, see Adrian Room, *Dictionary of Pseudonyms*, 3rd edn (Jefferson, North Carolina: McFarland & Co., 1998), pp. 30–1.
65. English College, Rome, *Collectanea* F, f. 90 onwards, transcribed in *Unpublished Documents Relating to the English Martyrs*, vol. I, 1584–1603, ed. John Hungerford Pollen, Catholic Record Society, vol. 5 (London: CRS, 1908), pp. 345–60 (quotation p. 347). See also Dillon, *Construction of Martyrdom*, p. 109.
66. Garry Wills, *Witches and Jesuits* (New York: Oxford University Press, 1995), p. 96; P. J. Holmes, *Elizabethan Casuistry*, Catholic Record Society, vol. 67 (London: CRS, 1981), pp. 64–5. Some English Catholics are given as examples in Johannes Deckherrus, *De Scriptis Adespotis Pseudepigraphis, et Suppositis Conjecturae* (1686), e.g. pp. 85–8, 337.
67. Analysis of the audience's role at such events is a crucial theme in Monta, *Martyrdom*.
68. The *OED* cites five examples of the spelling – three Scotch – between 1552 and 1651.
69. III ii 255–6. Cf. *Julius Caesar*, I iii 81; *Hamlet*, I iii 12.
70. The Bodleian text (generally inferior) reads 'lives'.
71. The fact that the copyist of this ballad renders the name of William Leigh, who tried over three days to convert Thewlis to Protestantism, as 'p[ar]son Lie', may indicate that puns on names were not observed only when martyrs were in question.
72. This has obvious counterparts in heraldic symbolism; for a seventeenth-century treatise on Catholic heraldry, see Thomas Shirley, 'The Catholike Armorist', 3 vols., Queen's College, Oxford, MS 141–3.
73. Stanley Morison, *The Likeness of Thomas More* (London: Burns & Oates, 1963), pp. 68–9. Mark Robson, 'Posthumous Representations of Thomas More: Critical Readings' (PhD, Leeds University, 1996), contains extensive discussion of puns on More's name.
74. BL Add. MS 21,203, f. 23a.
75. *Providence in Early Modern England* (Oxford: Oxford University Press, 1999); this anecdote is discussed on pp. 242–3.

76. Pliny, *Natural History*, 22:4, 6–8, quoted from the translation by W. H. S. Jones (London: William Heinemann, 1951), pp. 298–301.
77. This in turn might have tapped into, and subverted, the popular providentialist notion that no grass would grow on the scene of a crime or injustice: see Jacqueline Simpson, 'Beyond Etiology: Interpreting Local Legends', *Fabula*, 24:3/4 (1983), pp. 223–32.
78. For one example of the European response, see A. J. Loomie, *Spain and the Jacobean Catholics*, vol. 1 of 2, Catholic Record Society, vol. 64 (London: CRS, 1973), pp. 110–11, describing James I's fury at Spanish verses about the straw. On the events surrounding Garnet's execution, see the forthcoming work of Anne Dillon (and I would also like to acknowledge here her detailed and insightful reading of this chapter).
79. Foley IV, pp. 121–2, quoting from Gerard's *Narrative*; see also the more detailed description in BL Add. MS 21,203: 'a face of a man in glorious maner, havinge w[i]th all proportions most exactelye, bearde, mouthe, eies, foreheade, and upon his heade a crowne, a crosse in the foreheade and a starre, and in the lower parte of his face, as the chinne a Cherub' (f. 22b). An extensive bibliography on the topic is given in Walsham, *Providence*, pp. 243–4; see also her 'Miracles', p. 795.
80. As a point of comparison, see Challoner, ed. Pollen, p. 406 (martyrdoms of Thomas Reynolds and Bartholomew Roe).
81. If not more so: there are three sixteenth-century references to 'garneter' in the *OED*, but only one to 'garnet' with the meaning of jewel. See also Camden, *Remaines* (1637 edn), p. 117.
82. Verstegan to Persons, mid-August 1592, quoting an earlier letter of Garnet's to Verstegan: transcribed in Anthony G. Petti (ed.), *The Letters and Despatches of Richard Verstegan*, Catholic Record Society, vol. 52 (London: CRS, 1959), pp. 67–9 (quotation p. 67).
83. II iii 4–5. See Garry Wills, *Witches and Jesuits* (Oxford/New York: Oxford University Press/New York Public Library, 1995), chapter 5; H. L. Rogers, 'An English Tailor and Father Garnet's Straw', *RES*, 16 (1965), pp. 44–9. Wills observes that the controversy over the miracle of the straw arose just before *Macbeth* may have been first performed (p. 103). On Garnet's aliases, see Foley IV, p. 38.
84. *Construction of Martyrdom*, pp. 95–6 (discussing William Allen's *An Apologie and True Declaration*).
85. There may be a subsidiary pun here on 'grain'. Beads, especially those on a rosary, were sometimes described as grains (from the Latin *grana*), and blessed grains – rosary beads blessed by the Pope – were among the popish objects condemned by polemicists (e.g. Francis Bunny, *An Answer to a Popish Libell* (1607), p. 34). The *OED* also cites 'dyed in grain' as a phrase denoting objects dyed scarlet.
86. Verstegan, *Letters*, ed. Petti, p. 69. 'Garlick' is identified by Petti as an alias: Nicholas Garlick was martyred some years earlier, in 1588.
87. Cf. the insightful discussions of this passage in Dillon, *Construction of Martyrdom*, pp. 104–5; Peter Marshall, *Beliefs and the Dead in Reformation England*

(Oxford: Oxford University Press, 2002), pp. 243–4; and Geoffrey Hill, 'The Absolute Reasonableness of Robert Southwell', chapter 2 in *The Lords of Limit* (London: André Deutsch, 1984). My own account has benefited from all of these. A more straightforward account of Pilchard's execution can be found in Foley III, p. 429.

88. Stonyhurst MSS, *Anglia*, vii, n. 26. 'Catalogue of Martyrs, 1587–1594.' Quoted from *Unpublished Documents*, ed. Pollen, pp. 288–9. Gerard's emphasis is all the more striking because Pilchard's name is sometimes spelt 'Pylcher'.
89. *The Great Cat Massacre* (this edn Harmondsworth: Penguin, 1985), pp. 12–13.
90. Challoner and Foley do not use the stories. See comments in Walsham, 'Miracles', p. 783.
91. See (for instance) Foley I, p. 392; cf. the exchange between William Allen and Alphonsus Agazzari discussed in Dennis Flynn, *John Donne and the Ancient Catholic Nobility* (Bloomington: Indiana University Press, 1995), pp. 107, 216 (note 26).
92. See Edmund Spenser, *Selected Shorter Poems*, ed. Douglas Brooks-Davies (London: Longman, 1995), appendix, discussing 'The Shepherd's Calendar', November, line 16; *The Faerie Queene* (London: Longman, 1980 edn), p. 591.
93. Quoted from the translation in Pollen (ed.), *Unpublished Documents*, p. 318, and alluding to Tobit 6, v.5–9 (cf. Southwell's *The Triumphs Over Death* (1595), fol. E2a–b). Southwell continues: 'They will come to Peter's hands, that out of their mouths he may take the coins of the tribute, wherewith to discharge the debt that Catholics owe to supreme Caesar.' The reference is to Matthew 17, v.26, where Simon Peter is told to catch a fish which will have in its mouth enough money to pay the tax levied for the upkeep of the temple; cf. also Matthew 22, v.21, and Mark 12, v.17. See also Kilroy, *Edmund Campion*, p. 211.
94. See Hill, *Lords*, p. 31.
95. For a Catholic ballad on Tobias and the angel, see BL Add. MS 15,225, fols. 19–20a.
96. See Anthony G. Petti, 'Unknown Sonnets by Sir Toby Matthew', *Recusant History*, 9:3 (1967), pp. 123–58 (sonnet quoted p. 143). Petti suggests that this sonnet might refer either to the author or to his father of the same name, the Archbishop of York; and Matthew Jnr was himself a convert to Catholicism.
97. On this, see L. E. Whatmore, 'The Venerable Thomas Pylcher, c.1557–1587', 6 parts, *Southwark Record*, 1964–5 (i.e. Sept. 1964, pp. 18–25; Oct. 1964, pp. 16–20; Dec. 1964, pp. 20–4; Feb. 1965, pp. 21–6; Sept. 1965, pp. 14–17; Dec. 1965, pp. 21–7), part 5, pp. 16–17.
98. R. H. d'Elboux, 'The Venerable Thomas Pylcher', *Biographical Studies 1534–1829*, 3:5 (1956), pp. 334–7, referring to L. E. Whatmore, 'Thomas Pilchard of Battle (1557–1587)', *Sussex County Magazine*, May 1942. See also John Jones, *Balliol College* (Oxford: Oxford University Press, 1988), p. 79.
99. Cf. proverb cited in *OED*: *To take sturgeons with pilchards*, to get large returns for a small outlay.

100. The most recent account of Postgate's life is W. J. Sheils's life in the *ODNB*. See also Elizabeth Hamilton, *The Priest of the Moors* (London: Darton, Longman & Todd, 1980), and David Quinlan, *The Father Postgate Story* (Whitby: Horne & Son, 1967). 'Poskett' is an alternative spelling. For the circumstances surrounding his execution, see J. P. Kenyon, *The Popish Plot* (this edn London: Pelican, 1974), pp. 204–5, 207, 246, 250, 312.
101. Ward lived at Danby Castle, about seven miles from Postgate's cottage at Ugthorpe: Dom Bede Camm, *Forgotten Shrines* (1st edn London: Macdonald & Evans, 1910), p. 283. I am grateful to Judith Smeaton of the North Yorkshire Record Office and Fr Terence Richardson of the Postgate Society for help with this section.
102. *Englands Reformation* (1710 edn), Canto IV, p. 103. 'Blakamor' is an old name for the Yorkshire moors and the surrounding area. A side-note adds further topographical detail: 'His Cell was upon a Lingy [i.e. heathery] Moor, about two miles from *Mulgrave-Castle*, and five Miles from *Whitby*.' See Challoner, ed. Pollen, pp. 547–9. 'Blakamor' was used by Postgate as one of his aliases (*ODNB*).
103. Two texts of this anonymous ballad can be found in BL Add. MS 15,225 (dated by the cataloguer to the reign of James I, and transcribed in H. E. Rollins, *Old English Ballads* (Cambridge: Cambridge University Press, 1920), no. 16) and, with significant variants, in *The Song of Mary, the Mother of Christ* (1601). I discuss the latter in 'What is a Catholic Poem? Explicitness and Censorship in Tudor and Stuart Religious Verse', chapter 6 in Andrew Hadfield (ed.), *Literature and Censorship in Renaissance England* (Basingstoke: Palgrave, 2001), pp. 101, 109.
104. Camm, *Forgotten Shrines*, p. 289. Camm also describes it as being traditionally sung at Catholic funerals in the district. Nicholas Rigby was appointed to his ministry at Ugthorpe in 1827; see David Quinlan, *The Whitby Catholics (640–1957)* (2nd printing, Farnworth: Catholic Printing Company, 1945), p. 16.
105. 'This affecting Hymn gave the first idea of Printing as (*sic*) small collection here in 1805, when our new Chapel was opened': George Leo Haydock, *A Collection of Hymns* (1st edn Whitby 1805; 3rd edn, printed under the title *A Collection of Catholic Hymns*, Whitby and York, 1823), quotation from 3rd edn, p. iv (Postgate's hymn is printed at pp. 43–5 of this edition). For Gilbert, see Dominic Aidan Bellenger, *The French Exiled Clergy in the British Isles after 1789* (Bath: Downside Abbey, 1986), p. 57; W. J. Nicholson, 'Nicholas Alain Gilbert, French Émigré Priest, 1762–1821', *Northern Catholic History*, 12 (1980), pp. 19–22, 32. I am grateful to Alex Fotheringham for the last two references.
106. Letter to Knaresborough from John Danby, 17 February 1707/8, preserved in Knaresborough's 'Collections for "The sufferings of the Catholics"': Hull University Library, DDEV/67/2. Thanks to Kate Boyce for checking this reference. This attitude can be found elsewhere among Knaresborough's correspondents, though not obviously in Knaresborough himself. See (e.g.) DDEV/67/2, 'Collections for "The sufferings of the Catholics"', letter from

John Yaxlee, 17 July 1707, from Coxhoe, on the origins of the place-name 'Dryburn'.
107. Camm, *Forgotten Shrines*, p. 288.
108. Camm, *Forgotten Shrines*, pp. 298–302. The relics were officially recorded at the Office of the Vice-Postulation of the Cause of the Martyrs of England and Wales (Quinlan, *Father Postgate Story*, p. 41). See also Hamilton, *Priest of the Moors*, pp. 49–52.
109. Hamilton, *Priest of the Moors*, p. 76.
110. '. . . my informant, a good Catholic, seventy-six years of age, who was born at Ugthorpe, said that she had been told by her grandmother that Father Postgate was the first to bring the daffodil to that part of the country' (Camm, *Forgotten Shrines*, p. 291).
111. *Catholic Magazine* (1838), quoted in Camm, *Forgotten Shrines*, p. 293.
112. See Dom Aidan Bellenger, 'Dom Bede Camm (1864–1942), Monastic Martyrologist', in Diana Wood (ed.), *Martyrs and Martyrologies*, Studies in Church History, 30 (Oxford: Blackwell for Ecclesiastical History Society, 1993), pp. 371–81.
113. *Priest of the Moors*, p. 80.
114. See *The Canonisation of the Forty English and Welsh Martyrs* (London: Office of the Vice-Postulation, 1970), preface.
115. Postgate was beatified in 1886 (*ODNB*). On lay 'canonisations', see Walsham, 'Miracles', p. 791. On the cause of the English martyrs prior to 1929, see the articles by Aloysius Smith and Ronald Knox in Dom Bede Camm (ed.), *The English Martyrs* (Cambridge: W. Heffer & Sons, 1929), and the article by John Hungerford Pollen in the *Catholic Encyclopaedia*, 'English Confessors and Martyrs, 1534–1729' (www.newadvent.org.cathen/054749.htm, accessed May 2006); thereafter, see *Canonisation of the Forty . . . Martyrs*.
116. John 8:59.
117. Thomas M. McCoog, SJ, *The Society of Jesus in Ireland, Scotland and England 1541–88*, Studies in Medieval and Renaissance Thought, vol. 60 (Leiden: E. J. Brill, 1996), chapter 4, esp. pp. 174–7.
118. See Introduction, pp. 12–13.
119. John Gerard, *Autobiography of an Elizabethan*, trans. and ed. Philip Caraman (1st edn London: Longmans, Green & Co., 1951), chapter 9; Suzanne Gossett (ed.), *Hierarchomachia: Or, The Anti-Bishop* (London: Bucknell University Press, 1982), pp. 264–9. See also Michael Hodgetts, *Secret Hiding-Places* (Dublin: Veritas, 1989).
120. A priest-hole with wall paintings is referred to in John Barclay's *Argenis* (1625), pp. 12–14 (cited and discussed in Fleming, *Graffiti*, pp. 62–3).
121. *The Second Spring* (London: Thomas Richardson & Son, 1852), pp. 17–18. The quotation is commented on by Leo Gooch, '"Chiefly of Low Rank": The Catholics of North-East England, 1705–1814', in Marie B. Rowlands (ed.), *Catholics of Parish and Town, 1558–1778* (London: Catholic Record Society, 1999), chapter 11, quotation p. 237.
122. *Forgotten Shrines*, preface: 'Englishmen of all creeds have grown more sympathetic of late, as they have come to know something of the true story of that long persecution . . .' (p. vii).

123. *English Catholic Community, 1570–1850* (1975: this edn London: Darton, Longman & Todd, 1979), chapter 7, section 2.
124. Campion to Richard Stanihurst, March 1571: quoted and translated in Colm Lennon, *Richard Stanihurst the Dubliner, 1547–1618* (Dublin: Irish Academic Press, 1981), p. 33.
125. The identification is consolidated by J. E. Bamber, 'The Skull of Wardley Hall', *Recusant History*, 16:1 (1982), pp. 61–77. Barlow's head was impaled and Downes's trepanned, which may explain the confusion. On Barlow, see *ODNB*, and W. E. Rhodes (ed.), 'The Apostolical Life of Ambrose Barlow', *Downside Review*, 44 (1926), pp. 235–52. Wardley Hall is now the residence of the Catholic Bishop of Salford.
126. E.g. Edward Baines, *The History of the County Palatinate and Duchy of Lancaster*, rev. and ed. James Croston, 5 vols. (Manchester and London: John Heywood, 1888–93), vol. III, pp. 291–5; N. G. Philips (artist), *Views of the Old Halls of Lancashire and Cheshire . . . With Descriptive Letterpress by Twenty-Four Local Contributors* (London: Henry Gray, 1893), pp. 47–51 (text contributed by William E. A. Axon).
127. 'The Skull-House', John Roby, *Traditions of Lancashire*, 6th edn (Manchester and London: John Heywood, 1906), pp. 312–21 (quotation p. 321). This compilation was first published in 1829 (*ODNB* under Roby).
128. Quoted in Bamber, 'Skull', p. 66.
129. For instance, in Baines's account (see above, note 126), the Downes story is dominant, though an alternative tradition deriving from Barritt is reported, in which the skull belongs to a priest.
130. This piece of oral reportage is attributed to the great-grandson of a man who was there when the skull was discovered in the wall: see Henry Vaughan Hart-Davis, *History of Wardley Hall, Lancashire* (Manchester and London: Sherratt & Hughes, 1908), chapter VI. An additional story related by Hart-Davis, of how a labourer in the early nineteenth century diverted himself by faking spectral noises by weights drawn across the floors, suggests how supernatural tales can stimulate copycat activity and thus become self-perpetuating. On the place of hoaxes in stimulating oral traditions about ghosts, see David J. Hufford, *The Terror that Comes in the Night* (Philadelphia: University of Pennsylvania Press, 1982), pp. 13–14.
131. *Manchester City News*, 7 December 1895. See also Camm, *Forgotten Shrines*, pp. 202–46. Gillow's account is amplified in Hart-Davis, *History of Wardley Hall*.
132. Hufford, *Terror*, pp. 13–14.

CONCLUSION: ORALITY, TRADITION AND TRUTH

1. For the full quotation, see Introduction, p. 1.
2. On truth-claims, see Bernard Williams, *Truth and Truthfulness* (Princeton: Princeton University Press, 2002).
3. See Introduction, pp. 17–18.

4. 'How Myths are Made', chapter 1 in *Witches, Druids and King Arthur* (London: Hambledon, 2003), quotation p. 24. I am grateful to Arnold Hunt for this reference. See also Adam Fox, *Oral and Literate Culture in England, 1500–1700* (Oxford: Clarendon, 2000), conclusion; and David Vincent, *Literacy and Popular Culture* (Cambridge: Cambridge University Press, 1989), pp. 5–6.
5. 'The "Common Voice": History, Folklore and Oral Tradition in Early Modern England', *P & P*, 120 (1988), pp. 26–52, revised in *The Social Circulation of the Past* (Oxford: Oxford University Press, 2003), chapter 10 (quotation p. 391). See also Alexandra Walsham, 'Reformed Folklore? Cautionary Tales and Oral Tradition in Early Modern England', chapter 6 in Adam Fox and Daniel Woolf (eds.), *Oral Culture in Britain, 1500–1850* (Manchester: Manchester University Press, 2002). On an early historian of oral tradition, Giambattista Vico, see Patrick H. Hutton, 'The Problem of Oral Tradition in Vico's Historical Scholarship', *Journal of the History of Ideas*, 53:1 (1992), pp. 3–23.
6. On the effects of post-structuralism on oral history, see Joan Sangster, 'Telling Our Stories: Feminist Debates and the Use of Oral History', chapter 8 in Robert Perks and Alastair Thomson (eds.), *The Oral History Reader* (London: Routledge, 1998).
7. See the discussion by Gwyn Prins, 'Oral History', chapter 6 in Peter Burke (ed.), *New Perspectives on Historical Writing* (Oxford: Polity, 1991); and below, pp. 152–3, for the views of Catholic writers on textual interpretation.
8. However, as Woolf comments, there is 'no reliable correlation between Catholicism and a predisposition to accept tradition in contexts where religious truth was not at stake': *Social Circulation*, p. 363.
9. See George H. Tavard, *The Seventeenth-Century Tradition* (Leiden: E. J. Brill, 1978).
10. The Dogmatic Constitution on Divine Revelation *Dei Verbum* contains the key twentieth-century Catholic pronouncement on the interrelationship of Scripture and tradition: see Ronald D. Witherup, *Scripture: 'Dei Verbum'*, in the series 'Rediscovering Vatican II' (New York: Paulist Press, 2006), esp. pp. 57, 74–5, 88–100. See also Yves M.-J. Congar, O. P., *La Tradition et les Traditions*, 2 vols. (1960, 1963), trans. Michael Naseby and Thomas Rainborough as *Tradition and Traditions* (London: Burns & Oates, 1966).
11. George H. Tavard, *Holy Writ or Holy Church?* (London: Burns & Oates, 1959), p. 62 onward. On polemic relating to the idea of the visible church, see Peter Milward, *Religious Controversies of the Jacobean Age* (London: Scolar, 1978), pp. 217–26; T. H. Watkins, 'The Percy-Fisher Controversies and the Ecclesiastical Politics of Jacobean Anti-Catholicism, 1622–5', *Church History*, 5:7 (1988), pp. 153–69; and Peter Lake, 'Calvinism and the English Church, 1570–1655', *P & P*, 114 (1987), pp. 32–76. The topic was a particularly obvious one to receive attention in formal oral disputations: for one such, see Robert Dodaro, OSA, and Michael C. Questier, 'Strategies in Jacobean Polemic: The Use and Abuse of St Augustine in English Theological Controversy', *JEH*, 44:3 (1993), pp. 432–49 (esp. pp. 437–9, 443–4, 447–9).

12. *Of the Auctorite of the Word* [1544?], f. D8a. Bonner was the Bishop of London at the time; on his conservatism, see his entry in *ODNB*. Tavard, *Holy Writ*, comments on the inconsistency of Catholic answers to Protestant arguments (p. 195).
13. See Brian Cummings, 'Reformed Literature and Literature Reformed', chapter 31 in David Wallace (ed.), *The Cambridge History of Medieval English Literature* (Cambridge: Cambridge University Press, 1999), pp. 834–8.
14. For a survey of Reformation and present-day opinion, see John Barton (ed.), *The Cambridge Companion to Biblical Interpretation* (Cambridge: Cambridge University Press, 1998).
15. *The Church-History of Brittany* (1668), f. íia.
16. Thomas Bayly, *An End to Controversie* (1654), p. 92, quoted and discussed in Tavard, *17th-Century Tradition*, p. 132 (who compares it to Newman's ideas on the development of doctrine).
17. See F. J. Crehan, SJ, 'The Bible in the Roman Catholic Church from Trent to the Present Day', chapter VI in S. L. Greenslade (ed.), *The Cambridge History of the Bible: The West from the Reformation to the Present Day* (Cambridge: Cambridge University Press, 1963), p. 199; Tavard, *Holy Writ*, chapters VIII and XII; Walter J. Ong, *The Presence of the Word* (New Haven: Yale University Press, 1967), p. 276; Gabriel Moran, *Scripture and Tradition* (New York: Herder & Herder, 1963), pp. 34–8, 52–4, 63–9 (commenting on the 'lack of precision in terminology' on p. 93). For a hostile MS response to the Tridentine decrees, see F. S., 'Scripture and Tradition', BL Add. MS 25279 (cited in Fox, *Oral and Literate Culture*, p. 407). On Counter-Reformation views on tradition in the English context, see Alexandra Walsham, 'Unclasping the Book? Post-Reformation English Catholicism and the Vernacular Bible', *Journal of British Studies*, 42:2 (2003), pp. 141–66.
18. From Session 4 of the Council of Trent, 8 April 1546: translation taken from Norman P. Tanner, SJ, *Decrees of the Ecumenical Councils*, 2 vols. (London/Washington: Sheed & Ward/Georgetown University Press, 1990), vol. 2, p. 663.
19. See below, pp. 157–8.
20. On Catholic approaches to tradition, see Moran, *Scripture*. On the Church of England's approach to tradition, see Henry Chadwick, 'Tradition, Fathers and Councils', in Stephen Sykes and Jonathan Knight (eds.), *The Study of Anglicanism* (London: SPCK, 1988), pp. 100–15; and Stanley L. Greenslade, 'The Authority of the Tradition of the Early Church in Early Anglican Thought', and Gareth Vaughan Bennett, 'Patristic Tradition in Anglican Thought, 1660–1900', pp. 9–33 and 63–87 in *Tradition im Luthertum und Anglikanismus, Oecumenica* (1971/2). See also Walsham, 'Reformed Folklore.'
21. This summary of Reformist views is indebted to Tavard, *Holy Writ*, chapter 6, esp. p. 86 (Luther); pp. 92–3 (Melanchthon); pp. 106–9 (Calvin).
22. *The Eclipse of Biblical Narrative* (New Haven: Yale University Press, 1974), pp. 54–5.

23. Richard Hooker, *Of the Lawes of Ecclesiastical Polity*, Book I, ed. A. S. McGrade (Cambridge: Cambridge University Press, 1989), pp. 110–11 (quotation p. 110).
24. See Walsham, 'Reformed Folklore?', section 1.
25. *A Saxon Treatise Concerning the Old and New Testament* (1623), f. e2b. For the perceived Catholic tendency to point to the church as a means of concluding debate, cf. George Gifford, *A Dialogue Between a Papist and a Protestant* (1582), f. 2a. For the acknowledgement in Catholic apologetics of this tendency towards circular reasoning, see Tavard, *17th-Century Tradition*, chapter 3. See also Introduction, p. 15, for the argument that unlearned Catholics were capable of defending their church convincingly in debate.
26. John Foxe's *Acts and Monuments* depicts Divine Justice weighing the word of God against man's traditions: see Marsha S. Robinson, *Writing the Reformation* (Aldershot: Ashgate, 2002), p. 29, commenting on a woodcut in the 1576 edition, p. 771. See also Walsham, 'Reformed Folklore?', pp. 175–6.
27. Quoted from BL MS Egerton 2877, f. 183a. See my discussion of the incident in chapter 3.
28. Richard H. Popkin, *The History of Scepticism from Savonarola to Bayle* (this edn. Oxford: Oxford University Press, 2003), esp. chapter 1.
29. See Tavard, *Holy Writ*, pp. 37, 53–6, 187; and under term in F. L. Cross (ed.), *The Oxford Dictionary of the Christian Church*, 3rd edn, rev. E. A. Livingstone (Oxford: Oxford University Press, 1997). For typical English Protestant uses of the term, see John White, *The Way to the True Church* (2nd impression, 1610), esp. chapters 4–6, and his *A Defence of The Way to the True Church* (1614), chapters 26–27, 35. For typical and untypical English Catholic uses, see below. On Christian Pyrrhonism as practised by Catholics, see Popkin, *Scepticism*, esp. chapter 3.
30. See David Cressy, *Literacy and the Social Order* (Cambridge: Cambridge University Press, 1980), p. 3.
31. *A Briefe Discourse of Certaine Points of the Religion* (1582), f. 29a; cf. his *A Dialogue Between a Papist and a Protestant* (1582), f. 60a, and the discussion of Gifford in Jeffrey Knapp, *Shakespeare's Tribe* (Chicago: University of Chicago Press, 2002), p. 31 onwards.
32. See preface and notes to *Religio Laici* in Paul Hammond (ed.), *The Poems of John Dryden*, vol. II, 1682–5 (London: Longman, 1995). All quotations from the poem are taken from this edition. Simon's *Histoire Critique du Vieux Testament* (1678) had been translated into English by Henry Dickinson (not himself a Catholic) and published in 1682 as an anti-atheistical gambit. On Simon's thought and contemporary reception, see also Phillip Harth, *Contexts of Dryden's Thought* (Chicago: University of Chicago Press, 1968), chapter 6 *et passim*; 'Interpretation, History of', in *The Oxford Companion to the Bible*, ed. Bruce M. Metzger and Michael D. Coogan (New York: Oxford University Press, 1993), p. 323; Jonathan I. Israel, *The Radical Enlightenment* (Oxford: Oxford University Press, 2001), pp. 99–102, chapter 24 and p. 576. On Simon's influence in England, see Gerard Reedy, SJ, *The Bible and Reason* (Philadelphia: University of Pennsylvania Press, 1985), chapter 5; and Harold Love, *The Culture*

33. Following his *Histoire Critique du Vieux Testament* (1678), Simon was expelled from the Oratory in Paris. See *New Catholic Encyclopaedia*, vol. 4; Dryden, *Poems*, ed. Hammond, vol. II p. 81.
34. Conversely, Protestants could praise Simon for rescuing the Scriptures from error and combating deism – just as Dryden himself does in other parts of the poem. See Dryden, *Poems*, ed. Hammond, vol. II p. 82; Harth, *Contexts*, pp. 183, 193–6 (though cf. Israel, *Radical Enlightenment*, p. 452).
35. See glosses for these lines in *Poems*, ed. Hammond, vol. II pp. 124–5; Reedy, *Bible and Reason*, pp. 114–18; and Harth, *Contexts*, p. 202. My reading differs from the latter. Harth rightly points out that lines 252–3 have often been mistakenly cited as proof that Simon was a scoffer at religion, and suggests instead that Dryden is implying that Simon is a Protestant at heart; however, this is hard to reconcile with Dryden's picture of Simon as throwing doubt on Scripture. Dryden seems instead to be temporarily casting Simon as a secret freethinker for strategic purposes.
36. Harth, *Contexts*, pp. 202–3.
37. *Poems*, ed. Hammond, vol. II notes, pp. 124–5.
38. Quoted from *The Poems of John Dryden*, vol. III (1686–93), ed. Paul Hammond and David Hopkins (Harlow: Longman, 2000), Part 2, lines 212–13, 216–21. See also the introduction to the poem, p. 34.
39. Cf. *Religio Laici*, lines 342–55.
40. See Harth's discussion of tradition in the poem: *Contexts*, pp. 281–4, 288–9. I would wish to qualify his suggestion that Dryden 'ignored' the Blackloists, and suggest that the poem draws on Blackloist metaphor while maintaining a more mainstream understanding than theirs of the balance between Scripture and tradition. Anne Barbeau Gardiner points out that Dryden follows the Catholic theologian Abraham Woodhead in his use of the word 'traditive': 'Abraham Woodhead, "The Invisible Man": His Impact on Dryden's "The Hind and the Panther"', *Recusant History*, 26:4 (2003), pp. 570–88.
41. See Tavard, *Holy Writ*. Robert Morgan comments that 'the authority to define and defend the pattern of Christian truth devolved upon an episcopal leadership authenticated by its standing in an apostolic succession and able to provide a visible focus for unity': 'The Bible and Christian Theology', chapter 8 in John Barton (ed.), *The Cambridge Companion to Biblical Interpretation* (Cambridge: Cambridge University Press, 1998), p. 119.
42. See Introduction, p. 14; Tavard, *Holy Writ*, pp. 72–6. The Blackloists take their name from 'Blacklo', an alias of Thomas White's.
43. *Exomologesis* (1st edn 1647), p. 194, discussed in Tavard, *17th-Century Tradition*, p. 118 (see also pp. 178–9).
44. On the Blackloists, see Dorothea Krook, *John Sergeant and his Circle* (Leiden: E. J. Brill, 1993); Beverly C. Southgate, *Covetous of Truth* (Dordrecht/London: Kluwer Academic Publishers, 1993), '"Cauterising the Tumour of Pyrrhonism":

Blackloism Versus Scepticism', *Journal of the History of Ideas*, 53 (1992), pp. 631–45, and '"White's Disciple": John Sergeant and Blackloism', *Recusant History*, 24:4 (1999), pp. 431–6; Jeffrey R. Collins, 'Thomas Hobbes and the Blackloist Conspiracy of 1649', *HJ*, 45:2 (2002), pp. 305–31. Blackloist thought on Scripture and the rule of faith is discussed in Harth, *Contexts*, chapter 8, and Tavard, *17th-Century Tradition*, chapter 10 (p. 223 specifically on Sergeant). See also the *ODNB* articles on Sergeant, Rushworth and White.

45. This tract was written by William Rushworth but edited and published after Rushworth's death by Thomas White, who added to it in a later edition of 1654: see Beverly C. Southgate, 'A Note on the Authorship of Rushworth's *Dialogues*', *Notes and Queries*, 226 (1981), pp. 207–8. See also Thomas White, *An Apology for Rushworth's Dialogues* (1654); Serenus Cressy, *The Church-History of Great Britain* (1668), fols. é3b, íia, and *Exomologesis*, section 2. On Rushworth, see *ODNB* and Tavard, *17th-Century Tradition*, chapter 7 (written in the belief that White was the author of the *Dialogues*).

46. *17th-Century Tradition*, p. 179.

47. There were several editions in 1665: quotations are taken from Wing S5295. Many of Sergeant's points are anticipated in a less systematic manner in writings by other members of the group: e.g. John Belson, *Tradidi Vobis* (1662).

48. *The Rule of Faith: Or an Answer to the Treatise of Mr. I. S. Entituled, Sure-Footing, &c.* (2nd edn 1676), p. 319. Edward Stillingfleet's *A Reply to Mr. J. S. his 3^d Appendix* (1675) is bound together with this edition in some copies (e.g. the British Library's).

49. *A Brief Treatyse Settynge Forth Divers Truthes* (1547), f. D8r, quoted in Ellen A. Macek, *The Loyal Opposition*, Studies in Church History 7 (New York: Peter Lang, 1996), p. 121. I am grateful to James Austen for this reference.

50. On the relationship of orality and Scripture, see William A. Graham, *Beyond the Written Word* (Cambridge: Cambridge University Press, 1987).

51. On the limits to Sergeant's notion of oral tradition, see Tavard, *17th-Century Tradition*, p. 225.

52. See also *Rushworth's Dialogues*, dialogue 2.

53. On this point more generally, see Bruce M. Metzger, *The Canon of the New Testament* (Oxford: Clarendon, 1987).

54. Cf. Tavard's discussion of Serenus Cressy's thought: *17th-Century Tradition*, pp. 116–18.

55. Cf. Donne, Satire 3: 'ask thy father which is [true religion] / Let him ask his ...' (quoted from *Selected Poetry*, ed. John Carey (Oxford: Oxford University Press, 1996), lines 71–2, p. 8).

56. On Catholicism's concern to dissociate itself from ideas of a 'secret tradition', see Moran, *Scripture and Tradition*, p. 31.

57. *Devotions*, 3rd edn (1684), p. 170. These verses appear to paraphrase a passage from Henry Turberville, *A Manual of Controversies* (1654), p. 108. John Sergeant wrote the dedication to the second edition of the *Devotions* (1672).

58. Tavard, *17th-Century Tradition*, pp. 188, 196.

59. *17th-Century Tradition*, pp. 237–9.

60. *The Rule of Catholick Faith*, trans. Edward Sheldon (1660), p. 1.
61. *Rushworth's Dialogues*, fols. ***5b–6b, p. 48.
62. On the ubiquitous idea that the father should be the primary instructor within a household, see (e.g.) Sir Robert Filmer, *Patriarcha and Other Writings*, ed. Johann P. Sommerville, Cambridge Texts in the History of Political Thought (Cambridge: Cambridge University Press, 1991), 'Patriarcha', p. 12.
63. Bossy, *English Catholic Community*, esp. pp. 60–74.
64. By emphasising Sergeant's thought rather than his political machinations, this chapter can be read as qualifying John Bossy's judgment that 'Sergeant's career . . . was a long, skilful, but increasingly desperate rearguard action' (*English Catholic Community*, p. 67).
65. This is one of the central arguments in *English Catholic Community*.
66. On the low ratio of Catholic priests to lay people at this date, see Alexandra Walsham, 'Translating Trent? English Catholicism and the Counter-Reformation', *Historical Research*, 78 (2005), pp. 288–310, reference p. 294.
67. For a classic discussion of the relationship between religion and intellectualism, see Max Weber, *The Sociology of Religion*, trans. Ephraim Fischoff (London: Methuen, 1965), chapter 12.
68. Bossy, *English Catholic Community*, chapter 7; Marie B. Rowlands, 'Recusant Women, 1560–1640', chapter 5 in Mary Prior (ed.), *Women in English Society, 1500–1800* (London: Methuen, 1985).
69. See Introduction, pp. 13–14, and the definition of 'socialisation' in William Outhwaite and Tom Bottomore (eds.), *The Blackwell Dictionary of Twentieth-Century Social Thought* (Oxford: Blackwell, 1993).
70. See Harth, *Contexts*, pp. 252–3; *ODNB* under Sergeant; Tavard, *17th-Century Tradition*, pp. 237–8 and chapter 12.
71. Bossy, *English Catholic Community*, p. 68.
72. Bossy, *English Catholic Community*, pp. 25, 32, 49, 60, 70–1.
73. See Robert Perks and Alastair Thomson (eds.), *The Oral History Reader* (London: Routledge, 1998), part 1, for a comprehensive survey of the arguments for the validity of oral evidence.
74. See Introduction, esp. p. 15.
75. On post-Reformation Catholic catechisms, see Patricia Demers, *Heaven Upon Earth* (Knoxville: University of Tennessee Press, 1993), chapter 4; Ian Green, *The Christian's ABC* (Oxford: Clarendon Press, 1996), appendix 1; Sister Marian Norman IBVM, 'John Gother and the English Way of Spirituality', *Recusant History*, 11:6 (1972), pp. 306–19.
76. *Popular Culture in Early Modern Europe* (London: Temple Smith, 1978). See also Introduction, pp. 17–18.
77. See Phebe Jensen, 'Singing Psalms to Horn-Pipes: Festivity, Iconoclasm, and Catholicism in *The Winter's Tale*', *Shakespeare Quarterly*, 55:3 (2004), pp. 279–306; and Alexandra Walsham, 'Holywell: Contesting Sacred Space in Post-Reformation Wales', chapter 11 in Will Coster and Andrew Spicer (eds.), *Sacred Space in Early Modern Europe* (Cambridge: Cambridge University Press, 2005).
78. *The Pilgrim's Progress*, ed. Roger Pooley (London: Penguin, 2005).

79. This formulation is indebted to Philip V. Bohlman, *The Study of Folk Music in the Modern World* (Bloomington: Indiana University Press, 1988), chapter 2.
80. For the definition of 'oral history', see Introduction, p. 18.
81. These similarities are apparently fortuitous (Stanley Hauerwas, personal communication, 2005).
82. Stanley Hauerwas and William H. Willimon, *Resident Aliens* (Nashville: Abingdon, 1989) and *Where Resident Aliens Live* (Nashville: Abingdon, 1996). See also Stanley Hauerwas and Samuel Wells (eds.), *The Blackwell Companion to Christian Ethics* (Malden, Mass./Oxford: Blackwell, 2004).

Index

Acquaviva, Claudio 145
Adams, Thomas 204
Ady, Thomas 78
Aelfric 155
Agazzari, Alphonsus 138
Alane, Alexander 153
Aldcliffe Hall, Lancaster 131
Alençon, Duc d' 138
All Souls' Day 58
allegory 65, 67, 104
Allen, William 97
Allen's 'Articles' 16, 95–103
Anderton, Robert 124–5, 126
Andrew, St 117
Andrewes, Lancelot 188
anecdote ix, 2, 3, 20, 24, 139
animadversion 10
animism 204
annotation of texts 84
anonymity 8
anti-Catholicism ch. 2, 155
Antiquarian and Topographical Cabinet 191
antiquarians 2, 5, 6, 24, 25, 37, 40–1, 48, 67–8, 147–8, 151
apocalyptic writing 91, 93
architectural memorialisation 115
Ariosto, Ludovico 76
'art of memory' 20
Aubrey, John 5, 61, 62–4, 75, 79, 179, 204
Augustine of Hippo, St 95, 113, 115
Austin, John 162

B., I. 105
Babington, Anthony 65
Bagshaw, Christopher 79
Baker, Augustine 176
Bale, John 64, 66–7
ballads ix, 1, 2, 3, 4, 10, 13, 15, 16–17, 20, 112–13
Ballin, Rosetta 49–50
Bamber, Edward (alias Reading) 119–20
Barbauld, Anna 195

Barclay, John 228
Barham, R. H. 191
Barkworth, Mark 125–6, 127
Barlow, Dom Edward Ambrose 115, 147–8, 150
Barlow, Thomas 26
baroque viii
Barritt, Thomas 147
Bartholomew, St 117
Baxter, Elizabeth 142
Bellarmine, St Robert 102
Bellenger, Dom Aidan 141
Belson, John 234
Bentley, Richard 191
Berkshire: see Enborne
Berry, Mary 191
Bible:
    Apocrypha: see Tobit
    New Testament: see Corinthians, Revelation, Thessalonians
    Old Testament: see Ezekiel, Isaiah, Kings, Psalms
    reading 15
    relationship of Scripture with oral tradition 160–1
Black Mass 59–60
Blackamor, Yorkshire 140, 141
Blacklo: see White, Thomas
Blackloists 1, 13, 152, 159–65
    See also Rushworth, William; Sergeant, John; White, Thomas
Blackman, Mr 9
Blount, Edward 80
Blundell, William 112, 124
Blundell family 112
Boast, John 131
Bohlman, Philip V. 129
Bonner, Edmund, bishop 106, 113, 153
Book of Sports 61–2
Bossy, John 52, 146, 163
botanists: see herbals, plants
Bourne, Henry 63

Bovet, Richard 30
Bowles, William Lisle 191
Bradefalk, Kent 27
Brannon, Philip 42
Brayley, E. W. 41–2
Bristow, Richard 97, 212
Broke, T. 215
Brooks, Chris 49
Brown, Humfrey 188
Brown, James 191
Brown, Theo 48
Bull, John 210
Bunny, Edmund 84, 177
Bunyan, John 166
Burke, Peter 166
Burnet, Gilbert, bishop 9
Byrd, William 118, 125–7
Byron, George Gordon Noel, Lord 192

Calvin, John 155
Cambridgeshire: see Wisbech Castle
Camden, William 56, 63, 132
Camm, Dom Bede 141, 142–4, 145–6
Campion, Edmund, St ix, 8, 56, 79, 108, 118, 122–4, 132, 146, 212
'Campion' as surname 132, 224
Candlemas 4, 58
canon, expansion of viii
Canter, Laurence 143
carols 5–6
Cary, Elizabeth, Lady Falkland viii
Cary, Patrick 32–3
Caryll family 207
Castle, Terry 51
casuistry 12
catechisms 165
Catherine of Aragon 50
Catholic Relief Acts 52
Catholic revival 5
    current interest in Catholic writing viii
    See also: Gothic revival
Catholic survivalism 58
Cecil, Robert 107, 108
Cecil, William, Lord Burghley 65, 67
Challoner, Richard, bishop 131, 140, 144
Challoner, Sir Thomas 30
Charke, William 108
Charles I 62
charms: see spells
Chaucer, Geoffrey 207
Chetham, Kent 67–8
Christchurch, Hampshire 4
Christmas 5, 79
church papists 4, 5, 107
Clerkenwell Priory 30

Clifford family 153
Colchester, Essex 9
Coles, William 204
collective memory: see cultural memory; historical memory
confessorship ix, 12, 114, 115, 120–2, 129–30, 132
conformists 4, 6
conservatives, religious 5
conversation 2, 3
conversion 12
Cooke, Alexander 13
Corbett, Richard 77–8
Corinthians, Epistle to the 124
Cornwallis, Sir Thomas 215
Corpus Christi play 5
Cosen, Richard 9
Cosen family 9
Cosin, John, bishop 49
Council of Trent 154, 160
Covell, William 57
Crashaw, Richard 177
creeds 156
Cressy, Serenus 153, 159, 187, 234
Cromwell, Thomas 64, 66
Crowley, Robert 93–4
Crum, Ralph Adams 192
crypto-Catholics: see church papists
Culpeper, Nicholas 73–4
cultural memory 21–2
Cumberland, Earl of: see Clifford family
Cummings, Brian 10

Dalrymple, Sir David 36
Danby Castle, Yorkshire 227
Danby, John 142
Darnton, Robert 137
Davidson, Peter viii
debates: see dialogues
Dei Verbum 230
Deloney, Thomas 173
Devon: see Tavistock
dialogues, controversial 83–5
Dickinson, Henry 232
Dillon, Anne 115
disputations 12, 20
dissenters 6
dissolution of the monasteries 23–4, 26, 31, 48, 49
Dobin, Howard 65, 67
Donne, John 113, 234
Dorchester, Dorset 137, 139
Dorset: see Dorchester
Doughtie, Edward 2
Downes family 147
Downes, Roger, Earl of Wardley 147–8

Drake, Nathan 81
drama 2, 10, 13, 20
    continuance of religious drama after the Reformation 5
Drexelius, Jeremias 204
Dryden, John 79, 157–9, 161
Duffy, Eamon 4, 57, 87
Dugdale, William 186

Edolph, Sir Thomas 27
educated, the 7
    See also: literacy
Egton, Yorkshire 115, 142
    See also: St Hedda's Church
Eisenstein, Elizabeth 74
Elcius, Peter 120, 217
Elderton, William 123
elegy 95
Elizabeth I 9, 16, 28, 50, 108, 138
Elton, G. R. 64, 66
Enborne, Berkshire 103, 110–11, 156
English College, Rome 8, 59
English language, difficulties with among Catholics 8–9
English Martyrs' Church, Sleights, Yorkshire 143
English Reformation historiography vii
epigrams 10, 105
equivocation 12–13
Essex 88
    See also: Colchester
executions 12, 20, 118–20
exiles 128–30, 144
Eyston, Charles 23, 24, 25
Eyston, Edward Francis 22, 23
Ezekiel 92

Fairfax family 31
fairies 14, 68, 75–9, 179
Falkner, John Meade 36
Favour, John 4, 5
Featley, Daniel 12
Fermor family 207
festivity 6, 166
    religious festivals 5
    See also: hospitality
'feudalism' 18
Fieldcock, Roger 125
Filmer, Sir Robert 235
Fisher, Samuel 12
Fitzsimon, Henry 105
Fitzwilliam Virginal Book 89
folklore 2, 37, 55–8, 63–4
Forbes, Patrick 100–1, 106
Foucault, Michel 114
Fountains Abbey, Yorkshire 38

Fox, Adam 17, 106
Foxe, John 124, 232
Freeman, William (alias Mason) 132
Frei, Hans 155
French Revolution 50–1
Freud, Sigmund 51–2
Fulke, William 3, 208, 213
Fuller, Thomas 26

Gabalis, Comte de 80
Gannon, Fr 143
Gardiner, Stephen 215, 217
Garlick, Nicholas, Ven. 127, 135
Garnet, Henry, SJ 125, 134–7
Gasquet, Francis Aidan, cardinal 42
Gerard, John 134, 137, 139, 145
ghost stories 24, 27, 30, 47–8, 137
Gibson, Edmund 26
Gifford, George 156, 232
Gilbert, Nicholas Alain 141, 143
Gillow, Joseph 148
Gilpin, William 41
Glastonbury, Somerset 23
Glastonbury Thorn 203
Gloucestershire: see Wanswell
Goody, Jack 72
Gordon, Anna, Lady 100–1
Gordon Riots 52
Gostwyke, Roger 188
Gothic architecture 189, 193
    See also: antiquaries; ruins
Gothic drama 48
Gothic fiction 2, 24, 36–7, 48–54, 148
    psychoanalytical criticism 51–4
Gothic Revival 42, 49
Graham, Kenneth W. 33
grammar 10
Gray, Thomas 39, 191
    imitations of *Elegy* 42
Gregory XIII, Pope 144
Gregory, Brad 115
Grigson, Geoffrey 73
Grose, Francis 38, 46, 193
Guise, Duke of 9

Habermas, Jürgen 18
Hackett, Helen 90
Haggerty, George E. 51
hagiography 114
Haigh, Christopher 16, 20
Hale, Thomas 88
Hall, Joseph 1, 149–52, 155, 167
Hamilton, Donna viii
Hamilton, Elizabeth 142
Hampshire: see Christchurch; Netley Abbey

Harington, Sir John 200, 214
Harland, John 128
Harrab, Thomas 104, 105
Harris, Tim 18, 177
Harvey, John 76
Hauerwas, Stanley 167–9
Haydock, George Leo 141
Heal, Felicity 94
Helme, Elizabeth 191
Henry VIII 48, 50, 65, 67, 87, 90
heraldry, Catholic 224
herbals 73–4
Herrick, Robert 62
Heywood, John 176
Hickeringill, Edmund 26
Hierarchomachia: Or, the Anti-Bishop 228
Hieron, Samuel 97–8, 99, 102, 104
High Churchmen 24, 26, 27
historical memory 21, 172
historical trauma 21–2
Hobart, John 215
Hobbes, Thomas 77–9
Hogg, James 194
Hoghton, Richard 129
Hoghton, Thomas 128–30
Holy Office 164
holy wells 56, 69
Homer 63, 80
Hooker, Richard 155, 188
hospitality 94–5
Houghton, Norfolk 35
Howard, Philip, Cardinal 9
Hufford, David 148
Huggarde, Miles 16
Hutton, Ronald 18, 55, 58, 150

idolatry, definitions of ix
ignorance, fear of 5, 13, 81
illiteracy 10, 18
  link with religious conservatism 3, 14, 19
illustration 10
Inchbald, Elizabeth 49
Inquisition 164
inscriptions 20, 130–1
internationalism, Catholic 7, 8
Interregnum 5
invisible church 163
Ireland 20, 146
  See also: St Patrick's Purgatory
Ireland, William Henry 195
irrational, the 52–3
Isaiah 90

Jackson, Ken vii
Jackson, Thomas 70–2, 74, 75, 81
James I 61

James, M. R. 36–7
James, St 117
Jefferson, Joseph 192
Jelin, Elizabeth 21
Jenkins, David, bishop 188
Jensen, Phebe 84
Jerningham, Edward 192
Jerome, Stephen 109
Jesoppe, Mr 137
Jesuits 12, 15
Johnson, Samuel 36
jokes 137
  See also: puns
Jollett, Thomas 125–6, 127
justification by faith 11

K., E. 77
Keate, George 39, 42–4
Kennett, White 187
Kent: see Bradefalk; Chetham; St Radegund
  Abbey
Ker, Ann 191
Kerman, Joseph 126, 127
Kiely, Robert 52
Kilroy, Gerard ix
Kings, Book of 119
Kirk, Robert 205
Kirkstall Abbey, Yorkshire 47
Knaresborough, John 119–20, 142
Kunzle, David 93

laity, Catholic 19, 162–4
Lambarde, William 68
laments 7–8, 83, 87–92, 93–4
Lancashire viii, 5, 119, 128
Lancashire witches 60
  See also: Aldcliffe Hall; Lancaster; Sefton;
  Wardley Hall
Lancaster 119, 131, 147
Langdon, Thomas 87–8
Larkham, Thomas 65, 67, 77, 208
Latin viii, 6–7, 109–10
  See also: liturgy; Mass
Laud, William, Archbishop 5
Laudianism 187
Lee, Sophia 49–50
Leigh, William 224
Lemnius, Levinus 72
letters 2
Lévy, Maurice 51
Lewis, Sir Berkeley 39–40, 42
Lewis, Matthew 49
libels 8, 13, 82–5, 106–13
Lincolnshire: see South Kyme
linguistic concerns of Reformation 10, 20
L'Isle, William 155

literacy 17
  association with progress 14
literates' view of illiterates ix, 13, 56–7, 69–70
  communicating to both literates and illiterates 10, 13–16
'Little John Nobody' 7–8, 9, 19
liturgical fragments 14, 57, 64, 66
liturgical parody 10, 59–60
liturgical year 5, 6, 73
liturgy 2, 7, 78, 126
  changes in liturgy 6
Lloyd, William 187
Lluelyn, Martin 26
Lodge, Thomas 79
Loe, William 18, 177
London 124
  See also Clerkenwell Priory; St Paul's Cathedral; Tower of London; Tyburn
lower orders, Catholicism among 20
Ludlam, Robert 127
Luther, Martin 155
Lyke-Wake Dirge 62, 69

manuscript circulation ix, 16, 17, 82
manuscript miscellanies 6, 86
Marcus, Leah 61
marginalisation 18
Marian veneration 4
Marotti, Arthur F. vii, ix, 115
Martin, Gregory 95, 213
martyr-narratives ch. 4 *passim*
martyrs ix, 12, 21, 112–13, 114–15, 150
Marvell, Andrew 31–2
Mary I 16
Mary Stuart 49, 50
Mason: see Freeman, William
Mass, the 4, 7, 9, 57, 155
  See also: Latin, liturgy
Mathew, Tobie 138
McCoog, Thomas M. 115
McLuhan, Marshall 179
medieval church art 3
  See also: ruins
medieval devotion 6
medievalism:
  afterlife of medieval Catholicism 3
Melanchthon, Philip 155
Mercurian, Everard 145
metre 104
Michael, the archangel 138
Miles, Robert 50
Milner, John 42
Milton, John 73
minority languages, missionaries' use of 20
miracles 57, 79
Mitford, Mary Russell 45

mnemonic 20, 83, 108, 115, 116
Monta, Susannah Breitz 115
Montague, Viscount, of Cowdray 185
Monte, Philippe de 127–46
Moody, Henry 191
More, Hannah 189
More, St Thomas 87, 133, 134, 153
More, Sir William 215
Morrice, Richard 142
Mosse, Miles 202
motets 115, 125–7
Mulgrave Castle, Yorkshire 141, 227
Munday, Anthony viii
music 20

Napier, John 61
Nashe, Thomas 205
Neale, J. M. 42
Netley Abbey, Hampshire 37–47
  The Ruins of Netley Abb[e]y 43
new historicism vii, 114
Newman, John Henry, Cardinal 145
newsgathering and dissemination 18, 118, 122
Newton, Thomas 72
Nicholls, Norton 39
nonconformists 26
Norfolk 35
  See also: Houghton
Northampton 109
nostalgia, pro-Catholic 3–5, 22, 89
Numan, Philips 79
Nun Appleton House 31
Nutter, John 112

Oldcorne, Edward 134
Ong, Walter 13, 85
onomastics ix, 20, 115, 131–2
oral history 18, 150
oral tradition and traditions ix, 1, 14–15, 18, 70, conclusion, 223
oral transmission 1, 2–3, 6, 9, 14, 18, 149–50, 151, 152, 167
  relationship with literate culture 13, 56
  relationship with print 13, 17, 64, 66–7, 96, 98, 151
  relationship with Scripture 160–1
  relationship with written communication ix, 13, 17, 64, 66–7, 96, 150–1
  residual orality 13
  See also: rule of faith
orality 17–18
  association with factual distortion 59, 150
  Catholics' oral challenge 16, 82
  difficulties for Catholics 8, 9
  difficulty of censoring 3
  importance in pre-literate cultures 13

Ossory, Lady 39
Otto, Rudolf 6
Ovid 63

paganism 57–8, 63, 75
Parkinson, John 204
Parlor, John 19
parrhesia 12, 121
Paul VI, Pope 144
Paul, St 117
Pearce, William 44
pedlars 17
Penry, John 76
Percy, Thomas 78, 206
Persons, Robert 13, 89
Petre, Sir William 185
Petre family 207
Phillips, Peter 210
Piers Plowman 92
Pilchard/Pylcher, Thomas 136–40
Pilgrimage of Grace 87
Pittilesse Mother, A (anon.) 177
plant names 72–4
plants 72
Plato 70
Plautus 63
Pliny 134
Plot, Robert 202
Poeton, Edward 58
poetry 2
  See also: ballads; popular verse; psalms
polemic ix, 2, 4, 6, 12, 14, 57, 58, 63, 67–8, 77, 80, 96, 105, 116, 149, 153, 155
Pope, Alexander 79–81
popes 13
  See also: Gregory XIII; Paul VI; Urban VII; Urban VIII
'Popish Plot' 140
popular culture 17–18, 20
  and politics 18
  sophistication of popular literature 19–20
popular opinion 3
popular verse 121
  See also: ballads
Porte, Joel 53
Postgate, Nicholas 115, 140–4, 145–6
Pounde, Thomas 120
prayer 20, 57, 58, 150
preachers 15, 76, 111–12, 156
  difficulties faced by Catholic preachers 9
preaching in vernacular 9
Prideaux, Thomas 215
priest-holes 145, 146
priests, Catholic 8–9, 12, 19
  See also: Jesuits, secular priests

print 10
  Catholic use of print 16
  difficulty of access for Catholics 9
  mainstream publication of Catholic material 16
  popular print 10, 16–17, 76
  printed poetical miscellanies 6
  Protestant use of print 14, 16
prison 20
prophecy 64–5
Protestantism:
  and evangelism 10, 183
  suspicion of illiterates 74
proverbs 20
psalms 115, 125–6, 127
pseudonyms 3, 8, 132, 144
Pugin, A. W. N. 42
puns 131–40
Punter, David 51
purgatory 62
puritanism 3, 5, 61, 121, 156, 165, 166
Pylcher, Thomas: see Pilchard

Questier, Michael 12

Radcliffe, Ann 49
Radegund, Abbey of, Kent 27
Ralegh, Sir Walter 210
Ranger, Paul 44
Raphael, the archangel 138
Reading, Edward: see Bamber, Edward
recusancy 5
'recusant' writing ix
Reedy, Gerard 70
Reeves, Mr 142
relics 134–5, 146
Revelation, Book of 91, 92
reversal 92–4
rhetoric 10–11, 106, 110
Rhodes, John 99–100, 103, 213
  The Countrie Man's Comfort 93
Richards, John Inigo 44
riddles 104
  See also: allegory
Rievaulx Abbey, Yorkshire 38
Rigby, Nicholas 141
Rishton, Edward 212
Rites of Durham 184
ritual 137
Robartes, Fulke 188
Robin Hood 177
Roby, John 147
romance 2
Rome: see English College, Rome
Rooker, Michael 'Angelo' 192

Roscarrock, Nicholas 186
Royal Society 74
Royalists 5
Rudgley, William 58
ruins 1, 3, 37–9
rule of faith 152, 156–64, 166
rumour 18
Rushworth, William 12, 13, 159–60

sacramental theology 57
sacrilege 23–4, 25, 30, 32–3, 40
sacrilege narratives ix, 20, 23, 24–5, 30–47
Sacrilege a National Sin 27
Sade, Marquis de 50
St Hedda's Church, Egton Bridge, Yorkshire 142
St Patrick's Purgatory 56, 69, 79
St Paul's Cathedral 107
saints 3, 116–20
Sander, Margaret 9
Scot, Reginald 76
Scotland 20
Scott, James C. 92–3
secular priests 12
Sefton, Lancashire 112
Selden, John 173
Seneca 71
Sergeant, John 152, 159–67
sermons 2, 10, 13, 14, 20, 65, 67, 71, 165
    See also: preachers
Shagan, Ethan 18
Shakespeare, William viii
    Sonnets 3
    Hamlet 21
    Henry IV 133, 134
    Macbeth 135, 178
    Midsummer Night's Dream, A 206
Shaw, John 5
Sheldon, Edward 162
Shirley, Thomas
signatures 204
silencing, perceived 8
similitudes 72
Simon, Richard 154, 157–8, 161
Simpson, Robert 127–8
Sinclair, George 56
singing 2
    See also: ballads; psalms
Skelton, T. 191
Slegg, Edward 107
Sleights, Yorkshire 143
Smith, Richard, theologian 160
Smith, Richard, Bishop of Chalcedon 144
Smyth, John, of Nibley 69
solidarity among Catholics 7
Somerset: see Glastonbury

Song of Mary, the Mother of Christ, The 227
Sotheby, William 46–7
South Kyme, Lincolnshire 206
Southwell, Robert, St viii, 8, 138
spells ix, 1, 3, 14, 58–9, 60–1, 63, 65–7, 150
Spelman, Clement 187
Spelman, Sir Henry 23, 25–8
    The History and Fate of Sacrilege 25–7, 35, 42
    De Non Temerandis Ecclesiis 26
Spencer, Herbert 204
Spenser, Edmund 77, 138
Sprat, Thomas 74, 75–6
Staffordshire 99
Stanihurst, Richard 79, 229
Stephen, St 117
Stephens, Jeremy 25, 187
Steward, Richard 186
Stillingfleet, Edward 70, 164, 234
Strawberry Hill 33, 49
Stubbes, Philip 65, 67
Studley Royal, Yorkshire 38
Stukeley, William 185
superstition, perceived 3, 4, 13
Sutcliffe, Matthew 84, 108
Sympson, Agnes 56

Talbot, Peter 15
Tarletons Newes out of Purgatorie 69
Tavard, George 160, 162
Tavistock, Devon 65, 67
Taylor, Walter 26, 30, 39–45, 47
Tertullian 135
Theocritus 63, 74
Thessalonians, Epistle to 152
Thewlis, John 116–18, 133
Thomas, Keith 55, 73
Thwaites, Isabel 31
Tillotson, John 160, 164
tithes 26
Tobit, Book of 138
toleration 84
topography 123
    See also: ruins
Topsell, Edward 200
Touchet, Anselm 186
Tower of London 124
tradition 6
    place in Protestant thought 154–5
    relationship between Scripture and tradition 153–6
    See also: oral tradition
Tresham, Sir Thomas 131
trials 12, 20, 95
Trigge, Francis 173
Trinity 11

truth-claims 151
truth-telling 13
Turberville, Henry 234
Turner, Robert 204 n 69
Turvey House, Ireland 146
Tyburn 124

Udall, Ephraim 28
Ugthorpe 115, 143
uneducated, attitudes towards 7, 8, 163–4, 165
   See also: illiteracy
Urban VIII, Pope 144, 185

Vallenger, Stephen 108
Valsergues, Jean Albin de 97
Vansina, Jan 47
Vaughan, Henry 204
Vaughan, Richard, Bishop of Chester 112
vernacular 6–7
Véron, François 162
Verstegan, Richard 135
Vico, Giambattista 230
Victoria County History 192
Virgil 63, 75

Wadding, Luke 183
Wales 20
Walpole, Horace 33–6, 37, 39, 49
Walpole, Sir Robert 189, 190
Walpole family 35
Walsham, Alexandra 134
'Walsingham' 89–90
Walton, Isaak 28
Wanswell, Gloucestershire 69
Ward, Thomas 140
Wardley Hall, Lancashire 115–16, 147–8, 150

Warner, Richard, *Netley Abbey: A Gothic Story* 44–5
   Collections for the History of Hampshire 44, 215
Warner, William 76
Watt, Tessa 86
Weever, John 23, 30
Westminster Abbey 88
Whigs 190
Whitby, Yorkshire 227
White, John 64, 66, 67, 232
White, Richard 113, 212
White, Thomas (alias Blacklo) 159–60, 162
Whitgift, John, Archbishop 28
Whittle, Anne 60
Wiburn, Percival 109, 110–11
Williams, Gryffith 187
Willis, Browne 39–41, 42, 45, 193
Winifred, St 166
Wisbech Castle, Cambridgeshire 79
women's writing viii
Wood, Ralph 142
Woodhead, Abraham 233
Woolf, D.R. 68, 150
Wootton, John 38
word-choice 11–12
Worthington, Thomas 212
Würzbach, Natascha 86

Yonge, Charlotte M. 192
York Minster 188
Yorkshire 115, 140–3
   See also Blackamor; Danby Castle; Egton; Fountains Abbey; Kirkstall Abbey; Mulgrave Castle; Rievaulx Abbey; St Hedda's Church; Sleights; Studley Royal; Ugthorpe; Whitby; York Minster